CONVERTIBLE DEBENTURES/BONDS

CONVERTIBLE DEBENTURES/BONDS

EXPERIENCE OF INDIAN PRIVATE CORPORATE SECTOR

Dr. O. P. GOYAL

GIAN PUBLISHING HOUSE
DELHI-110007

GIAN PUBLISHING HOUSE
29/6 SHAKTI NAGAR, DELHI-110 007

ISBN 81-212-0122-5

Price : Rs. 360.00

PRINTED IN INDIA
Published by Mrs. Gayatri Garg for Gian Publishing House, Delhi-110007 and Printed at Suman Printers, Delhi-110 053

To

Asha, my wife;

Alpana, my daughter; and

Prashant & Anish, my sons.

PREFACE

One of the operational postulates of the Indian Private Corporate Sector has since 1978 been to reduce its dependence steadily on commercial banks and other finance intermediaries in matters of procurement of funds, be it for short term or of long term nature, and thus become 'self-reliant' in this regard. This change has however not been intuitive, self-moving and unwrinkled. Rather it has come to be forced upon by the events which characterized the period of more than one and a half decade. For long, commercial banks could not make it a secret that they are "over-financing" the Companies of the Private Corporate Sector. Findings of the numerous Committee/Study Groups/Working Groups appointed by the Government of India/Reserve Bank of India intersidereal 1968-79 made this point abundantly clear. As a matter of fact the acceptance of the virtuous recommendations of these, including that of Dehejia (1969), Tandon (1975) and Chore (1975) Committee, brought about a marked shift in the policies of the Union Government and Reserve Bank of India concerning the subject of financing the corporate sector in general and its constitutent private corporate sector in particular.

The culminated impact of all this has been the appearance of Convertible and Non-Convertible Debentures/Bonds on the scene of Indian Capital Market rather in a big way during the years which followed 1978. Virtually a scramble was further noticed among public limited companies of the private corporate sector for convertible debentures/bonds. Also it was, however, observed that the investing public did not reveal the same degree of pull and enchantment for each and every issue of convertible debentures/bonds; the variation in its response being wide to the extent that it necessitated in certain cases resort to the services of underwriters. When convertible debentures/bonds came to be used more both extensively and intensively then several other interesting aspects attracted our attention from the stand point of study in depth. The chief of them being as thus. How much funds have actually been mobilized by the private corporate sector through ths issuance of convertible debentures/bonds over the years? What have been the terms of the funds so raised? What has been the response of the investing public to the various issues of convertible debentures/bonds ? What considerations are kept in mind by investing public while purchasing, selling and retaining an investment in convertible debenture/s ? How to evaluate the successfulness/unsuccessfulness of the different issues of convertible debentures/bonds from the angle of issuing companies and their corporate managements, managers/underwriters to issues, investors and the State ? Under what distinctive circumstances and for what category of funds ('Debt' or 'Equity') the convertible debentures/bonds should be employed ? Has the climate been set for raising of funds on a continual basis through the issuance of convertible debentures/bonds ? Since there existed no such study which might have covered these and other related issues of the security 'convertible debentures/bonds' with reference to Indian experience and alongside the comparable position of 'non-convertible debentures/bonds', we ventured to complete one on, Convertible Debentures/Bonds: Experience of Indian Private Corporate Sector'.

The task that we accomplished through this study has been quite exhaustive so as to cover almost all the major issues. This study thus presents: the major trends of the funds raised via convertible and non-convertible debentures/bonds on the basis of a census survey of public limited listed companies of the private corporate sector with reference to the period 1978-82; four separate lists of the appropriate yardsticks need to be used for pronouncing the success/failure of the issues of convertible debentures/bonds from the view point of concerned companies, investors, economy and an integrated analysis; and, the results secured on applying these to the actual issues. One case study each of the most successful and unsuccessful issue of convertible debentures/bonds and a representative issue of non-convertible debentures/bonds have further been included in this work with a view to facilitate a thorough investigation. This has been followed by an analysis of the considered opinions secured on leading questions/issues from the chairmen/corporate finance executives of all the debenture issuing companies, distinguished academics, office bearers of the main stock exchanges, managers/underwriters/brokers to issues and a select group of existing/prospective investors. This helped us greatly in appraising our findings which emerged from the experience of Indian Private Corporate Sector, Government Guidelines related to the issuance of debentures, provisions of Income Tax and Wealth Tax Acts and then in finally making our constructive recommendations on the subject.

As would have been, all the finance experts, debenture issuing companies and the investors must find this work not only of academic interest but also of significant value in offering useful suggestions to resolve some of their practical problems.

October 22, 1987
Department of Commerce
M.D. University, Rohtak.

O.P. GOYAL

ACKNOWLEDGEMENTS

My sincere thanks are due to the Indian Council of Social Science Research, New Delhi for approving and financing this research project. I am however personally responsible for whatever has been stated in this research report by way of facts, opinions and inferences.

I also thank Dr. V.K. Agarwal, Department of Commerce, Shyam Lal College, University of Delhi, Delhi, for the help rendered by him to me in the collection and tabulation of statistical material for this project. He also assisted in many analyses at the final stages. And the words would be insufficient to express my heart-felt *gratitudo* to my father, Shri G.S. Gupta, and friend, Dr. O.P. Lathwal, who have unintermittently extended their angelic support for the completion of this work.

O.P. GOYAL

CONTENTS

1

OVERTURE

- FRAMEWORK OF ECONOMIC, FISCAL AND MONETARY POLICIES
- POKE ON 'SELF-RELIANCE'
- LANDSCAPE OF CONVERTIBLE AND NON-CONVERTIBLE DEBENTURES/ BONDS
- THE INSPIRATION DERIVED FOR THIS STUDY
- SHOVEL BOARD OF EXISTING LITE- RATURE
- CONCEPTUAL FRAMEWORK
- THE RALLYING POINTS OF THE STUDY
- IMPORTANT HYPOTHESIS
- THE MAJOR TASK
- LOGIC OF THE PERIOD:1978-82
- MESSAGE OF THIS STUDY
- ORGANIZATION OF THIS WORK

FRAMEWORK OF ECONOMIC, FISCAL AND MONETARY POLICIES AS CONTEMPLATED IN THE SEVENTH FIVE YEAR PLAN : 1985-90

IN a mixed economy such as ours, the programs of investments are to be harnessed both through direct public sector outlays and through influencing and regulating the flow of resources in the private sector.[1] Thus, in addition to the program of public sector investment, a plan of development is expected to contain a set of policies designed to bring about the desired pattern of investment in the private sector too. Accordingly, the major task of the fiscal policy as it concerns to industry has been set at enabling it to raise a much greater part of the resources needed for its expansion from internal resources and the capital market than heretofore.[2] And, the monetary policy fantasized that the private sector industries must be unwaveringly emboldened to seek a much larger volume of support from the capital market, and on a selective basis public sector enterprizes may also be stimulated to resort to it.[3] The strategy pronounced is palpable from the intent of the financing pattern of investment of the Seventh Five Year Plan : 1985-90. Thus of the total investment of Rs. 54,236 crores for the private corporate sector as much as 53 per cent (Rs. 28,779 crores) is proposed to be financed via their own savings, 28 per cent (Rs. 15,191 crores) through its recourse to the household sector savings via the capital market, 15.3 per cent (8,266 crores) by resorting to the credit assistance extended by the public finance institutions, and the rest 3.7 per cent (2,000 crores) by foreign borrowings. Similarly, of the total investment of Rs. 1,54,218 crores, as envisaged for the public sector, 32 per cent (Rs. 57,422 crores) would be forthcoming by way of their own savings,[4] 56 per cent (Rs. 87,062 crores) by draft on private savings and around 12 per cent (Rs. 18,000 crores) by foreign borrowings.[5]

POKE ON 'SELF-RELIANCE'

1.2 In the context it would be *ad rem* to recall that the need for 'self-reliance' was first of all came to be explicitly stated in the country's Third Five Year Plan : 1961-66 as thus :

> "The balance of payments difficulties the country is facing are, it must be stressed, not short run or temporary ; they will continue for several years to come. The external assistance is essential for this period, but the aim must be to make the economy more and more self-reliant, so that it is able to support within a period of 10 or 12 years an adequate scale of investment from its own production and savings. Normal inflow of capital may continue but reliance on special forms of external assistance has to be reduced progressively and eliminated."[6]

Fitly, therefore, well step out programs were drawn for realizing the goal of self-reliance during the Fourth through Sixth Five Year Plans.[7] That the Government has been straightforward and unfeigned in its endeavors on this score is conspicuous from the copious Study Groups/Committees formed intersidereal October 1968 and December 1982 for making a probe in depth into the problem as to how to effectuate the objective of self reliance on the one hand, and streamline the lending systems of the commercial banks and improve the effectiveness of monetary policy as an instrument for promoting the basic aims of planned economic development on the other. Thus the purpose and direction of commercial bank lending in the country was questioned by the National Credit Council's Study Group No. 2 appointed in October 1968 under the Chairmanship of *Shri V.T. Dehejia* "to examine the extent to which credit needs of industry and trade were likely to be inflated and how such trends could be checked."[8] Its Report commented extensively on the shortcomings of the prevalent system of lending to industry and came to the conclusion that the security-oriented approach to lending had led to over-financing of industry in relation to production trends as also with reference to inventory in industry.[9] The Industrial Licensing Policy Inquiry Committee set up under the stewardship of *Shri S. Dutt* in July 1967 submitted its Report in 1969 ;

it contained highly treasured recommendations in respect to the manner in which the licensing system could be modified to serve the cause of self-reliance.[10] The *Narasimham* Study Group on Bills instituted by the Reserve Bank of India (RBI) in 1970[11] and the Study Group to Frame Guidelines For Follow-up of Bank Credit, created by the RBI in July 1974 under the Chairmanship of *Shri Prakash Tandon*, again highlighted the serious weaknesses of the then pattern of lending followed by banks. The following annotation from the Report of the Tandon Study Group (1975) is worth gripping :

> "The problem of potential imbalance in demand for and supply of funds is accentuated by the manner in which banks extend credit under the present cash credit system of lending. Under this system, the level of advances in a bank is determined not by how much a banker can lend at a particular point of time but by the borrower's decision to borrow at that time. This makes credit planning difficult in banks. Also, cash credit advances are repayable on demand only in name. To the extent that outstandings in the cash credit account never fell below a certain level during the course of a year, there is an element of what is called a 'hard core' borrowing which is in reality a quasi-permanent lock up of bank funds in the borrower's business." (Paragraphs 3.12 to 3.20)[12]

In June 1977, the Ministry of Law, Justice and Company Affairs (Department of Company Affairs) of the Government of India constituted a High Powered Committee for Review of the Companies Act and the Monopolies and Restrictive Trade Practices Act under the Chairmanship of Justice *Shri Rajinder Sachar* ; it submitted its Report on August 31, 1978. As it ought to be in the light of its long list of terms of reference, it's indeed an encyclopedic and commendatory work on the subject. While it is neither covetable nor doable to reiterate all what has been said in this Report, yet it would be quite fitting to run our eye's over the remarks adduced hereunder :

(*i*) "There are various areas in which corporate discipline cannot be achieved by mere amendments of both the

Acts. Since the independence of the Country and particularly after the role that has been developed for the public financial institutions, the industrial growth has come to be what it is today ; but at the same time, it is not the Companies Act or the MRTP Act which can take care of the total financial discipline that is required for management of corporate sector whether it be in public or private sector." (Paragraph 17.106.)[13]

(*ii*) "The racket of inter-corporate investment has led to widespread sickness in the industry for the sake of building industrial empire. I feel that the inter-corporate investment should be banned. But the question is raised that in the interest of the growth of the economy, it will be better to permit investment rather than allow the funds to lie idle. There are very few companies which have really surplus capital if the liabilities are offset. Today with five to ten per cent share capital the industries are run with the support of the financial institutions and banks. It is, therefore, necessary that diversion of funds may be prevented." (Paragraph IV of the Note of *Shri K.P. Tripathi.*)[14]

While reviewing the monetary and credit trends in March 1979 the then Governor of RBI stressed the need for exercising continued restraint on the further expansion of credit. He indicated to the bankers that there is the need for considering certain long-term issues relating to banking operations. And in his letter dated the 16th March 1979 addressed to all scheduled commercial banks he indicated :

"I would like to initiate action on certain structural matters which need further examination. It is necessary to take a fresh look at another major problem faced by banks in implementing the credit regulatory measures, viz., the extensive use of the cash credit system. Its drawbacks have been pointed out by various Committees in the past including the Tandon Committee, which suggested the bifurcation of credit limits into a demand loan and a fluctuating cash credit component. Although the banks were advised to implement this recommendation, I am afraid, the progress achieved has been very slow. Clearly, this problem needs to be looked into further and for this purpose I propose to set up immediately a small Working Group, to report to me.........on the reforms to be introduced."[15]

Thus came into existence in 1979 the RBI's Working Group to Review the System of Cash Credit headed by *Shri K.B. Chore* which submitted its Interim Report in May 1979 but final Report only in August 1979. This Group *a fortiori* feels that there is :

"the need for reducing the over dependence of the medium and large borrowers : both in the public and private sectors-on bank finance for their production/trading purposes. There has been hitherto a belief among the banking and industrial circles that it is the responsibility of the commercial banks to provide at all times the entire working capital requirements of the industrial sector. Consistent with this belief, it has been hitherto taken for granted that the surplus cash generation of a unit should be available for its expansion, although there are term lending institutions to provide for such capital expansion programmes. Whatever might be the justification for such a belief in the past, there is need for a serious rethinking on the subject in the present context.........An equitable distribution of the scarce resources under the present day circumstances would be possible only if the available scarce funds are utilized for genuine short term requirements of this sector. So, the net surplus cash generation of an established industrial unit should be utilised partly at least for reducing borrowing for working capital purposes. This principle should also apply to the trading sector. In other words, the established units should not divert their cash generation exclusively for expansion purposes which should legitimately be financed by promoter's own funds by way of deposits or issue of share capital or debentures and institutional agencies." (Paragraph 5.7.)[16]

Dr. Manmohan Singh, the then Governor of the RBI established another Committee to Review the Working of the Monetary

System in December 1982 under the Chairmanship of Professor *Sukhamoy Chakravarty* in order to undertake an in-depth study of the working of the monetary system as a whole. On April 10, 1985 it submitted its Report and made as many as 243 observations and recommendations ; of these, following should not be missed :

(*i*) "Bank lending essentially retains its security orientation despite the application of more sophisticated norms. The present credit appraisal procedures do not prevent utilisation of credit facilities over and above what is justified on the basis of cash flow analysis, so long as the drawing power is not exhausted. As the Stock statements are available once a month or less frequently, and their submission can be delayed if it suits the borrower, the drawing power based on the latest available stock statement does not necessarily represent current credit requirements." (Paragraph 11.20.)[17]

(*ii*) "The cash credit system, in our view, suffers from two serious drawbacks which have important implications for the working of the monetary system. Under the cash credit system the task of cash management is passed on by the borrower to the bank. Another related aspect of the cash credit system which has received somewhat less attention is the considerable benefit derived by the borrowers akin to interest income on their temporarily surplus funds. The surplus funds credited to the cash credit account reduce interest costs at the rate charged which now stands at 17.5 per cent per annum, a level of return on surplus funds not available to other sectors of the economy." (Paragraph 11.37 and 11.38.)[18]

(*iii*) "The large public sector and private sector units need to build a strong financial structure so that they are able to transmit growth impulses to the rest of the economy on a sustained basis and not get bogged down from time to time with financial crises with their fall out on smaller borrowers." (Paragraph 11.45.)[19]

THE REMINISCENCE

1.3 Until the close of 1970 the procurement of funds by the private corporate sector did not pose any severe problem, may it be for short-term or of long-term nature. Both commercial banks and finance institutions use to come to its rescue like 'shock-absorbers' during the conditions of depressed money and capital market. The short term credit could be had from the banks not only 'on tap' but also it was reasonably priced, ability-criterion-based, quite flexible and growth inducive. By and large, banks even did not bother for the 'rolling-over' of this credit time and again, aside its frequent utilization for financing the long-term credit needs. Obviously, therefore, there was no can of worms for the settled companies in securing debt for meeting working capital needs. Almost the similar position prevailed in respect to the raising of long-term investible debt funds because the industrial finance institutions had, by then, no lengthy list of their commitments. Nevertheless this situation underwent drastic changes during the periods of Fourth and Fifth Five Year Plans on account of the Government's unabated passion for the corporate sector to attain 'self-reliance' in as short a span of time as it could be conceived of. The acute oil crisis[20] and registering of two-digital inflation almost every year during these Plans[21] further jack up the Government's thirst to do something on this front nimble-footed.

POLYCHROMATIC WHEREWITHAL OF HEAVING FUNDS AND OPTIMAL CAPITAL STRUCTURE

1.4 The modulations in the environment forced the managements of the private sector companies to fall back on such means of raising capital funds which were sparingly used by them thus far. Provisions in the Memorandums and Articles of Associations of every company include the list of the sources which can be tapped for gathering the required money resources. Pre-eminent of these are : issuance of equity and preference shares, borrowings from banks and finance institutions, acceptance of deposits from public, issuance of debentures—non-convertibles and convertibles—*et caetera*. Recurrent issue of equity and preference shares is evaded on account of the well known limitations of this method of augmenting moneys. Sequel to this company's capital base is widened which may have unsmiling purports. Not only the profitability and the managerial structure of the concerned company may stand adversely affected, it would add to its burden regarding the amount of profits to be distributed by way of dividends.[12] Borrowings from banks and other finance intermediaries too may not now be easy to get hold of consequential to the acceptance and implementation of a good number of recommendations of the variors Study Groups/Committees referred to above. *Ergo*, the corporate managements turn aside to the alternative means of debt capital like accepting deposits from the public and issuing convertible and/or non-convertible debentures/bonds.

MAXIMIZATION OF "OWNERS' WEALTH" AND "PROFITS" AND AN OPTIMAL CAPITAL STRUCTURE

1.5 True that raising of debt capital is relatively cheaper *vis-a-vis* the risk capital the corporate managements must not forget that in doing so they have to bring off an optimal capital structure—proper mix of debt and equity capital—for the enterprizes under their charge as it is one *sine qua non* for the maximization of "Owners' Wealth" and "Profits"; albeit, opportune mix of debt capital with the funds contributed by the owners confide in the peculiar circumstances of the concerned enterprize and the legal environment within which it is operating. *Enfin* the enterprize ultimate objective of maximizing the owners' wealth is so much interwoven with optimum capital structure that the latter is defined as the "relationship of debt and equity securities that maximizes the value of the firm's common stock in the marketplace" by keeping the overall cost of capital at the minimum possible level.[22]

LANDSCAPE OF CONVERTIBLE AND NON-CONVERTIBLE DEBENTURES/BONDS

1.6 Such being the case the corporate managements of the private sector companies set about to accept deposits from the individual/institutional surplus spending units and inlet for the floating of convertible and non-convertible debentures/bonds. Thus came in sight on the financial tableau of the Indian

Capital Market the Convertible and Non-Convertible Debentures/Bonds. And now there seems to be a scramble on the part of Indian Public Limited Companies to raise funds through the means of convertible and non-convertible debentures/bonds. It can be well reckoned from the simple fact that during the year 1983 as many as 110 non-government companies were granted approval by the Controller of Capital Issues (CCI) for the issuance of debentures—convertibles and non-convertibles put together worth Rs. 584.23 crores in sharp contrast to stunted sum of Rs. 48.75 crores for 13 companies during 1978.[23]

GUIDELINES FOR ISSUE OF DEBENTURES : DROP BY DROP PALLIATION TO PUFF UP THEIR PROGRESSIVE ATTRACTIVENESS

1.7 To actuate the issuance of debentures and raise through them the requisite money for meeting the working capital requirements the CCI on behalf of the Government of India, porched out on September 13, 1978 the guidelines for the issuance of "rights debentures" by public limited companies. Limited as these were in terms of their provisos allowing the companies to ascend their funds, the Government considered it expedient just after the lapse of nearly two years to revise its guidelines in order to make them more liberal, flexible, and attractive. The CCI came out with a new set of guidelines on October 27, 1980 for the floatation of debentures by the public limited companies ; these, it may be acclaimed, were supplemental to and not in supersession of the earlier guidelines issued in 1978. Despite the introduction of several favourable features in the guidelines the obtained results were rather perfunctory. And, non-convertible debentures as a source of raising long-term funds remained almost hermetically sealed. This situation compelled the Central Government to seek an expert opinion in respect to the measures which should be taken for the promotion of a Secondary Market for Debentures—both convertibles and non-convertibles—so that these may emerge as potent instruments of raising both debt and equity capital for our industrial enterprizes. Accordingly, RBI set up a Working Group under the Chairmanship of *Mr. N.N. Pai*, Chairman, Industrial Development Bank of India, for the fulfilment of the above referred desire of the Government. While Pai Committee submitted its Report in December 1981, it is yet to be made public.[24] However, the recommendations of this committee are under active consideration of the Government.[25] And, on April, 17, 1982, as a vanguard to the comprehensive measures expected to be announced by the Government, the CCI revised its guidelines for the issuance of convertible and non-convertible debentures by public limited companies. Emphasis in revised guidelines is on popularizing both the Secured Convertible Debentures/Bonds (CDs) and the Secured Non-Convertible Debentures/Bonds (NCDs) with the Indian Public Limited listed Companies through overtly allowing more favourable terms for the floatation of NCDs *vis-a-vis* CDs on the one hand, and by withdrawing the concessions hitherto enjoyed by the class of CDs, on the other. The details of the Guidelines issued by the Controller of Capital Issues (CCI) from time to time may be perused in Annexe : I.

THE INSPIRATION DERIVED FOR THIS STUDY

1.8 The foregoing milieu explains as to why do we these days, come across quite incessantly wirh maganetized announcements of one or the other company belonging not only to the private corporate sector but also to public sector offering CDs or NCDs to the surplus spending units of the economy. In terms of the present policy of the Union Government, the RBI also seems to be seriously concerned with the problem of the creation and development of a 'Secondary Market' for debentures/bonds. And, it is these developments of the Indian Capital Market which inspired us to undertake a research study into the experience of Indian Private Corporate Sector in point of meeting its capital needs through retailing in particular the CDs. At the outset it appears as if the NCDs may not gain the same degree of popularity as is the case with the CDs, and as an obvious consequence may not be able to evolve itself as a matching instrument of raising funds for the corporate sector, the Government is quite keen that these too are welcome with equal enthusiasm by the investing public. In view of this as also to obtain a comparative picture we intend to cover in this study the experience of the Indian Private Corporate Sector as it relates to the issuance of NCDs too. Even so, our prime emphasis in this work would be on CDs.

SHOVEL BOARD OF EXISTING LITERATURE

1.9 The devibity observed on several counts in the studies so far completed by individual researchers both in and outside the country on the subject of 'Convertible Debentures/Bonds' further encouraged the author to select this study for research. The review of the important studies is presented hereunder.

Weston & Brigham's Empirical Study

1.10 An empirical study was accomplished in United States of America by *Weston & Brigham* on the usage of convertible bonds with a view to gain insight into the corporate planning that lies behind the decision to issue convertibles as also to discover their distinguishing features. 215 public issues of convertible bonds worth $ 1,080 million floated during the period 1961-63 were selected for the purpose. The main findings of this study were : (i) of the total issues 76 per cent were offered by 42 well renowned US Companies to the public and the size of their issues and maturity periods ranged between $ 5 million and $ 20 million, and 20 and 25 years, respectively ; (ii) these convertible bonds were rated capitally below the straight debt securities ; (iii) the preponderance number of companies floated such bonds for raising equity capital in sharp contrast to the setting in India where they are used partly for raising equity capital and partly for debt capital-the former being generally in a less proportion than to the latter ; (iv) the comparatively large corporations covered in the sample were free from any sort of pressures in point of using convertibles for raising the required funds ; (v) about 88 per cent of the companies which issued convertibles have had sinking fund provisions for the redemption ; and (vi) greater number of corporations which resorted to this means did not frame any clear cut guidelines for the conversion of convertibles into equity shares.[26]

Studies Replenished by Indian Academics

1.11 In India not even one thorough and blanket study on the subject under search has so far been concluded ; no doubt, a few individual researchers did make desperate attempt in this direction and their findings have been pulverized via articles/papers put out mostly in the Economic Times and the Financial Express either in their Daily Issues or in Special Supplements. The outcome of some of the investigations have also appeared in the celebrated magazines like Business Standard and Chartered Accountant, and as distinct Chapters in the works of distinguished academics in the area of financial/investment management. The gist of the serious fact finding enquiries/explorations is adduced in a nutshell here. The subsequent para concerns with the Research Papers which captivated our attention in the Economic Times.

1.12 *Narendra J. Sheth* has discussed in his papers, 'Convertible Debentures, Bonds : Relevance to Financing of New Projects' (October 1980),[27] and 'Convertible Bonds/Debentures : A Perspective on Conversion Price' (April 1982),[28] the extent to which convertible bonds can become effective instruments for the financing of new projects through reviving the market for equity shares especially in the context of despondency of Indian Capital Market, and the plight of conversion in the event of the issue of bonus shares following the issue of convertible debentures/bonds but prior the right/option of conversion is enjoyed by the debentureholders/bondholders. The importance of debentures, measures needed to develop them as a potential means of financing investment by medium and large public limited companies and for developing a secondary market for them in India constitute the main theme of *M.D. Mukhi's* essays entitled, 'Debentures : Steps Needed to Develop It' and 'Debentures : Need for A Secondary Market' (January 1981),[29] and of *N.V. Venkataraman's* paper captioned, 'Debentures : Rising Importance'. (April 1981).[30] The way bonds are defined, their different variants and the purposes for which they are utilized in USA, UK and in our Country, have been highlighted in *S.R. Kashekar* research paper, 'Bonds—The British Way' (April 1981)[31] and in *M. Krishnan*

Kutty's article, 'Bonds of Public Bodies.' (April 1981.)[32] *Sudhi R. Sengupta* in his search pieces titled, 'Working Capital : Debentures & Deposits As Sources' and 'Working Capital : Interests of Investors' (June 1981)[33] discussed in an interesting manner the relative merits and demerits of enhancing working capital funds through debentures and acceptance of deposits from public, on the one hand, and, how to make these sources more attractive to the savers, on the other. Similarly, *V.D. Datar* spurred out the benefits received through convertible debentures, both by the issuing company and the investing public, when compared with other modes of raising capital like acceptance of deposits from public, and preference and equity shares, in his paper entitled, 'Convertible Debentures : A Utility Analysis'. (April 1982.)[34] Pointing out the two components of the yield—an interest rate yield and yield from capital gains—on convertible debentures and different yield concepts in vogue—flat yield (or running yield), gross flat yield and redemption yield (or yield to maturity), *Swapan Kanti Chaudhuri* in his exploratory and suggestive endeavour entitled, 'Convertible Debentures : Components of Yield' (October 1982),[35] has attempted the calculation of redemption yield through solving the given present value equation for 'k' (the internal rate of return per annum) in the case of a sample of public issues. It is also emphasized that : "Change in interest rate seems to have less impact on yields than volatility of shares' market prices. This may imply two things : firstly any attempt to make convertible debentures more attractive by increasing the interest rate by a percentage point or so, as has been done in recent past, will be met with limited success ; secondly, investors be cautious in predicting the expected market price of shares which is subject to its own vagaries."[36] The preliminary findings of the pilot survey undertaken by the author with the assistance of *V.K. Agarwal* also appeared in the Saturday Supplement on Finance of the Economic Times in its issue of May 8, 1982 with the title, 'Convertible Debentures/Bonds : Experience of Private Corporate Sector.'[37] It covered all the Indian Companies which floated convertible debentures/bonds during the period 1978-81 and it concentrated on four basic aspects :

one, pinpointing the virtues of convertible debentures/bonds which create lasciviousness in the minds of investors towards them *vis-a-vis* other forms of investments ; second, presenting an overview of the profile of the issues of convertible debentures/bonds for the period 1978-81 ; third, undertaking a critical study of the different issues of the convertibles with a view to assess the 'fate' with which they have met in order to draw out lessons for the companies intending to enter the so called 'secondary market' on the one hand, and for the prospective investors, on the other ; lastly, discovering the areas in which improvements are urgently called upon so as to sustain the steadily growing interest of the investors in the convertibles. Being quite lengthy the entire findings of this Pilot Survey would not be reiterated here excepting that it may be stated that the main inferences did provide necessary indoctrination for this unexpurgated study. Also it seems pertinent to draw attention towards this overriding conclusion of our pilot study :

> "The companies desirous of raising funds by this means must realise that their issues can succeed only when the market price of their shares continues to register a steady rise which would be possible only when these are enlisted on one of the Stock Exchanges in India alongwith that of the one situated at Bombay in the category of volatile and active scrips. Not only that the corporate managements of such companies must keep the public well informed about their current and planned operations on a continuous basis, the convertibility price has also got to be kept at the minimum possible low level in relation to the prevailing shares market price at the time of issuance."[38] And, "In order to sustain the interest of investors in the convertibles it may be stressed that the issuing company must continue to offer more and more attractive terms compatible of course to its own interests both short and long term."[39]

1.13 The papers appeared in the Financial Express can now be taken up for their scrutiny. *P.K. Balakrishnan* explained in his article titled, 'Rate of Return on Convertible Debentures' (January 1981), how to work out the rate of return on such investments on the basis of discounted cash flow technique and concluded that : "The investment is highly remunerative and very suitable for all investors, small and large, particularly those who can afford to keep the capital locked up and utilise the interest only for day-do-day use".[40] 'Management of Convertible Debentures', an article produced by *G. Prasad and K. Viyyanna Rao*, appeared in two parts in October 1981. In it the authors have described the way issues of convertible debentures are being managed in India. And, while doing so they arrived at the conclusion that while convertible debentures have become one of the promising instruments for meeting the requirement of finance by the companies in Indian private corporate sector, the use of this mode of financing is still at an embryonic stage viewed in the context of both the spread and intensity of use. Due to lack of perfect knowledge on this method of raising finance, the Indian Companies are deficient in visualising the situations at which these issues can be made and in formulating the conversion terms to their advantage.[41] To what extent the issuing company's overall impressive financial record, incentives like the facility of conversion at par, rates of dividend and other advantages have influenced the public response to convertible debentures constitute the crux of the discussion in *K.S. Ramachandran's* paper titled, 'Why this Scramble For Convertible Debentures ?' (February 1982.)[42] In his paper, 'Convertible Debenture Profit' (May 1982), *A.S. Moses* after having examined the different modes employed for computing return on such securities concludes that the true return on a convertible debenture can be determined by first estimating the expected cash inflows and outflows relating to the investment in the debenture over its life and then using discounted cash flow techniques for determining the return. While the investors can use this return both for ranking the alternative investment opportunities and for selecting only those investments with returns higher than their minimum expected return, companies can use it for determining the terms of its convertible debenture issue ; the terms of issue having determined in such a manner that while prospective investors are offered an attractive investment with a high return, the company at the same time obtains finance at as low a cost as possible.[43] *M.D. Mukhi's* essay titled, 'Debentures : Prolific Source of Funds for Companies' (April 1983) summarizes the policy measures taken by the Government since 1978 for making secured debentures as a prolific source of raising finance by the corporate sector.[44]

1.14 The Research Bureau of Business Standard in its Study entitled, 'Debenture Issues And Equity Prices : A Case Study of Seven Companies' (January 1982), has examined the prices movements of equity shares of the sample companies with the tacit presumption that ingraining a provision for the conversion of at least a small portion of the debentures into equity shares is the surest way to activate the secondary market ; a rise in the prices of equity shares will have an instant impact on the response of ordinary investors towards debentures. Reckoning compound weekly growth rates of equity prices the Bureau reaffirmed that the scramble for convertible debentures during their pre and post periods has been primarily on account of their convertible component and not owing to their debenture segment. Further, no strong correlations have been found between the rise of net worth and rise in the equity prices of the companies issuing convertible debentures. And in order to render debentures more alluring to the ordinary investor several refinements have been called for such as an automatic provision for a hike in the rate of interest payable, an annual buy-back provision at par-value, fixing the face value in a manner that the residual portion after conversion comes to Rs. 100, making provision for conversion not only at the earlier stage but also towards the end, educating properly the investing public about the benefits of investment in debentures, etc.[45] *N.P. Sinha* in his article entitled, 'Convertible Debentures—An Analytical Study', which appeared in the Chartered Accountant (September 1982), however, confined his efforts only to the enumeration of the strategic factors which governs the issue of convertible debentures illustrating the computation of the rate of return through Discounted Cash Flow Method and the deterrents which inhibit the universal acceptance of the debentures as an attractive form of investment.[46]

1.15 *S.L.N. Simha, D. Hemalatha and S. Balakrishnan* in their title, 'Investment Management : Introduction to Securities Analysis' (1979), devoted a distinct appendix on 'Analysis of Convertible Debentures'. It is here that they have dealt briefly with the evaluation of an investment opportunity in convertible debentures by undertaking both an analysis of its debt-servicing capacity as well as equity earnings prospects.[47] Critical appraisal of the September 1978 and October 1980's Guidelines in respect to 'Rights' and 'Public' debentures, respectively, has been attempted alongside the inclusion of certain meaningful suggestions for improving market for debentures by *S.C. Kuchhal* in Chapter 25 of his work entitled, 'Financial Management : An Analytical and Conceptual Approach' (1982).[48] In Chapter 32 of the title under reference Kuchhal has further described the merits, demerits and dilution effect on earnings per share of the security convertible debentures/bonds apart enumerating the key factors behind the decision to raise funds through them in India.[49] *Prasanna Chandra* in his title, 'Financial Management : Theory and Practice' (1984) devoted a specific Chapter on 'Debentures with Subscription Rights and Conversion Features' aside covering the general description of the debt investment in Chapters entitled, 'Equity, Preference and Debenture Capital,' and 'Market for Long-term Securities in India'.[50] In the specific chapter, Prasanna Chandra has made an appreciable attempt to calculate the value, rate of return to debentureholder and cost of Debenture with Subscription Rights, value, rate of return to debentureholder and cost of Partly Convertible Debenture and conversion and investment value of Fully Convertible Debenture.[51]

CONCEPTUAL FRAMEWORK

Debenture/Bond :

1.16 An explicit definition of the term 'debenture/bond' is even not contained in the Companies Act, 1956 of our Country. It's Section 2 (12) only jabber out that :

> "Debenture" includes debenture, stock, bond and other securities of a company, whether constituting a charge on the assets of the company or not".[52]

On analysis, it can be deduced that 'debenture' is document issued by a company by way of an evidence of debt to the holder which usually arise out of a loan and most commonly secured by a charge on its assets—the latter condition is however not an essentiality. Alternatively, 'Debenture' is an instrument used for raising necessary funds and it represents the contract of a company with the holder or owner to pay the latter a definite sum of money at a stipulated time together with periodic payment of interest. Are 'debentures' and 'bonds' synonymous or there exists some difference ? No answer is furnished by our Companies Act, 1956, as also by the interpretation attached to the contents, of Section 2(12) by us above. In the context it may be recalled that the term 'debentures' and 'bonds' have distinct meanings. The term 'bond' in United States, refers to a long term contract under which borrower agrees to make payments of interest and principal, on specific dates to the holder of the bond.[53] *Weston and Brigham* looked at it simply as a long term promissory note,[54] while *Gitman* states that bond certificate is a certificate indicating the fact that a corporation has borrowed a certain amount of money which it promises to repay in the future.[55] Considering bond as a debt *Archer, Choate & Racette* gave it the connotation of some form of long term interest being debt.[56] Thus 'bond' is a long-term debt financing source which have traditionally been issued with ripen period of 20 to 30 years.[57] The specific promises and details of the issue are mentioned in the bond indenture—a legal document that spell out the rights of both the bondholders and the issuing corporation.[58] And, an important provision incorporated in this indenture relates to the collateral against which the relevant bond is being floated and a mention of the name of a trustee (which is usually a bank), who represents the bondholders for making sure that the terms of the indenture would be carried out in toto. Obviously, therefore, bonds in USA are secured by a lien on specific tangible assets or a guarantee by the parent company which ensures the bondholders about their legal entitlements to receive interest and repaying back of principal amounts on due dates irrespective of the fact that corporation earns profits or runs into losses. In case the corporation fails to pay or repay any amount to its bondholders then they can be satisfied by selling the security on which they have their charge.

1.17 A 'debenture', on the other hand, is an unsecured promissory note which is supported by the general credit-worthiness of the firm.[59] *Eugene F. Brigham and Louis C. Gapenski* have, therefore, preferred to call it as an 'Unsecured Bond' which provides no lien against specific property as security for the obligation.[60] Debentureholders are, therefore, like other common creditors whose claims are protected by property not otherwise pledged. And, hence, debenture is a promissory note issued by a company and usually not secured by a mortgage or lien or any specific property.[61] In some cases the debenture bond may specify that claim to assets is secondary to the claims of other bondholders. Under the circumstance, this class of debentures are called 'Subordinated Debentures'. And, the claims of the holders of such debentures are considered only after having fully satisfied the senior claims.[62] In USA the issuance of unsecured debentures is possible because here companies are absolved of the necessity of assigning a charge on specific assets and keeping a detailed records of the same. Aside, they also have the freedom to dispose off the assets without first getting released the title on them. In sharp contrast to what is observed for the American Corporate Sector the vocable 'Bonds' and 'Debentures' are used interchangeably in the Indian Corporate Sector perhaps on account of the overriding fact that both have to be secured as per the Guidelines issued by the Controller of Capital Issues. Accordingly, we have used the terms. 'Debentures' and 'Bonds' as synonymous in this study.

Clan of Debentures/Bonds :

1.18 In India debentures/bonds are categorized broadly into four classes : (a) registered and bearer debentures ; (b) redeemable and irredeemable (perpetual) debentures ; (c) secured and unsecured debentures ; and, (d) convertible debentures. The Registered Debentures are registered in the books of the company alongwith the names, addresses and other particulars of debentures issued to different holders. They are transferable in the same way as shares i.e. only through a transfer deed,

Interest on such a debenture is payable to the registered holder or to the order of the registered holder. A company may issue Bearer Debentures also. In case of such debentures the company keeps no register of debentureholders and they are transferable by a mere delivery of the debenture to the transferee. Payment of interest is made on production of coupons attached with the debentures. But if such debentures are secured then their record has to be kept in the Register of charges on Company's Assets.

1.19 Generally the debentures issued by a company are redeemable and in case of such debentures the principal money is paid off to the investor on the expiry of a specified term. Further such debentures may be redeemed either at the issue price (at par) or at a higher price (at premium) or at the price prevailing in the market. Redeemed debentures can be reissued by the company unless any provision to the contrary, whether express or implied, is contained in the articles, or in the conditions of issue, or in any contract entered into by the company ; or unless the company has, by passing a resolution to that effect or by some other act, manifested its intention that the debentures shall be cancelled. Irredeemable Debentures, known also as 'Perpetual Debentures', are issued with no fixed date of redemption and are repayable either in the event of winding up or on the happening of some serious contingency or on the expiration of some remote period.

1.20 Debentures may be either secured or unsecured. Debentures carrying charge on the assets or property of the company are deemed as 'secured' and when there is an absence of such a charge in favour of the debentureholders then they are termed as 'unsecured'. As has already been observed in India the CCI gives permission only for the issuance of secured debentures/bonds. Convertible Debentures are those which can be converted, in part or full, into ordinary shares of the same company at the option of the debentureholders under specified terms and conditions. (See, please, para 1.22 of this Chapter for the full description of Convertible Debentures/ Bonds).

1.21 Aside convertible bonds, secured bonds, unsecured debentures, redeemable and irredeemable bonds/debentures, corporations in USA are further found floating certain new variants of bonds such as 'Mortgage Bonds', 'Income Bonds', 'Zero Coupon Bonds', etc., the actual terms of Issues of these bonds, however, are designed as per the corporate policies of different corporations. Thus while under an issue of 'mortgage bonds' the corporation pledges its certain assets as security in favour of the bondholders, 'income bonds' are riskiest in the sense that interest is payable only if the issuing firm earns sufficient profits. In an eventuality when the company is even not able to meet its other expenses, it would not be obligatory on its part to pay interest on these bonds.[63] Consequent upon the high degree of risk associated with them these bonds are very sporadically issued. Innovations that took place in early 1980's in USA in the sphere of long-term debt financing would be further inquisitive as they led the way of the introduction of another variety of bonds, namely, the 'Zero Coupon Bonds' (ZCB) which are also known as 'Discount Bonds'. Since such bonds are offered at a substantial discount i.e., much below their par values, these have also come to be called by the name 'Original Issue Discount Bonds'.[64] ZCBs provide not only a large measure of call protection but also certain tax advantages. The larger the discount offered on this kind of bonds, the greater would be the attraction from the angle of their content of a capital gain and lower would be their yield in terms of coupon rate (interest rate) as compared to a situation if the bonds would have been sold at par.[65] Undoubtedly the foregoing discussion is quite significant from the view point of academic interest, our primary concern in this study is with the secured debentures/bonds offered to public by the listed public limited companies in India.

Convertible and Non-Convertible Debentures/Bonds :

1.22 The phrases Convertible Debentures/Bonds (henceforth abridged as 'convertibles' or CDs) and 'non-convertible debentures/bonds' (henceforth called 'non-convertibles' or NCDs) have common connotations both in India as well in USA. In India while convertibles are the securities which can be exchanged, in part or full, into equity shares of the issuing company at the option of the debentureholders/bondholders on the stipulated terms of conditions announced at the time of their issuance, non-convertibles are those which cannot be exchanged for equity shares and thus, are like ordinary or straight debentures/bonds.[66] *Eugene F. Brigham* construed convertibles to denote those securities which are convertible into shares of common stock at a fixed price at the option of the bondholders.[67] For *Fisher and Jordan*, "Convertible bonds give the owner the right to exchange the security for a given number of shares of common stock of the issuer during a specified period of time."[68] This term came to be explained by *Archer, Choate and Racette* as, "Some bonds, usually debentures, are convertible at the option of the holder into common stock of the issuing firm on specific terms"[69]; this explanation imply that convertible bonds are usually debentures. *Weston & Brigham* viewed "Convertible Securities" to refer to "bonds or preferred stocks that are exchangeable into common stock at the option of the holder and under specified terms and conditions."[70] Likewise, *Jack Clark Francis* also observed that : "A convertible security is usually a preferred stock or bond that can be converted into common stock."[71] Convertibles thus possess certain discriminative features such as : provision of conversion into equity shares ; pre-announcement of a specific conversion ratio and conversion price ; and, the specific period after the lapse of which permissible portion of convertibles is exchanged for equity shares.

Nature of Funds Raised through Convertibles : Is it a Debt or an Equity Capital ?

1.23 No dispute is found as to the nature of capital raised through non-convertibles ; all agree that it's a debt capital. Howbeit, the position is respect to the nature of funds gathered through convertibles differs. As disseminated above, in USA and some other Western Countries the funds raised wherewithal convertibles are clubbed as 'Equity Capital' perhaps on the analogy that they generally are fully (100 per cent) convertible in equity shares and it seems, rightly also, that the underlying intention of the issuing company is also to raise equity capital. Conversion, however, is permitted only after the lapse of a stipulated period of time. Clearly, therefore, even under a situation where the convertibles are fully convertible and the intention of the issuing company is to raise equity capital it appears more logical to treat the capital so gathered as debt capital till the date conversion is affected. And in case a part of it is kept convertible, then the portion which is declared as convertible is regarded as equity capital, that too, from the date conversion is affected, and the rest as debt capital. In contrast to this, eminent academics like *Eugene F. Brigham and Louis C. Gapenski* are of the opinion that Convertible Debentures/Bonds are primarily the source of raising debt funds. They thus, state that, "Convertibles offer a company the chance to sell debt with lower interest rate."[72] *Brigham and Gapenski's* suasive version has fully been supported by his contemporary thinkers. *Herbert B. Mayo* accordingly observed that, "technically convertibles are 'debt'."[73] He further stated that, "convertible bonds are debt instruments that may be converted at the holder's option into the stocks of the issuing company."[74] Similarly, *Stanley Huang* opined quite pertinently that : "The convertible bond is debt of the issuing corporation. It has a fixed claim on the earnings and assets of the corporation ahead of common and preferred stocks."[75] The same inference flows from what has been asserted by *Franks & Scholfield* : "A Convertible debenture or loan stock carries all the rights of non-convertible stock, but in addition entitles holders to convert into ordinary shares of the company at a specified time. Until and unless converted, convertibles are exactly the same as debentures and loan stocks, carrying an interest rate of the legal rights of the relevant security."[76] In the Indian Context, the instrument of convertible debenture is basically employed for raising debt capital. It is true both on legal and conceptual grounds. Official Guidelines issued on April 17, 1982 by the CCI in respect to the issuance of secured convertibles and non-convertibles by the listed public limited companies also made this point amply clear through the indusion of the statement which read as thus : "The debt equity ratio, including the proposed debenture issue will not normally exceed 2 : 1. For this purpose, 'debt' will mean all term loans, debentures and bonds with an initial maturity period of five years or more, including interest accrued thereon."[77] In brevity, the portion of the convertibles which is likely to be converted can rightfully be deemed as a source of raising equity capital and the rest as that of debt capital for the purpose of analysis by us.

Species of Convertibles (CDs)

1.24 In order to attract the surplus spending units to invest in debentures, Indian Companies have evolved a family of CDs suiting to the variety of motives with which they save money through introduction of 'sweeteners' in the terms and conditions on which they are placed in the market specially in respect to subscription rights and conversion features, we may mention in the context specifically the three variants of CDs.

(*i*) *Debentures with Subscription Rights* : While the debentures with subscription rights do not permit the conversion of either in full or part any portion of their face value into equity shares, they come to acquire the characteristics of CDs due to the fact that the holders of such debentures are allowed to obtain equity shares on terms and conditions announced at the time of their issuance by paying additional money. Thus in this case the face value of CDs is kept in tact. These also cover debentures/bonds issued to the existing shareholders of the issuing company in a specified proportion of their equity holdings.

(*ii*) *Partly Convertible Debentures* : Partly Convertible Debentures are those in which a part of the face value of a debenture is kept convertible into equity shares of the issuing company after the lapse of a specified period of time and at a specified price either at the option of the debentureholder or on an automatic basis. Issuance of such debentures is not only most popular with the debentures issuing companies but they are also prized by the investing public.

(*iii*) *Fully Convertible Debentures* : In case of fully convertible debentures the whole of the face value of a debenture is converted into equity shares of the concerned company after a specified period of time or after certain intervals either automatically or at the option of the debentureholders. These debentures are sparingly issued by the Indian companies as they are likely to affect capital structure and profitability presumably to their disadvantage. Even so, the employment of this variant of CDs is commended under the situation when the company is having a corporate plan to raise the base of its equity capital but is posed with an immediate problem of the shortage of long term funds.

THE ROOT OF EXCELLENCE IN CONVERTIBLE DEBENTURES :

1.25 The fancy for CDs is increasing as a means of raising funds needed to meet both the working capital as well the investment capital required for financing expansion, modernization, diversification, buying of balancing equipments including the R&D programs. A few companies have also used them for gathering resources which may be required to implement their amalgamation proposals. Indian Companies' longingness to this means of convoke funds is quite understandable. They cost less for the issuing company, the maximum burden of rate of interest being 13.5 per cent per annum until recently in sharp contrast to 19.26 per cent for annum as charged generally by commercial banks on their loans apart an obligation to bear some actual out-of-pocket expenses by the loanee. Commitment to pay interest is confined only up to the period and for the portion for which the conversion is not affected ; true that the burden of interest is also required to be borne on the permissible convertible portion till the date actual conversion is affected. Equity base of the company remains naive if it aggrandize its resources through the issuance of CDs. *Ipso facto* the question of the dilution in management would remain lockout. It is possible to fit the conversion period in accordance with gestation period of the project for the financing of which necessary funds are augmented through CDs, in such a manner so that earning per share is in no way adversely affected. And, once the project sees its successful completion it would start contributing to the earnings of the enterprize which in their turn assist in maintaining the hitherto earnings per share. (E.P.S.) The above aspects, it may be sweared, extends great solace in maintaining the already attained standards of profitability. Generally the redemption of CDs is done after the lapse of Seven Years and that too in specified instalments. Consequently the cash outflow on this count remain at a level which may ensure a satisfactory liquidity position for the company. The CDs are superior *vis-a-vis* the debt raised from public finance intermediaries. At the time of declaration of dividends while no permission is required from the debenture-holders, it would be obligatory in case a clause is included in the loan-agreement if debt is arranged through some public financial institution ; it is certainly a blinking condition to fulfil for the corporate management of the concerned company. Although setting of the purchase conditions in the event of mergers and amalgamations is done commonly through equity shares, it is no more a secret that CDs present a better means of paying this consideration.

1.26 From the angle of investors CDs fall in the category of preferred savings instrument. They offer to them full safety of their funds since CDs in India are issued only after the creation of a charge on company's assets Easy marketability of CDs at the Stock Exchanges satisfies the liquidity motive of the investors. The added feature of conversion of a part or the whole of it into equity shares either at the face value or at a much lower price than what is found prevalent in the market grants them the right to avail the advantage of capital appreciation meaning thereby possessing a right to enjoy the fruits of company's growth.[78] Furthermore, interest payable on CDs is in no way less lucrative ; as a matter of fact it is higher in contrast to several other saving instruments that are available to them for investment.

COLLATING CDs WITH THE DEPOSITS FROM THE PUBLIC, PREFERENCE AND EQUITY SHARES :

1.27 Deposits from public include the deposits accepted by the public limited companies (non-banking and non-financial) from the public for a period ranging between 3 months to 3 years in terms of Companies Amendment Act 1974 (Section 58-A and 58-B)[79] and the Companies (Acceptance of Deposits) Rules 1975 as amended to this date. These are in the nature of debt instrument. A preference share, in terms of Section 85 (1) of the Indian Companies Act, is that part of the share capital of the company which fulfils the following requirements, namely :

(*a*) that as respects dividends, it carries or will carry a preferential right to be paid a fixed amount or an amount calculated at a fixed rate, which may be either free of or subject to income-tax ; it means that dividend must be paid to the preference shareholders before the holders of equity shares receive anything ; and

(*b*) that as respects capital, it carries or will carry on a winding up or repayment of capital, a preferential right to be repaid the amount of the capital paid up or deemed to have been paid up, whether or not there is a preferential right to the payment of either or both of the following amounts, namely :

(*i*) any money remaining unpaid, in respect of the amounts specified in clause (a) upto the date of the winding up or repayment of capital ; and

(*ii*) any fixed premium or premium on any fixed scale, specified in the memorandum or articles of the company.[80]

But this right to receive the capital back in priority to the equity shareholders is said to be exhaustive i.e., it implies that there is no right to receive anything more, and, therefore, if it is desired that the preference shareholders should also participate in the surplus assets, then, this right must be expressly given to them. While legally preference shareholders are considered owners of the firm since no debtor-creditor relationship exists as occurs between the firm and the debenture/bondholders, from the point of view of financial theory they are more closer to the form of debt-financing. And, Equity Share Capital means all share capital which is not preference share capital.[81]

1.28 Though in recent years the quantum of deposits accepted from public by the non-banking non-financial companies has shown a spurt, it must be recognised that Public

Deposits is an uncertain source of finance so long as it may imply a panic to withdraw the same by the depositors consequential to a slight rumour about the financial position of the company.[82] Further the Government is gradually hightening its restrictions on the acceptance of such deposits. Thus, the overall limit of fixed deposits accepted from public and shareholders has been brought down to 25 per cent of their aggregate paid up capital and free reserves with effect from April 1,1981 from 35 per cent prior to the above date. Then the companies are not allowed to accept deposits for more than 3-years and that too with an initial minimum of Rs. 1,000 and thereafter in multiples of Rs. 500—a sum which is indeed obdurate for small and middle class savers. The company is obliged to deposit in a scheduled bank or invest in specified securities before April 30th each year a sum not less than 10 per cent of the amount of its deposits maturing during the year ended on March 31st of the following year. Moreover, the effective cost of Public Deposits to the company comes much more than what is indicated by the interest payable on them. The interest paid on them is not allowed in its entirety from Income Tax Under Section 40 A (viii) of the Income Tax Act, 15 per cent of such interest paid is disallowed as a business expenditure whereas 100 per cent of the interest paid on CDs is an allowable expenditure under Income Tax Act. Consequently, the effective rate of interest borne by the company on public deposits amount to $R \times .15 \times T/1\text{-}T$; here R=Rate of Interest on Deposits ; T=Rate of Income Tax paid to Government on its Rs. 1 profit. Assuming that the company is paying 15 per cent interest on public deposits and 60 per cent tax on its profits its effective rate would be :

$$15 \times .15 \times .60/1\text{-}60 = 3.38$$

i.e., 15 per cent+3.38 per cent

=18.38 per cent.[83]

In the absence of such restrictions and restrictive treatment of interest paid under the Income Tax, CDs are obviously superior to the Public Deposits from the angle of both the issuing company and the investors.

1.29 As compared to preference shares also the CDs have an edge. The interest paid on CDs is a permissible business expenditure for income tax purposes and the company can continue to enjoy this tax advantage until they are converted/redeemed. The dividend rate on preference shares has varied between 9.5 per cent and 11 per cent, whereas on CDs interest was payable until recently at the rate of 13.5 per cent which should have been preferable to the investors. Again, preference hareholders do not have any voice in the management of the company. Equity shares too poses larger problems in contrast to CDs for the companies as a means of augmenting their capital resources. The expectations of investors in respect of dividends are relatively high as the same are determined by the prevalent structure of interest rates on the one hand, and a plus for the risk, on the other. Low profit margins and absence of information about the prospects of company to the prospective investors make the task of issuing equity capital quite formidable. Investors plump for CDs as compared to shares offered by new companies because no gestation period is involved in respect to the return on investment in case of the latter. CDs are more successful in attracting funds from institutional investors which may not otherwise be purchasing equity shares or at best may hold a small percentage of total investment in ordinary shares. Other merits of CDs *vis-a-vis* equity shares have already been highlighted by us in the preceding paras.

OTHER RELEVANT CONCEPTS

(*i*) *Capital Market : Primary & Secondary Capital Market*

1.30 The term 'Capital Market' has a wide connotation. Since the term in this wide sense is not relevant to the context under consideration, in a restricted sense it signify the institutional mechanism or market through which the requirement of long-term funds of the private corporate sector in India is met. Viewed in this manner, the capital market includes individual investors, national level industrial finance institutions, state level financing institutions, Life Insurance Corporation of India, Unit Trust of India and General Insurance

Corporation of India. Commercial banks are excluded because they provide basically short-term working capital finance and the term loan facility that they provide is backed up to a greater extent by a corresponding refinance facility from the Industrial Development Bank of India. However, their role as Managers to Issues can not be overlooked.

1.31 Primary capital market is concerned with the initial issues of shares and securities. It is basically a distribution market for new issues and its primary function is to affect transfer of investible funds to the users who need them for productive purposes. The primary market therefore becomes active only when new issues are floated. The Secondary Capital Market is the market where after the initial issue the securities are bought and sold. The two markets are, however, mutually interrelated and interdependent and the development of both has to proceed hand in hand.

(*ii*) *Public Limited Listed Companies* :

1.32 In terms of Section 3 (1) (iv) to be read alongwith Section 12, 12 (2) (a) and Section 13 (3) of the Companies Act, 1956 a public limited company is an association comprising of seven or any higher number of members, which is registered under the Companies Act, 1956 or Companies Acts previously in force, and which is not a private company within the meaning of the Act. The articles of such a company do not contain provisions restricting the number of its members or excluding generally the offer or transfer of shares or debentures to the public. On principle, any member of the public who is willing to pay the price may acquire shares or debentures of it. Also, only shares and debentures of public companies are capable of being dealt in on a stock exchange. The liability of the members of such a company is limited by its memorandum to the amount, if any, unpaid on the shares respectively held by them or to such an amount as the members may respectively, through a guarantee, undertake to contribute to the assets of the company in the event of its winding up.[84] Those public limited companies of the private sector the securities of which have been admitted for trading privileges on

Stock Exchange/s are clubbed as Public Limited Listed Companies. In the context, it may be mentioned that the Securities Contracts (Regulation) Rules 1957, promulgated by the Government of India under the Securities Contracts (Regulation) Act, 1956 and the Stock Exchange Bye Laws and Regulations approved by the Government under the Act prescribe the requirements a company must comply with before its shares can be listed on any recognised Stock Exchange. And, the listing regulations of all the recognized stock exchanges in India are uniform.

(*iii*) *Transactions in the Listed Securities* :

1.33 Under the bye-laws and regulations of the recognized stock exchanges transactions in listed securities may be either :

(*a*) For 'spot delivery' i.e., for delivery and payment on the same day as the date of the contract or on the next day ; or

(*b*) For 'hand delivery', i.e., for delivery and payment within the time or on the date stipulated when entering into the bargain which time or date shall not be more than fourteen days following the date of contract ; or

(*c*) For the 'clearing' of the account i.e., for clearance and settlement through the clearing house ; or

(*d*) For 'Special delivery' i.e., for delivery and payment within any time exceeding fourteen days following the date of the contract as may be stipulated when entering into the bargain and permitted by the Governing Board or the President.

1.34 Business for spot delivery or hand delivery can be done in cleared as well as non-cleared securities, but business for the clearing can be done in cleared securities alone. Business for special delivery may be entered into in cleared or non-cleared securities after obtaining permission as provided in the bye-laws. The 'Cleared Securities' refer to the securities included in the list of such securities by the Governing Body of a recognized stock exchange subject to the fulfilment of certain specified conditions ; such an inclusion entitle these securities for dealing them on the concerned/stock exchange/s. While 'Spot delivery' contracts are exempted from the Act, 'Special Delivery Contracts' are rare. Trading on the stock exchange mostly relates to those on hand delivery and clearing which informally are still known by the name forward trading though the Government of India has banned such transactions at all the Stock Exchanges through the issuance of a notification on June 27, 1969 under Section 16 of the Securities Contracts (Regulation) Act, 1956. Thus the forward trading continues to exists under the garb of "Group 'A' Securities" (at Bombay Stock Exchange), "Hand Delivery/Paid up" (at Calcutta Stock Exchange), "Specified Shares" (at Delhi Stock Exchange), "Cleared Securities" (at Madras Stock Exchange) and so forth.

VOLATILE AND NON-VOLATILE SHARES

1.35 All shares of listed companies can be categorized into 'Volatile' and 'Other than Volatile Shares'. And, by 'Volatile' shares, we would mean those which witness either steady growth or wide range of fluctuations in their prices on account of they being actively traded. These are usually of "Cleared" list, but in certain cases they may also belong to the "non-cleared" list. All shares other than volatile would be clubbed into "Other than Volatile Shares".

TERMS OF CONVERSION

1.36 These cover conversion ratio, conversion price and conversion value in case of convertible debentures/bonds. The 'conversion ratio', which is also termed as rate, refers to the number of shares of common stock that may be obtained by converting a convertible debenture/bond. 'Conversion Price' is usually stated as formal part of the terms of the issue. It indicate the actual price to be paid for the shares to be obtained at the time of conversion by the convertible debenture/bondholder. And, the 'Conversion Value' of a convertible security is obtained by multiplying the conversion ratio by the current market price of the share.

THE RALLYING POINTS OF THE STUDY

1.37 The discussions in the preceding paras exhort us to make convertible debentures/bonds issued by the listed public limited companies of the private corporate sector during the period 1978-82 as its nucleus of indepth quest ; though side by side the merited audit of the Issues of Non-Convertible Debentures/ Bonds has also been undertaken with a view to put forward also the relevant analysis in respect to them and compare and contrast the findings concerning with convertibles with that of the non-convertibles. The centre of our attention is proposed to be focussed on such cardinal aspects as tracing out the history of convertibles in India, the pattern of the approvals granted by CCI during the period 1978-82 for the issuance of CDs and NCDs by the public limited listed companies of the private corporate sector, appraising these issues by selecting appropriate criteria with an angle to discover the fate with which they met, and reckoning of values and rates of returns to the debentureholders of variegated character by selecting specific issues to represent them. The detailed analysis of the issues of CDs is, however, intended to be restricted only to cover those which have come to be offered to public ; consequently, therefore, the issues of CDs offered on rights basis have been excluded. This exclusion is justifiable because such convertibles are attached to the limited category of investors holding the special status of existing shareholders of the concerned company. Employing the determinative trends, captious and dispassionate culmination of upshots and the set of proposed values in respect to CDs, two case studies—one for the successful and another for the unsuccessful Issue of CDs—have further been undertaken with a view to investigate in details the variables which contributed to the successfulness and unsuccessfulness of the chosen issues. A case study of an Issue of Non-Convertible Debentures has also been included to serve the similar objective. The Case Studies have been followed by an analysis of the responses filled in the Questionnaires addressed to the Corporate Executives, prominent academics/office bearers of leading Stock Exchanges/Managers to Issues/Underwriters to Issues/Brokers, and the select group of existing and prospective investors on the one hand, and a critical audit of the existing Government Policy in respect to the issuance of debentures, relevant provisions of the Income Tax Act and the present state of affairs of the Secondary Market for Debentures in India, on the other. And, the Study comes to an end with a set of recommendations which, if implemented in true spirit, should not only allow the companies of Indian Private Corporate Sector to employ debentures on a continual basis for raising long-term funds on most appropriate terms but should also enlighten the investors in regard to the aspects that need to be borne in mind at the time of purchasing, selling and retaining this class of securities. Not only this, these should abet development of an effective market for debentures in India.

IMPORTANT HYPOTHESES

1.38 The main propositions on which this study is based are :

— of the two, namely convertible and non-convertible debentures/bonds, the former is an easy mode for raising the funds from the angle of corporate managements and the investing public ;

— issues of convertible debentures/bonds of such companies whose shares are of volatile nature, witnessing a rising trend in their market prices, and which are accompanied with attractive terms of conversion/conversion rates, timing of conversion and conversion price are likely to meet with more success as against the issues of convertibles floated by such companies whose shares are of non-volatile category, witnessing either a constant or declining trend in their market prices, and are accompanied with rather less lucrative terms of conversion ; and

— not only the much publicized higher returns on the variegated issues of convertibles/non-convertibles are misleading, these securities neither provide adequate liquidity nor expected returns to the investors.

THE MAJOR TASK

1.39 The major task which this Study intends to accomplish is comprised of :

— tracing out the history of convertible debentures/bonds in India ;

— undertaking a census survey of companies which have raised funds by issuing convertible and non-convertible debentures/bonds between the years 1978 and 1982 and analyzing the trends in the issuance of the debentures of both categories in terms of face value, amount of issue, timing of issue, volume of funds raised, terms and conditions of issue, as also on the basis of industry-, region-, and age-wise classifications of the issuing companies ;

— adjudging the successfulness and unsuccessfulness of the different issues of convertible debentures/bonds from the view point of the concerned company, its corporate management, investors, managers to issues, and the economy on the basis of the bunch of appropriate yardsticks such as dates of opening the subscription lists, amount of issues, number of times the issues have been oversubscribed or undersubscribed or just fully subscribed, total number of issues of convertibles floated during the entire period under analysis by different companies, market values of the shares in number of times to their face values at the time of the floatation of relevant issues, number of times the conversion price is to the face values of correlated shares, insertion of news items about the working of the concerned company on a regular basis, advertised returns and expected benefits in terms of the likely percentage increase in the market values of convertibles and possibility of similar increase in the market values of associated shares and the expected benefits on account of bothof them as measured through benefit indices at the time of convertibility, volatile and non-volatile nature of the relevant shares, and the costs of specifically selected issues. In doing so statistical tools like coefficient of correlation, coefficient of determination standard deviation, coefficient of variation, etc. have further been employed at the appropriate place ;

— assessing in a realistic manner the investment opportunities entailed by convertible debentures/bonds through the computation of values and rates of returns to the holders of specific issues representing different varieties of CDs with the help of Internal Rate of Return Method on the one hand, and advertized returns, on the other ;

— undertaking one case study each of the successful and unsuccessful issue of convertible debentures/bonds and one to represent an issue of non-convertible debentures/bonds with a view to identify the variables responsible for the successfulness/unsuccessfulness and evaluate the role played by the concerned issue of debentures/bonds in improving the financial resources of the company on the one hand, and in its overall performance, on the other ;

— appraising critically the official guidelines laid down from time to time in respect to the issuance of secured convertible and non-convertible debentures/bonds, relevant provisions of the Income Tax Act in order to adjudicate their subservience to the objectives of companies and the investing public. Alongside this an exercise has also been undertaken for reviewing the existing situation of the secondary market for debentures in India ; and

— suggesting out on the basis of our main inferences and analysis of responses recorded from the Chairmen, corporate finance executives of all the debenture issuing companies, prominent academics, office bearers of the leading Stock Exchanges, Managers to Issues/Underwriters/Brokers to the various issues of debentures under reference and a select group of existing and prospective investors, the most conducive theoretical and operative framework which may permit the companies of Indian Private Corporate Sector employing of these instruments on a continual basis for raising funds on most benign terms, warrant the investing public on the considerations to be kept in mind while purchasing, selling and retaining such securities in their portfolio and abet development of an effective secondary market for debentures/bonds in India.

LOGIC OF THE PERIOD : 1978-82

1.40 While 1982 has come to be selected inadvertently it benig the year in which this research project got its final approval-our choice for 1978 is marked by the year when Government of India first of all issued its Guidelines for the issuance of "Rights" Debentures by Public Limited Companies. And it is since then that a real spurt in the floatation of debentures has been witnessed. As a matter of fact, the whole period of 1978-82 can be regarded quite important from the view point of issuance of CDs and NCDs. This is however not to deny that the period following the year 1982 has not been significant from this angle.

MESSAGE OF THIS STUDY :

1.41 The significance of this research work lies in the dissemination of most critical information not only to the corporate managements of the companies interested in meeting their capital requirements by issuing CDs or NCDs but also to those who are anxious in investing their savings in these saving instruments. The corporate managements would find answers to such strategic questions as to when, for what purposes and amounts, and under what terms and conditions it would be most beneficial to raise funds through CDs/NCDs. Similarly, the investing public should find this study interesting as it is to enlighten them about the real benefits which they would obtain through investment in such kind of securities aside cautioning them about the situations under which they could be deceived by the shrewd managements/managers handling such issues. The findings of this work would further assist them in resolving some of their problems concerning with the management of investment in debentures such as : how to make a judicious selection among the number of similar securities offered almost at the same point of time by different companies ; when and which is to be disposed off ; and, for how long and which one of these are to retained.

1.42 The financial intermediaries, whose services are engaged in the issue of such securities as Managers of Issues would also find it of their concern as it would make them aware of the effectiveness of the alternate strategies, policies and measures which could be adopted for deposing desired success in the Issues which they choose for the purpose apart signalizing them about the most appropriate timings for the floatation of such issues. The information to be released by this study on the expectations of the investing public from such securities and on the investment opportunity entailed in this means of corporate financing should further be found useful to them in counselling with the corporate managements craving to raise funds by floating CDs/NCDs. The sections of this work wherein we have identified the gaps in the official guidelines for the issuance of CDs/NCDs, pitfalls in the relevant provisions of Income Tax Act, and the essential conditions for and the measures required to develop an effective secondary market for debentures in the country should point out to the necessity to affect improvements on the indicated lines in the existing statutory operative framework for debentures by the Government in particular by the CCI, Ministry of Finance and the RBI. The national theorist in financial management too are likely to value this work as it also includes an outline of the most conducive theoretical model for such securities keeping in view the Indian environment as also the interests of all concerned parties with the issues of CDs/NCDs.

1.43 The pre-eminence of this study shall in no way be less from the macro angle i.e., from the view point of the nation's economy. One, it spotlights the magnitude of funds mobilised in the private corporate sector during the period 1978-82 for the capital formation through the issuance of CDs/NCDs. To the extent these funds have been subscribed by individual investors, particularly the small investors, it might be taken to mean that some portion of such savings have been mobilised by these securities which otherwise would perhaps frittered away into unproductive outlets. And, to the extent this premise stands established by the relevant data this research report can also said to have endeavoured to highlight the part these securities can play in controlling the inflationary conditions in the economy. Two, the present day position of the country is such which could be considered to have been circumferenced by the oppositly moving twin forces. While the financial needs of the corporate sector are growing steadily alongwith the strides of industrial growth, the former sources of commercial banks and other finance institutions have been issued directives not to channelise their funds to the private corporate sector in a big and in an indiscriminate way on account of the hard need felt for deploying them for the growth of more strategic sectors of the economy in terms of the country's well conceived planning objectives for benefitting the maximum number of people in an equitable manner. Undisputably, the increasing demand for funds by the private corporate sector can not be questioned on the grounds of they being unjust ; truly speaking they are fully justified so long as they contribute to the attainment of a higher rate of growth in the sector industry of our economy. What is further pertinent in this context is that the RBI's and Government's above referred dictates to commercial banks and other finance institutions too are well thought out and in tune with the judicious needs of the day. Under the circumstances, it is essential that the Government's endeavour to create and develop a secondary market for debentures/bonds in the country must meet with a grand success. And, it is here that this study is to contribute its most.

ORGANIZATION OF THIS WORK

1.44 Aside the Chapter First, which is in our hands, this research report has three more Chapters making the organization of this study to spread over in all the Four Chapters. Chapter Second describes the research methodology employed for the accomplishment of the set in task besides presenting in its beginning a succint view of the various constituents of the Indian Corporate Sector in general and Private Corporate Sector in particular. Thus it highlights the spirit of research design, universe of the study, observational units and sampling framework, sources from where the essential data/information has been gathered, pattern of analysis undertaken, statistical tools used and crucial variables involved for the examination of our hypotheses and establishment of the determined objectives.

1.45 The major results alongside the proposed analysis have been placed in Chapter Three which is comprised of seven distinct sections. While an attempt has been made to trace out the history of the origination of Convertible Debentures/ Bonds in India in Section : One, macro and microsopic trends of interest in respect to the total approvals granted by the CCI for the issuance of CDs/NCDs during the period 1978-82 have been presented in Section : Two. Apart highlighting industry-, age-, and region/state/Union-territory-wise drifts regarding CDs/NCDs, minute details of the Issues of CDs floated by Public Limited Listed Companies of the private corporate sector have further been thrashed out in this Section. The subsequent Section : Three stands fully devoted for adjudging the successfulness and unsuccessfulness of the Issues of CDs offered to Public on just, admissable and cogent set of proposed yardsticks from the angle of companies and managers to issues involved in them on the one hand, and investors and the nation's economy, on the other. We have pierced through the values of the cost of raising funds, expected market price and rates of return reckoned out with the help of internal rate of return method on the randomly selected issues of debentures aside comparing these rates of return with the advertised rates in Section: Four. The proposed case studies of CDs and NCDs and the analysis of the responses recorded in the Questionnaires addressed to the Corporate Executives of the Companies which floated CDs/NCDs, Office Bearers of the Stock Exchanges/Managers to Issues/Eminent Academics/Underwriters to Issues/Brokers and to a select group of investors constitute the subject matter of Sections Five and Six, respectively. And a critical appraisal has been attempted in Section-Seven of this Chapter in regard to the present Government Policy/Official Guidelines concerning with the issuance of debentures, relevant provisions of the Income Tax Act and the existing state of affairs of the secondary market for debentures. In the concluding Chapter Fourth, a set of recommendations have been included on the basis of our major inferences drawn in regard to the issues chosen by us for an indepth study of Convertible Debentures/Bonds. In brief, these focus on how the interests of different groups of people, institutions, and the State would stand served best in the kind of securities we are dwelling upon.

NOTES

1. Government of India, Planning Commission, New Delhi, '*The Seventh Five Year Plan : 1985-90, Volume-I : Perspective, Objectives, Strategy, Macro-Dimensions and Resources*', 1985 Chapter 6, p. 68.
2. Ibidem, p. 71.
3. Ibidem, p. 72.
4. It is inclusive of the savings of Rs. 8,266 crores of public sector financial institutions.
5. Government of India, Planning Commission, New Delhi, '*The Seventh Five Year Plan : 1985-90, Volume-I,*' *Op. Cit.*, p. 48.
6. Government of India, Planning Commission, New Delhi, '*Draft Fifth Five Year Plan : 1974-79, Volume I*'. *p. 3*.
7. For instance several sectoral programs aiming at self-reliance in food, oil and fertilizers were taken up in Fourth through Sixth Five Year Plans. For details, see, please, Government of India, Planning Commission, New Delhi, Fourth through Sixth Five Year Plans.
8. Dehejia Study Group's Report was submitted in September 1969.
9. RBI, '*Report on Currency and Finance, 1969-70*', *p. 106, and* RBI, '*Report of the Study Group to Frame Guidelines for Follow up of Bank Credit*', Bombay, 1975, p. 10.
10. Government of India, '*Report of the Industrial Licensing Policy Inquiry Committee*', New Delhi, 1969. The Committee was appointed in July 1967 under the Chairmanship of Shri S. Dutt which submitted its Report in July 1969.
11. RBI, '*Report of the Working Group to Review The System of Cash Credit*', Bombay, 1979, p. 20.
12. RBI, '*Report of the Study Group to Frame Guidelines for Follow up of Bank Credit*, Chapter 15 tit'ed, *Summary of Observations And Recommendations*' Bombay, 1975, p. 67.
13. Government of India, Ministry of Law, Justice and Company Affairs, Department of Company Affairs, '*Report of the High Powered Expert Committee On Companies & MRTP Acts*'. New Delhi, August 1978, p. 206.
14. Ibidem, p. 298.
15. Quoted from the RBI's Report of the Working Group to Review the System of Cash Credit, Bombay, 1979, p. 1.

16. RBI, '*Report of the Working Group to Review The System of Cash Credit*', Op. Cit., p. 28.
17. RBI, '*Report of the Committee to Review the Working of the Monetary System*', Bombay, April 1985, pp. 306-307.
18. Ibidem, p. 307.
19. Ibidem, p. 308.
20. The acute oil crisis is visible from the goodly rise registered in the imports of Petroleum Oil and Lubricants between 1970-71 and 1981-82 which not only mounted pressure on the already meagre foreign exchange resources available with the Government but further aggravated the unfavourable balance of payments position ; thus, the imports rose to Rs. 560 crores in 1973-74 and reached to the peak of Rs. 5622 crores in 1982-83 from a bare sum of Rs. 136 crores in 1970-71. *Source*: Government of India, Ministry of Finance (Economic Division), '*Economic Survey*: *1985-86*' New Delhi, 1986, p. 163.
21. The Index Number of Wholesale Prices (Base : 1970-71 = 100) for All Commodities rose to 346.3 during the last week of 1984-85 from 108.2 during the last week of 1971-72 indicating thereby an overall percentage increase of over 220 in a span of thirteen years and an average percentage increase of 17 per annum. *Source*: Government of India, Ministry of Finance (Economic Division), '*Economic Survey*: *1985-86*', New Delhi, 1986, p. 153.
22. Solomon, Ezra and Pringle, John J., '*An Introduction to Financial Management*', Prentice Hall of India Private Limited, 1978.
23. See, please, Table 2.1 of Annexe II for details.
24. For details, see, please, RBI's N.N. Pai Committee's Report, December, 1981.
25. As a matter of fact it is understood that strategic portions of some of the recommendations of the Pai Committee have already been taken care of by the CCI while issuing the Guidelines for the issuance of Debentures in April 1982.
26. Brigham, Eugene F. '*An Analysis of Convertible Debentures*: *Theory and Some Empirical Evidence*', Journal of Finance 21, March 1966, pp. 35-54.
27. Sheth, Narendra J., '*Convertible Debentures, Bonds*: *Relevance to Financing of New Projects*', the Economic Times, Bombay, October 7, 1980, p. 5.
28. Sheth, Narendra J., '*Convertible Bonds* : *A Perspective On Conversion Price*', *Saturday Supplement*, The Economic Times, Bombay, April 10, 1982, p. IV.
29. Mukhi, M.D., '*Debentures*: *Steps Needed to Develop It*', Part I, The Economic Times, Bombay, January 23, 1981, pp. 5-8 ; and,

'*Debentures* : *Need for a Secondary Market*', Part II, The Economic Times, Bombay, January 24, 1981 p. 5.

30. Venkataraman, '*Debentures* : *Rising Importance*', The Special Survey on Investment, the Economic Times, Bombay, April 23, 1981, pp. I-IV.
31. Kashekar, S.R., '*Bonds—The British Way*', Special Survey on Investment, the Economic Times, April 23, 1981, pp. I-IV.
32. Kutty, M. Krishnan, '*Bonds of Public Bodies*', Special Survey on Investment, the Economic Times, April 23, 1981, pp. I-IV.
33. Sengupta, Sudhi R., '*Working Capital*: *Debentures and Deposits as Sources*', The Economic Times, Bombay, June 4, 1981, p. 5 ; and '*Working Capital* : *Interests of Investors*', The Economic Times, Bombay, June 5, 1981, p. 5.
34. Datar, V.D., '*Convertible Debentures*: *A Utility Analysis*', Mid-week Review on Investment, the Economic Times, Bombay, April 7, 1982, p. IV.
35. Chaudhuri, Swapan Kanti, '*Convertible Debentures*: *Components of yield*', the Economic Times, October 16, 1982, pp. 5-6.
36. Ibidem.
37. Goyal, O.P. & Agarwal, V.K : '*Convertible Debentures/Bonds* : *Experience of Private Corporate Sector*', *Saturday Supplement on Finance*, the Economic Times, Bombay, pp. VII-VIII.
38. Ibidem, p. VII.
39. Ibidem.
40. Balakrishnan, P.K., '*Rate of Return on Convertible Debentures*', Financial Express, Bombay, January 3, 1981.
41. Prasad, G., & Rao, K. Viyyanna, '*Management of Convertible Debentures-I*', and '*Convertible Debentures-II*', Financial Express, Bombay, October 27, 1981, p. 5, and October 28, 1981, p. 7, respectively.
42. Ramachandran, K.S., '*Why this Scramble For Convertible Debentures?*', Financial Express, Bombay, February 2, 1982, p. 5.
43. Moses, A.S., '*Convertible Debenture Profit*', Financial Express, Bombay, May 15, 1982, p. 5.
44. Mukhi, M.D., '*Debentures* : *Prolific Source of Funds for Companies*', Financial Express, Bombay, April 28, 1983, p. 5.
45. Research Bureau, Business Standard, '*Debenture Issues & Equity Prices* : *A Case Study of Seven Companies,*' Business Standard, January 29, 1982.
46. Sinha, N.P., '*Convertible Debentures—An Analytical Study*', The Chartered Accountant, Volume XXXI, No. 3 September 1982, pp. 222 & 226.

47. Simha, S.L.N., Hemalatha D., & Balakrishnan, S., '*Investment Management : Introduction to Securities Analysis*', Institute for Financial Management & Research, Madras, December 1979, pp. 773-76.

48. Kuchhal, S.C., '*Financial Management : An Analytical & Conceptual Approach*', Chaitanya Publishing House, Allahabad, 1982, Chapter 25—'Debentures Rights & Public', pp. 483-94, and Chapter 32—'Convertible Bonds and Loans' pp. 587-607.

49. Ibidem.

50. Chandra, Prasanna, '*Financial Management : Theory and Practice*', Tata McGraw-Hill Publishing Company Ltd., New Delhi, 1984, Chapter 21—'Equity, Preference and Debenture Capital,' pp. 493-06 ; Chapter 22—'Market for Long Term Securities in India', pp. 507-41 ; and, Chapter-28, 'Debentures With Subscription Rights and Conversion', pp. 635-48.

51. Ibidem.

52. Government of India, Ministry of Law, Justice and Company Affairs, '*The Companies Act, 1956*', p. 5.

53. Brigham, Eugene F., and Gapenski, Louis C., '*Financial Management : Theory & Practice*', the Dryden Press, Tokyo, 1985, p. 611.

54. Weston, J. Fred, and Brigham, Eugene F., '*Managerial Finance*', the Dryden Press, Tokyo, Seventh Edition, 1981, p. 785.

55. Gitman, Lawrence J., '*Principles of Managerial Finance*', Harper & Row Publishers, New York, Third Edition, 1982 p. G-3.

56. Archer, Stephen H., Choate, G. Marc. & Racette George, '*Financial Management*', John Wiley & Sons, New York, Second Edition, 1983, p. 80.

57. Brigham, Eugene F., & Gapenski, Louis C., Op. Cit. p. 611.

58. Ibidem, p. 612.

59. Mayo, Herbert B., '*Basic Investments : An Introduction*, The Dryden Press, Hinsdate, Illnois, 1980, p. 172.

60. Brigham, Eugene F. & Gapenski, Louis C., Op. Cit., pp. 612-13.

61. Johnson, Timothy E., '*Investment Principles*', Prentice-Hall Inc., Englewood Cliffs, N.J., Second Edition, 1983, p. 453.

62. Sharpe, William F., '*Investments*', Prentice Hall Inc., Englewood Cliffs, N.J. Second Edition, 1981, p. 276.

63. Mayo, Herbert B., Op. cit., p. 172.

64. Brigham, Eugene F. & Gapenski, Louis C., Op. Cit. p. 614.

65. Fisher, Donald E. & Jordan, Ronald J., '*Security Analysis and Portfolio Management*', Prentice-Hall Inc., Englewood Cliffs, N.J. Third Edition, 1983, p. 366.

66. Simha, S.L.N., Hemalatha D., & Balakrishnan S., Op. Cit., pp. 250-53.
67. Brigham, Eugene F. and Gapenski, Louis C., Op. Cit., p. 613.
68. Fisher, Donald E. & Jordan, Ronald J., Op. Cit., p. 402.
69. Archer, Stephen H., Choate, G. Marc and Racette, George., Op. Cit., p. 80.
70. Weston, J. Fred and Brigham, Eugene F., Op. Cit., p. 878.
71. Francis, Jack Clark, '*Investments : Analysis and Managements*', McGraw Hill Book Co., New York, Second Edition, 1976, p. 24.
72. Brigham, Eugene F. and Gapenski, Louis C., Op. Cit., p. 690.
73. Mayo, Herbert B., Op. Cit., p. 172.
74. Ibidem, p. 390.
75. Huang Stanley, '*Investment Analysis and Management*', Winthrog Publishing Inc., Cambridge Massachusetts, 1981, p. 334.
76. Franks, J.R. & Scholefield, H.H., '*Corporate Financial Management*', Gower Press, Teak Field Limited, England, Second Edition, p. 177.
77. Kapur, D.K., '*Management of Capital Issues*', A Publication of PHD Chamber of Commerce and Industry, New Delhi, May 1983, p. 100.
78. Fisher, Donald E., and Jordan Ronald J., Op. Cit., p. 438.
79. See, for details, Government of India, Ministry of Law, Justice and Company Affairs, '*The Companies Act, 1956*', New Delhi, pp. 37-39.
80. Ibidem, pp. 59-60.
81. Section 85(2) of the Companies Act, 1956, Op. Cit., p. 60.
82. The Textile Industry of Bombay and Ahmedabad did experience such a panic during the depression of the Thirties.
83. Datar, V.D., Op. Cit., p. IV.
84. The Companies Act, 1956, Op. Cit., pp. 9-16.

2

THE SETTING AND THE METHOD OF STUDY

- PROFILE OF INDIAN CORPORATE SECTOR
- THE UNIVERSE AND THE SURVEY POPULATION
- SELECTING THE OBSERVATIONAL UNITS AND AN ELUCIDATION OF THE ISSUES FLOATED ON "RIGHTS" BASIS
- EXCULPATION FOR OBTRACIZING THE ISSUES OF NCDs FOR BLOW-BY-BLOW INVESTIGATION
- STRIKING FEATURES OF THE SAMPLE
- SOURCES AND METHODS EMPLOYED FOR DATA COLLECTION
- PATTERN OF ANALYSIS UNDERTAKEN, STATISTICAL TOOLS/ MODELS EMPLOYED AND VARIABLES INVOLVED
- THE DISPOSITION

PROFILE OF INDIAN CORPORATE SECTOR

AS is the case with most of the developed and developing countries of the world, Corporate Sector has been the nucleus of the industrial progress of our country too. The modernity, substantial degree of self-reliance, diversification and use of high level of technology that are now marked in our industrial sector have been the overweening impacts of the cardinal role played by the corporate sector during the planned era. The Industrial Policy Resolution of 1956, as modified from time to time, germinated an eloquent groundwork for the Government's industrial policies which strived at not only bringing about precipitated growth of employment and output but also at accomplishing certain socio-economic objectives, such as, regional diffusion of growth, promotion of village and small industries, prevention of monopolies and concentration of economic power in sporadic hands by acquiescing the public corporate sector to play a leading role, partly as a catalyst, in moulding and accelerating the process of industrialization within the pragmatic structure of 'mixed economy' on the one hand, and Socialistic Pattern of Society, on the other.[1] The objective of self reliance would also receive support via an appropriate policy mix to be created to sought protection for domestic industry from all relevant angles covering both internal and external variables.[2] In years ahead sector industry, as contemplated by our planners, would thus continue to play a pioneering role in accomplishing the determined targets of overall economic growth ; although the undercurrent stress is on better efficiency, reduction of cost, improvement of quality through absorption of new technology, greater attention to economies of scale and greater competition.[3]

2.2 *Ergo*, it seems contextual to adorn succinctly the components of our Corporate Sector and the growth registered by its various sub-parts during the period of our Study. With its two wings—public and private—in India Corporate Sector is, as per the Companies Act, 1956 and registration-wise, comprised of companies limited by shares, companies with unlimited liability, and companies with liability limited by guarantee. The total number of these three categories of companies stood at 72,611 as on March 31, 1982 as against 48,341 at the beginning of April 1, 1978, thereby indicating an increase of 24,270 i.e. over 50 per cent between 1977-78 and 1981-82.[4] In terms of ownership and nature of membership, all companies are categorized into Government and Non-Government[5] and Public and Private Companies. The number of Government Companies stood at 894 (with a total paid up capital of Rs. 13,309 crores) and 745 (with Rs. 8,527 crores), and those belonging to Non-Government segment at 71,508 (with Rs. 4,961 crores) and 47,549 (with Rs. 4,070 crores) on the aforesaid dates ; it indicates an increase of 149 (20 per cent) and 23,959 (over 50 per cent) in the number of Government and Non-Government Companies, respectively. Of the total increase of 149 in Government Companies, the number of public limited companies rose by 72 (24 per cent) and that of the private limited companies by 77 (over 17 per cent). In contrast to this the public and private limited companies of the Non-Government category registered a rise of 2,141 (nearly 27 per cent) and 21,818 (slightly more than 55 per cent), respectively. This means that the numerical growth of the private limited companies has been more scenical both in the case of Government and Non-Government segments. Appertaining to the growth of paid up capital, it may be mentioned that in the case of Government Companies it rose to Rs. 13,309 crores as on March 31, 1982 from Rs. 8,527 crores on April 1, 1978 (i.e. by Rs. 4,782 crores or about 56 per cent). Similarly, the paid up capital of Non-Government Companies increased to Rs. 4,961 crores from Rs. 4,070 crores (i.e. by Rs. 891 crores or nearly 22 per cent) during the aforesaid period. It may be further noted that of Rs. 4,782 crores raised by way of paid up capital by the Government Companies, as much as Rs. 4,218 crores (i.e. 88.2 per cent of the total) are accounted by private limited companies, and the remaining sum of Rs. 563 crores (11.8 per cent) is obligated by public limited companies. In contrast to this, of an increase of Rs. 891 crores registered by Non-Government Companies, Rs. 603 crores (i.e. 67.7 per cent of the total) relates to the public limited companies, and Rs. 288 crores (32.3 per cent) to private limited companies. Despite these constituent-wise erratic trends observed in the growth of paid up capital of the various classes of Indian Companies, the overall growth noticed in paid up capital during the period 1977-82 can rather be considered perceptive ; true, of course, is the fact that the bulk portion of it has come to be contributed by private limited companies of Government and Non-Government sector taken together. Furthermore, while the Non-Government Companies eclipsed the Government Companies in point of their growth measured in terms of their number (Non-Government Companies=23,959 and Government Companies=149), it is the latter which wrapped in clouds as far as the paid up capital is concerned (Government Companies=Rs. 4,782 crores, and Non-Government Companies=Rs. 891 crores) ; the latter trend is however not to be looked upon with a surprise in view of the massive investments that are being made by the Government of India during its Five Year Plans. On the whole growth of the public limited companies, both in terms of numerical expansion and paid up capital, has far lagged behind than that of private limited companies during the period under review ; thus the number and paid up capital of public and private limited companies registered a rise of 2,213 and Rs. 1,166 crores in sharp contrast to 21,895 and Rs. 4,506 crores, respectively. The figures of paid up capital may be looked upon from another angle also. As on March 31, 1982, the average paid up capital of public limited companies stood at Rs. 0.47 crores (Rs. 5,005 crores/10,541) as compared to Rs. 0.21 crores (Rs. 13,265 crores/61,861) in the case of private limited companies. (See, please, Table 2.2 of Annexe II, for details.) If the progress registered in the paid up capital is interpreted on the criterion of improvement in financial soundness then the obvious inference would be that the financial base of both the public and private limited companies of India, as it exists today, is rather impecunious. This state of affair clearly points out to the need for strengthening the base of long term funds in the case of all categories of companies in general, and in case of public limited companies, in particular, for it is these which are strategic from the angle of the industrial development of our country. Aside, it is these companies which have been incited to move forward in the direction of attaining 'self-reliance'. Also it is for them the CCI first of all opened its permissions to float secured convertible and non-convertible debentures/bonds. One more point may however be made explicitly clear in this regard. Until recently it is the companies of the private corporate sector alone which use to amplify capital through the issuance of CDs/NCDs. However, as of late the public sector companies/corporations too have started raising funds through the floatation of debentures. Since this study is restricted to the Issues of CDs/NCDs floated by public limited listed companies of the private corporate sector only, the matching Issues of public sector organizations have not been analyzed by us. Even so, the relevant details of the Issues of Bonds placed in the market by the public sector companies/corporations for augmenting their long-term capital resources alongside the pertinent Government Guidelines have been included in Annexe : III for the perusal of those who are interested in them.

THE UNIVERSE AND THE SURVEY POPULATION

2.3 All the public limited companies registered under the Indian Companies Act, 1956 under its various clauses and companies deemed to have been registered constitute the 'Universe' of this Study. Of these, only those which are found functioning in the private corporate sector and which have been granted approvals by the CCI for the issuance of Convertible/Non-Convertible Debentures/Bonds during the period beginning from January 1, 1978 till the close of December 31, 1982 make up the 'Survey Population' for this research endeavour. As it is, the Universe of this work is comprised of 8,328 companies as on April 1, 1978 and 10,541 as on March 31, 1982. (See, please, Table 2.2.) And, the 'Survey Population' is 284 public limited companies of the private corporate sector which received approvals from the CCI for raising funds worth Rs. 1,072.55 crores via issue of CDs/NCDs during the period under reference. Of these 284 companies,

91 companies heightened their resources equivalent to Rs. 643.98 crores by issuing CDs either on the basis of Public Issues or by way of Rights Issues offered to their existing shareholders/debentureholders, and the rest 193 aggrandize the needed capital through issuing NCDs worth Rs. 428.57 crores. (Please refer to Table 3.1 of Annexe : VI)

CALCULUS OF SURVEY POPULATION : THE PERTINENT SUBSTRATUM

2.4 In order to understand the integral of 284 companies catalogue as our survey population as also to put on an overview of the varied sources tapped by the public limited companies of the private corporate sector during the period 1978-82, we may add here a fitting newsy passage.

2.5 As may be perused from Table 2.1 of Annexe : II, Non-Government Companies mainly reinforce their funds either by way of initial issues,[6] further issues,[7] bonus issues, loans from public finance institutions or with the help of debentures/ bonds. Thus between January 1, 1978 and December 31, 1982, the CCI granted its approvals in all to 2,397 non-government companies for a sum of Rs. 3,412.77 crores ; of these, approvals to 289 companies (12.06 per cent of the total) for a sum of Rs. 1,104.33 crores (32.36 per cent) concerned with the issuance of debentures/bonds--convertibles and non-convertibles both, while the remaining, namely, to 2,108 companies (87.94 per cent of the total) for Rs 2,308.44 crores (67.64 per cent) with the Initial Issues, Further Issues, Bonus Issues, Loans, etc. Of the 289 companies which received the favour of CCI's approvals for the issuance of debentures/bonds worth Rs. 1,104.33 crores as many as 284 companies are public limited companies which secured permission to float debentures for Rs. 1,072.55 crores ; the rest 5 are private limited companies to whom CCI accorded sanctions to issue debentures/bonds worth Rs. 31.78 crores. (Also see, please, Table 3.1 of Annexe : VI, for necessary details.) In the context, it would be of further relevance to note that from out of 284 companies, as many as 91 public limited companies entered the capital market for the issuance of CDs for an aggregate sum of Rs. 643.98 crores, and the remainders i.e., 193 for the NCDs worth Rs. 428.57 crores. Again out of 91 public limited companies which resorted to the issuance of CDs, 40 of them placed their Issues worth Rs. 203.05 crores on Rights basis and 51 offered their Issues involving Rs. 440.93 crores to the Public. While the year-, and date-wise details of the approvals granted by the CCI to public limited companies of the private corporate sector for the issuance of CDs/NCDs between the period January 1, 1978 and December 31, 1982 may be seen in Table 2.3 through 2.7 of Annexe : II, cumulative figures may be visualized in Table 3.1 of Annexe : VI.

SELECTING THE OBSERVATIONAL UNITS AND AN ELUCIDATION OF THE ISSUES FLOATED ON "RIGHTS" BASIS

2.6 Focussed as this study is on CDs, only 51 public limited companies of the private corporate sector which obtained consent from the CCI to float the Public Issues of CDs for Rs. 440.93 crores during the period 1978-82 constitute our observational units for the proposed exhaustive analysis. Those private sector's public limited companies which issued CDs on Rights basis have consciously been excluded from within the purview of our observational units for two testatory reasons. One, such CDs are offered only to a select group of investors, and hence, are primarily meant to benefit an already identified class of investors. Thus they possess a restricted scope of investment meaning thereby that the general public is not involved in them in a substantial manner. Second, the requisite informations for the proposed analysis are not available.

EXCULPATION FOR OSTRACIZING THE ISSUES OF NCDs FOR BLOW-BY-BLOW INVESTIGATION

2.7 193 public limited companies which resorted to the issuance of NCDs have been precluded from the gamut of observational units selected for an indepth investigation on several counts. First, the NCDs are traded at the Stock Exchanges only sporadically and whatever transactions take place they are generally at a price which is far below their face values.[8] Second, a good proportion of the investors are not substantially interested in NCDs because they do not carry with them the convertibility clause which entitle them to acquire equity shares and through these some amount of capital gain after the lapse of some time-interval. No doubt, the interest rate offered on them until recently was higher at 15 per cent as against 13 5 per cent on CDs but this incentive seems to be less gorgeous to the investors *vis-a-vis* the one presumed in the shape of capital appreciation.

STILL INCLUDED IN THIS STUDY ARE THE EYE-CATCHING LINEAMENTS OF THE ISSUES OF NCDs AND A CASE STUDY OF AN ALIKE ISSUE

2.8 Unstirred by these facts we would highlight, of course, *intra muros* for this work, the flagrant hallmarks of the Issues of NCDs. Further, one case study has also been included of an Issue of NCDs selected on a widely agreeable scale of yardsticks with a view to present a comparable picture of this category of debentures with that of CDs on the one hand, and to probe into the question as to how NCDs can be made fruitful to the investors and an effective source of mustering capital supplies by the Indian Companies, on the other.

STRIKING FEATURES OF THE SAMPLE

2.9 All the 51 public limited companies included in our sample are listed at one or the other Stock Exchange of our country. In terms of number and amount these companies represent 17.96 per cent and 41.11 per cent of our survey population, respectively. The detailed profile of our sample companies covering the name, year of incorporation, location of the registered office, nature of the industry to which it belongs, information as to the fact whether the concerned company is covered by Monopolies and Restrictive Trade Practices Act, 1969 or not, purpose/s for which fund raising has been approved, date on which consent has been granted by CCI, actual date of issuance, face value of convertible debenture/bond, nature of convertibility clause added i.e. whether partially convertible or fully convertible, conversion ratio, conversion period, interest rate offered, the total amount of issue and the portions offéred on rights basis and to public, the number of times the public issue has been oversubscribed/undersubscribed/just fully subscribed, benefits offered to debentureholders during the conversion period by way of Bonus Shares/ Rights Equity Shares, market price of the equity shares of the concerned company measured in number of times to their face value at the time of issuance of CDs, conversion price announced *vis-a-vis* the face value of the relevant equity shares, policy of insertion of news items regarding company's progress/future programs of expansion, modernization, diversification, etc., benefit indices, the expected benefits to the debentureholders at the time of conversion on account of difference observed in the market price of equity found prevalent at the time of issuance of CDs and the announced conversion price (expressed in terms of percentages over the face value of CDs), etc. are *àvue d'oeil* of the Table 3.6 of Annexe VI. The clubbing of these companies on such bases as MRTP companies/other than MRTP companies, industry group, Region-, and Age-wise distribution have been displayed in Table 3.2 through 3.5 of the above Annexe ; alongside the sample companies comparative information is however also included in these tables for those public limited companies which have offered their CDs on rights basis as well those which have floated the issues of NCDs. The final point that we would like to mention about our sample is this that it is decisively representative from the angle of both our universe as well as the survey population for it includes all the public limited companies of the private corporate sector which have entered the capital market for raising funds through the floatation of Public Issues of CDs.

SOURCES AND METHODS EMPLOYED FOR DATA COLLECTION

2.10 This study has been completed with the help of both secondary and primary data. The main sources from which we have collected secondary data include the Records available in the Office of the Controller of Capital Issues including its official Press Releases, Prospectuses & Brochures issued by the companies, the Stock Exchange Official Directory, Bombay,

Madras Stock Exchange Official Year Book, Delhi Stock Exchange Official Year Book, 1985, Directory of Joint Stock Companies in India, 1980, Directory of Joint Stock Companies in India, 1984, Directory of Joint Stock Companies in India, Volume One (A-DEL), Registration & Liquidation of Joint Stock Companies in India 1980-82, and 1983-84, Kothari Economic and Industrial Guide of India, Annual Reports of the concerned companies for the year 1978 through 1982, Daily Quotation Lists of the market prices of the shares and debentures of the different Stock Exchanges, Five Year Plans, Economic Surveys, Report of the Study Group to Frame Guidelines for Follow up of Bank Credit 1975 (Tandon Committee), Report of the Working Group to Review the System of Cash Credit, 1979 (Chore Committee). Reports on Currency & Finance, Report of the High Powered Expert Committee on Companies & MRTP Acts, August 1978, News Papers in particular the Financial Express and the Economic Times, Eminent Indian Journals like the Chartered Accountant, Commerce, Capital, Business standard, and the important works of Western and Indian researchers as have already been mentioned by us in the preceding Chapter while presenting a survey of the existing literature. Some of the gaps observed in the secondary information were filled in through establishing personal contacts with the corporate executives/stock exchange office bearers/managers and underwriters to the public issues floated by the sample companies.

2.11 The secondary data has been supplemented by the primary information gathered on the subject through mailing distinct structured questionnaires, covering of course both close-ended and open-ended questions, to the three categories of polity concerned with the subject being probed into. Thus Questionnaire-I was mailed to the Chairmen/Finance Executives of all the 284 public limited companies of the private corporate sector, which resorted to the issuance of CDs/NCDs with a view to solicit cruical information on the relevant issues of debentures and their considered views on the appropriate yardsticks that should be employed for adjudging the successfulness/unsuccessfulness of the CDs/NCDs, factors which should weigh in drawing the most salubrious design of terms of conversion, official guidelines, rationalization of the relevant tax provisions of the Income Tax Act, etc. Another Questionnaire was transmitted to 500 Office Bearers of the recognised Stock Exchanges (Presidents, Secretaries, and Executive Directors/Managers to Issues/Eminent Academics/Underwriters to Issues with the specific objective of seeking their considered opinions on such questions as : How do they look towards the CDs/NCDs as a means of corporate financing in the context of Indian environment? ; What do they feel about the terms on which Indian Companies are issuing CDs/NCDs? ; What could be the indicators of successfulness/unsuccessfulness for such securities from the view point of concerned companies? ; Is there any need to affect modifications in the CCI's guidelines relating to the issuance of debentures, and in the existing provisions of the Income Tax Act from the angle of making them more lucrative to the issuing companies and the existing/prospective investors? ; what role the finance intermediaries can play in popularizing such securities in India? ; In what manner the market ability of such securities and effective return on them can be improved? ; What other measures should be taken to promote an effective secondary market for debentures in India? ; Can we think of drawing some lessons on the subject from the experiences of Corporations employing such securities for raising long-term funds in developed countries such as United States of America/United Kingdom? And, to as large as 1,500 investors, chosen on a random basis to represent existing/prospective and prudent/ imprudent investors, regions/states, big/medium/small-sized groups was dispatched Questionnaire : 3. The primary aim of addressing an exclusive questionnaire to them was to secure their opinions on such aspects as the factors which they generally consider while subscribing to such securities, computation of short and long run gains, expectations in regard to the return on their investment in CDs/NCDs, influence of the aggressive selling tactics adopted by corporate managements/managers/ underwriters handling/standing sideby the issues, awareness found among them about the pitfalls of such securities, and the modifications desired by them in the existing legal environment surrounding the debentures in order to make these as their first choice, etc. Since the response actually received from all categories of respondents was rather trifling, they were approached personally. And, we were successful in securing filled in Questionnaires from 105 corporate executives (nearly 37 per cent of the total), 126 office bearers of stock exchanges/ eminent academics/managers, underwriters and brokers to issues (25 per cent), and 704 investors (47 per cent). The response rates accomplished as thus finally can be deemed satisfactory for two weighty reasons. One, due care was taken by the researcher while approaching the respondents so as to ensure that they should not impair their character of truly representing the respective universe/survey population/stratums proposed to be covered on the one hand, and for protecting the authenticity of the information actually filled/got recorded by the respondents in the questionnaires through performing the exercise of editing them then and there as also recording certain additional informations on the basis of personal interviews/observations, on the other. Needless to mention that the primary information thus secured amply helped us not only in undertaking a critical resume of our findings but also in confidently venturing upon making appropriate recommendations on vital issues concerning with the subject under examination. The Annexe IV and Annexe V subsume the contents of questionnaire 1 through 3, and the list of eminent corporate executives, office bearers of stock exchanges, and academics from whom the filled in questionnaire were actually secured for the benefit of those readers who may feel curious in knowing such details.

PATTERN OF ANALYSIS UNDERTAKEN, STATISTICAL TOOLS/MODELS EMPLOYED AND VARIABLES INVOLVED

2.12 The whole analysis has been shaped directly to fit the logical needs of our objectives/propositions. Thus the details ferret out from the Stock Exchange Official Directory, Bombay such as the name of the company, maturity period, interest rates offered, etc. on the Series of Debentures issued by the Indian Companies during the post independence era, have been highlighted in order to bring in broad daylight the history of the origination of CDs in India. While the macro trends observed in the raising of funds during the period under review through debentures have been described in terms of the nature of the debentures floated, the number of public limited companies, and the amount involved in various kinds of debentures, the portions of the issues placed to the public and in the market on rights basis, categorization of companies of CDs/NCDs issuing companies on the basis of MRTP/Other than MRTP companies, industry groups/nature of product/s and/ or service/s produced/ rendered, age-groups namely Old Public Limited Companies of the Private Corporate Sector ($OPLC_{pr}$), Middle Aged Public Limited Companies of the Private Corporate Sector ($MAPLC_{pr}$) and Relatively New Public Limited Companies of the Private Corporate Sector ($RNPLC_{pr}$) and Region/State/Union territory-wise location, and the year-wise approvals, the microscopic trends of curiosity has come to discussed on the basis of the pristine and the aftermost company to get the CCI's approval, ranges of face values, interest rates and the 5 per cent premium offered at the time of redemption, spectrum of purposes, the two components of CDs, interval between the dates of consents and actual dates of openings of the issues of CDs, the kind of conversion involved (fully convertible, partially convertible and rights to subscribe, and issue of shares in lieu of interest accrued), conversion ratio and period. For highlighting both the composite and micro trends of interest absolute increase/decrease, average and percentage variation of the concerned variable has been computed, mentioned and interpreted.

2.13 After enumerating the just, admissible and cogent scale of yardsticks for adjudging the successfulness/unsuccessfulness from the angle of different interest groups of populace, the successfulness and unsuccessfulness of the different Public Issues of CDs has been examined first of all distinctly in the light of the considerations of issuing companies, investors and the economy, and then on the basis of an integrated analysis in order to reach conclusive results. Thus, we have reckoned as to the number and their percentage to total public issues which came to be oversubscribed/undersubscribed, general range of oversubscription computed by simply looking at the number of times issues have been oversubscribed, and adjusted range of oversubscription calculated by adjusting the number of times with the volume of funds raised for the purpose from the view point of issuing companies, their corporate managements, managers/underwriters/brokers to issues. Alongside, the possible reasons responsible for undersubscription in case of certain public issues of CDs have been critically analyzed. The number of times the market prices are of the equity shares of different PLC_{pr} at the time of issuance of CDs to public and interest rates and 5 per cent premium offered, announced conversion ratio, conversion price, conversion period, ancillary benefits etc. accompanying the various Public Issues of CDs have been compared in order to assess their relative attractiveness to the investors. While doing so we have contrasted the monetary benefits, specially in the form of promised capital gains calculated as percentages to the face values of CDs and on the premise that debentureholders continue to hold the alloted CDs until the date of effectualization of conversion, shut in the various issues of CDs floated by different PLC_{pr}; the fallacy found in the aforesaid tacit assumption has, however, been conjure up the readers. To facilitate an undefiled analysis synthesizing the considerations of affected companies and investors, successfulness and unsuccessfulness of CDs has been appraised on such criterion as the volatile and non-volatile character of relevant equities, and percentages of increases/decreases registered in the prices of concerned equity shares/convertible debentures since the enlistment of convertible debentures on the stock exchange/s.

2.14 Dexterity in the above analysis has been attained through the computation of coefficient of correlation ('r'.) coefficient of determination ('r^2'), standard deviation ('σ') and coefficient of variation ('C.V.') for the weekly/monthly prices of 27 (from out of 42) Public Issues of CDs and those of the relevant Equity Shares as quoted at their parent stock exchanges with an object to ascertain the relationship between the two, prices of convertibles and shares, and the degree of significance. Furthermore, illustrative values of the cost, market price and the rates of return have been reckoned out by employing Internal Rate of Return for the selective public issues of debentures with a view to demonstrate as to the extent such measures can be used for evaluating the successfulness/ unsuccessfulness of the CDs by the issuing companies and investors. To serve the cause of latter the rates of return computed as above have also been compared with the corresponding advertised rates of return. We have however distinguished the three variants of CDs for calculating the aforesaid values, namely, debentures with a Right to Subscribe, partially convertible debentures/bonds and fully convertible debentures/bonds. In the case of '*Debentures with a Right to Subscribe*' the market price, rate of return to the debentureholder and the cost of the debenture to the issuing company has been computed by feeding relevant data in the following equations :

(*i*) Market Price of Debenture :

$$P_d = \sum_{t=1}^{n} \frac{I_t}{(1+k)^t} + \frac{a(M_i - S_i)}{(1+k)^i} + \frac{R}{(1+k)^n}$$

Here,

P_d = Price of the Debenture at the time of its issuance ;

I_t = Interest Payment at time 't' ;

a = Number of Equity Shares the holder of one debenture can subscribe to at the end of the ith period ;

M_i = Market price of the share after the end of ith period ;

S_i = Price at which the shares are to be subscribed at the end of ith period ;

R = Redemption price of the debenture at the end of ith period ; and

k = Required Rate of Return by the investors'

(ii) Rate of Return to the Debentureholder :

$$\text{Face Value of Debenture} = \sum_{t=1}^{n} \frac{I_t}{(1+r)^t} + \frac{a\,(M_i - S_i)}{(1+r)^i} + \frac{R}{(1+r)^n}$$

Here,

'r' represents 'rate of return'.

(*iii*) Cost of Debenture to the Issuing Company

$$NS_a = \sum_{t=1}^{n} \frac{I_t\,(1-T)}{(1+kd)^t} + \frac{a(bM_i - S_i)}{(1+kd)^i} + \frac{R}{(1+kd)^n}$$

Here,

NS_a = Net Subscription amount realized by the firm per debenture on its issuance ;

It = Interest Payment at time 't' ;

T = Tax Rate applicable on the company ;

a = Number of Equity Shares the holder of one Debenture can subscribe to at the end of ith period ;

M_i = Market Price per share at the end of ith period;

b = Proportion of M_i the firm can realize net by issuing additional equity shares to public at time i, under the given regulations of the Controller of Capital Issues ;

S_i = Subscription Price per share at the end of the ith period ;

R = Redemption Rate at the end of n th period ; and

Kd = Cost of Debenture to the company.

The formulas used for the computation of aforesaid values in the case of an Issue of '*Partly Convertible Debentures/Bonds*' are as given under :

(*i*) Market Price of the Debenture :

$$P_d = \sum_{t=1}^{n} \frac{I_t}{(1+k)^t} + \frac{aM_i}{(1+k)^i} + \sum_{J-m}^{n} \frac{F_j}{(1+k)^j}$$

Here,

P_d = Price of the Convertible Debenture at the time of its issuance ;

I_t = Interest received by the debentureholder at the end of period t ;

n = The total life of the Debenture ;

a = Number of Equity Shares which would be received by the debentureholder at the time of affecting of the part-conversion after the lapse of ith period ;

M_i = Price per equity share at the end of ith period ;

F_j = Instalment of repayment of the principal amount at the end of j th period ; and

k = Investors' Required rate of return.

(*ii*) Rate of Return to the Debentureholder :

$$\text{Subscription price} = \sum_{t=1}^{n} \frac{I_t}{(1+r)^t} + \frac{a\,M_i}{(1+r)^i} + \sum_{J-m}^{n} \frac{F_j}{(1+r)^j}$$

Here,

r = Rate of Return.

(*iii*) Cost of Partly Convertible Debenture :

$$NSa = \sum_{t=1}^{n} \frac{I_t\,(1-T)}{(1+kd)^t} + \frac{aM_ib}{(1+Kd)^i} + \sum_{j-m}^{n} \frac{F_j}{(1+kd)^j}$$

Here,

NSa = Net Subscription Price Realised at the time of issue ;

b = Proportion of M_i that will be realizable net if the firm were to issue equity shares to public ; and

Kd = Discount Rate representing the Cost of Capital.

And, the price, rate of return, and the cost of a '*Fully Convertible Debenture/Bond*' has been computed by employing the following given formulas :

(*i*) Market Price of the Debenture :

$$P_{d,t} = \sum_{q=t+1}^{m} \frac{I}{(1+r)^{t+1}} + \frac{CR \times Mcm}{(1+r)^{m-t}}$$

Here,

$P_{d,t}$ = Price of Debenture if it is held for conversion defined at time t (t=0,......n) ;

I = Periodic Interest Receivable till the time of conversion is reached ;

m = Time of conversion ;

CR = Conversion Ratio ;

Mcm= Price for Equity share at time 'm' i.e. at the time of conversion ; and

r = Investors' Required Rate of Return.

(*ii*) Rate of Return to the Debentureholder

$$\text{Subscription Price} = \sum_{t=1}^{m} \frac{I}{(1+r)^{t}} + \frac{CR \times Mcm}{(1+r)^{m}}$$

Here,

'r' represents the rate of return.

(*iii*) Cost of the fully convertible debenture

$$Nsa = \sum_{t=1}^{m} \frac{I(1-T)}{(1+kd)^{t}} + \frac{CR \times Mcm \times b}{(1+kd)^{t}}$$

Here,

Nsa = Net Subscription Realised from debenture at the time of its issuance ;

T = Tax-Rate.

b = Proportion of Mc, m that will be realisable net if the firm were to issue equity shares to public ; and

kd = Discount Rate representing the cost of Capital.

As regards the computed values of rates of return it may be observed that it is with the help of these coupled with the inferences concerning interest rates and 5 per cent premium offered, likely capital gains and other ancillary benefits that we have made an attempt to assess the investment opportunities entailed by CDs.

2.15 The number of PLC_{pr} and the magnitude of funds raised by them both in absolute and relative terms through the issuance of debentures during the different years and in the total period under reference, and the role these funds have played in controlling the inflationary trends via curbing the demand for and increasing the supply of various kinds of goods/services constitute the main stream of our analysis which paved our way for evaluating the success/failure of this saving instrument from the angle of the Indian economy as a whole.

2.16 It is at this junxture that we set down to affect refinements in our major findings concerning with both the successfulness/unsuccessfulness of the Issues of CDs/NCDs. And, it is from this angle that we added to our analysis one case study each for a successful and unsuccessful issue of CDs and one for an unsuccessful issue of NCDs as identified on the basis of scores of scales. A vast multitude of information relating to each issue preferred for the case study such as the incorporation and history of the company, product lines, management, and an array of financial data particularly concerning with sales, profits, dividends, capital structure, market price of shares, etc. have been thoroughly investigated so as to unearth among other things the main factors which led to the success/failure of the given issue and, accordingly highlight the facets that should invite the attention of prospective companies/investors interested in this instrument to serve their respective causes. Employing the tools of common statistics like number, averages, percentages and ranks we have also analysed on different bases such as industry-wise, region-wise etc., and from the same angle, the responses recorded by corporate executives, office bearers of the stock exchanges/ Managers, Underwriters and Brokers to Issues/Academics, and individual investors on such issues as the reasons which prompted PLC_{pr} to issue CDs/NCDs, purposes for which funds have been so raised, methods used for the redemption of debentures on their maturity, measures that should be taken by the companies issuing CDs, suggestions for making CDs/NCDs more popular, break-up of the investments made by individual investors in the variety of savings instruments, variegated reasons favouring CDs and factors governing the selection of the specific issues of CDs by investors. A brief critical review of the guidelines issued from time to time for the issuance of debentures, existing provisions of Sections 80 cc, and 80L of the Income Tax Act, and the present state of affairs of the Secondary Market for debentures in India has further been undertaken keeping in view the considered opinions expressed by company executives/eminent academics/investors in order to facilitate finale inferences of this study.

2.17 The gamut of inescapable conclusions drawn on the basis of diversified indepth analysis as described in the preceding paras have then been used to examine the validity found in our hypotheses on the one hand, and for drawing logical conclusions on the broad issues raised in this work, on the other.

THE DISPOSITION

2.18 udged by style the research design of this study is primarily descriptive-cum-diagnostic. It is descriptive in so for as we have concerned ourselves with the portrayal of the idiosyncratic features of convertibles in general and of the Issues of CDs/NCDs floated by PLC_{pr} during the period under review, it assumes diagnostic character when we have examined the success/failure of various issues on a wide range of yardsticks to satisfy the interests of concerned companies, investors and the nation's economy. Since this study is the first of its kind narrating at length the experience of the Indian Private Corporate Sector in point of raising long term funds through the issuance of Convertible Debentures/Bonds, it can also be regarded as an exploratory to some extent,

NOTES

1. Government of India, Planning Commission, '*The Seventh Five Year Plan: 1985-90, Volume II: Sectoral Programmes of Development*', New Delhi, October, 1985, p. 167.
2. Ibidem.
3. Government of India, Planning Commission, '*The Seventh Five Year Plan : 1985-90, Volume I : Perspective, Objectives, Strategy, Macro Dimensions and Resources*', Forward written by *Shri Rajiv Gandhi*, New Delhi, October, 1985, p. VI.
4. Sources : (i) Government of India, Ministry of Industry and Department of Company Affairs, Research and Statistics Division, '*Directory of Joint Stock Companies in India, Volume One (A-DEL)*, New Delhi, 1986, pp. VII-XII ; (ii) For the period 1959-60 to 1979-80 : Government of India, Ministry of Law, Justice and Company Affairs, Department of Company Affairs, Research and Statistics Division. '*Directory of Joint Stock Companies in India* Volume, I. New Delhi, 1980, p. ii, and, (iii) For the years 1980-81 and 1981-82 see please, Government of India, Ministry of Law, Justice and Company Affairs, Department of Company Affairs, Research and Statistics Division, '*Registrations and Liquidations of Joint Stock Companies in India ; 1980-82*', New Delhi, 1982, p. iii.
5. 'Government Company means any Company in which not less than 51 per cent of the paid up share capital is held by the Central Government, or by any State Government or Governments, or partly by the Central Government and partly by one or more State Government and includes a company which is a subsidiary of a Government Company as thus defined.' *Source* : See, please, Government of India, Ministry of Law, Justice and Company Affairs, '*The Companies Act, 1956*', Section 617, p. 336.
6. The equity shares/preference shares floated in the market by the newly incorporated companies are given the caption of 'Initial Issues' by the Controller of Capital Issues as per the provisions of the Capital Issues (Control) Act, 1947.
7. The equity shares/preference shares floated by the existing companies are covered under the head, 'Further Issues'.
8. The common practice observed at the Stock Exchanges has been that the NCDs are traded at a price which is 10 per cent below than their face values if the interest rate offered is 15 per cent, and at a discount of 15 per cent if the interest rate offered is 13.5 per cent. The posture towards them may however take a sympathetic turn if the managements of the companies buoyed up the Issues of NCDs with the enchantments that the debentureholders would also soon be having a chance either to invest in equity shares or in CDs on rights basis; surely, it applies to those companies which for one or the other reason have a good effigy in the minds of investors.

3
MAJOR RESULTS

— **SECTION ONE** : UNCOVERING THE HISTORY OF THE ORIGINIATION OF CONVERTIBLE DEBENTURES/BONDS IN INDIA

— **SECTION TWO** : COMPENDIUM OF DETERMINATIVE TRENDS

— **SECTION THREE** : ADJUDICATING THE SUCCESSFULNESS/UNSUCCESSFULNESS OF THE PUBLIC ISSUES OF CONVERTIBLE DEBENTURES

— **SECTION FOUR** : PIERCING THROUGH THE VALUES OF THE MARKET PRICE, RATE OF RETURN AND THE COST OF IMPORTANT VARIANTS OF CONVERTIBLE DEBENTURES

— **SECTION FIVE** : CASE STUDIES

— **SECTION SIX** : ANATOMIZATION OF THE RECORDED RESPONSES

— **SECTION SEVEN** : APPRAISAL OF THE CONTEMPORARY GOVERNMENT POLICY/OFFICIAL GUIDELINES, PERTINENT PROVISIONS OF THE PRESENT STATE OF AFFAIRS OF THE SECONDARY MARKET FOR DEBENTURES

THE findings and the pertinent analysis are summarized in this Chapter which has seven distinct sections. While a candid and almost *ad infinitum* attempt has been made to trace out the history of the origination of convertible debentures/bonds in India in Section-One, determinative trends of macro and microscopic interest, classifying broadly the connected PLC_{pr} on such bases as MRTP and Other than MRTP Companies, industry-group-, region/state/union-territory-, and age-wise, have been fit to be seen with a fine tooth comb for the CDs in general and Public Issues of CDs in particular, and in a nutshell for the NCDs in Section Two. Section Three includes the passable yardsticks set out by us with an open mind for adjudicating the successfulness/unsuccessfulness of the issues of CDs covering the variegated interest groups, namely, the issuing companies and their corporate managements, managers to issues, institutions offering their underwriting services to make up the deficiencies in the public subscription, investors, and the nation's economy on the one hand, and the results arrived at on testing the various public issues of CDs floated by public limited companies of the private corporate sector during the period : 1978-82, on the other. The values cast up by employing the precept of Internal Rate of Return for the market price, rate of return, and the cost of 3 distinct varieties of CDs have been highlighted in the subsequent Section Four. For the purpose, we have randomly selected the Usha Alloys & Steels Company Limited, Calcutta (Issue of 1982) to typify CD issued with Rights to Subscribe to Equity Shares, J.K. Synthetics Limited, Kanpur (Issue of 1982) to symbolize the partly convertible debenture, and Straw Products Limited, Jaykaypur (Orissa), (Issue of 1981) to delineate the fully convertible form of CD. The rates of returns so reckoned have been contrasted with the returns advertised by the concerned companies via brochures and/or insertion of prepossessing advertisements in the different news papers with a view to guage the element of truth found in the latter. Next Section Five adorns this study with the Case Studies of Reliance Textile Industries Limited (re-named as Reliance Industries Limited since January, 1986), Bombay's Public Issue for Rs. 24 crores comprising of 19,20,000 Debentures of Rs. 125 each for cash of par (Third Series) (June 10,1981) chosen as an indicative of a successful venture, Sukhjit Starch & Chemicals Limited, Phagwara's Public Issue of 1,00,000-13.5% Secured Convertible Debentures of Rs. 100/- each for cash at par (January 18, 1982) selected to represent an unsuccessful endeavour, and J.K. Synthetics Limited, Kanpur's Issue of 5,00,000—13.5% Secured (Second Series) Redeemable Debentures of Rs. 100/- each for cash at par (August 10, 1981) to stand for an instance of an unsuccessful issue of NCDs; indicidentally it may be noted that this Issue proved unsuccesful from all angles. We, however, embarked to complete these case studies after having discussed the precise grounds justifying their opportuneness. As to why a case study to sketch an issue of successful NCDs has not been included we may add to whatever has already been said elsewhere that quite a good number of companies enter into prior arrangements with either some finance institution or non-profit earning organisation like Military Organizations, Charitable Trusts, etc. to subscribe to their issues of NCDs from out of employees' provident funds or similar other funds available with them. As a matter of fact these institutions remain in search of such securities which carry no risk and can also ensure a fairly good return. And, as we all know, NCDs meet both of these requirements.[1] This widely observed feature of the Issues of NCDs, which drained all possibilities of evolving a judicious scale of yardsticks for evaluating their successfulness, coupled with an almost callous attitude of corporate managements in point of releasing needed informations embittedly led us to drop in the idea of inclusion of a case study of a successful issue of NCDs. The responses recorded by all categories of our respondents have been interpreted in Section-Six. And the last Section Seven has been devoted to the critical examination of the Government Policy/Official Guidelines relating to the issuance of debentures, provisions of Section 80 cc, 80L, and such other pertinent clauses of the Income Tax Act, and the present state of affairs of the secondary market for debentures in India.

SECTION ONE

UNCOVERING THE HISTORY OF THE ORIGINATION OF CONVERTIBLE DEBENTURES/BONDS IN INDIA

3.2 To unearth the history of the emergence of CDs on the scene of Indian Corporate Sector being our earnest desire, the researcher tapped all conceivable sources like available literature on the subject including the records found in the Office of the Controller of Capital Issues, establishing personal contacts with corporate executives, executives of stock exchanges and finance institutions, brokers etc. but no authentic information could be gathered pertaining to the premier company and the earliest issue on this score. However, whatever we could collect in this respect is presented hereunder.

3.3 In the post-independence era Naskarpara Jute Company was primal to raise capital through the floatation of series of debentures carrying an interest rate of 6.50 per cent and a maturity period of 1947-69.[2] Around Fifties Ferro Alloys (7-$\frac{3}{4}$ per cent), Surat Electricity (8 per cent), Swastik Rubber (8 per cent), Bombay Sub-urban Electric Supply (One Series carrying an interest of 8 per cent, and another carrying 8.5 per cent), Larsen & Toubro (8 per cent), India's Premier Automobiles, Indian Aluminium, and Andhra Foundry and Machine Company Limited placed to the public the Series of Convertible Debentures/Bonds.[3] While the larger details of the above issues of CDs are not available, it is well known that the public issue of Convertible Bonds offered to the public in May, 1966 by the Standard Mills for an amount slightly over Rs. One crore did not meet with success. Not only that this issue remained undersubscribed, bonds worth nearly Rs. 37 lakhs were required to be subscribed by the underwriters. And of the 65 issues of public debentures during 1966-70 only 4 issues provided for conversion facilities ; the response to these also being none-too-encouraging. A relatively good response was, however, evinced by the public to the four issues of the CDs put forwarded by the Standard Mills Company Limited, Bharat Bijli (10 per cent), Camphor and Allied Products Limited (11 per cent), and National Machinery Manufacturing during the period 1971-77.[4]

SECTION TWO

COMPENDIUM OF DETERMINATIVE TRENDS

MAJOR TRENDS

3.4 As may be seen in Table 3.1 of Annexe VI, the CCI granted permission in all to 284 Public Limited Companies of private corporate sector (PLC_{pr}) to raise funds for a sum of Rs. 1,072.55 crores through the issuance of CDs/NCDs during the period 1978-82 ; of this sizeable portion of Rs. 643.98 crores (slightly over 60 per cent of the total amount) came to be claimed by CDs of 91 companies (slightly over 32 per cent of total number) and the residual by NCDs (Rs. 440.93 crores or nearly 40 per cent, and 193 companies or about 68 per cent). Thus, while in terms of the number of the PLC_{pr} which secured consent the NCDs markedly superseded the CDs ; it is latter which are more expressive from the angle of amount raised. And, clearly, it is the amount raised which is of vital significance. Worthwhile it would be further to mention here that from out of the total consents worth Rs. 643.98 crores relating to CDs, as much as Rs. 440.93 crores (68.47 per cent of the total) were extended by 51 PLC*pr* (56 per cent of the total) to the public for their subscription in sharp contrast to Rs. 203.05 crores (31.53 per cent) by 40 PLCpr (43.96 per cent) placing their issues in the market on rights basis.

MRTP & OTHER THAN MRTP COMPANIES

3.5 In the context of composite trends it would be of fresh interest to spot out from Table 3.2 of Annexe VI that out of 284 PLCpr, 149 with aggregate approvals worth Rs. 811.19 crores for the issuance of CDs/NCDs during the period under reference (52.46 per cent and 75.63 per cent, respectively) are covered under one or the other clause of MRTP Act. In the like manner, of 91 PLCpr which secured permission to float CDs, 40 with a sum of Rs. 514.86 crores (about 44 per cent and 80 per cent, respectively) fall in this category ; in the latter the proportion of PLC_{pr} placing their issues to the public being 23 and Rs. 351.93 crores (57.5 per cent and 68.35 per cent respectively). The corresponding position in respect to PLC_{ps} enjoying the privilege to place NCDs being 109 and Rs. 296.33

crores during the same period (56.48 per cent and 69.14 per cent, respectively). Both in the case of CDs and NCDs the left out portions (CDs= the number of PLCpr 51 or 56 per cent, and an amount of Rs. 129.12 crores or about 20 per cent; NCDs=84 PLCpr or 43.52 per cent, and amount of Rs. 132.24 crores or 30.86 per cent) represent the segment which has been clubbed by us under the caption, 'Other than MRTP Companies'.

3.6 On interpretation the above analysis obviously stears us to infer that during the period January 1, 1978 to December 31, 1982 : (i) of the total amount raised via debentures by the PLCpr over three-fifths has been through the issuance of CDs, although the number of companies involved in their case has been less than half *vis-a-vis* to those finding their convenience to opt for NCDs ; (ii) more than half of PLCpr which fall back upon CDs preferred to offer over two-third of these debentures to public in contrast to the rights basis ; and, (iii) in the case of both CDs and NCDs, the PLCpr falling under MRTP Group have dominated the scene, be it judged in terms of their number or the amount of funds raised ; this domination, however, being more pronounced in the case of CDs. Evidently, this means that among PLC_{pr}, those which are relatively large-sized i.e. in possession of huge asset base have made the most of this means.

YEAR-WISE DELINEATION

3.7 Meaningful year-wise trends can now be discriminated in tables already under consideration. Among the different years covered by the period 1978-82, the maximal approvals were accorded by the CCI for the issuance of CDs/NCDs taken together during the year 1982 i.e., to 90 PLC_{pr} (31.69 per cent of the total) for a sum of Rs. 516.20 crores (48.13 per cent), and the minimum during the year 1978 i.e., to 13 PLCpr (4.58 per cent) for an amount of Rs. 48.75 crores (4.54 per cent). As a matter of fact there has been a steady increase in the CCI's approvals for the purpose since 1978 excepting of course during 1980, the shortfall of which seems to have been recouped in the successive year 1981 ; the approvals which declined to Rs. 66.95 crores in 1980 from Rs. 114.00 crores in 1979 again registered a steep rise to Rs. 326.65 crores in 1981. Thus the retrogressive direction observed in CCI's concurrences in 1980 appears primarily the consequence of administrative delays on the part of the Offices of CCI and the concerned companies.

3.8 The year-wise features are closely alike for both CDs and NCDs ; minor deviations are, however, observed in case of that part of CDs which is offered on rights basis and the one put up for sale to the public. Furthermore, it is true for MRTP Companies ; other than MRTP Companies indicate aberrant tendencies. (For full details see, please, column 3 through 7 of Table 3.1 and column 3 through 12 of Table 3.2 of Annexe VI).

INDUSTRY-WISE DRIFTS

3.9 284 PLCpr which received CCI's consent for 51 Public Issues of CDs, 40 Issues of CDs placed on Rights Basis, and 193 Issues of NCDs during the period under review have been classified in 15 Industry Groups in Table 3.3 (Annexe VI) on the basis of the nature of product/s and/or service/s produced/rendered by them for/to the society as followed by the Department of Company Affairs, Ministry of Industry and Department of Company Affairs, Government of India, New Delhi ; we have not adopted the broad industrial classification designed by the Reserve Bank of India (Basic, Capital, Intermediate, and Consumer Goods Industries) for the purpose of our analysis because it is not likely to present an elaborate picture in this respect. Thus a pore over the table under analysis reveals that the maximum number of Public Issues of CDs have been approved by CCI in favour of PLC_{pr} engaged in the production of 'Iron, Steel, and Non-Ferrous Metal' (11 or 21.6 per cent of the total) followed by 'Cotton Textiles' (10 or 19.6 per cent), 'Chemicals' (9 or 17.6 per cent), 'Silk, Rayon and Woollen Textiles' (8 or 15.7 per cent), 'Engineering' (6 or 11.8 per cent), 'Hotel' (2 or 3.9 per cent), and 'Tobacco', 'Rubber and Rubber Manufacturing', 'Paper and Paper Products', 'Commerce', and 'Jute Textiles' (1 each or 1.96 per cent each). However, on the basis of amount allowed to be raised the industry group 'Silk Rayon and Woollen Textiles' with Rs. 99.80 crores or 22.6 per cent of the total ranks first. And, 'Iron, Steel and Non-Ferrous Metal' (Rs. 84.85 crores or 19.2 per cent), 'Engineering' (Rs. 63.40 crores or 14.4 per cent), 'Cotton Textiles' (Rs. 61.25 crores or 13.9 per cent), 'Chemicals' (Rs. 51.13 crores or 11.6 per cent), 'Tobacco' (Rs. 30 crores or 6.8 per cent), and 'Hotel' (Rs. 22.50 crores or 5.1 per cent) occupies the subsequent rank second through seventh, respectively. If the number of Public Issues of CDs and the amount involved therein are analyzed in chorus then it would be noted that it is the Public Issues of CDs claimed by the PLC_{pr} of the above seven industrial groups (47 or over 92 per cent) which have accounted for the chunk portion of the total amount raised (Rs. 412.93 crores or about 94 per cent).

3.10 The relative position of the Issues of CDs to be placed on Rights Basis is as thus. The first place in terms of the number of approvals is occupied by the PLC_{pr} found engaged in 'Commerce' (10 or 25 per cent of the total). This group is followed by those engrossed in 'Chemicals' and 'Cotton Textiles' (7 or 17.5 per cent each), 'Engineering' (6 or 15 per cent), 'Paper and Paper Products' (3 or 7.5 per cent). 'Silk, Rayon and Woollen Textiles', and 'Iron, Steel and Non-Ferrous Metal' (2 or 5 per cent each), and 'Aluminium', 'Sugar' and 'Hotel' (1 or 2.5 per cent each). Howbeit, in terms of amount to be mobilized through such CDs the dignity group is, 'Silk, Rayon and Woollen Textiles' (with Rs. 60.80 crores or 29.94 per cent) ; other industrial groups next in order being, 'Chemicals' (Rs. 46.26 crores or 22.8 per cent), 'Cotton Textiles' (Rs. 41.96 crores or 20.7 per cent), 'Engineering' (Rs. 18.85 crores or 9.3 per cent), 'Commerce' (Rs. 18.68 crores or 9.2 per cent), 'Aluminium' (Rs. 10.45 crores or 5.15 per cent), 'Paper and Paper Products' (Rs. 2.80 crores or 1.4 per cent), 'Iron, Steel and Non-Ferrous Metal' (Rs. 2.25 crores or 1.1 per cent), and 'Sugar' and 'Hotel' (Rs. 50 Lakhs or 0.25 per cent each). On the combined scale of the number of issues approved and the amount allowed to be raised the premium industrial groups for this class of CDs can be considered as comprising of 'Silk, Rayon and Woollen Textiles', 'Chemicals', 'Cotton Textiles', 'Engineering', 'Commerce' and 'Aluminium, for they count for 82.5 per cent (33) of the total number of rights issues approved and over 97 per cent (Rs. 197 crores) of the total amount sanctioned.

3.11 Turning to the issues of NCDs, it may be mentioned that the PLC_{pr} tied up with 'Chemicals' enjoy the apex place having secured the consent to float 53 (27.5 per cent of the total) Issues involving a sanction of Rs. 115.45 crores (26.9 per cent). The next in order being those occupied in 'Engineering' (49 or 25.4 per cent and Rs. 77.27 crores or slightly higher than 18 per cent), 'Cotton Textiles' (27 or 13.99 per cent and Rs. 61.50 crores or 14.35 per cent), 'Iron, Steel and Non-Ferrous Metal' (20 or 10.4 per cent and Rs. 41.60 crores or 9.71 per cent), 'Silk, Rayon and Woollen Textiles' (11 or 5.7 per cent and Rs. 35.78 crores or 8.35 per cent), 'Commerce' (7 or 3.6 per cent and Rs. 36.30 crores or 8.5 per cent), 'Paper and Paper Products' (4 or 2.1 per cent and Rs. 16.60 crores or 3.87 per cent), and 'Hotel' (3 or 1.6 per cent and Rs. 11.20 crores or 2.6 per cent). These eight industrial groups thus caused the floatation of over 90 per cent (174) of the entire lot of NCDs approved by CCI during the period 1978-82 involving more than 92 per cent (Rs. 395.70 crores) of the total consented amount.

3.12 If we put all the varieties of debentures at one place then it is observed that PLCpr belonging to the family of 'Chemicals' occupy the first place with permltted approvals for 69 Issues (24.3 per cent of the total) involving a sum of Rs. 212.84 crores (19.8 per cent of the aggregate). Next in order on this score comes, 'Silk, Rayon and Woollen Textiles' (21 or 7.4 per cent and Rs. 196.38 crores or 18.3 pcr cent), 'Cotton Textiles' (44 or 15.5 per cent and Rs. 164.71 crores or 15.4 per cent), 'Engineering' (61 or 21.5 per cent and Rs. 159.52 crores or 14.9 per cent), 'Iron, Steel and Non-Ferrous Metal' (33 or 11.6 per cent and Rs. 128.70 crores or nearly 12 per cent), 'Commerce' (18 or 6.3 per cent and Rs. 59.98 crores or 5.6 per cent), 'Tobacco' (4 or 1.4 per cent and Rs. 38.75 crores or 3.6 per cent), 'Hotel' (6 or 2.1 per cent and Rs. 34.20 crores or 3.2 per cent), and soforth.

3.13 Since the industry-wise tendencies observed in respect to the different categories of debentures on the one hand and debentures as a whole, on the other, are quite inconsistent with each other, it is difficult to infer anything worthwhile in regard to the relationship of industry group or nature of products/ services with the raising of funds either through CDs NCDs. Even so, it can be broadly concluded that PLCpr engaged in those product/service lines which offer faster opportunities of growth/diversification such as Chcmicals, Silk, Rayon and Woollens, Engineering, etc. or which further ensure lucrative and faster returns like Cotton Textiles, Hotel, and Commerce have relatively preferred to augment their resources through the means of CDs/NCDs as against those found operating in the industry groups of 'Tea Plantation', 'Sugar', 'Jute Textiles', 'Rubber and Rubber Manufacturing', and 'Electricity Generation and Supply'.

AGE-WISE SWINGS

3.14 All companies covered by this Study have been first classified into six logically created age-groups and then with a view to promote a facile and purposeful analysis these age-classes have appropriately been clubbed to constitute three broad categories, namely : Old PLCpr (OPLCpr), Middle Aged PLCpr (MAPLCpr), and Relatively New PLCpr (RNPLCpr).[5]

3.15 As may be browsed in Table 3.4 (Annexe . VI) the number of Public Issues of CDs and the amount approved during the period 1978-82 by CCI in favour of OPLCpr, MAPLCpr, and RNPLCpr stood at 14 and Rs. 160.05 crores (i.e. 27.45 per cent and 36.3 per cent) 27 and Rs. 223.30 crores (52.9 per cent and 50.6 per cent), and 10 and Rs. 57.58 crores (19.6 per ccnt and 13.1 per cent), respectively. Evident from this is one tendency. The major portion of the CCI's approvals in this regard (over 80 per cent in terms of number, and nearly 87 per cent of the total amount) has come to be claimed by $OPLC_{pr}$ and $MAPLC_{pr}$, as against $RNPLC_{pr}$ which issued CDs to the public rather in a small magnitude.

3.16 The whereabouts of CDs placed on rights basis, however, disclose a different story. The OPLCpr secured permission for this variant of CDs only for 5 Issues (12.5 per cent) which involved a sum of Rs. 38.7 crores (19.1 per cent).

In contrast to this, $MAPLC_{pr}$ and $RNPLC_{pr}$ accounted for 16 Issues for a sum of Rs. 83.9 crores (40 per cent and 41.3 per cent), and 19 Issues for an amount of Rs. 80.6 crores (47.5 per cent, and 39.7 per cent), respectively. Thus it is obvious that resort to CDs on rights basis has been maximum on the part of $RNPLC_{pr}$. and the least by $OPLC_{pr}$. The position of $MAPLC_{pr}$ though lie afar to $RNPLC_{pr}$ in terms of the number of issues approved, it is almost at the same level judged by the amount raised.

3.17 If the findings arrived at in para 3.15 and 3.16 above are intermingled then we reach to two important conclusions. One, the Old and Medium-Aged PLC_{pr}, which *inter alia* represents a group of companies covering well established and renowned ones, seem to be more confident in raising long term funds through the Public Issues of CDs as compared to Relatively New PLCpr, which in its turn tacitly implies that both the existing and prospective investors repose more confidence in the former as compared to the latter. Two, it is the Relatively New and Medium-Aged PLCpr put together which have augmented their resources rather in a big way through the instrument of CDs (with 72 Issues or 79.12 per cent, and Rs. 445.33 crores of 69.15 per cent) in contrast to OPLCpr (19 Issues or 20.88 per cent and Rs. 198.75 crores or 30.86 per cent) which means that the latter are more sound financially as against the former i.e., availability of internal resources for financing working capital and other expansion/replacement/modernization/diversification programs is found in larger magnitude with the OPLCpr as against the RNPLCpr and MAPLCpr.

3.18 In regared to NCDs the most *ad rem* direction is that the MAPLCpr have taken the lead both in point of securing the permission for the number of Issues and amount raised (125 Issues or 65.3 per cent and Rs. 292.19 crores or 68.19 per cent). These have come to be followed by OPLCpr (44 Issues or 22.80 per cent, and Rs. 91.25 crores or 21.29 per cent), and RNPLCpr (23 Issues or 11.92 per cent, and Rs. 45.13 crores or 10.53 per cent). The pertinent inferences on the above basis are : (i) the RNPLCpr seem to be hesitant in raising their long term resources through NCDs perhaps on account of the perception that their efforts in this direction might not meet with success ; associated with this, however, is another fact that their total needs for long term funds too are not very high; (ii) the $OPLC_{pr}$ possessed as they seem to be with adequate long term funds, are not hard pressed for amplifying their resources through the floatation of NCDs; and (iii) the $MAPLC_{pr}$ have been found enthusiastic for enhancing their resources via NCDs for more than one reason. Their need for long term funds seems to be higher as a consequence of the corporate strategies to bring about modernization in their production processes coupled with simultaneous determination to implement the devised expansion programs. Also, they appear to be rather assured that the NCDs floated by them would be welcome by the existing as well as prospective investors.

REGION/STATE/UNION TRRITORY-WISE INCLINATIONS

3.19 As may be perused in Table 3.5 (Annexe VI) all the PLCpr included in this work fall within the geographical boundaries of Five Regions, 12 States, and One Union Territory.[6] And, the features worthmentioning of this distribution are as thus. Region-wise. Western Region occupies the place of pride in respect to the Public Issues of CDs ; secured approvals during the period 1978-82 having stood at 26 or 50.98 per cent for a sum of Rs. 223.23 crores or 50.63 per cent. Other places of respect are commanded in sequence by the Eastern Region (11 consents or 21.57 per cent for Rs. 105.75 crores or 23.98 per cent), Central Region (3 Issues or 5.88 per cent, for Rs. 60.65 crores or 13.75 per cent), Northern Region (8 permissions or 15.69 per cent, for Rs. 33.88 crores or 7.67 per cent), and Southern Region (3 Issues or 5.88 per cent, for Rs. 17.50 crores or 3.97 per cent). If we peep into what is there behind the scene of these regions, it is noticed that the PLCpr beloning to the State of Maharashtra who have been benefitted most by the CCI's consents in respect to the Public Issues of CDs (13 Issues for a sum of Rs. 158.73 crores which constitute 25.5 per cent, and nearly 36 per cent of the respective totals), and next in order comes the PLC_{pr} of the states of West Bengal (10 Issues of Rs. 95.75 crores i.e. 19.61 per cent, and 21.72 per cent), Gujarat (13 Issues for Rs. 64.50 crores i.e. 25.49 per cent and 14.63 per cent), Uttar Pradesh (2 Issues of Rs. 30.65 crores i.e. 3.92 per cent and 6.95 per cent), Madhya Pradesh (1 Issue of Rs. 30 crores i.e. 1.96 per cent and 6.80 per cent), Delhi (3 Issues for Rs. 24 crores i.e. 5.88 per cent and 5.44 per cent), Tamil Nadu (2 Issues for Rs. 15 crores i.e. 3.92 per cent and 3.40 per cent), Orissa (1 Issue for Rs. 10 crores i.e. 1.96 per cent and 2.27 per cent), Punjab (5 Issues for Rs. 9.80 crores i.e. 9.80 per cent and 2.22 per cent), and Andhra Pradesh (1 Issue for Rs. 2.50 crores i.e. 1.96 per cent and 0.57 per cent).

3.20 As regards the Issues of CDs approved by CCI for floatation on rights basis during the aforesaid period, Western Region again attracts our attention having emerged the pre-eminent region on this count also (with 30 Issues for Rs. 183.55 crores i.e. 75 per cent, and 90.4 per cent of the respective totals); rest of the four regions share the remaining portion of these issues of CDs i.e., Eastern Region 3 Issues for Rs. 14.70 crores (7.5 per cent and 7.2 per cent), Southern Region 5 Issues for a sum of Rs. 4.25 crores (12.5 per cent and 2.1 per cent), and Northern Region 2 Issues for a bare sum of Rs. 0.55 crore (5 per cent and 0.3 per cent). State-wise, again Maharashtra stands at the top with 24 Issues of CDs on rights basis for Rs. 153.96 crores (60 per cent and 75.8 per cent). And, next to it in order are found Gujarat (6 Issues or 15 per cent for Rs. 29.59 crores or 14.6 per cent), and West Bengal (3 Issues or 7.5 per cent for Rs. 14.70 crores or 7.2 per cent). The remaining 7 Issues or 17.5 per cent for Rs. 4.80 crores or 2.4 per cent are obliged by the PLC_{pr} located in the States of Andhra Pradesh, Kerala, Tamil Nadu and Punjab.

3.21 On consigning to oblivion the regional features one point is very luminous. It is the PLCpr situated in industrially developed states/metropolitan city like Maharashtra, Gujarat, and West Bengal (Calcutta) which have availed the highest number of sanctions involving the largest amount in the case of both the CDs placed to the public and on rights basis; their aggregate contribution having stood at 69 Issues for a total sum of Rs. 517.23 crores which constitute nearly 76 per cent and over 80 per cent of the respective totals. Almost alike trends are noticeable in hespect to the Issues of NCDs. Thus the Western Region with 106 Issues or 54.92 per cent for Rs. 239.10 crores or 55.79 per cent has come to be followed by Eastern Region (with 38 Issues or 19.69 per cent for Rs. 78.77 crores or 18.34 per cent), Central Region (13 Issues or 6.74 per cent for Rs. 47.25 crores or 11.03 per cent), Northern Region (16 Issues or 8.29 per cent for Rs. 33.25 crores or 7.76 per cent), and Southern Region (20 Issues or 10.36 per cent for Rs. 30.20 crores or 7.05 per cent). Further, developed states/metropolitan city like Maharashtra, Gujarat, and West Bengal (Calcutta), which put together account for 142 Issues or 73.6 per cent for Rs. 312.27 crores or 72.9 per cent, have a whip hand over the NCDs market.

MICROSCOPIC FEATURES OF CURIOSITY

3.22 Side by side the macro trends, the features of microscopic interest of the Issues of CDs/NCDs as approved by the CCI between 1978 and 1982 may now be highlighted. The significant trends from this angle, as would be obvious from the perusal of the contents of Table 2.3 through Table 2.7, are adduced hereunder.

[I] THE PRISTINE AND THE AFTERMOST COMPANY :

3.23 Metal Box Company of India Limited, Calcutta, has been the first in receiving permission from CCI to float an Issue of CDs on 17.7.1978 for heaving a sum of Rs. 2 crore-Rs. 1.50 crore from the public and the rest Rs. 0.50 crore from its existing members. Analogously, the aftermost company which succeded in yielding accent to issue CDs to the public has been the Indian Rayon Corporation Limited, Veraval; it secured CCI's accent on 23.11.1982 for augmenting a total sum of Rs. 21 crores-Rs. 4.9 crores from the public and the remaining from its existing members.[7] The parallel premier and latest counterparts in the case of NCDs have been Madura Coats Limited, Madurai, and Kanoria Chemical & Industries Limited, Calcutta, respectively. The CCI admitted the former on 18.2.1981 for a sum of Rs. 3.50 crores and the latter on 10.12.1982 for an amount of Rs. 2.50 crores.[8]

[II] RANGES OF FACE VALUES, INTEREST RATES & 5 PER CENT PREMIUM PROFERRED :

3.24 On the whole the face value of CDs issued during the period 1978-82 has ranged between Rs. 10 (Metal Box Co. of India Ltd., Calcutta which secured CCI's consent on 17.7.1978) and Rs. 1,000 (Daccan Sugar and Abkari Company Limited, and Sirpur Paper Mills Limited, which received CCI's permissions on 24.2.1981 and 2.11.1982, respectively). In the context it may be mentioned that for the minimum and the highest face values put together there have been only three cases as referred to above. Further, in the case of CDs placed in the market to the public the face value has only varied between Rs. 10 and Rs. 500. What is more relevant is the fact that in over fifty per cent of the Issues of CDs the face value has been Rs. 100. And, wherever it has been higher or less the Issue has either been found fully offered on a rights basis or partly on a rights basis and partly to the public. It may be recaptulated here that this trend is in consonance with the latest CCI's guidelines governing the issuance of debentures. These state that, "The face value of the debentures will ordinarily be Rs. 100 each"[9].

3.25 The correlative position in respect to NCDs has been as follows. While it is true that the face value of NCDs has varied in a wide domain of Rs. 10 (Andrew Yule Company Limited, Calcutta, and Perfect Circle Victor Limited, Bombay which obtained approvals on 13.3.1978 and 31.12.1981, respectively) and Rs. 5,000 (Industrial Credit and Investment Corporation of India, Bombay, to which permission was granted on 20.5.1978), it has been Rs. 100 in most of the Issues (nearly 95 per cent of the total).

3.26 The rates of interst offered on CDs and NCDs varied between 10.5 per cent and 14 per cent per annum, and 6.5 per cent and 15 per cent per annum, respectively. Barring few cases the rate of interest offered on these has in fact been as per the Guidelines approved by the CCI from time to time. And, the exceptions to this rule are found only in Issues offered on Rights Basis.

3.27 There has been no Issue of Convertible Debentures which carried the benefit of 5 per cent premium on redemption, as the same is not allowed under the aforesaid Guidelines. However, most of the Issues of NCDs came to enjoy this advantage as soon as CCI permitted PLCpr on April 17, 1982 to grant a premium upto 5 per cent at the time of their redemption. In short, the above analysis leads us to conclude that the Issues of CDs/NCDs offered by PLC_{pr} to the public are completely governed in respect to their face values, interest rate offered and granting of the benefit of 5 per cent premium on redemption by the Guidelines issued from time to time by the CCI.

III. SPECTRUM OF PURPOSES :

3.28 The CCI's Guidelines prescribe that these debentures can be issued either "to raise long term funds for the financing of any expansion or diversification project or to augment the long term resources of the company for working capital requirements."[10] Accordingly, CDs in India have largely been buoyed up by PLCpr during the period under review to augment their base of long term funds needed for meeting the working capital requirements, and financing expansion, replacement and modernization, and diversification projects. Two ssues of CDs (Straw Products Limited, Jaykaypur, Orissa, and Ferro Alloy Corporation Limited, Tumser which received consents on 1.4.1981 and 29.9.1981, respectively), have the aim of raising long term funds for financing new projects; one issue. (Mukand Iron & Steel Works Limited, Bombay, which secured consent on 28.11.1981) has the objective of amplifying medium term funds; one issue (May & Baker Limited, Bombay, which obtained approval on 24.9.1982) has the twin purpose of raising funds for modernization and affecting reduction in the holdings of Non-Residents; and, one issue (Daccan Sugar & Abkari Company Limited, Madras, which secured permission on 24.2.1981) has been for boosting long term funds for the company's rehabilitation program. In sharp contrast to this, the chunk portion of the Issues of NCDs aim at augmenting the companies' long term resources needed by way of working capital, while a few of them have also been for implementing the programs relating to amalgamation/transfer of business. Thus it is abundantly clear that in actuality the Controller of Capital Issues has allowed the floatation of CDs/NCDs by PLCpr for the sepectrum of purposes which is much wider than what has statutorily been stipulated.

PUBLIC ISSUES OF CONVERTIBLE DEBENTURES/ BONDS: THRASHED OUT IN MINUTIAE

3.29 Excluding the Issues of CDs put up on rights basis by PLC_{pr}, exhaustive details have been included in Table 3.6 (Annexe VI) of those which have been approved by CCI for sale to the public during the entire period 1978-82. As may be seen in this table, the total number of such issues add up to 51 for a total sum of Rs. 440.93 crores. Of these, 4 PLC_{pr} abandoned their plan to utilize their consents involving a sum of Rs. 9.80 crores. These are : Cheviot Company Limited, Calcutta (Rs. 1 crore), Rajasthan Spg. & Wvg. Mills Limited, New Delhi (Rs. 5 crores), Mohta Industries Limited. Ludhiana (Rs. 1.30 crores), and Nagarjuna Steel Limited, Hyderabad (Rs. 2.50 crores). While the exact reasons have not been made public by the corporate managements of first three companies, in the case of last one the approval was cancelled by the CCI on April 16, 1983. Our enquiries made from other sources, however, reveal that the other three companies seem to have decided not to enter the debenture market primarily due to two reasons. One, not-too-good an opinion is found about the financial position of these companies in the minds of prospective investors. Two, the equities of these companies are traded at different stock exchanges rather sporadically. Consequently, we are left out with 47 Issues of CDs for the purposes of our diagnostic and suggestive investigation. Before we switch over to this we may, however, mention here some other features of importance of these Issues which are obvious from a quick look of the table under scrutiny.

[I] THE TWO COMPONENTS OF THE ISSUES OF CDS :

3.30 Of the 51 Public Issues of CDs, as many as 48 are characterized with the possession of two components : a portion which has been offered to the Public, and also another portion which has been placed in the market on Rights basis ; the amount offered to public and placed on rights basis being Rs. 216.95 crores (49.20 per cent of the total) and Rs. 224.53 crores (50.80 per cent), respectively. Likewise, from out of 47 actual Public Issues of CDs, 43 possess the above two components ; the corresponding amounts involved being Rs. 212.55 crores or or 49.30 per cent, and Rs. 218.58 crores or 50.70 per cent. It indicates that the ratio between the funds raised from the public and the existing members has been nearly 50:50.

(II) INTERVAL BETWEEN THE DATES OF CONSENTS & ACTUAL DATES OF OPENINGS OF THE ISSUES :

3.31 There is observed a time gap between the dates on which CCI communicated its approvals and the actual dates on which the different Issues of CDs actually came to be opened. This time gap has been maximum (11 months and 7 days) in the case of Tata Engineering & Locomotive Company Limited, Bombay which received the consent on 12.9.1979 and opened its issue on 6.10.1980, and minimum (1 month and 2 days) for Reliance Textile Industries Limited, Bombay which secured the consent on 14.5.1981 and opened its Issue on 16.6.1981. For rest of the companies this gap has been 2 to 5 months. While there have been certain uncontrollable factors in the case of Tata Engineering & Locomotive Company Limited, Bombay which led to considerable delay in the actual effectualization of the CCI's consent, the strategic planning on this score of Reliance Textile Industries Limited, Bombay, needs to be regarded more precise—an aspect worth distinguishable and admiring.

(III) THE KIND OF CONVERSION INVOLVED :

3.32 From the angle of the kind of conversion involved all the Issues of CDs can be clubbed into four categories, namely, Partly Convertible CDs (38 Issues), With a Right to Subscribe (08), Fully Convertible (03), and With a Proviso to Issue Equity Shares in Lieu of interest Accrued on CDs (01). The information about Nagarjuna Steel Company, Hyderabad, is not available ; but then it is not significant in the light of the fact that the approval to this company was cancelled by the CCI. Even if we exclude 3 other companies which did not avail their consents for the issuance of Partly Convertible Debentures, it can be safely inferred that it is the Partly Convertible variant of CDs (35 or 75 per cent of the total number of *de facto* Issues) which have tyrannize the scene. And, these have come to be followed by CDs covetous by Right to Subscribe (8 or over 17 per cent), Fully Convertible (3 or over 6 per cent), and CDs carrying the clause of Issuing Equity Shares in lieu of Interest Accrued (1 or over 2 per cent).

(IV) CONVERSION RATIO & CONVERSION PERIOD :

3.33 In the case of Fully Convertible Debentures issued by the Metal Box of India Limited, Calcutta, Tata Engineering & Locomotive Company Limited, Bombay, and Straw Products Limited, Jaykaypur the conversion ratio has been 'One Equity Share for One Debenture At Par', '2 Equity Shares for One Debenture At a Premium of Rs. 175', and '25 Equity Shares for One Debenture At a Premium of Rs. 10 per Share', respectively, indicating thereby that no uniformity is found in the conversion ratios of all the three companies. A similar position is obtained for Partly Convertible Debentures. As a matter of fact both the conversion ratio and the concomitant terms have come to be announced differently by almost all the companies involved in the issuance of Partly Convertible Debentures. Even so, it may be noted that the orbit of convertibility has been between 10 per cent and 60 per cent of the face value of the debenture. On this score homogeneity is again missing in the Issues of CDs accompanied with a Right to Subscribe. And, the conversion ratio of CDs of I.T.C. Limited Calcutta, came to be stated as '10 Equity Shares in Lieu of Interest At Par.'

3.34 In regard to the period of conversion too, no likeness is noticed—it having varied from 3 months (Punjab Anand Batteries Limited, Mohali) to a blending of 3 and 7 years (The Tata Engineering & Locomotive Company Limited, Bombay). A close view of the various Issues of CDs floated during the period under review reveals that the majority of the companies have kept the conversion period in the vicinity of few months to one year. Furthermore, the period of conversion has been kept on a higher side only by those PLCpr which are older in age and are well famed for their financial soundness and integrity and quality of management.

SECTION THREE

ADJUDICATING THE SUCCESSFULNESS/ UNSUCCESSFULNESS OF THE PUBLIC ISSUES OF CONVERTIBLE DEBENTURES

HUNT FOR THE JUST, ADMISSIBLE & COGENT FRAMEWORK OF YARDSTICKS

3.35 Literally speaking there are 3-segments of our populace who may have their differing interests in the public issues of CDs. These are : (i) the companies issuing such debentures, their corporate managements, managers and underwriters to issues ; (ii) the existing and potential investors ; and, (iii) the economy which in the setting of our country represent the State including the entire mechanism created for managing an overall speedy growth. Accordingly we may prepare a check list of the criteria need to be employed for adjudging the success or failure of the various Public Issues of CDs. This, however, is not a simple task. In particular it would be strenuous to prepare distinct checklists to serve the cause of different interested parties because their decisions are influenced by the perceptions they have about each other. Even so it would be desirable first to prepare separate check-lists and then an integral one to facilitate a crystal clear analysis. So we proceed ahead on the task set.

CHECK LIST FOR COMPANIES, THEIR CORPORATE MANAGEMENTS AND MANAGERS/UNDERWRITERS TO ISSUES.

(*a*) *Over-Subscription* :

3.36 Managers/Underwriters to Issues would consider any Public Issues of CDs as successful if it is fully subscribed/ oversubscribed since it would soon alleviate them from their obligations. Over subscription of an issue also adds to their celebrity in this area of business. For companies and their corporate managements 'oversubscription' again present an important measurement for evaluating the success of an Issue; conversely, if an Issue remains 'undersubscribed' it is to be regarded as an unsuccessful endeavour. The criterion of over subscription ensures the managements of the concerned companies that the required funds stand augmented and they can go ahead in implementing the planned programs. An oversubscribed issue further spawn confidence in them about the appropriateness of plans, aside creating a perception that investors repose confidence in their concerns.

(B) 'Number of times an issue is oversubscribed' :

3.37 Hence, greater the number of times an issue is oversubscribed ameliorate indicator it would be of the success and *vice-versa* of the issue under reference. Beyond doubt, there exists a substantial amount of truth in this. A word of caution in this regard, however. The criterion of the number of times an Issue is oversubscribed needs to be interpreted with reference to the total amount involved in the Issue. If the total amount to be raised through an Issue is meagre the number of times it has been oversubscribed would carry a different meaning in contrast to a situation where the amount involved is huge. Thus it is obvious that this indicator would present the correct picture of successfulness/unsuccessfulness only when the number of times of the oversubscription is duly adjusted keeping in view the amount involved.

(C) Impact on the Capital Structure :

3.38 What impact the raising of long-term funds through the issuance of CDs to public has on re-shaping the company's capital structure could still be another vital criterion for examining the success/failure of an Issue. If they have assisted in moving forward in the creation of an optimal capital structure for the company we can safely regard it as a sign of success because it is likely to contribute to the maximization of owners' wealth and *vice-versa.* Since the computation of an optimal capital structure involves numerous complexities, we have not been able to examine every issue on this score saving, of course, those for which case studies have been completed in this Study. Also we have reckoned out the cost of different variants of CDs to illustrate the significance of this yardstick; the issues to represent the various variants of CDs having selected on the basis of stratafied random sampling.

(D) Market Values of Equity Shares and Convertible Debentures and the Volume of Training :

3.39 The quotations of the prices of the relevant equities/ debentures and the data bearing information on the magnitude of trading in them on different Stock Exchanges relating to the period prior to and after the actual allotment of concerned CDs can further be used for appraising the success/failure of various Issues. Given the framework of conversion ratio, higher the price of the equity share as against the announced conversion price, higher would be the benefit in the form of capital gain at the time of the conversion to the debentureholder. Therefore, if during the period following the allotment of CDs the market value of the relevant equity share/convertible debenture keeps on rising then it would mean a rise in the likely capital gain if the debentureholder retains the debentures and *vice-versa.* Besides there being a direct utility of these criteria from the angle of investors, the prudent managements having their commitments toward corporate plans for the growth of institutions under their charge would also admire the message these yardsticks leave for them. Thus no company can think of using this instrument of raising long-term funds on a continuous basis unless it ensures a steadily rising trend in the market price of its equity share and debenture and a fairly good volume of trading in them at different stock exchanges. An upward trend in prices/volume of trading would signify to the management that existing/soon-to-be class of investors continues to repose confidence both in them and the company. Hence, it can go ahead.

CATALOGUE OF BENCHMARKS FOR INVESTORS

(A) Terms of conversion and sources of capital gain :

3.40 Be it a case of existing or prospective investor, over-subscription of an issue simply provides a psychological satisfaction to him and nothing more than that. Secured as the CDs are, safety considerations of investors stand taken care of. By virtue of this element, they are less risky also. So for them the prime consideration is the 'return on their investment'. While in the ultimate analysis they should logically be interested in the 'redemption yield computed by employing internal rate of return method', they are found interested in immediate gains in the short run. These immediate gains take the shape of interest rate yield and capital gains. Since the interest rate yield can be taken as given, we can evaluate the worth of the various public issues of CDs from their angle on the basis of :

—extent of conversion;

—timing of conversion;

—conversion price; and

—market price of CDs.

Higher the proportions, shorter the duration and the minimum the price is of the conversion, greater would be the likely capital gains to the debentureholder provided the associated equity share either witnesses an upward increase in its price or its price remains constant at the peak level already attained. The debentureholder is likely to have his capital gains generally in a graduated declining manner if any one or all of the situations mentioned here are found prevalent : (i) the price of equity share start witnessing downward trend soon after the Issue of Debentures comes to close or comes to be quoted at a price lower than the level already attained before the issuance of CDs or the upward quotations as observed at the time of issuance of CDs prove once-time feature; (ii) the conversion price is announced at a fairly high premium thus leaving a narrow gap between the market price of the equity and the price which the investor would be required to pay for acquiring them at some future date; (iii) the proportion of the CDs to be converted into equity share is kept on a lower side; and (iv) the date of conversion is kept at a far distance.

3.41 Price at which a CD is quoted during the periods preceding and subsequent to its date of conversion it would further determine the capital gain an investor is likely to secure from this security. Alongside the concerned equity, if the market value of CD also indicates a steady upward movement, then it would further imply an additional gain to an investor and *vice-versa*.

(B) Auxiliary benefits affixed with the public issues of CDs :

3.41 Auxiliary benefits affixed with the Public Issues of CDs to be given affect before the actual effectualization of conversion can additionally be utilized for determing the fortune of the variegated public issues of CDs from the standpoint of investors. These benefits have normally been to the debentureholders by way of assurances to extend the benefits given to the shareholders during the period of conversion such as the issue of bonus shares and making available equity shares on rights basis etc. or promise to effect reduction in the announced premium at which the defined portion of convertible debenture is to be converted into equity shares if bonus shares are issued. It needs no reiteration that the larger and more lucrative benefits on the pattern cited above would go to enhance the success of such securities. Obviously, the absence of such benefits are likely to affect adversely the response of investors for such securities.

(C) Adjuvant Criteria :

3.42 Sidelong the above, investors' interests can be safeguarded if we adjudge the issues of CDs under reference on such bases as :

— whether the associated equity shares of the companies issuing public CDs are of 'Volatile' or 'Non-Volatile' nature;

— comparison between the advertised rates of returns with those which are realized *de facto*; and

— the progress being registered by the companies and their programs of future expansion/diversification. Interested as the debentureholders are in such aspects, it must be seen that do the companies insert, on a regular basis, 'News Items' in the prominent news papers with a view to furnish the investors with the type of information they are interested in ?

SCALE OF TOUCHSTONES FROM THE VIEW-POINT OF 'ECONOMY'

(I) Magnitude of Aggregate Funds Mobilized :

3.43 The thrust of the Government's Policy being on the attainment of 'self-reliance' by the private corporate sector in point of its need for long-term funds, it would be irrelevant to distinguish between different kinds of secured debentures, namely, convertible debentures-offered to public and those placed on rights basis-and non-convertible debentures. Hence, it seems rational if the success/failure of the variegated kinds of debentures is adjudged clubbing them at one place. On doing so, the first important criterion on which we can examine the success of the various Issues of CDs/NCDs floated during the period 1978-82 can be the 'magnitude of the aggregate long-term funds mobilized by the PLC_{pr} through these instruments during the period under review'. This magnitude can be measured both in absolute terms as well a percentage to total permissions granted by CCI for raising fresh capital through all available modes by non-government companies. An increase in the proportion of CCI's consents for debentures in its total approvals over the years would indicate success for this saving instrument and *vice-versa.*

(II) Debentures and Their Role in Restraining Inflationary Trends :

3.44 Related to the above is another quite meaningful aspect. The extent to which these funds have come to be contributed by the category of individual investors, particularly by those who have meagre savings, it can be rightly interpreted that the floated debentures have assisted in mobilizing at least a portion of household savings which otherwise might have either remained idle or misspend. From this flows our argument that debentures via mobilisation of savings for productive purposes not only assist the nation's growth process but also in controlling the inflationary conditions in the economy broadly in two ways : one, by holding back the people to spend their savings on unproductive items or just keeping them in an idle form, and, second, through increasing the aggregate supply of goods/services in the economy.

AN INTEGRAL CHECK LIST

3.45 On the whole a Public Issue of CDs can be deemed successful if it :

- involves sizeable amount;
- comes to be held widely;
- receives an overwhelming response dipted via commendable number of times the issue is oversubscribed;
- lean towards the creation of an optimal capital structure coupled with minimum possible cost of the issue for the company;
- carries an attractive rate of interest (preferably with a proviso to affect revision in it as and when CCI permits it), and a frame of the terms of conversion (highest possible ratio of conversion, shortest possible duration of conversion, and conversion either at par or minimum possible price of the associated equity) which may ensure debentureholders about the maximum possible capital gains;
- advertizes the rate of returns in a manner which is not misleading; and
- comes to be backed up by a competent and sincere corporate management who can devise really worthwhile projects, take all necessary measures which may either steadily increase or maintain the market price of the associated equity and the CDs at the different stock exchanges, lead to the categorization of equity as 'Volatile', and insert news items in the important dailies highlighting the company's progress and future programs.

It is obvious from the integrated check list that there exists no conflict between the benchmarks for judging the success/failure of the Issues of CDs either from the viewpoint of the companies or investors, and even from the angle of the economy. As a matter of fact they supplement each other. A word of caution may be added here. The above criteria would settle the problem by and large from the short run perspective. In the long-run debentureholders/prospective investors would be found-interested in the liquidity, redemption yield to be computed with some time-adjusted technique, fulfilment of the promises given in respect to the announced auxiliary benefits, survival and prosperity of the company accompanied with a laudable image about it in the society, and so forth. Similarly, the companies and their corporate managements would be keen to raise long-term funds at the minimum possible committed interest rates, though they may not mind in compensating the debentureholders in the shape of higher capital gains which may accrue on account of rising market values of associated equity shares/debentures, allotment of additional equity shares on rights basis or of bonus shares. Saving those who wish to maximize returns in the short-run, it should not make any material difference for the prudent and farsighted investors, however. In fact, those who fall in higher income brackets would welcome a return in the form of capital gains for it may help them in their tax-planning exercise. In the light of present day Government Policy they may have fierce yearn for strengthening their long-term resources in as much magnitude as possible and that too on a continual basis till such funds take forward the company's capital structure towards an optimum level. This desire has the background of attaining self-reliance in point of their long-term capital needs covering as well the permanent portion of working capital requirements. This being the situation, the prudence, ingenuity, competence, creativity, sincerity and integrity of the corporate managements on the one hand, and meritoriousness of the designed project(s), to be gauged through their technical, economic and commercial viability, should constitute important criteria for evaluating the success/failure of the Issues of CDs.

CATECHISM OF PUBLIC ISSUES OF CONVERTIBLE DEBENTURES/BONDS ON DISPASSIONATE GROUND

3.46 Reference to Column 18 of Table 3.6 reveals that information in respect to 'oversubscription' is available only about 41 Issues of the Public CDs. A perusal to this discloses that of the 41 Public Issues of CDs, as many as 36 i.e. 87.5 per cent came to be oversubscribed, and the rest 5 i.e. 12.2 per cent stood undersubscribed; the range of oversubscription having varied between 1.9 times (East India Hotels Limited, Calcutta) and 72 times (Hindustan Development Corporation Limited, Calcutta) indicating thereby an average range of 8.5 times. If we leaf through on Issue-to-Issue position, it is evident that the Public CDs of Hindustan Development Corporation Limited, Calcutta, floated on 6.5.1981 for a sum of Rs. 1.50 crores, witnessed the highest oversubscription of 72 times. And, they have been followed by Straw Products Limited, Jaykaypur on 18.8.1981 for Rs. 10 crores by 25 times, Lohia Machines Company, Kanpur, on 7.9.1982 for Rs. 5.65 crores by 13 times, Camphor and Allied Products Limited, Bombay, on 29.1.1981 for Rs. 1 crore by 12 times, Tata Iron & Steel Company Limited, Bombay, on 14.12.1981 for Rs. 30 crores by 10.2 times, Jyoti Limited, Baroda, on 12.11.1981 for Rs. 2 crores by 9 times, ITC Limited, Calcutta, on 29.11.1982 for Rs. 30 crores by 8.9 times, Voltas Limited, Bombay, on 6.5.1981 for Rs. 5 crores, and Shri Dinesh Mills Limited, Baroda, on 4.8.1981 for Rs. 1 crore by 8.7 times each, Indian Rayon Corporation Limited, Veraval, Gujarat, on 16.3.1981 for Rs. 10 crores, Reliance Textile Industries Limited, Bombay, on 16.6.1981 for Rs. 24 crores, J.K. Synthetics Limited, Kanpur, on 3.2.1982 for Rs 25 crores, and Indian Rayon Corporation Limited, Veraval, on 25.1.1983 for Rs. 21 crores by 8 times each, and soforth; the latitude of oversubscription being between 1.9 and 7 times for the rest of the Issues. Clearly thus 13 from out of 41 Issues came to be oversubscribed by near or more than the average number of times. Even so, on the above criterion it can be deduced safely that bulk of the Public Issues of CDs have been successful from the watchtower of managers/ underwriters to issues and also to some extent the PLCpr and their corporate managements.

ANECDOTE OF UNSUCCESSFUL PUBLIC ISSUES OF CDs

3.47 Before we further examine in depth the success/failure of the aforesaid 36 Issues on other criteria, let us probe into the reasons which led to the undersubscription of the Public CDs putforwarded by the Sukhjit Starch and Chemicals Limited, Phagwara, the Ahmedabad Shri Ramkrishna Mills Company Limited, Ahmedabad, the Premier Mills Limited, Udampur, the General Industrial Society Limited, Calcutta, and the Guest Keen Williams Limited, Calcutta. The factors contributing to this rather abhorrent situation seems to be copious. First, the associated equity shares of these companies are of non-volatile nature. Consequence to this either no stock exchange quotations for the concerned equity and debenture are available or these are rare or relate to a particular stock exchange. To substantiate, the equity shares of Sukhjit Starch & Chemicals Limited came to be traded and quoted only for a couple of days, that too on the Delhi Stock Exchange, during the period just anterior to the opening of its Issue of CDs to the public. And, since then no quotation either in regard to equity or debenture is obtainable. Likewise the equity shares are traded and quoted only at Ahmedabad Stock Exchange, that too rarely, in the case of the Ahmedabad Shri Ramkrishna Mills Company Limited, Ahmedabad. And, no quotation for this Mills' debentures, even of Ahmedabad Stock Exchange, is attainable. Exactly the same is true for General Industrial Society Limited, Calcutta, excepting the fact that in this case Delhi Stock Exchange is found involved. And, quotations for the debentures of Guest, Keen Williams Limited are not traceable on any other Stock Exchange excepting the one found situated at Calcutta. Second, the terms of conversion have some what been uninviting in all the five Issues as compared to their counterparts. For instance, the Issue floated by Premier Mills Limited stated that only '30 per cent of the Convertible Debenture would be converted into 2 Equity Shares At Premium of Rs. 5 per share within a period of 3 years.'[11] This framework of the terms of conversion needs to be interpreted with reference to an additional information. The market price of the equity share of the Premier Mills at the time of the opening of the issue of CDs stood barely at 1.7 times of its face value which incidentally happens to be the minimum. Likewise, the terms of conversion announced by Guest Keen Williams Limited read as: '25 per cent Conversion in two stages : first within 6 months of the date of allotment of debentures and Second 2 years after the first conversion, into 5 Equity Shares of Rs. 10 each at par.'[12] And those of the Ahmedabad Shri Ramkrishna Mills Co. Limited, the Sukhjit Starch & Chemicals Limited, and the General Industrial Society Limited read as under respectively :

(i) 'Rs. 20 of the face value of each Debenture of Rs. 120 held by the holder..... shall carry an obligation on the company to issue two Equity Shares of Rs. 10 each at par..... on 30.6.1982 .. in effect it means conversion of bare 16.67 per cent of the face value of the debenture which is lowest of all.'[13];

(ii) 'Each Debenture Holder .....be allotted by and receive from the company two Ordinary Shares .....against the partial redemption of an amount of Rs. 20 from the nominal value of the Debenture..... i.e. conversion ratio being only 20 per cent.'[14]; and

(iii) 'Allotment of 3 Equity Shares of Rs. 10 each at par on 1.1.83..... including a conversion ratio of 30 per cent.'[15]

Third, no additional benefits like assurance of issuing Bonus Shares and/or Rights Equities came to be attached with the CDs issued by the Sukhjit Starch & Chemicals Limited, and those of the General Industrial Society Limited. Fourth, there also appears to be a lapse on the part of concerned corporate managements alongside the managers and underwriters to these Issues in point of the formulation of appropriate market strategy. A fact which is simply borne out by the situation that none of them even bother to insert 'news items' in different news papers commonly subscribed by the prospective investors detailing the company's past record of performance, present financial position, and future growth plans. Fifth, the market prices of the equity shares of the companies issuing CDs at the time of entering into the market for issuance of CDs to the public have not been much captivating to the investors; these having ranged between 2 and 2.8 times of the respective face values. In the context it would be pertinent to mention that in as many as 17 PLC_{pr} the corresponding market prices varied between 4 and 10 times. Sixth, the reckoned percentages of benefits computed taking into account the number of equity shares to be allotted on conversion, their market price at the time of the issuance of CDs and the price on which these would be made available to the debenture-holders are found to be varying between 14 and 36 in the case of aforesaid five Issues *vis-a-vis* 50 and 345 in as many as 16 oversubscribed Issues. Last but not least the terms of redemption of these Issues too have not been fetching in the sense that they did not carry with them buy back clause or any other kind of option which could have imbibed in them a higher degree of liquidity an aspect to which is given a high weightage by the investors. Thus it is abundantly clear that the above referred Issues proved unsuccessful not only from the stand point of concerned companies but also came to be discarded by the investors on syllogistic grounds.

3.48 Undersubscribed Issues of CDs mobilized a total sum of Rs. 25.85 crores which constitute a tiny proportion of 6 per cent of the total funds actually mobilized for the private corporate sector by 47 Public Issues of CDs during the period 1978-82. If we calculate their shares in the aggregate funds raised during the aforesaid period by PLC_{pr} through the issuance of both CDs and NCDs, then it further stands reduced to bare 2.4 per cent. Further it turns to a negligible proportion i.e. 1.1 per cent if the total approvals granted by CCI to raise fresh capital for Rs. 2308.44 crores via debenture issues, initial issues, fresh issues, bonus issues, loans, etc. are taken in to account. (Also, see please, Table 2.1, for details).

AN INDEPTH PROBE INTO THE 36 PUBLIC ISSUES OF CONVERTIBLE DEBENTURES :

3.49 Out of 47 Public Issues of CDs, as many as 36 of them emerged out successful on the criterion of 'oversubscription'; information on this score not being available in respect to 6 such Issues and the rest 5 being undersubscribed. (See, please, Column 18 of Table 3.6, for details). In so far as the managers/underwriters to issues are concerned the inference flowing on the above basis seems correct. To some extent, it also serves the cause of issuing companies and their managements. But then this criterion neither reveals the whole truth nor assists in arranging the various Issues in descending order on the basis of their success either from the viewpoint of issuing companies and their managements, investors and economy or in presenting an overall position on the basis of an integral scale of yardsticks. Hence the need for employing other criteria.

3.50 Let us start with an adjustment in the criterion of oversubscription by taking into account the magnitude of funds involved in various issues under analysis. Thus the highest amount of Rs. 47.25 crores is entailed by the public issue of CDs placed in the market by the Tata Engineering and Locomotive Company Limited (TELCO) and it stood oversubscribed by as many as 6 times. Next in order are found the issues putforwarded for an even amount by Tata Iron and Steel Company Limited (TISCO) for Rs. 30 crores (oversubscribed by 10.2 times), the Gwalior Rayon Silk Mfg. (Wvg.) Company Limited (Gwalior Rayon) for Rs. 30 crores (oversubscribed by 6 times), and the ITC Limited for Rs. 30 crores (oversubscribed by 8.9 times), respectively. Third, Fourth, and Fifth places in this regard are occupied by those of the J.K. Synthetics Limited (JKS) for Rs. 25 crores (oversubscribed by 8 times), the Reliance Textile Industries Limited (Reliance) for Rs. 24 crores (oversubscribed by 8 times), and the Kesoram Industries and Cotton Mills Limited (Kesoram) for Rs. 21 crores (oversubscribed by 6.7 times) and the Indian Rayon Corporation Limited (Indian Rayons) for Rs. 21 crores (oversubscribed by 8 times). The comparable issue of the Ahmedabad Shri Ramkrishna Mills Company Limited (Ramkrishna Mills) convoluted the least amount of Rs. 0.60 crores and that too remained undersubscribed. In order to guage the relevance of the above we may proceed a step further. An oversubscription by 6 times of of the TELCO's issue worth Rs. 47.25 crores means that investors were prepared to invest as high a sum as Rs. 283.50 crores as compared to Rs. 108 crores which they proffered to place at the disposal of the Hindustan Development Corporation Limited for its debentures worth Rs. 1.50 crores and which came to be oversubscribed by the highest number of times i.e. 72. The corresponding figures for TISCO, Gwalior Rayon, ITC, JKS, Reliance, Kesoram and Indian Rayons stood at Rs. 306 crores, Rs. 180 crores, Rs. 267 crores, Rs. 200 crores, Rs. 192 crores, Rs. 140.7 crores and Rs. 168 crores, respectively. On this more realistic criterion of public response TISCO's issue (Rs. 306 crores) occupies the place of pride followed by the Issues of TELCO (Rs. 283.50 crores), ITC (Rs. 267 crores). JKS (Rs. 200 crores), Reliance (Rs. 192 crores), Gwalior Rayon

(180 crores), Indian Rayons (Rs. 168 crores), and Kesoram (Rs. 140.7 crores). The matching position for the remaining Issues can be computed likewise. Incidentally, the coming forth order of the successfulness of various Issues on above criterion would be of real value to the issuing companies and their corporate managements.

3.51 While we have interrogated the public issues of CDs on the criteria of their accomplishments in the sphere of optimal capital structure, real cost of issuing such securities, value and return to the debentureholders over a period of time, worthwhileness of the projects financed alongside the quality of managements in the subsequent sections of this Chapter, other yardsticks chosen for the purpose from the standpoint of issuing companies, investors and the economy may now be taken up. As has already been emphasized the number of times the market price of the associated equity share is as compared to its face value at the time of the opening up of a public issue of CDs vitally affect the response of potential investors as it influences the likely capital gains to them depending of course on the announced terms of conversion. It is observed in this regard in Column 20 of Table 3.6 that the market price of the equity share stood top-most (10 times of the face value) for the Reliance Textile Industries Limited, followed by the Indian Rayon Corporation Limited (9 times on 25.1.1983 and 7.8 times on 16.3.1981), the Hindustan Development Corporation Limited (7.5 times) the Kesoram Industries and Cotton Mills Limited (6.5 times), the J.K. Synthetics Limited and the Indian Hotels Company Limited (6 times each), the Gwalior Rayon Silk Mfg. (Wvg.) Company Limited and the Bharat Vijay Mills (5 times each), the Zenith Steel Pipes and Industries Limited, and the Straw Products Limited (4.8 times each), the Raymond Woollen Mills Limited (4.5 times), the Star Industrial and Textile Enterprises Limited (4.2 times), and the Elecon Engineering Company Limited, the Usha Alloys and Steels Company Limited and the Gujarat Steel Tubes Limited (4 times each).

3.52 The criterion of benefit indices may now be employed for appraising the oversubscribed public issues of CDs. Benefit

Indices, which have been computed by dividing the amount of expected benefit per equity share reckoned on the basis of its market price found prevalent at the time of floatation of the issue by the conversion price multiplied by 100 (B.I. $= \frac{\text{Amount of Expected Benefit Per Equity Share}}{\text{Conversion Price}} \times 100$), indiate the amounts of benefits expressed in percentages which are likely to be attained by the debenturcholders per equity share. An over view of the Column 23 of Table 3.6, which displays these indices, brings to our notice that on this score the Public Issues of Kesoram Industries and Cotton Mills Limited stood at the top with as high a benefit index as 550. It has come to be followed by the Public Issues of CDs placed by Hindustan Development Corporation Limited (328.57), Reliance Textile Industries Limited on 3.10.1979 (First Series), and on 16.6.1981 (Third Series) (300 each), Indian Rayon Corporation Limited (the one floated on 16.3.1981) (290), ITC Limited (268), Tata Iron and Steel Company Limited (240), Indian Rayon Corporation Limited (the one putforwarded on 25.1.1983) (221.43), Zenith Steel Pipes and Industries Limited and Punjab Anand Batteries Limited (220 each), J.K. Synthetics Limited (200), Voltas limited (170), Usha Alloys and Steels Limited and Gujarat Steel Tubes Limited (166.67 each), and soforth. In the case of remaining public issues of CDs of the identical nature, Benefit Index has varied between 25.7 (Shree Dinesh Mills Limited) and 150 (Raymond Woollen Mills Limited, Gwalior Rayon Silk Mfg. (Wvg.) Company Limited and Ranbaxy Laboratories Limited). The above analysis clearly indicates that while on the minimum side the Benefit Index has been 25.7, it touched the peak of 550 on its higher side. And, if the benefit indices of all the concerned issues are perused then it is further obvious that no consistancy is observed between them. What is, however, most relevent is the fact that this measure suffers from an important lacuna. It only calculates the expected gains to the debentureholders at the time of conversion per equity share, which would not present a true picture unless we also take into account the number of equity shares likely to be obtained by them as per the announced conversion ratio. The debentureholders are not keen in the benefit per equity share, but in the aggregate gains.

3.53 Keeping in view the prevalent market prices of associated equities at the time of the floatation of Issues, conversion ratios and conversion prices, the picture that emerges in respect to likely capital gains to the debentureholders computed as percentages to the face values of the related CDs is as thus. This benefit is at its extremity of 345 per cent for the debentures issued by the Hindustan Development Corporation Limited, and dips gradually to 140 per cent for the Straw Products Limited, 80 per cent for the Tata Iron and Steel Company Limited, 75 per cent each for the Reliance Textile Industries Limited (16.8.1981) and the Usha Alloys and Steels Limited, 68 per cent for the Voltas Limited, 62.50 per cent for the Gujarat Steel Tubes Limited, 60 per cent each for Reliance Textile Industries Limited (30.10.1979) and the Ferro Alloys Corporation Limited, 58.8 per cent for the Star Industrial and Textile Enterprizes Limited, 58 per cent for the Indian Rayon Corporation Limited (16.3.1981), 55 per cent each for the Zenith Steel Pipes and Industries Limited and the Indian Rayon Corporation Limited (25.1.1983), 53.6 per cent for ITC Limited, and 50 per cent each for Bharat Vijay Mills Limited and J.K. Synthetics Limited. (See, Please, Column 23 of Table 3.6 for the similar details concerning with the rest of the Issues). This set of statistics too does not furnish us with a fully reliable picture for two important assumptions which are found to be tacitly underlying in them. One, the market prices of the associated equities would remain constant till the dates of actual conversions are reached. Second, debentureholders would continue to hold the allotted CDs until the effectualization of conversion. In real life situations both of these assumptions may not prove true, however. As a matter of fact market prices of the relevant equities did vary since the enlistment of different CDs at the stock exchanges. (See, Please, Column 9 of Table 3.7). And the researcher's interactions with the debentureholders reveal that not all of them wait to realize these capital gains. The prudent class of debentureholders no sooner conjure up by the favourable market prices of CDs ensuring a higher return compared to possible capital gain may decide to dispose off their debenture holdings much earlier to reaching the date of conversion.

3.54 The extent of conversion and the paronymous terms, the period of conversion, offered affiliated benefits during the conversion period, the practice of insertion of 'news items' on a regular basis, etc. for the oversubscribed Public Issues of CDs are depicted in Table 3.6. (See, Please, Columns 12, 13, 19, and 22). The triffling differences as they portray, these criteria too do not come to our rescue in accomplishing the task we are involved in. Still we may highlight some features of interest concerning the above. Accordingly, the maximal conversion ratio i.e. 60 per cent of the face value of CDs has been that of the Issue floated by Camphor and Allied Products Limited. But then this conversion, though at par, came to be effectutated after the lapse of a relatively long period of 4 years. Next in sequence comes the CDs' Issue of Ferro Alloys Corporation Limited wherein this ratio has been kept at 56 per cent of the face value of debentures to be actuated at a premium of 40 per cent after the expiry of 3 years. Broadly it is noticed that wherever the conversion ratio has been higher, it has been allowed on premium and after the intermission of a comparatively long period. Further, most of the Issues under reference carry with them one or other kind of promise to benefit debentureholders during the interlude of conversion And, the number of PLC_{pr} which have the proclivity of infixing news items in important news papers on regular basis have been bare five, namely, the Reliance Textile Industries Limited, the Tata Engineering and Locomotive Company Limited, the Indian Rayon Corporation Limited, the Tata Iron and Steel Company Limited and the Lohia Machines Limited; the rest of the PLC_{pr} either did not put up 'news items' at all or did so casually.

A MORE PRAGMATIC ASSAY

3.55 It being the situation, let us now employ another trio of criterion for adjudging in a pragmatic manner the success of public issues of CDs. Whether the associated equities have been of 'volatile' or 'non-volatile' nature. How much increase/ decrease has been registered in the prices of concerned equity shares and convertible debentures since the enlistment of the latter on the stock exchange/s ? The relationship between the prices of equity shares and those of convertible debentures has been examined with the help of statistical tools like Coefficient of Correlation ('r'), Coefficient of Determination ('r^2') Standard Deviation ('σ'), and Coefficient of Variation (C.V.) with a view to reach some expressive conclusions. It may however be added that for the purpose we could gather the required weekly/monthly prices of Equity Shares and Convertible Debentures as quoted on their respective parent stock exchanges only in respect to 27 Public Issues from out of 42 Issues which came to be oversubscribed. The obtained results on the basis of percentage increase/decrease registered in the prices of associated equity shares since the enlistment of CDs on parent stock exchanges and the corresponding percentage increase/decrease registered in the prices of CDs until the effectualization of their conversions are summarized in Table 3.7.In it 'Category A' includes those public issues of CDs which have been put out by PLC_{pr} whose equity shares are volatile and active as are also found enlisted on various stock exchanges, and 'Category B' represent other than those which stand covered by 'Category A'.

3.56 On running our eyes over the values of Coefficient of Correlation ('r'), Coefficient of Determination ('r^2') Standard Deviation ('σ') and Coefficient of Variation (C.V.) for the public CDs issuing Companies in Category 'A' (15 PLC_{pr}) and Category' B' (12 PLC_{pr}), it is abundantly clear that : generally there is found a positive relationship between the market prices of equity shares and convertible debentures i.e. the market prices of convertible debentures are positively influenced by the market prices of associated equity shares; the values of 'r' having found positive in case of 14 out of 15 PLC_{pr} falling in Category 'A' and in 9 out of 12 PLC_{pr} bracketed in Category 'B'. On comparing the values of 'r' relating to PLC_{pr} of Category 'A' with those of Category 'B' it is further noted that these have been much higher in most of the cases falling in the former category *vis-a-vis* the latter where not only the values have been at a low ebb in the large number of cases but there have been as many as three companies in contrast to one found in the former where the values of 'r' have been negative. All this leads us to infer that in the case of PLC_{pr} having volatile equity shares the degree of positive relationship between prices of equity shares and CDs is found greater as against those PLC_{pr} whose equity shares are of non-volatile nature. While this fact is not clearly borne out by the corresponding values of the 'r' for equity shares and CDs as they take into account the deviations in prices from their mean values which in this case may not represent a true picture on account of wide gap observed both in the face values of the Equity Shares and CDs, but the correlative values of C.V. for the equity shares/convertible debentures amply testify the above. Thus, wherever the values of C.V. have been higher the values of 'r' have also stood at a high ebb and *vice-versa*. To substantiate, values of C.V. for Equity Shares and CDs stood at 40.64 and 10.98 for Delhi Cloth and General Mills Company Limited and the corresponding value of 'r' has been found as high as +0.97. Likewise, the similar values for the (i) Tata Engineering and Locomotive Company Limited, (ii) Metal Box Company of India Limited, (iii) Voltas Limited, (iv) Zenith Steel Pipes and Industries Limited, (v) East India Hotels Limited, (vi) Lohia Machines Limited, and (vii) Reliance Textile Industries Limited (Third Series) stood, respectively as under:

(i) C.V. = Equity Shares : 30.80 and CD : 22.56 and r = + 0.82;

(ii) C.V. = Equity Shares 16.80, and CD : 21.00 and r = + 0.95;

(iii) C.V. = Equity Shares : 15.44, and CD : 19.95 and r = + 0.89;

(iv) C.V. = Equity Shares : 12.43, and CD : 6.45, and r = + 0.82;

(v) C.V. = Equity Shares : 12.12, and CD : 11.96, and r = + 0.94;

(vi) C.V. = Equity Shares : 12.09, and CD : 28.79, and r = + 0.98; and

(vii) C.V. = Equity Shares : 10.16, and CD : 14.56, and r = + 0.82.

The above is true not only for those equity shares and CDs associated with PLC_{pr} belonging to Category 'A', but is also correct for the under mentioned PLC_{pr} falling under Category 'B':

(i) Indian Hotels Company Limited-
C.V. = Equity Shares : 16.00, and CD : 10.08 and r = 0.86.

(ii) Usha Alloys and Steels Limited.
C.V. = Equity Shares : 10.85 and CD : 5.48, and r = + 0.87.

As is obvious from the above, positive impact of prices of equity shares on the prices of CDs is more widespread in case of PLC_{pr} whose equity shares are volatile *vis-a-vis* those which are possessed by equity shares of non-volatile list. This fact is further found re-inforced by another round of minute scrutiny of these values. From out of 15 companies of the volatile list, as many as 14 have the positive values of 'r'. Thus only one PLC_{pr}, namely, J.K. Synthetics Limited has a negative value of 'r'. Even this solitary case seems to have arisen on account of the relatively short span of conversion period which consummated fast for its effectualization. In sharp contrast to this, there have been as many as three out of twelve companies of the non-volatile list which witnessed negative values of 'r'. Furthermore, the range of positive values of 'r' for the companies of the volatile list has been higher i.e. + 0.86 ; and +0.56 and + 0.98 and that of the non-volatile list has been lower i.e. + 0.21 and +0.87 which indicates that this relationship is of greater degree and significance for the former as compared to the latter, an aspect which is duly corroborated by the respective values of coefficient of determination ('r^2'), they having varied between 0.31 and 0.97 for the companies of volatile list and between 0.04 and 0.75 for the companies of non-volatile list. On the whole, therefore, it can be derived that the volatile character of the equity shares generally has a positive impact on the number of times an Issue would be oversubscribed as it provides a potential opportunity to the investors for maximizing their capital gains via either through disposing off the CDs prior to the reaching of actual dates of their conversions or through selling the acquired equities/non-convertible portions of CDs on the most opportune prices. It would be befitting to recaptulate in the context that despite large sums involved in the issues floated by the PLC_{pr} of Category 'A' the number of times of over-subscription has been over 8 times in 7 cases, 6 times in 3 cases and between 2 to 5 times in rest of cases ; the relative position being 3, 2, and 7 cases respectively. (Refer please to Table 3.6). As might have been visualized by now, this set of criterion as well do not help us much in preparing a list of successful issues of CDs in a desending order except facilitating the the general inference that Public Issues of CDs which are having the backing of volatile equity shares are likely to be received with greater enthusiasm by the investors provided they are coupled with handsome benefits.

3.57 Transposing to the task of appraising the Public Issues of CDs from the standpoint of nation's economy, it may be stated at the out set that assessing the contribution of funds raised by PLC_{pr} via each Issue of CDs in restraining inflationary pressures in the country would not have any practical significance as the amount involved, howsoever voluminous it may be, in an Issue would only constitute infinitesimal proportion of the total money supply found in circulation. As a matter of fact the total funds raised by an individual PLC_{pr} during the whole period under study through the different variants of the debentures too would make up a negligeable proportion of the country's money supply. Hence, the significance of this yardstick is only from the viewpoint of whole private corporate sector. And in this regard it can be said that with the steadily growing amounts of funds the private corporate sector is mobilizing through this means its contribution to the promotion of this cause is increasing.

3.58 Considering the absolute amounts of funds raised through all kinds of CDs during the entire period of 1978-82 by those PLC_{pr} whose Public Issues came to be oversubscribed, it is obvious from the contents of Table 3.8 and 3.9 that Reliance Textile Industries Limited stands atop for it could successfully float in a short span of five years as many as four Issues of CDs for a sum of Rs. 91.80 crores. Reliance has come to be followed by Tata Engineering and Locomotive Company Limited (with one issue for Rs. 47.25 crores), Indian Rayon Corporation Limited (2 Issues for Rs. 31.00 crores), Tata Iron and Steel Company Limited, Gwalior Rayon Silk Mfg. (Wvg.) Company Limited and ITC Limited (One Issue each for Rs. 30 crores), J.K. Synthetics Linited (One Issue for Rs. 25 crores), Keshoram Industries and Cotton Mills Limited (One Issue for Rs. 21 crores), Delhi Cloth and General Mills Company Limited, and Indian Hotels Company Limited (One Issue each for Rs. 15 crores), Dunlop India Limited (One Issue for Rs. 12 crores), Straw Products Limited and Kothari (Madras) Limited (One Issue each for Rs. 10 crores), East India Hotels Limited and Ferro Alloys Corporation Limited (One Issue each for Rs. 7.50 crores), Mukand Iron and Steel Works Limited (One Issue for Rs. 7 crores), Metal Box Company of India (Two Issues for Rs. 6 crores), Ahmedabad Advance Mills Limited (One Issue for Rs. 6 crores), Lohia Machines Limited (One Issue for Rs. 5.65 crores), Elecon Engineering Company Limited (One Issue for Rs. 5.50 crores), Voltas Limited and Gujarat Steel Tubes Limited (One Issue for Rs. 5 crores each), Raymond Woollens Mills Limited and Zenith Steel Pipes Industries Limited (One Issue each for Rs. 4.80 crores), Ranbaxy Laboratories Limited (One Issue for Rs. 4.50 crores); Star Industrial and Textile Enterprizes Limited (One Issue for Rs. 4.25 crores), Bharat Steel Tubes Limited (One Issue for Rs. 4 crores), Bharat Vijay Mills (One Issue for Rs. 3.40 crores), Mahindra Mills Limited (One Issue for Rs. 3 crores), Fibre Glass Pilkington Limited (One Issue for Rs. 2.63 crores), Rustom Mills and Industries Limited, Vardhman Spg. and General Mills Limited and Shree Digvijay Woollen Mills Limited (One Issue each for Rs. 2 crores), Hindustan Development Corporation Limited, Usha Alloys and Steels Limited, and Cellulose Products of India Limited (One Issue each for Rs. 1.50 crores) and Camphor and Allied Products Limited, Shree Dinesh Mills Limited and Punjab Anand Batteries Limited (One Issue each for Rs. 1 crore).

3.59 If the Issues of CDs and NCDs floated during the period under review are put together then also it is noted that the Reliance Textile Industries Limited has been most successful in raising long term funds through this mode ; it mobilized Rs. 91.83 crores via four issues of CDs and one issue of NCDs. The Tata Engineering and Locomotive Company Limited's second place in this regard has remained undisturbed for the amount involved in the alone issue of CDs has been to the tune of Rs. 47.25 crores. The order of rest of the PLC_{pr} has, however, been changed. Thus if these companies are arranged in a descending order from the angle of aggregate funds accumulated through the issuance of CDs/NCDs during the aforesaid period then the obtainable position is as thus. Next in order have been Gwalior Rayon Silk Mfg. (Wvg.) Company Limited (with two Issues of CDs/NCDs for Rs. 45 crores), J.K. Synthetics (4 Issues for Rs. 38 crores), ITC Limited (2 Issues for Rs. 35 crores), Indian Rayon Corporation Limited (3 Issues for Rs. 32 crores), Tata Iron and Steel Company Limited (One Issue for Rs. 30 crores), Keshoram Industries and Cotton Mills Limited (3 Issues for Rs. 29.50 crores), East India Hotels Limited (2 Issues for Rs. 17.50 crores), Delhi Cloth and General Mills Company Limited and Indian Hotels Company Limited (One Issue each for Rs. 15 crores), Ferro Alloys Corporation Limited (3 Issues for Rs. 14.25 crores), Mukand Iron and Steel Works Limited (4 Issues for Rs. 14 crores), Straw Products Limited (2 Issues for Rs. 12 crores), Dunlop India Limited (One Issue for Rs. 12 crores), Voltas Limited (3 Issues for Rs. 10.30 crores), Kothari (Madras) Limited (One Issue for Rs. 10 crores), Raymond Woollens Mills Limited (2 Issues for Rs. 9.30 crores), Ahmedabad Advance Mills Limited (2 Issues for Rs. 7 crores), Zenith Steel Pipes India Limited (2 Issues for Rs. 6.05 crores), Metal Box Company of India and Gujarat Steel Tubes Limited (2 Issues each for Rs. 6 crores), Lohia Machines Limited (One Issue for Rs. 5.65 crores), Elecon Engineering Company Limited (One Issue for Rs. 5.50 crores), Bharat Steel Tubes Limited (2 Issues for Rs. 5.25 crores), Jyoti Limited (2 Issues for Rs. 2 crores) Ranbaxy Laboratories Limited (One Issue for Rs. 4.50 crores), Mahindra Mills Limited (3 Issues for Rs. 4.25 crores), Star Industrial and Textile Enterprizes Limited (One Issue for Rs. 4.25 crores), Bharat Vijay Mills Limited (One Issue for

Rs. 3.40 crores), Fibre Glass Pilkington Limited (One Issue for Rs. 2.63 crores), Hindustan Development Corporation Limited (2 Issues for Rs. 2.25 crores), Rustom Mills and Industries Limited and Vardhman Spg. and General Mills Limited and Shree Digvijay Woollen Mills Limited (One Issue each for Rs. 2 crores), Shree Dinesh Mills Limited (2 Issues for Rs. 1.50 crores), Usha Alloys and Steels Limited and Cellulose Products of India Limited (One Issue each for Rs. 1.50 crores) and Camphor and Allied Products Limited and Punjab Anand Batteries Limited (One Issue each for Rs. 1 crore).

3.60 The listing done in the preceding para of the successful and oversubscribed public issues of CDs on the above criterion can be further refined by employing the results which are now available in respect to the criteria included in the integral check list, excepting the illustrative values of the market price, rate of return and the cost of important variants of convertible debenture using internal rate of return method. Since these values have been computed and highlighted in the successive section, the final list, as planned, has been drawn in the lead-in paragraph of Section-Five.

SECTION FOUR

PIERCING THROUGH THE VALUES OF THE MARKET PRICE, RATE OF RETURN & THE COST OF IMPORTANT VARIANTS OF CONVERTIBLE DEBENTURE

3.61 Pursuant to the proposed objective, we have chosen the public issues of CDs as floated by the Usha Alloys and Steels Limited, the J. K. Synthetics Limited and the Straw Products Limited to be token of CDs with a Right to Subscribe, Partly Convertible Debentures, and Fully Convertible Debentures, respectively.[16] As indicated in the preceding Chapter the relevant values of the market price, rate of return and cost of the concerned debentures have been arrived at by employing Internal Rate of Return Method.

USHA ALLOYS & STEELS LIMITED'S PUBLIC ISSUE OF REDEEMABLE SECURED DEBENTURES WITH A RIGHT TO SUBSCRIBE TO EQUITY SHARES : JANUARY 19, 1982.

Highlights of the Issue :

3.62 Usha Alloys and Steels Limited, Calcutta opened its issue of 1,50,000 13.5% (Plus 1% if equity dividend exceeds 15%) Redeemable Secured Debentures of Rs. 100/- each for cash at par with a right to be offered to subscribe for 3 Equity Shares of Rs. 10/- each at a premium of Rs. 5/- per share for each such Debenture held on January 19, 1982. While it was to close on Monday the 1st February 1982, it came to be closed early on the already announced Friday the 22nd January 1982. As the Company paid dividend @ 20 per cent during the year 1980-81, these debentures automatically carried a firm assurance of the payment of interest @ 14.5 per cent for the year 1981-82. Other highlights of this Issue have been as thus : (i) the debentures will mature for redemption at par on the expiry of 10 years from the date of their allotment with an option to the company to redeem the debentures at par in one or more instalment after the expiry of the 7th year from the date of their allotment ; (ii) interest will be payable half yearly on 31st March and 30th September each year ; (iii) no capital gain tax liability will arise on account of subscribing to equity shares ; however the debentureholder can claim set off of the short term capital loss he might incur on selling the Debenture against his income from any other source ; (iv) the company will be free from any tax liability not only during the year of this Issue but also in two successive years ; and (v) as may be perused in the brochure issued for private circulation, and reproduced here, the company claimed an actual return of 79.5 per cent in one year for a short term investor who will sell his shares and debentures after one year, of 89.5 per cent in the first year for a long term investor who will retain debentures but sell shares, and a recurring return of 54 per cent (at 13.5 per cent interest) and of 58 per cent (at 14.5 per cent interest) from 2nd to 10th year on investment in debentures which would be of Rs. 25 ; total investment in debentures and shares Rs. 145 less current market price of 3 Equity Shares Rs. 120.

BASIC DATA & PRESUMPTIONS

3.63 The market price of the equity share of the company, which was Rs. 40 at the time of the issuance of debentures reduced to an average price of Rs. 23 between the date of enlistment of the debentures on the stock exchanges situated at Calcutta, Bombay and Delhi and the date for exercising the right to subscribe. (See, Please, 'Daily Quotation Lists', Delhi Stock Exchange Limited, Delhi). Keeping in view the prevalent structure of market interest rates, the required rate of return for the investors is presumed at 16 per cent per annum payable in two half yearly instalments @ 8 per cent for a period of 6 months. We are further assuming for the purpose of envisaged computations that the interest rate for the first year will be 14.5 per cent and 13.5 per cent in the subsequent years.

COMPUTING THE VALUES

(*a*) *Market Price of the Debenture* :

3.64 Employing the equation given below, the market price of the debenture under reference has been computed for the associated equity for its price of Rs. 40 and Rs. 23 separately as thus.

$$P_D = \sum_{t=1}^{n} = \frac{It}{(1+k)^t} + \frac{a(Mi+Si)}{(1+k)^i} + \frac{R}{(1+k)^n}$$

Fitting the concerned data into the above equation for the equity market price of Rs. 40, we get,

$$= \frac{7.25}{(1+0.8)^1} + \frac{7.25}{(1+0.8)^2} + \frac{6.75}{(1+.08)^3} + \ldots + \frac{6.75}{(1+.08)^{20}}$$

$$+ \frac{3(40-15)}{(1+.08)^2} + \frac{100}{(1+.08)^{20}}$$

$$= \text{Rs. } 152.90$$

On an average equity market price of Rs. 23, the price of the debenture would be :

USH ALLOYS & STEELS LIMITED

Registered Office: 11, Sooterkin Street, Calcutta 700 072.

ISSUE OF 1,50,000 - 13.5% (WITH ADDITIONAL INTEREST OF 1% IF EQUITY DIVIDEND EXCEEDS 15%) REDEEMABLE SECURED DEBENTURES OF RS.100 EACH FOR CASH AT PAR WITH A RIGHT TO BE OFFERED TO SUBSCRIBE FOR 3 EQUITY SHARES OF RS.10 EACH AT A PREMIUM OF RS.5 PER SHARE FOR EACH SUCH DEBENTURE HELD.

Issue opens on 19th January, 1982
and closes on 1st February, 1982
Earlier closing 22nd January, 1982

INTRODUCTION

Usha Alloys & Steels Limited (UASL) was promoted in the year 1971 by Usha Martin Black Limited, for manufacture of Steels and steel products. The Company's steel plant for manufacture of high/low carbon alloy steel billets was set up at Adityapur near Jamshedpur in 1974 with an annual licensed capacity of 50,000 tonnes. In 1975-76 UASL had acquired a Rolling Mill at Agra which manufactures rolled products for use in the construction activities etc. The products of the Company have acquired good reputation in the market. With the production of Stainless steel and other popular grades of forging quality steel, UASL has already entered sophisticated high quality steel market.

PAST PERFORMANCE AT A GLANCE

- **SALES in 1980-81 rose to Rs. 2173.63 lacs from Rs. 240.34 lacs in 1974-75**
- **RESERVES as at 31st May 1981—Rs. 218.62 lacs from Rs. 18.90 lacs as at 31st May 1979—a phenomenal spurt of over 1056%**
- **PROFIT BEFORE TAX rose from Rs. 25.72 lacs in 1979-80 to Rs. 149.52 lacs in 1980-81. An incredible increase of 481% in just two years.**
- **For the year ended 31st May 1981 the company earned 131.1% on its Equity Capital.**

FINANCIAL HIGHLIGHTS

The Company has made remarkable growth since its inception which would be evident from the following figures.

	Rs. in lacs		
Year ended 31st May	**1981**	**1980**	**1979**
Gross Fixed Assets	499.92	381.44	359.97
Turnover	2173.63	1450.74	1259.73
Gross Profit	176.29	120.41	47.63
Profit Before Tax	149.52	98.37	25.72
Profit After Tax	149.52	98.37	25.72
Equity Capital	114.05	114.05	107.83
Reserves	218.62	94.76	18.90
Net Worth	332.67	208.81	126.73
Dividend %	20	10	Nil
PER SHARE OF Rs. 10			
Earnings (Rs.)	12.85	8.37	2.12
Dividend (Rs.)	2.00	1.00	-
Net Worth (Rs.)	29.16	18.30	11.80
Market price of Equity Share on Diwali Day	34.50	22.50	12.75

BOARD OF DIRECTORS

Mr. B. K. Jhawar
— Chairman

Mr. Brij K. Jhawar
— Vice Chairman & Managing Director

Mr. P. Sen Gupta

Mr. M.D. Kapila

Mr. R. K. Saboo

Mr. S.K. Bose

Mr. M.M. Vadi

HIGHLIGHTS OF THE ISSUE

- Interest at 13.5% or more*
- Right to Subscribe for 3 Equity Shares of Rs. 10/- each at a premium of Rs. 5/- (market price on 27.11.1981 Rs. 40/-) within one year of allotment
- No Capital Gains Tax Liability on your subscribing to Equity Shares.
- Unlike Convertible Debentures the amount pertaining to Equity Shares to be paid only at the time of offer
- Fully Secured
- Easy Marketability as Debentures will be listed on Stock Exchanges at Calcutta, Bombay & Delhi.
- The Debentures will mature for redemption at par on the expiry of 10 years from the date of their allotment with an option to the Company to redeem the debentures at par in one or more instalment after the expiry of the 7th year from the date of their allotment.

* As the Company has paid 20% dividend for the year 1980-81 the interest for 1981-82 will be 14.5%

ATTRACTIVE RETURNS

Whichever way you look at it

IA If you are a short term investor and you sell your shares and debentures after one year

		Rs. p.
Interest on one debenture @ 14.50% p.a. for one year		14.50
Sale proceeds of 3 equity shares (Market Quotation as on 27.11.81—Rs. 40)		120.00
Sale proceeds of one debenture of Rs. 100 after offer for shares discounted @ 16% yield		90.00
		224.50
Less—		
Cost of one debenture	100.00	
Cost of 3 equity Shares	45.00	145.00
Net profit in one year	...	**79.50**

A return of 79.5% in one year

IB And let us look at the cost of Equity to you—In that case you hold the shares and sell the Debentures.

	Rs.
—Amount paid for 3 Equity Shares	45
—Discount on sale of Debenture after the offer for shares	10
Cost of 3 Equity Shares	55
∴ Cost per Equity Share against the market price of Rs. 40/- on 27.11.81.	**Rs. 18.33 p**

IIA If you are a long term investor and retain debentures but sell shares

Investment in 1 Debenture		**Rs. 100**
Interest for 1 year	14.50	
Capital appreciation on 3 equity shares (market quotation on 27.11.81— Rs. 40/- equivalent to Rs. 120/- less Rs. 45/- cost of 3 equity Shares)	75.00	
Return in first year		**89.5%**

IIB And look at the recurring Return from 2nd to 10th year
Investment in Debentures reduced to only Rs. 25 (total investment in Debentures & Shares Rs. 145 less current market price of 3 equity shares Rs. 120)

Hence Yield on investment

i) At 13.5% interest $\left(\frac{13.5 \times 100}{25}\right)$ — **54%**

ii) At 14.5% interest $\left(\frac{14.5 \times 100}{25}\right)$ — **58%**

And remember—that No Capital Gains tax liability will arise on your subscribing to Equity Shares under this scheme. However, you can claim set off of the short term capital loss you might incur on selling the Debenture against your income from any other source.

ISSUE OPENS ON 19TH JANUARY 1982

Managers to the Issue
J. M. FINANCIAL & INVESTMENT CONSULTANCY SERVICES PVT. LTD.
Merchant Banking Division
112, Jolly Maker Chambers No.2,
Nariman Point, Bombay-400 021

STRICTLY PRIVATE AND CONFIDENTIAL
(FOR PRIVATE CIRCULATION ONLY)

The information given in this brochure is for private circulation only

TATA PRESS Limited Bombay 400 025

Designed and produced by Pressman Advertising & Marketing Pvt. Ltd

$$P_D=\frac{7.25}{(1+.08)^1}+\frac{7.25}{(1+.08)^2}+\frac{6.75}{(1+.08)^3}+\ldots\ldots$$

$$+\frac{6.75}{(1+.08)^{20}}+\frac{3(23-15)}{(1+.08)^2}+\frac{100}{(1+.08)^{20}}$$

$$=\text{Rs. } 109.17$$

The market price of the Debenture of Rs. 152.90 implies a gain of Rs. 52.90 per debenture and partly explains as to why the Issue under analysis witnessed oversubscription by 4.3 times. It however reduced to bare Rs. 9.17 per debenture consequent upon the reduction of the market price of the equity to an average level of Rs. 23 by the time of exercising the subscription right ; the price of debenture at Rs. 109.17 is marginally higher than its face value meaning thereby a virtual absence of any attraction to a long term investor to retain these debentures.

(*b*) *Rate of Return to the Debentureholder :*

3.65 Using the aforesaid market prices of equity, the rate of return to the debentureholder would be as calculated hereunder.

$$\text{Face value of Debenture}=\sum_{t=1}^{n}\frac{It}{(1+r)t}+\frac{a(Mi-Si)}{(1+r)t}+\frac{R}{(1+r)n}$$

At the equity's market price of Rs. 40:

$$100=\frac{7.25}{(1+r)}+\frac{7\ 25}{(1+r)^2}+\frac{6.75}{(1+r)^3}+\ldots\ldots+$$

$$\frac{6.75}{(1+r)^{20}}+\frac{75}{(1+r)^2}+\frac{100}{(1+r)^{20}}$$

r=16 per cent per half year or 32 per cent per annum.

At the equity's market price of Rs. 23:

$$100=\frac{7.25}{(1+r)}+\frac{7.25}{(1+r)^2}+\frac{6.75}{(1+r)^3}+\ldots+\frac{6.75}{(1+r)^{20}}$$

$$+\frac{24}{(1+r)^2}+\frac{100}{(1+r)^{20}}$$

r=9 per cent for a half year period i.e. 18 per cent per annum.

COLLATION WITH THE PROCLAIMED RATES:

3.66 For a short term investor the company publicized that he would be getting a return of 79.5 per cent in one year. In actuality, however, it calculates to only 32 per cent per annum. Similarly, a long term investor in effect is going to receive a bare return of 18 per cent *vis-a-vis* the notified return of 89.5 per cent. On this basis one can safely deduce how deceitful and tricky the advertized returns could be from the standpoint of an investor.

(*c*) *Cost of the Debenture :*

3.67 For working out the cost of the Debenture the equation given below is employed.

$$NSa=\sum_{t=1}^{n}\frac{It(1-T)}{(1+kd)t}+\frac{a(bMi-Si)}{(1+kd)i}+\frac{R}{(1+kd)^n}$$

While 'b' is presumed to be 0.8, 'NSa' would be equal to Rs. 88 per debenture without any tax liability taking into account Rs. 18 Lakhs as an expenses of the Issue as per the information included in the Prospectus issued by Usha Alloys and Steels Limited at page 4. Hence,

$$88=\frac{7.25(1-0)}{(1+kd)}+\frac{7.25(1-0)}{(1+kd)^2}$$

$$+\frac{6.75(1-0)}{(1+kd)^3}+\ldots+\frac{6.75(1-0)}{(1+kd)^{20}}$$

$$+\frac{3(0.8\times 23-15)}{(1+kd)^2}+\frac{100}{(1+kd)^n}$$

kd=9 per cent for a period of half year or 18 per cent for a period of one year.

It means that the real cost of the long term funds raised through the Issue of Debentures under reference to the Usha Alloys and Steels Limited boils down to 18 per cent per annum. Judged by the structure of current market interest rates the reckoned cost can in no way be regarded as cheap. Hence it can be persuasively inferred that seemingly this Issue has belittle to contribute towards developing an optimal capital structure for the firm.

J.K. SYNTHETICS' PARTLY CONVERTIBLE DEBENTURES: FEBRUARY 3, 1982

FOCAL POINTS OF THE ISSUE

3.68 On February 3, 1982, J.K. Synthetics Limited came out with an Issue of 15,62,500 13.5 per cent secured convertible debentures of Rs. 160/- each for cash at par offered to the public for an amount of Rs. 25 crores with an obligation to convert 25 per cent of its face value i.e. Rs. 40/- into two equity shares of Rs. 10/- each at a premium of Rs. 10/- per share on January 1, 1983; however, in the event of issue of bonus shares by the company during the conversion period the number of equity shares to be issued in this respect would stand augmented in the same proportion. Besides an assured return @ 13.5 per cent per annum, the debentureholders would be benefitted by the additional incentive interest rate of 1 per cent per annum during any such financial year which has a precedent year in which the company's rate of dividend on equity excedeed 18 per cent per annum. Whatever interest is accrued, will be payable half-yearly on January and July First of each year and on the date of last redemption of Debentures. The balance of Rs. 120/- remaining after conversion is to be redeemed in one or more instalments commencing at the end of the seventh year and ending at the end of tenth year from the date of allotment.

CRUCIAL INFORMATION AND POSTULATES:

3.69 While the actual expenses incurred by the company for the floatation of this Debenture Issue amounted to Rs. 200 lakhs, the market price of its equity centred around Rs. 55 per share. And, the company enjoyed the no-tax liability position for the year 1982 through 1985. The Required Rate of Return for the investor is supposed at 16 per cent per annum i.e. 8 per cent half yearly and the market price of the equity share at the time of conversion as Rs. 55.

MEASURING VALUES:

(*a*) *Market Price of the Debenture* :

3.70 Employing the relavent equation and the above information/presumed figures, market price of the Debenture reckons out Rs. 205.49 as shown hereunder.

$$P_D=\sum_{t=1}^{n}\frac{It}{(1+k)t}+\frac{aMi}{(1+k)i}+\sum_{J-m}^{n}\frac{Fj}{(1+k)j}$$

$$=\frac{10.8}{(1.08)}+\frac{10.8}{(1.08)^2}+\frac{8.1}{(1.08)^3}+\ldots$$

$$+\frac{8.1}{(1.08)^{14}}+\frac{6.075}{(1.08)^{15}}+\frac{6.075}{(1.08)^{16}}$$

$$+\frac{4.05}{(1.08)^{17}}+\frac{4.05}{(1.08)^{18}}+\frac{2.025}{(1.08)^{19}}$$

$$+\frac{2.025}{(1.08)^{21}}+\frac{2\times 55}{(1.08)^{2}}+\frac{30}{(1.08)^{14}}$$

$$+\frac{0}{(1.08)^{15}}+\frac{30}{(1.08)^{16}}+\frac{0}{(1.08)^{17}}$$

$$+\frac{30}{(1.08)^{18}}+\frac{0}{(1.08)^{19}}+\frac{30}{(1.08)^{20}}$$

$$=\text{Rs. } 205.49$$

It may be noted that as against Rs. 205.49, the actual market price of the Debenture fluctuated in the proximity of Rs. 200/-. Clearly it indicates a satisfactory situation particularly in the light of the fact that the required rate of return has been presumed higher than the declared rate at which the interest will be paid as also in view of the fact that the market price of the equity share actually turned out to be lower than the level of Rs. 60/- per share as found prevalent on 16.12.1981 (See, Please, the Brochure brought out by the company for private circulation reproduced ahead).

(*b*) *Rate of Return to Debentureholder:*

3.71 Rate of Return to the debentureholder calculates at about 13 per cent half yearly or 26 per cent per annum as revealed by the results obtained through feeding the pertinent data in the formula given below.

Jaykaylon®

J.K. Synthetics LTD.

Regd. Office. Kamla Tower Kanpur

Issue of 15,62,500 13.5% Secured Convertible Debentures of Rs. 160/- each for cash at par.

HIGHLIGHTS

1. Capital Appreciation: Allotment of 2 Equity Shares of Rs. 10 each at a premium of only Rs. 10 per share.
2. Conversion: On 1.1.83—in less than a year.
3. Assured Returns: Interest @ 13.5% p.a. or more.
4. Safety: Fully secured.
5. Liquidity: To be listed on Delhi, Bombay and Calcutta Stock Exchanges.

PORTRAIT

J.K. Synthetics was incorporated in May 1943 as an investment Company, and it was in the year 1958 that the Company received a licence to manufacture Nylon/Perlon Yarn. The story of J.K. Synthetics is the story of Synthetic Fibre in India. J.K. Synthetics which made a modest start in 1962 as a manufacturer of Nylon Filament Yarn has, in the following years, rapidly expanded and diversified its base. Today the Company's activities include:—

- —Nylon/Polyester Filament Yarn.
- —Nylon Tyre Cord/Fabric
- —Polyester Staple Fibre
- —Acrylic Staple Fibre
- —Rayon Filament Yarn
- —Cement
- —Metallic Cops
- —Equipment for Synthetic Fibre, Chemical, Pharmaceutical & Fertilizer Industry
- —Hot and Cold Rolled Steel Products
- —Sulphuric Acid and Carbon-Di-sulphide

The Company's contribution to the development of indigenous technology has been well appreciated, the Company having been awarded the Indian Merchants' Chamber Award for 1979, for the improvement made in the technologies of Man-Made Fibres.

J.K. Synthetics is the only Company in India which has provided technical know-how for synthetic fibres in India and abroad. In fact, the Company has promoted Africa Synthetics Fibres Ltd, Kenya in 1975.

MANAGEMENT

J.K. Synthetics' management is highly professionalised and experienced and the Board of Directors consists of eminent persons:—

Dr Gaur Hari Singhania, Chairman and Managing Director

Shri Sohanlal
Shri Chiranjilal Jhunjhunwala
Sir Bhim Singh
Shri Narendrajit Singh
Shri Shripati
Shri S.P. Vishnoi (Nominee Director)
Shri Govind Hari
Shri Bharat Hari
Shri R.K. Daruwalla (Nominee Director)
Shri M.P. Chi[illegible]le (Nominee Director)

REWARDS TO AN INVESTOR SINCE 1961

Equity Shares of the Company are considered highly rewarding investment in the Country; the value of the equity shares of the Company having remarkable appreciation as can be seen from following tables:—

	No. of Shares	Cost Rs.
a. Investment in 1961	1000	10,000
b. 1966—Bonus issue—1:5	200	
c. 1968— " " —1:3	400	
d. 1970— " " —1:2	800	
e. 1974— " " —2:1	4800	
f. 1977— " " —2:3	4800	
	12000	10,000

	Rs.
Market value of 12000 shares @ Rs. 60/-per share (as on 16.12.81)	7,20,000
Plus: Dividend till date	1,42,260
	8,62,260
Less: Original Investment	10,000
Net appreciation	8,52,260

This Represents the appreciation at the rate of over 425% p.a. over a period of 20 years—An enviable record in the Indian Corporate History.

Besides impressive appreciation, this also reveals another fact that an original investment of Rs. 10,000/- has been recovered by dividend income more than 14 times during this period and still the original investor continues to receive dividend year after year. The Company has been paying dividend for the last 3 years @ 18%, and this means a dividend income of 216% p.a. (for the last 3 years) on an original investment of Rs. 10,000/-. An outstanding record by any standard.

FINANCIAL HIGHLIGHTS

Rs. in Lakhs

	Year ended 30.6.1962	31.12.1972	31.12.1980	For nine months ended 30.9.1981
Gross Sales and Other Income	28	3674	17726	15082
[illegible] Block	158	3576	14118	16200
[illegible] Profit	6	767	1533	1402
Profit after tax	(10)	344	670	738
Dividend	-	18%	18%	[illegible]
Capital Equity	125	300	1506	1506.6
Preference		[illegible]	185	185
Reserves	3	[illegible]	[illegible]	5020
Net Worth	128	[illegible]	5787	6526.6
Net Worth per Equity Share (Rs.)	10.24	70*	38.39**	43.32

* After bonus Issues of 1:5 in 1966, 1:3 in 1968 and 1:2 in 1970

** After Bonus issues of 2:1 in 1974 and 2:3 in 1977

J.K. Synthetics — where results are a true measure of performance.

FUTURE PROSPECTS

The Company has embarked on major capital expenditure programmes which are expected to be completed by 1983. The programmes costing Rs. 178 crores include the following:—

1. Substantial expansion in the capacity for the manufacture of Polyester Filament Yarn by 6000 tonnes per annum.
2. Substantial expansion in the capacity for the manufacture of Polyester Staple Fibre by 6000 tonnes per annum.
3. Increase in Nylon Tyre Cord Fabric capacity by 1960 tonnes per annum and Tyre Cord Yarn by 1400 tonnes per annum.
4. Setting up a new plant for production of White Cement with a capacity of 50,000 tonnes per annum.
5. Setting up a third Cement Unit at Nimbahera (Dist. Chittorgarh) with an annual capacity of 4,20,000 tonnes of Portland Cement.
6. Modernisation in the Nylon Filament Yarn division resulting in increase in production capacities.
7. Installation of balancing equipment in the Acrylic Fibre Division for processing of fibre waste.

A major portion of the cost of Rs. 178 crores is being financed by Internal Accruals.

With the completion of schemes mentioned above by 1983 the turnover is expected to be around Rs. 400 crores for the year 1984 and it is expected to increase further in the following years when all the schemes reach their rated capacities. The Company has been advised that in view of the various expansion schemes underway no income tax liability is expected not only for the current year but also for the next few years.

OBJECT OF THE ISSUE

The object of the present issue of Convertible Debentures of an aggregate value of Rs. 25 crores is to raise Rs. 21 crores for meeting a part of the estimated cost of PFY project and Rs. 4 crores to augment long term resources for working capital requirements of the Company.

J.K. SYNTHETICS SECURED CONVERTIBLE DEBENTURES

Main Terms

Out of the total issue of Rs. 25 crores, Rs. 13 crores are reserved for preferential allotment

—Rs. 5.5 crores for existing share and Debentureholders. (Equity Shareholders to use—Pink form and others to use—Green)
—Rs. 1.5 crores for fixed depositors. (Use Grey coloured form).
—Rs. 4 crores for Indian non residents and persons of Indian origin resident abroad. (Use Blue coloured form)
—Rs. 2 crores for promoters, business associates, friends, relatives, employees and Directors (Use Yellow coloured form)

Each Debenture carries an obligation on the part of the Company to issue 2 shares of Rs. 10/- each at a premium of Rs. 10/- per share. The conversion shall take place on 1st January, 1983 i.e. in less than a year's time.

Interest @ 13.5% plus additional interest @1% p.a. in case the Company declares a dividend exceeding 18% on its equity capital for the immediately preceding year.

Redemption in one or more instalments commencing at the end of 7th year and ending at the end of 10th year from the date of allotment.

These Convertible Debentures will be listed for dealing on Delhi, Bombay and Calcutta Stock Exchanges.

The Debentures will be fully secured by a mortgage over a part of the fixed assets of the Company.

WHY YOU SHOULD INVEST IN J.K. SYNTHETICS CONVERTIBLE DEBENTURES

YIELD

Convertible Debentures of Rs. 160/- each are being offered in February 1982 and the 25% conversion into two equity shares will be on 1.1.83 at a price of only Rs. 20/- per share. Assuming interest at a minimum rate of 13.5% and the market price of Rs. 60/- per equity share (as on 16.12.81), the debentureholder will get a return of over 60% by 1.1.83. If annualised this works out to 65.59%

1. Investment in One Debenture		Rs. 160/-
2. Profit after conversion from 2 Equity Shares between the market value of Rs. 60/- and conversion price of Rs. 20/-	Rs. 80.00	
Plus: Interest on Investment @ 13.5% for nine months	Rs. 16.20	
Total return in eleven months	Rs. 96.20	

LOOK AT THE RECURRING RETURN

Each Convertible Debenture costs Rs. 160/-. The profit on the two Equity Shares is Rs. 80/- (present market value Rs. 120/- less original cost of Rs. 40/-) Thus net investment in the debentures is reduced to Rs. 40/- However, the Debentureholder will continue to get an annual interest of Rs. 16.20 (at the minimum rate of 13.5% p.a.) on the non convertible portion of Rs. 120/-. A return of Rs. 16.20 on the net investment of Rs. 40/- provides a **recurring minimum yield** of 40.5% p.a. on a safe and marketable security. This is the minimum yield. If a higher rate of interest becomes payable on the Company declaring a dividend of more than 18% or market price of the Company's Equity Shares increases then:—

If market price per equity share	Interest rate on Debentures 13.5 %	14.5 %
Rs.	Annual Recurring Yield Rate	
62.50	46.28%	49.71%
65	54 %	58 %
67.50	64.8 %	69.60%
70	81 %	87 %

ISSUE OPENS ON 3RD FEBRUARY 1982

The subscription list for J.K. Synthetics Convertible Debentures will open on 3.2.82 and close on 13.2.82 or earlier but not before 6.2.82. The Minimum application is for 4 convertible debentures and thereafter in multiples of 2. The amount payable is Rs.80/- on application and the balance Rs. 80/- on allotment.

Managers to the Issue

STATE BANK OF INDIA
Merchant Banking Division
Central Office, Madame Cama Road, Bombay-400 021

H. L. Financial Consultants & Management Services Private Limited
Stock Exchange Towers, 12th Floor, Dalal Street, Fort, Bombay 400 023.

D S P Financial Consultants Limited
814, Raheja Chambers, 213, Backbay Reclamation, Bombay 400 021.

The information given in this brochure is for private circulation only.

$$\text{Subscription Price} = \sum_{t=1}^{n} \frac{It}{(1+r)t} + \frac{aMi}{(1+r)i} + \sum_{J-m}^{n} \frac{Fj}{(1+r)j}$$

$$+\frac{10.8}{(1+r)}+\frac{10.8}{(1+r)^2}+\frac{8.1}{(1+r)^3}+\ldots+\frac{8.1}{(1+r)^{14}}$$

$$+\frac{6.075}{(1+r)^{15}}+\frac{6.075}{(1+r)^{16}}+\frac{4.05}{(1+r)^{17}}+\frac{4.05}{(1+r)^{18}}+\frac{2.025}{(1+r)^{19}}$$

$$+\frac{2.025}{(1+r)^{20}}+\frac{110}{(1+r)^2}+\frac{30}{(1+r)^{14}}+\frac{0}{(1+r)^{15}}+\frac{30}{(1+r)^{16}}$$

$$+\frac{0}{(1+r)^{17}}+\frac{30}{(1+r)^{18}}+\frac{0}{(1+r)^{19}}+\frac{30}{(1+r)^{20}}$$

r=About 13 per cent half yearly or 26 per cent per annum.

JUXTAPOSITION OF THESE RETURNS WITH THE ANNOUNCED YIELDS

3.72 If the rate of return so arrived is contrasted with company's bold announcements, which may be perused in the brochure reproduced in the preceding above, then it is speciously observed that the actual return to the debenture-holder stands at a much low ebb than both the professed annualized return of 65.59 per cent and the recurring minimum yield of 40.5 per cent per annum. This again is another glaring instance of how the corporate management can tactfully befuddle the innocent class of investors.

(c) *Cost of Partly Convertible Debenture :*

3.73 The cost of partly convertible debenture would stand computed through incorporating the *ad rem* data of the selected Issue in the equation adopted for the purpose, namely;

$$NSa = \sum_{t=1}^{n} \frac{It(1-T)}{(1+kd)t} + \frac{aMib}{(1+kd)i} + \sum_{J-m}^{n} \frac{Fj}{(1+kd)j}$$

While 'b' is presumed to be equal to 0 8, for computing the value of 'NSa' and 'Tax Liability'. the information given in the 'Prospectus' issued by the company can be used. The

Expenses of the Issue have been equivalent to Rs. 200 lakhs. (See, Please, Prospectus of the Issue published by J. K. Synthetics Limited, Kanpur, page 22). Accordingly, 'NSa' stands equal to Rs. 147. And, the Company has claimed 'NIL' tax liability. Putting this information into the above equation we get ;

$$147=\frac{10.8(1-0)}{(1+kd)}+\frac{10.8(1-0)}{(1+kd)^2}+\frac{8.1(1-0)}{(1+kd)^3}+\ldots$$

$$+\frac{8.1(1-0)}{(1+kd)^{14}}+\frac{6.075(1-0)}{(1+kd)^{15}}+\frac{6.075(1-0)}{(1+kd)^{16}}$$

$$+\frac{4.05(1-0)}{(1+kd)^{17}}+\frac{4.05(1-0)}{(1+kd)^{18}}+\frac{2.025(1-0)}{(1+kd)^{19}}$$

$$+\frac{2.025(1-0)}{(1+kd)^{20}}+\frac{2\times 55\times .8}{(1+kd)^2}+\frac{30}{(1+kd)^{14}}$$

$$+\frac{0}{(1+kd)^{15}}+\frac{30}{(1+kd)^{16}}+\frac{0}{(1+kd)^{17}}$$

$$+\frac{30}{(1+kd)^{18}}+\frac{0}{(1+kd)^{19}}+\frac{30}{(1+kd)^{20}}$$

kd=12.5 per cent half yearly i.e. the annual cost of debenture being equal to 25 per cent.

If this cost of raising funds by J. K. Synthetics is evaluated on the criterion applied in the case of Usha Alloys and Steels Limited then the inference is obvious. The company has not been able to raise funds through this Issue at reasonable cost. Rather the cost company actually bears is on higher side. In fact it is higher than that of the Usha Alloys and Steels Limited. Apparently, therefore, this Issue must not have assisted the company in making any headway towards developing an optimal capital structure for it.

STRAW PRODUCTS LIMITED's PUBLIC ISSUE OF FULLY CONVERTIBLE DEBENTURFS : AUGUST 18, 1981

MAIN FEATURES OF THE ISSUE :

3.74 On August 18, 1981 Straw Products Limited came out with an Issue of 2,00,000 12% Secured Debentures of

Rs. 500 each for cash at par with option to receive 25 Equity Shares of Rs. 10 each at a premium of Rs. 10 per share in lieu of each Debenture, such option being exercisable within a period of 90 days after the expiry of 3 years from the date of allotment of the Debentures under reference. In cases of failure to exercise this option, the repayment of the debenture amount is to be affected at the end of 10th, 11th and 12th years in three instalments of Rs. 100, Rs. 200, and Rs. 200, respectively. The Debentures carried an interest @ 12 per cent per annum on the paid up value from the date of allotment, payable half yearly on 1st April and 1st October of each year. Additional interest @ 1 per cent per annum shall also become payable in any financial year if the average annual dividend on Equity Capital declared by the company for the 3 immediately preceding financial years exceeds 20 per cent.

DECISIVE INFORMATION

3.75 On an average the tax liability of the company has been @ 50 per cent. And, while total expenses of this Issue aggregated to Rs. 50 lakhs, the market price of the company's share averaged out Rs. 45 during the period of conversion.

CALCULATING THE VALUES

(*a*) *Price of the Debenture*

3.76 Utilising the aforesaid information alongside the presumption that the investors' required rate of return is 16 per cent per annum, the price of the Debenture comes to Rs. 847.60 as is evident from the result of the following equation.

$$P_{D,\,t} = \sum_{q=t+1}^{m} \frac{I}{(1+r)^q} + \frac{CR \times Mcm}{(1+r)^{m-t}}$$

$$= \sum_{t+1=1}^{6} \frac{30}{(1.08)^{6+1}} + \frac{25 \times 45}{(1.08)^6}$$

$$= \text{Rs. } 847.60$$

(*b*) *Rate of Return to the Debentureholder*

3.77 The rate of return to the Debentureholder calculates

to 19 per cent half yearly or 38 per cent per annum as per formula given below :

$$\text{Subscription Price} = \sum_{t=1}^{n} \frac{I}{(1+r)t} + \frac{CR \times Mcm}{(1+r)^m}$$

$$500 = \frac{30}{(1+r)} + \ldots + \frac{30}{(1+r)^6} + \frac{25 \times 45}{(1+r)^6}$$

r=19 per cent half yearly i.e. 38 per cent per annum.

(*c*) *Cost of the Debenture*

3.78 And the cost of debenture reckons at 8.75 per cent for a half year period or 17.50 per cent for one full year as shown below :

$$NSa = \sum_{t=1}^{m} \frac{I(1-T)}{(1+kd)t} + \frac{CR \times Mcm \times b}{(1+kd)t}$$

Where,

NSa=Rs. 475

b=0.6

Tax Rate=50 per cent

$$475 = \frac{30(1-.5)}{(1+kd)} + \frac{30(1-.5)}{(1+kd)^2} + \ldots + \frac{30(1-.5)}{(1+kd)^6} + \frac{25 \times 46 \times .6}{(1+kd)^6}$$

kd = 8.75 per cent for half year or 17.50 per cent for the full year.

3.79 The values of price and rate of return are quite alluring from the angle of debentureholders. Thus there seems to be no intention on the part of the company's management to cheat the investors in any manner. Perhaps it on this account that this Issue came to be oversubscribed by as many as 25 times. The value of the cost of the debenture is, however, not very favourable from the standpoint of the company.

SECTION-FIVE
CASE STUDIES

FINAL NOTE ON THE SUCCESSFULNESS AND UNSUCCESSFULNESS OF THE ISSUES OF CDs

3.80 As planned let us first present the final picture about the successfulness/unsuccessfulness of the public issues of the CDs putforwarded by the PLC_{pr} during the period 1978-82 on the basis of the criteria evolved for an integral check list on the one hand, and main results drawn in the preceding two sections, on the other. We may begin with the identification of those issues first which can be placed on persuasive grounds in the category of unsuccessful issues and then seriously ponder over the successful ones ; of course, in doing so we shall also search out the most unsuccessful and successful issues of public CDs. Of 51 PLC_{pr} Four, namely, Cheviot Company Limited (for an Issue worth Rs. 1 crore), Rajasthan Spg. & Wvg. Mills Limited (Issue for Rs. 5 crores), Mohta Industries Limited (Issue for Rs. 1.30 crores), and Nagarjuna Steel Limited (Issue for Rs. 2.50 crores) did not either avail consents or it came to be lapsed/cancelled out later on. Strictly speaking the related four Issues cannot be included in the list of unsuccessful public issues of CDs as there is no criterion on the basis of which their fate could be visualized in advance. Even so a few observations are worth mentioning. There seems to be some fault in the financial planning of the aforesaid companies as evidenced by their respective low profile at the stock exchanges. Not placing an issue in the market for which consent has already been obtained does affect adversely the reputation of the concerned company and its corporate management. Hence, the corporate managements should avoid the emergence of such situations.

3.81 The *de facto* public issues of CDs have thus been 47. Of these, the Issues floated by Sukhjit Starch and Chemicals Limited (for a sum of Rs. 1 crore), Ahmedabad Shri Ramkrishna Mills Company Limited (Rs. 0.60 crore), Premier Mills Limited (Rs. 5 crores), General Industrial Society Limited (Rs. 4 crores) and Guest Keen Williams Limited (Rs. 15.25 crores) remained undersubscribed, although but the Premier Mills

Limited a part of the issue has been on rights basis. The rights proportion varied between 10 per cent (Sukhjit Starch and Chemicals Limited) and over 57 per cent (Guest Keen Williams Limited). The probable factors which led to this rather unhappy situation in the case of these issues have already been discussed in para 3.47 of this Chapter. It may be noted here that under-subscription of an issue clearly implies its downright failure not only from the standpoint of its underwriters and managers but also from the perspective of the issuing company and its corporate management and the investors. On undersubscription, the underwriter/s is/are required to come to the rescue of the issuing company by making an offer to buy the unsubscribed portion of the issue as per the terms of the agreement. In the wake of none-too-encouraging position obtainable in respect to the market prices of the associated equity shares, terms of conversion, non-volatile character of equities/CDs, the overall return on such an investment to the underwriters is also not going to be higher, besides facing difficulty in liquidating such securities in case of need. Repetitive association with such Issues is further likely to impair the reputation commanded in this area of activity by the institutions who act as their Managers. For them the failure of an Issue means that the consultancy extended and the market strategy adopted for its floatation have not been of superb character. An undersubscribed issue signals its collapse to the issuing company in more than one way. It is an indication that the existing/prospective investors are not satisfied with the progress registered by the CDs issuing company in the recent past in general and on financial front including dividend policy, market price of the equity shares etc. in particular. Undersubcription also implies the non-approval of the program of diversification/expansion/modernization, etc. Even the wisely designed terms of conversion are not gratifying to them. In brief they do not feel complacent both about the quality of management of such a convertible debentures issuing company and its present and future financial worth. An under-subscribed issue of CDs would thus mar the possibility of such securities being employed on a continual basis for the purpose of amplifying long term funds. As a matter of fact the company involved in such an issue would not easily dare to approach the public again. That the Companies under review have since then not floated other issues of identical securities testify the expressed apprehension. The lack of enthusiasm observed on the part of existing/prospective investors in investing their monies in the Issues under consideration alone led to their undersubcriptions. Perhaps no other evidence is required for treating these issues unsuccessful from the elbow of investors. Suffice it should be to mention from their standpoint that all of these issues did not meet the motives of liquidity and a sufficiently attractive return on investment. The meagre importance these issues carry from the view point of nation's economy has already been highlighted in para 3.48.

3.82 In the absence of exact information regarding their undersubcription adequate it would be to mention as regards their relative unsuccessfulness that once an issue has not been welcome by the public it would merely be our conjecture to compare and on that basis deduce that a specific variable concerning with the frame of terms of conversion or any other aspect has contributed more/less to the failure. The hard fact remains that the investors did not feel attracted about the liquidity and gains offered in all of these issues primarily on account of the non-volatile nature of the correlated equities. In view of this, the only palatable crieria on which we can arrange them for denoting their relative unsuccessfulness are the total amount involved in each of them and the volume of funds offered to public. The higher the total amount involved and greater the volume of funds offered to the public lesser the degree of the failure of the issue being considered and *vice-versa*. Accordingly the position of these issues in an ascending order of unsuccessfulness is as follows. With a total amount of Rs 15.20 crores and the amount raised from public being Rs. 6.50 crores the Issue of Guest Keen Williams Limited can be deemed as the least unsuccessful. In ascendency, it is followed by Premier Mills Limited with a total amount of Rs. 5 crores, the entire sum having offered to public; General Industrial Society Limited-amount involved and offered to public being Rs. 4 crores and Rs. 2.80 crores, respectively; Sukhjit Starch and Chemicals Limited-amount involved and offered to public being Rs. 1 crore and Rs. 90 lakhs respectively; and, Ahmedabad Shri Ramkrishna

Mills Company Limited—amount involved and offered to public being Rs. 60 lakhs and Rs. 48 lakhs, respectively. As such, Ahmedabad Shri Ramkrishna Mills Company Limited's Issue stands identified as the most unsuccessful public Issue of CDs and therefore also for the proposed case study in this respect. Instead of this, we have, however, included the Public Issue of CDs putforwarded by Sukhjit Starch & Chemicals Limited to represent the case of an unsuccessful issue for certain weighty reasons. It is true that the Ahmedabad Shri Ramkrishna Mills Company Limited is older than the Sukhjit Starch & Chemicals Limited, the former having come into existence on 20.4.1907 and the latter on 16.3.1944, vibrant difference is not found in the total amount involved in both of these issues. This being the situation, among the two, the Sukhjit Starch & Chemicals Limited, is more widely held in sharp contrast to the Ahmedabad Shri Ramkrishna on the basis of the number of equity shares; on December 31, 1980, they being 3,59,000 in the case of former and only 12,282 in the case of latter. The record of dividend payment as created by Sukhjit during the period 1976-80 has been much impressive as compared to Ahmedabad Shri Ramkrishna; in the former case the rate of dividend has been 20 to 25 per cent *vis-a-vis* 10.8 to 12.8 per cent in the case of latter. Since these two aspects vitally affect the investing decisions of the investors, it seems more persuasive and unerring to select Sukhjit's Issue for the case study of an unsuccessful public issue of CDs for it would facilitate the type of analysis we intend to take up.

3.83 We are now left with 42 public issues of CDs which fall in the category of successful issues on the parameter of 'oversubscription'. Of these precise information about the number of times the Issue came to be oversubscribed is neither available nor has come to be disclosed to the author by the concerned PLCp/rManagers to Issues in respect to seven Issues put out by the Mahindra Mills Limited, Bharat Steel Tubes Limited, Vardhman Spg. and General Mills Limited, Ahmedabad Advance Mills Limited, Bharat Vijay Mills Limited, Dunlop India Limited, and Shri Digvijya Woollen Mills Limited. In the absence of exact information in regard to oversubscription and other scores, the line of argument advanced by us for the unsuccessful issues in the preceding para 3.82, the fact that in 6 cases the associated equity shares are of non-volatile nature, and the availability of rare quotations of the relavant equity shares/convertible debentures, it would be judicious if these issues are categorized simply as successful public issues of CDs and are not appraised and ranked for the comparative successfulness. Under the circumstances, these issues can be ranked for their allied successfulness, keeping in view the total amount entailed and the portion offered to the public through each one of them. On this basis the descending order that emerges is as follows.

(i) Dunlop India Limited for a total sum of Rs. 12 crores—Rs. 6.38 crores having offered to public ;

(ii) Ahmedabad Advance Mills Limited for a total sum of Rs. 6 crores—Bs. 2.81 crores having offered to public ;

(iii) Bharat Steel Tubes Limited for a total amount of Rs. 4 crores—Rs. 3 crores having offered to public ;

(iv) Bharat Vijay Mills Limited for Rs. 3.40 crores—Ks. 1.60 crores having offered to public ;

(v) Mahindra Mills Limited for Rs. 3 crores, the whole of it having offered to public ;

(vi) Vardhman Spg. & General Mills Limited for Rs. 2 crores—Rs. 1.47 crores having placed to the public ; and

(vii) Shri Digvijay Woollen Mills Limited for Rs. 2 crores—Rs. 1.19 crores having placed to the public.

3.84 The remainder 35 oversubscribed public issues of CDs can now be taken up for determining their relative triumph. From out of these, regular weekly/monthly price quotations of associated equity shares/CDs pertaining to as many as Eight Issues could not be garnished on account of they being on tap intermittently ; these Issues being those of Shri Dinesh Mills Limited for Rs. 1 crore (Rs. 60 lakhs having offered to public), Fibreglass Pilkington Limited for Rs. 2.63 crores (Rs. 1.73 crores having placed for subscription by public),

Jyoti Limited for Rs. 2 crores (Rs. 1 crore having meant for public), Star Industrial and Textile Enterprizes Limited for Rs. 4.25 crores (Rs. 2.25 crores having placed to the public), Elecon Engineering Company Limited for Rs. 5.50 crores (Rs. 2.80 crores being for public), Punjab Anand Batteries Limited for Rs. 1 crore (Rs. 50 lakhs being for the public), Cellulose Products of India Limited for Rs. 1.50 crores (Rs. 95 lakhs having meant for public), and Keshoram Industries and Cotton Mills Limited for Rs. 21 crores (Rs. 4.35 crores having offered to public). Obviously, therefore, we stand restrained for identifying and assessing the impact of the volatile nature of the associated equities on the successfulness of the aforesaid Issues of CDs. In view of this it seems logical on the earlier footings, to classify these issues in another category of successful public issues of CDs which may be designated as 'Relatively More Successful Public Issues of CDs'. And, their comparative degree of successfulness can be adjudged through applying the parameter of adjusted number of times an Issue has been oversubscribed i.e. the aggregate amount offered by the investing public for these issues ; these amounts having arrived at by multiplying the number of times an issue is over-subscribed with the total amount involved in it. On this basis Keshoram Industries and Cotton Mills Limited's issue stands atop in which the investing public applied for the subscription to the tune of Rs. 140.70 crores. It's followed by Elecon Engineering Limited (Rs. 37.40 crores), Star Industries & Textile Enterprizes Limlted (Rs. 27.20 crores), Jyoti Limited (Rs. 18 crores), Shri Dinesh Mills (Rs. 8.70 crores), Fibreglass Pilkington Limited (Rs 8.05 crores), Cellulose Products of India Limited (Rs. 3.45 crores), and Punjab Anand Batteries Limited (Rs. 2.60 crores). To this we may add that the above ranking is found unchanged even if these issues are appraised alongside such macro-focussed criterion as the total volume of funds raised through the issuance of both public as well as rights CDs/NCDs and the number of times the company entered the market during the period of our study for raising of long term funds through such securities. To substantiate, excepting three PLCpr, namely, Keshoram, Jyoti and Shri Dinesh, none else entered the market more than once. Keshoram, however, raised additional funds worth Rs. 8.50 crores through the issuance of two Issues of NCDs. Likewise, Jyoti floated an issue of NCDs worth Rs. 3 crores and Shri Dinesh an issue of NCDs for Rs. 0.50 crore. On adding these sums in the respective amounts, we find that with Keshoram the investing public was ready to place Rs. 149.20 crores and with Jyoti and Shri Dinesh Rs. 21 crores and Rs. 9.20 crores, respectively. This means an unaltered position in respect to the ranks of the aforesaid companies.

3.85 Leftover of 27 oversubscribed public issues of CDs can be clubbed into another two groups of successful issues, namely, 'Quite Successful Issues' and 'Most Successful Issues'. In the former category are included the public issues of Raymond Woollen Mills Limited for Rs. 4.80 crores (the whole of which having come to be placed at the disposal of public), Camphor and Allied Products Limited for Rs. 1 crore (Rs. 75 lakhs offered to public), Hindustan Development Corporation Limited for Rs. 1.5 crores (Rs. 75 lakhs for subscription by public), Rustom Mills & Industries Limited for Rs. 2 crores (Rs. 1.40 crores offered to public), Ferro Alloys Corporation Limited for Rs. 7.50 crores (Rs. 5 crores offered to public), Usha Alloys and Steels Limited for Rs. 1.50 crores (Rs. 90 lakhs being for public), Gujarat Steel Tubes Limited for Rs. 5 crores (Rs. 3 crores offered to public), Mahindra Mills Limited for Rs. 3 crores (Rs. 1.62 crores offered to public), Kothari (Madras) Limited for Rs. 10 crores (Rs. 6 crores for subscription by public), Indian Hotels Company Limited for Rs. 15 crores (Rs. 9.33 crores offered to public), Ranbaxy Laboratories Limited for Rs. 4.50 crores (Rs. 1.25 crores offered to public), and ITC Limited for Rs. 30 crores (Rs. 6.75 crores offered to public).

3.86 While all the above referred issues concern with those companies whose equity shares are of non-volatile nature, still we may analyze their fate utilising the information relating to different parameters in order to assess their comparative success within the group itself. Accordingly, ITC's Issue can be deemed to have witnessed the highest degree of success. No doubt that ITC's corporate management neither bothered to insert news items on a regular basis in the news papers and assured its prospective debentureholders about any other benefits nor cared to activitize trading in its equity shares at different stock exchanges, yet its issue witnessed oversubscription by 8.9 times seemingly on account of its attractive terms of conversion (10 Equity Shares in lieu of interest accrued at par in two instalments), and the expected benefit at the time of conversion having stood at 53.60 per cent of the face value of CD on the basis of the market price of its equity share being 3.68 times of its face value at the time of floatation of the Issue. Furthermore, the investing populace proferred as high as Rs. 267 crores at the discretion of the company. And, as ITC also entered the market with an issue of NCDs worth Rs. 5 crores, this amount reaches to the peak of Rs. 272 crores. Had the period of conversion been shorter (it being in two parts : one, after one year and four and half month, and another, two years and four and a half month), nature of equity share volatile, and regular insertion of news items by the ITC's management, then perhaps the fate of this Issue could have been still brighter for the obvious reason that these factors generally have a favourable impact on the market price of the equity shares and thereby on the expected percentage of benefits to the debentureholders on the one hand and the liquidity of the concerned CD and the possibility of earning larger capital gains via wider variations in the prices of equity share/CD both during and after the conversion period, on the other. A part of this inference is corroborated by the variations observed in the aforesaid variables relating to the Issue placed in the market by the Hindustan Development Corporation Limited (HDC) which on an identical pattern of appraisal, occupies the second place. Notwithstanding the apathetic attitude of HDC's management in respect to 'News Items' and 'Measures Ought to have taken for Propelling Trading in its Equity Shares', this Issue came to be oversubscribed by the maximum number of times i.e. 72 times implying thereby that the investors placed Rs. 108 crores at the discretion of HDC apart further allowing augmentation of funds through an Issue of NCDs for Rs. 0.75 crore. But then this Issue had three privileges. One, by nature it has been of Right to Subscribe to 6 Equity Shares per Debenture at a premium of Rs. 7.50 per share which means an announced conversion price of 1.75 times of the face value of equity shares obtainable at the time of issuance of CDs. Second, the market price of the company's equity share stood at as high as 7.50 times of its face value at the time when this issue came to be placed in the market. Third, which is a consequence of the above, expected benefit to the debenture-holders stood at the record level of 345 per cent. Indian Hotels Company Limited's (IHC) Issue, though not accompanied with magnetic terms of conversion (1 Equity Share for 25 per cent face value of CD at a premium of Rs. 15 per share after the lapse of 3 years from the date of allotment) and followed by regular corporate briefs and efforts to promote trading in the equity shares at different stock exchanges, yet it came to be oversubscribed by 6.63 times denoting the investors' preparedness to offer a sum of Rs. 99.45 crores in response to a demand for Rs. 15 crores. Behind this success are hidden the impact of such factors as : the market price of the IHC's epuity shares at the time of the issuance of CDs being 6 times of its face value, expected benefit at the time of conversion having reckoned at 35 per cent and the values of CV of Equity Shares and CDs at 16.00 and 10.08, respectively. The above record of IHC has elevated its Issue to the third position in the list of Quite Successful Issues. With an expected benefit of 34 per cent (market price of the equity being 3.50 times of its face value and the announced conversion of 1.80 times) at the time of conversion within the framework of 2 Equity Shares for 36 per cent face value of CD at a premium of Rs. 8 per share after the expiry of 18 months and values of CV for Equity Shares and CD being 8.79 and 4.79, respectively but with no consistancy on the score of advertizing the company's progress/future plans on a regular basis as also in respect to the measures required for making equity shares/CDs of volatile nature, the Issue worth Rs. 10 crores of Kothari (Madras) Limited came to be oversubscribed by 7 times indicating the investors' willingness to invest a sum of Rs. 70 crores and thus allowing this Issue to occupy the fourth position among the Quite Successful Public Issues of CDs. The position of the rest of the Issues and their relevant record is as narrated hereunder :

(i) Ferro Alloys Corporation Limited—Fifth Place : expected benefit 60 per cent reckoned out on the basis of 2.90 times market price of Equity Share and 1.40 times announced conversion price ; the Issue met with an oversubscription of 5.2 times within the conversion framework of, 'One Equity Share for 56 per cent Face Value of CD at a Premium of Rs. 40 per Share after the expiry of 3 years' implying thereby a response to invest a sum ol Rs. 39 crores as against the total demand for Rs. 7.50 crores followed by a further support of Rs. 6.75 crores by way of subscription to 2 Issues of NCDs floated by the Company during the period under review ; and, while the Company did not put corporate briefs in the news papers on a regular basis as also failed in bringing its equity within the fold of volatile category, the relatively good response from the side of investors seems to be the result of higher percentage of expected benefit (60) and values of CV for Equity Shares (13.06) and CD (3.66).

(ii) Rambaxy Laboratories Limited—Sixth Position : the Issue witnessed an oversubscription by 6.8 times assuring an availability of funds to the extent of Rs. 30.60 crores in response to a demand for Rs. 4.50 crores with values of CV for equity share and CD having stood a 7.61 and 7.76 respectively and an expected benefit of 37.5 per cent on a market price of equity shares of 2.50 times and an announced conversion price 'at par', and terms of conversion having set as, '5 Equity Shares for 22 per cent face value of CD'.

(iii) Gujarat Steel Tubes Limited—Seventh Position with a record of an oversubscription by 5.85 times and thus placing at the discretion of the company Rs. 29.25 crores against the demand for Rs. 5 crores aside the support of Rs. 1 crore in the shape of subscription to an Issue of NCDs. Although the concomitant terms of conversion, namely, '1 Equity for 30 per cent face value per CD at a premium of Rs. 50 per share after the lapse of 11 months' does not seem attractive at its first glance, the success of the Issue stands explained by the percentage of expected benefit which reckoned out at 62.50 on account of the market price of equity at the time of issuance of CDs having stood at 4 times of its face value and the announced conversion price at 1.50 times.

(iv) Raymond Woollen Mills Limited--Eighth Position: the investing public furnished the Mills with Rs. 19.20 crores in response to the demand for Rs. 4.80 crores indicating an oversubscription by 4.00 times; an additional amount of Rs. 4.50 crores placed at the disposal of the Mills by way of subscriptions to its Issue of NCDs; the percentage of expected benefit stood at 37.50 on the basis of the market price of equity share and announced conversion price of 4.50 and 2.00 times of its face value, respectively; the Mills management did not put up corporate briefs in the news papers and no steps were taken to enhance trading in its equity shares/ CDs at different Stock Exchanges; and, the associated conversion terms read as, 'Right to Subscribe to 5 Equity Shares per Debenture at a premium of Rs. 10 per Share after the expiry of six months from the date of allotment'.

(v) Camphor and Allied Products Limited—Ninth Position: oversubscribed by 12 times indicating a reposte to the tune of Rs. 12 crores against a call for Rs. 1 crore; terms of conversion were as thus, '2 Equity Shares for 60 per cent face value of CD at a premium of Rs. 50 per Share after the lapse of 4 years'; and, it involved an expected benefit of 28 per cent at the market price of Equity Share of 2.20 times of its face value and an announced conversion price of 1.50 times.

Although oversubscribed only by 6 times the Issue for Rs. 2 crores as placed by Rustom Mills & Industries Limited also occupies the ninth position because in it also the investing public showed its desire to invest to the tune of Rs. 12 crores; the substance of accompanying terms of conversion reciting as, '2 Equity Shares for 30 per cent face value of Debenture at a premium of Rs. 5 per share after the lapse of one year from the date of allotment'; and, it convoluted an expected benefit of 44 per cent at the market price and announced conversion price of 3.70 and 1.50 times of its equity share measured in terms of face value, respectively.

(vi) Usha Alloys & Steels Limited—Tenth Position with an oversubscription by 4.3 times indicating the investors' desire to invest to the extent of Rs. 6.45 crores against the demand for Rs. 1.50 crores and the Right to Subscribe for 3 Equity Shares per Debenture and a premium of Rs. 5 per Share within one year of allotment. While expected benefit in this Issue counted at 75 per cent on the basis of market price of equity shares of 4 times of its face value and announced conversion price of 1.50 times, the corresponding response from the side of investing public seems to be rather poorer due to more than one reason. First, the management of Usha Alloys neither seriously attempted to promote trading in its shares/debentures at different stock exchanges nor followed a policy of informing the public about its performance/future plans on a regular basis. Second, it advertised that the short term and long term investors would be receiving a return of 79.5 per cent in one year and 89.5 per cent per annum, respectively. In actuality, however, these returns computed at bare 32 and 18 per cent per annum. (See, Please, para 3.66 of this Chapter, for details). Third, the market price of the company's equity shares, which stood at Rs. 40 at the time of the floatation of this Issue, gradually started declining and averaged out at Rs. 23 at the time of exercising of subscription rights which clearly imply wiping off the expected benefit likely to accrue to the debentureholders from about Rs. 53 to Rs. 9 per debenture (see, please, para 3.64 of this Chapter) and benefit per equity share declined from Rs. 25 to bare Rs. 8. It seems that prospective investors had already anticipated these trends correctly, and therefore responded to this Issue in a rather blase manner.

3.87 Due to the non-availability of precise information in regard to the number of times the Mahindra Mills Limited's Issue of CDs came to be oversubscribed, we have excluded it from the category of 'Quite Successful Issues'. As a matter of fact, we have already included its analysis under the class of 'Successful Issues of CDs'.

3.88 Among the 'Most Successful Issues of CDs' are included 15 Public Issues of CDs proferred by 14 PLC_{pr}. These cover the Issue of Metal Box Company of India Limited (Metal Box) for Rs. 2 crores (Rs. 1.50 crores having offered to public), Reliance Textile Industries (Reliance) (First Series) for Rs. 7 crores (the whole placed for subscription by public), Tata Engineering and Locomotive Company Limited (TELCO) for Rs. 47.25 crores (Rs. 29.29 crores offered to public), Voltas Limited (Voltas) for Rs. 5 crores (Rs. 3 crores to be subscribed by public), Indian Rayon Corporation Limited (Indian Rayons) for Rs. 10 crores (Rs. 5.50 crores having offered to public)*, Straw Products Limited (Straw Products) for Rs. 10 crores (Rs. 6.50 crores having meant for contribution by public), Reliance Textile Industries Limited (Third Series) for Rs. 24 crores (Rs. 13 crores reserved for support by the public), East India Hotels Limited (East India) for Rs. 7.50 crores (Rs. 3 crores for the public). Tata Iron and Steel Company Limited (TISCO) for Rs. 30 crores (Rs. 12 crores for the public), Delhi Cloth & General Mills Company Limited (DCM) for Rs. 15 crores (Rs. 6 crores for the public), J.K. Synthetics Limited

*The Indian Rayons placed this Issue in the market on 16.3.1981. Another public issue of CDs for Rs. 21 crores came to be offered by the Indian Rayons on 25.1.1983. Although the CCI consented for it on 23.11.1982. Since our period of study is restricted only upto the close of December 31, 1982, we have not covered this Issue under the Category 'A' of Table 3.7, as also for want of relevant quotations at the time of collection of data. The aforesaid Issue has, however, been taken into consideration while analysing the success of the first Issue putforwarded by the Indian Rayons.

(J.K. Synthetics) for Rs. 25 crores (Rs. 12 crores for public), Mukand Iron & Steel Works Limited (Mukand Irons) for Rs. 7 crores (Rs. 4.55 crores for the public), Zenith Steel Pipes & Industries Limited (Zenith Steels) for Rs. 4.80 crores (Rs. 2.40 crores for the public), Gwalior Rayon Silk Mfg. (Wvg.) Company Limited (Gwalior Rayons) for Rs. 30 crores (Rs. 10 crores for the public), and Lohia Machines Limited (Lohia) for Rs. 5.65 crores (Rs. 4.05 crores for the public). Notwithstanding the fact that equities associated with all the above referred public CDs are of volatile nature and all Issues fall in the broad group of 'Most Successful Issues', they have come to be received by investing public with discrete warmth as is evidenced from the simple truth that an Issue involving meagre amount has come to be oversubscribed by a lesser number of times and an Issue for a higher amount has met with an oversubscription by a much greater number of times. On this basis and utilizing the meaningful informations pertaining to these Issucs on pre-laid down criteria we may further assign ranks to them.

3.89 The aggregate amounts placed at the discretion of the concerned PLC_{pr} by the investing public have, however, not been employed as such for ranking the Issues under consideration. The total amounts involved in different Issues are bound to differ, and at times significantly, depending upon the requirement for long term funds, which in its turn is determined by a number of factors such as the size of the ongoing operations, nature of product/service, the purpose and the nature of growth program, etc. Similarly, the number of times an Issue is over. subscribed depends upon the time element, availability of identical and other worthwhile securities, Government Policy concerning debentures, mood and the state of affairs found in the capital market and stock exchanges, etc. Hence, inconsiderable differences in the amounts of aggregate support by the investing public have been ignored if it is observed that: (i) the involved PLC_{pr} has been able to meet its requirement for the long term funds from time to time through the floatation of such securities; and/or, (ii) the amount of total funds raised either via similar type of debentures or its any other variant such as Rights Issues of CDs and/or Issues of NCDs during the period under review is found significant in absolute terms.

Ranking of Issues on the above basis is not only judicious but quite befitting from both micro and macro view points. To be able to raise successfully the desired volume of long term funds as and when the need arises by issuing one or the other type of debentures is most important for individual companies. From the economy's stand point the strategic criterion for adjudging the successfulness of debentures is the total volume of long term funds so raised and the extent of the self-reliance attained by the private corporate sector in point of such financial needs. The scale as devised above rightly meets the above objectives.*

3.90 If the record disclosed here has to be the testimony then the Third Series of Public Convertible Debentures put forth by the Reliance emerge out to be the utmost successful. Including this Issue, the Reliance entered the market with its debentures by the maximum number of times, namely, five times during the period 1978-82—two times with public issues of CDs for Rs. 31 crores; two times with Rights Issues of CDs for Rs. 60.80 crores; and, once with an Issue of NCDs for Rs. 0.03 crore. Total long term funds mobilized by Reliance through available variants of debentures thus aggregated to Rs. 91.83 crores, which is the highest of all PLC_{pr} under review. The investing public extended a total support of Rs. 294.83 crores to Reliance which is nearer to the maximal amount of Rs. 306 crores as given to TISCO for its solitary public issue of CDs. The factors contributing to this grand success have been many. The equity shares/convertible debentures of Reliance are of volatile nature, as is evident from the values of '$\overline{V}$' and

*This scale has not been consciously employed for ranking the Public Issues covered by the category of 'Quite Successful Issues' for more than one reason. During the five year period 1987-82, from out of 11 PLCpr, with which the Issues were associated, only four entered the marmet twice and the rest only once. It is difficult to draw out conclusive inference in respect to the extent such securities are depended upon by the associated PLCpr for augmenting their long term funds by considering their sole Issues as floated by most of them. It is only in the case of four PLCpr that the volume of funds raised through debentures touched the amount of Rs. 10 crores. Even if this scale is employed it is the rank of one Issue alone which is found affected. Hence, we avoided the use of this scale, which is rather complex, to the Issues which are not going to affect our generalized findings of this Study in any manner.

'CV' for its Equity Shares ('$\overline{V}$' = 14.63, and CV=10.16) and CDs of Third Series ('$\overline{V}$' 25.84, and CV=14.56). The corporate management of Reliance is keeping abreast its debentureholders with the company's progress/future programs of expansion/ diversification, etc. The terms of conversion which stipulated that company shall issue and allot one equity share for 20 per cent value of CD at a premium of Rs. 15 after the lapse of one year without any further act or application by the debenture-holders also seems to have been considered alluring by the investing public in the light of other surer associated benefits with thc Issue such as entitlements to Rights Debentures and to Bonus in the shape of reduction in conversion price and proportionate increase in the number of equity shares, and an expected benefit to the extent of 75 per cent of the face value of CD at the time of conversion on the basis of market price and announced conversion price of equity having stood at 10 and 2.5 times of its face value at the time of issuance of CDs under analysis. The consistent record of Reliance's progress and fulfilment of declared promises by its management has been still another significant factor contributing to the marked success of this Issue. (See, Please, Table 3.6 through Table 3.9, Annexe VI).

3.91 Reliance has come to be followed by the Issues of TELCO (one public Issue of CDs floated for Rs. 47.25 crores and whereby a support worth Rs. 283.50 crores came to be assured by the investing public), Gwalior Rayons (entered the debenture market two times for Rs. 45 crores—once with an Issue of CDs for Rs. 30 crores and another time with an Issue of NCDs for Rs. 15 crores, and secured support for an aggregate sum of Rs. 195 crores from the investing public) J.K. Synthetics (raised funds worth Rs. 38 crores via floatation of one Issue of CDs for Rs. 25 crores and three Issues of NCDs for Rs. 13 crores and with the investing public's support measuring to Rs. 213 crores) Indian Rayons (augmented Rs. 32 crores through two Issues of CDs for Rs. 31 crores and one Issue of NCDs for Rs 1 crore with an assured support of Rs. 253 crores), TISCO (gathered Rs. 30 crores via one Issue of CDs but with a maximum amount of assured support from the investors for Rs. 306 crores), East India (amplified its long term capital resources by Rs. 17.50 crores in two instalments—Rs. 7.50 crores through issuance of CDs and Rs. 10 crores via NCDs, registering an assurance from the investors to support to the extent of Rs. 24.25 crores), DCM (raised funds worth Rs. 15 crores via one Issue of CDs in which investing public offered to place with the company to the tune of Rs. 45 crores), Mukand Irons (augmented its long term resources by Rs. 14 crores through the floatation of one Issue of CDs for Rs. 7 crores and 3 Issues of NCDs for Rs. 7 crores and the support of investing public aggregated to Rs. 42 crores), Straw Products (heightened the long term resources by Rs. 12 crores via one Issue of CDs for Rs. 10 crores and one Issue of NCDs for Rs. 2 crores; but the support received from the investing public amounted to Rs. 252 crores) Voltas (raised funds worth Rs. 10.30 crores via floatation of one Issue of CDs for Rs. 5 crores and two Issues of NCDs for Rs. 5.30 crores and the support from the investing public amounted to Rs. 48.80 crores), Zenith Steels (issued CDs for Rs. 4.80 crores and NCDs for Rs. 1.25 crores for raising Rs. 6.05 crores to which investing public assured its support upto Rs. 19.49 crores), Metal Box (placed CDs for Rs. 2 crores and NCDs for Rs. 4 crores for accumulating long term funds worth Rs. 6 crores and investors' support amounted to Rs. 8 crores), and Lohia (raised Rs. 5.65 crores via one Issue of CDs to which investing public assured a support of Rs. 73.45 crores).

3.92 While the Issue-wise details of the factors which led to their varying degree of success can be seen in Table 3.6 through Table 3.9, discernible findings relating to overall impact of various factors on the success/failure of the public issues of CDs may be pinpointed here. The frame of terms, market price of the associated equity, and announced conversion price are appraised by the debentureholders in a composite manner in terms of percentage of expected benefit. And, wherever the percentage of expected benefit has been higher, the secured oversubscription has generally been higher irrespective of amount involved in an issue and *vice-versa.* To substantiate, with 140 per cent of expected benefit the Issue of Straw Products came to be oversubscribed by 25 times. The same is also true for TISCO (80 per cent and 10.2 times), Reliance (Third Series)

(75 per cent and 8 times), Voltas (68 per cent and 8.7 times), Indian Rayons (58 per cent and 8 times), J.K. Synthetics (50 per cent and 8 times), Lohia (40.8 per cent and 13 times), Gwalior Rayons (37.5 per cent and 6 times), TELCO (33.50 per cent and 6 times) and Mukand Irons (32.5 per cent and 5 times). Conversely, the Issue of Metal Box, which entailed an expected benefit of bare 7 per cent came to be oversubscribed only by 2 times. Likewise, DCM and East India's Issues met with a poor response (3 and 1.9 times respectively) on account of the low level of expected benefits (16 and 21 per cent respectively). Zenith Steels, however, constitutes an exception to above. On carefully observing the values of $\overline{V}$ and CV for associated equities and CDs on the one hand and the position of oversubscription on the other, it is clear that volatileness of the associated equity shares alone is not an adequate condition for the success of a public issue of CDs. Volatileness of correlated equity shares must be followed, and preferably with greater intensity, by the volatileness of the relevant CDs if it has to be an instrumental for the success of any Issue. This in fact has been the case with Reliance, Voltas, Straw Products and Lohia. Further, volatileness of equities and CDs must be accompanied by a certain minimum percentage of expected benefit; this minimum having determined presumedly by the investors' expectations in respect to the return on investment which in its turn is greatly influenced by the prevailing structure of interest rates. In the cases under investigation, the 'volatileness' seems to have assumed a role in the success of an Issue which entailed an expected benefit of more than 32 per cent. Neither positive nor negative impact is ascertainable with confidence of the announced ancillary benefits on the basis of public Issues under study. Thus there have been Issues (Zenith Steels and East India) which witnessed poor response inspite of the fact that they carried with them ancillary benefits. Also, in the absence of these (Voltas & TISCO) the Issues have been well received. However, on the basis of our analysis presented in regard to the Reliance Third Series of CDs it can be argued that ancillary benefits are likely to have a positive impact on the success of Public Issues of CDs provided, of course, the investors are hopeful that whatever benefits have been announced shall see

their transcription into a reality within the stipulated/reasonable period of time. Also the positive impact of the management's policy to put on corporate briefs regularly on the success of public Issues of CDs is discernible; although, the evidences of negative impact are lacking.

3.93 The above description clearly explains as to why we have chosen Reliance (Third Series) and Sukhjit Starch for case studies of successful and unsuccessful public Issues of CDs, respectively. In respect to the Issues of NCDs let us reiterate that there are valid difficulties in the identification of most successful/unsuccessful Issue of NCDs. Hence, we have selected, for our case study, J. K. Synthetics' Issue of Secured (Second Series) Redeemable Debentures put out on August 10, 1981 to betoken of NCDs keeping in view the overriding consideration that this Issue would provide us an opportunity to undertake the desired type of analysis for drawing meaningful inferences on this score. J. K. Synthetics is next to Reliance in so far as raising of funds through debentures is concerned ; it entered the market four times during the period 1978-82—3 times with NCDs and once with a public Issue of CDs. Moreover, it is a widely held and well managed PLC_{pr}. As would be evident soon, it has been able to create a good financial record to its credit. Its equity shares are listed on major stock exchanges of India and are of volatile nature. Truly speaking, the market price of its equity shares registered an almost six-fold rise between 1976 and 1981. Since inception, it has also issued Bonus Shares five times. Investors seem to repose confidence in J.K. Synthetics as its Issue of CDs putforwarded on February 3, 1982 for Rs. 25 crores was quite enthusiastically received by them. All these features of J.K. Synthetics allow us to presume that its Issue of NCDs was planned well. And, therefore, must also permit us to go into the required type of details.

1, A SUCCESSFUL PUBLIC ISSUE OF CDs : RELIANCE INDUSTRIES LIMITED—PUBLIC ISSUE FOR RS. 24 CRORES COMPRISING OF 19,20,000 DEBENTURES OF RS. 125 EACH FOR CASH AT PAR (THIRD SERIES) JUNE 10, 1981.

Incorporation and History of the Company :

3.94 A Company under the name and style 'Reliance Textile Industries Private Limited' was incorporated on February 11, 1966 in the State of Maharashtra which in the same year established a Synthetic Fabric Mill at Naroda near Ahmedabad. This Company was converted into a public limited company with effect from June 28, 1975 and a fresh certificate of change of name was obtained from the Registrar of Companies, Maharashtra, Bombay, on July 9, 1975.

3.95 In terms of High Court of Karnataka, Bangalore's order dated January 13, 1977 and High Court of Judicature, Bombay's order dated November 24, 1976, Reliance Textile Industries Limited amalgamated with a Company incorporated in the State of Karnataka on May 8, 1973 under the name Mynylon Limited with effect from July 1, 1975 and in consideration 59,50,000 fully paid up equity shares of Rs. 10 each were alloted by the latter to the shareholders of the former in accordance with the Controller of Capital Issues consent letter dated April 23, 1977 ; consequently the name of Mynylon Limited was changed to Reliance Textile Industries Limited with effect from March 11, 1977 and it was granted a fresh certificate of incorporation by the Registrar of Companies, Karnataka, Bangalore apart shifting its Registered Office from the State of Karnataka to the State of Maharashtra on Agust 4, 1977.

3.96 In order to enable the Company to comply with the listing formalities of the Stock Exchanges at Bombay and Ahmedabad, Shri Dhirubhai H. Ambani and Shri Natvarlal H. Ambani, in their own capacity and as joint and severally constituted attorneys of the other offerors, at the request of the Company made an offer for sale of 28,20,000 equity shares of Rs. 10/- each for cash at par to the general public by a letter of offer dated October 24, 1977. Accordingly, the Equity Shares of the Company came to be listed at the Stock Exchange of Bombay and Ahmedabad on January 23, 1978. Subsequently, the Equity Shares of the Company further came to be enlisted on other important Stock Exchanges of Country including that of Calcutta, Delhi and Madras.

3.97 Effective from July 1, 1981, the Company has taken over the undertaking of the Sidhpur Mills Company Limited in terms of the Scheme of Amalgamation approved by the High Courts at Bombay and Gujarat. And, it is with effect from June 27, 1985, when the Additional Registrar of Companies, Maharashtra, Bombay, issued a fresh Certificate of Incorporation, that the Company acquired present name, namely, Reliance Industries Limited.

PRESENT PRODUCT LINES

3.98 The Company's present range of product lines includes manufacturing, processing and trading of synthetic yarn and fabrics, and polyester yarn and polyester staple fibre. Further the projects for manufacturing of Purified Terephthalic Acid (PTA), Mono Ethylene Glycol (MEG), and Linear Alkyl Benzene (LAB) are under implementation. Also, the Company soon proposes so diversify its manufacturing activities so as to cover High Density Polyethylene (HDPE). Poly Vinyl Chloride (PVC), Polyester Industrial Yarn (PIY), and TV Colour Tubes and Glass Shells for Colour TV.

MANAGEMENT

3.99 The day to day operations of the Company are managed by Shri Dhirubhai H. Ambani, Chairman and Managing Director, Shri R.H. Ambani, Joint Managing Director, Shri N.H. Ambani, Shri M.D. Ambani, and Shri A.D. Ambani, Executive Directors subject to the overall superintendance and control by the Board which has seven other directors besides the above. They, however, base their decisions on the advice given by qualified and experienced professionals employed by the Company in technical, financial, marketing, legal and other key areas.

FINANCIAL HIGHLIGHTS

3.100 The financial position of the Company during the period 1978-82 can be gauged from the data presented in Exhibit 3.i and 3.ii. The Exhibit 3.i depicts the availability of funds and their application as at the end of December 31, 1978 through December 31, 1982. The significant trends both in respect to the volume and means used for raising funds and their application may be highlighted. Thus, the total volume of funds with Reliance rose to nearly Rs. 318 crores as at 31st December 1982 from nearly Rs. 48 crores as on December 31, 1978 indicating thereby an increase of over 562 per cent (or 6.6 times) in a period of 5 years. A probe into the composition of these funds further reveals that of the total funds of Rs. 318 crores as on December 31, 1982, Rs. 91.64 crores (28.79 per cent of the total) have been raised from the shareholders by way of Equity Capital (Rs. 18.60 crores or 5.85 per cent), Preference Share Capital (Rs. 5.79 crores or 1.82 per cent), and Reserves and Surpluses (Rs. 67.14 crores or 21.11 per cent), and the remaining Rs. 226.44 crores (71.21 per cent of the total) by way of loans ; the corresponding position as on December 31, 1978 stood as thus : of the total funds of Rs. 47.85 crores, Rs. 14.44 crores (30.18 per cent of the total) raised from shareholders by way of Equity Capital (Rs. 5.95 crores or 12.43 per cent), Preference Share Capital (0.30 crore or 0.63 per cent), and Reserves and Surpluses (Rs. 8.19 crores or 17.12 per cent), and the rest Rs. 33.41 crores (69.82 per cent) by way of loans. On a close scrutiny of these figures, it is observed that (a) the proportion of shareholders' funds has declined marginally from 30.18 per cent to 28.79 per cent and that of loan funds has gone up from 69.82 per cent to 71.21 per cent between December 31, 1978 and December 31, 1982 ; (b) while the equity capital of Reliance registered a rise of Rs. 12.65 crores (212.61 per cent) during the aforesaid period, the increase in reserves and surpluses has beenm ore pronounced i.e. of Rs. 58.95 crores (719.78 per cent) in the same period ; (c) the proportion of secured loans in the total loans has gone up from 83.18 per cent to 89.91 per cent on the aforesaid dates; and (d) the capital gearing ratio has further risen from

EXHIBIT 3.i : Sources and Uses of Funds of Reliance Textile Industries Limited (1972-82)

(Rs. in Crores)

Particulars	As at the end of December 31				
	1978	1979	1980	1981	1982
(1)	(2)	(3)	(4)	(5)	(6)
I. SOURCES OF FUNDS					
1. Shareholders' Funds	14.44	26.63	31.79	57.10	91.54
(a) Capital	6.25	7.84	12.36	16.97	24.39
	(5.95)	(7.54)	(12.06)	(16.67)	(18.60)
(b) Share Application Monies	—	—	—	0.002	—
(c) Reserves and Surpluses	8.19	15.80	19.43	40.12	67.14
(d) Sub Total (a+b+c)	14.44	26.63	31.79	57.10	91.54
2. Loan Funds	33.41	61.79	94.40	165.42	226.44
(e) Secured Loans	27.79	55.90	85.37	149.06	203.59
(f) Deferred Payment Liabilities	1.71	—	—	—	—
(g) Unsecured Loans	3.91	5.89	9.03	16.35	22.85
(h) Sub Total (e+f+g)	33.41	61.79	94.40	165.42	226.44
Total (1+2)	47.85	85.42	126.19	222.52	317.98

Exhibit 3.i (Contd.)

(1)	(2)	(3)	(4)	(5)	(6)
II. APPLICATION OF FUNDS					
1. Fixed Assets	25.03	37.74	57.95	105.56	314.61
2. Investments	0.04	0.07	0.08	0.07	0.12
3. Net Current Assets	22.78	47.61	68.16	116.88	3.25
(a) Current Assets	33.44	69.47	87.88	141.11	174.88
(b) Loans and Advances	1.64	2.89	7.42	15.44	16.65
(c) Sub Total (a+b)	35.08	72.35	95.29	156.55	191.53
(d) *Less* Current Liabilities and Provisions	12.30	24.75	27.13	39.66	188.28
(e) Sub Total (a+b+c)	22.78	47.61	68.16	116.88	3.25
Total (1+2+3)	47.85	85.42	126.19	222.51	317.98

Note : Figures in brackets indicate the amounts of equity capital.

Source: Reliance Textile Industries Limited, Annual Report for the year ended 1978 through 1982.

EXHIBIT 3.ii : Summary of Operational Results of Reliance Textile Industries Limited : 1978-82

Particulars	As at the end of December 31, 1978*	1979	1980	1981	1982
Sales (Rs. Crores)	120.11	155.13	207.68	301.66	406.33
Gross Profit** (Rs. Crores)	10.15	12.56	18.09	30.67	43.33
Net Profit (Rs. Crores)	6.56	8.21	11.21	19.70	29.16
Dividend Rate (In Per cent)	27.50	25.00	25.00	35.00	30.00
Earning Per Share (In Rupees)	11.01	10.89	9.30	11.82	15.68
Average Market Price Per Share (In Rupees)	33.00	75.00	86.00	90.00	162.00

Notes: *Relates to the period of 15 months ended on December 31, 1978.

**Profit Before Depreciation and Taxes but after Interest.

1 : 2.4 (Rs. 14.14 crores : Rs. 33.71 crores) to 1 : 2.7 (Rs. 85.74 crores : Rs. 232.23 crores).

3.101 On the side of employment of funds it may be noted that Rs. 314.61 crores (98.63 per cent) stood invested in fixed assets as at the close of December 1982 as against Rs. 25.03 crores (52.31 per cent) in December 1978. As a corollary to this the ratio of current assets to current liabilities reduced sharply from nearly 3 : 1 to almost 1 : 1 meaning thereby that the current assets are just adequate to meet the current liabilities.

3.102 The persual of the summary of operational results presented in Exhibit 3.ii discloses that Sales of the Company went up to Rs. 406.33 crores at the close of December 1982 from Rs. 120.11 crores in December 1978 indicating an increase of over 238 per cent; the gross profit rose to Rs. 43.33 crores from Rs. 10.15 crores or by 326.9 per cent ; and net profit to Rs. 29.16 crores from Rs. 6.55 crores or by 345.2 per cent. The impact of these figures is visible on variables which are of interest to the shareholders and prospective investors. Despite an increase registered in the Equity Capital, Earning per Share rose to Rs. 15.68 from Rs. 11.01 as on the dates under reference. The dividend rate came to be enhanced upto 35.00 per cent for the year ended in December 1981 from 27.5 per cent for the year ended in December 1978. This apart, Reliance declared two Bonus Shares. One, in 1980 in the ratio of 3 : 5 for a total sum of Rs. 4.52 crores and, Second in 1982 in the same ratio for Rs. 11.16 crores. Consequently, the average market price of the equity share touched the peak of Rs. 162 on December 31, 1982 from Rs. 33 on December 31, 1978.

PIONEERING ROLE OF RELIANCE IN POPULARIZING CDs

3.102 Immediately after the publication of Revised Guidelines for the issuance of Rights Debentures from the Office of the CCI, Reliance approached the public first on October 3, 1979 with an Issue of 1,40,000 11% Convertible Secured Debentures (Series I) of Rs. 500 each for cash at par. This Issue was for a total sum of Rs. 7 crores and it carried an option to convert 20 per cent of the face value of Debenture into four equity shares of Rs. 10 each at a premium of Rs. 15/- per share on

January 1, 1981. This Issue came to be oversubscribed by more than 6 times. Noticing the marvellous success of Reliance many other companies also came out with their Issues of CDs which resulted into a scramble for the issuance of CDs. In September 1980 Reliance too made another offer of 8,64,000 — 12% Secured Convertible Debentures (Series II) of Rs. 125 each for cash at par on Rights basis to the Shareholders and Debentureholders (other than Promoters and Non-Residents). This Issue, which also evinced an overwhelming response, aimed at raising Rs. 10.80 crores required for financing the replacement and modernization scheme taken up by the Company during the year 1980.

THE ISSUE

3.103 In 1981, the Company needed more long term funds for financing its planned programs of diversification and modernization. And, in pursuant to the Government Policy that the private corporate sector should become self-reliant in matter of its requirements for long term funds, the Company again decided to raise funds through the floatation of Convertible Debentures. Accordingly, it came out with another Public Issue for Rs. 24 crores comprising of 19,20,000—13.5% Secured Convertible Debentures (Series III) of Rs. 125 each for cash at par on June 10, 1981 with a proviso to convert 20 per cent of the face value of each Debenture into One Equity Share of Rs. 10/- at a premium of Rs. 15/- without any further act or application by the Debentureholder on August 31, 1982. The Debentureholders shall be entitled to receive interest at the aforesaid rate on the full face value of debenture up to the date of allotment of the said Equity Shares. After issue and allotment of Equity Shares on 31st August, 1982 the Company shall pay interest only on the balance face value of the Debenture i.e. Rs. 100/-. Such interest will be payable half yearly on last date of February and the last date of August in each year. After conversion, the balance amount of Rs. 100 shall be redeemed by the Company at par in four equal annual instalments of Rs. 25/- each on the expiry of 9th, 10th, 11th, and 12th year from the date of allotment of the Debentures. The Debentureholders were to be given further the benefit of the issuance of bonus shares if issued prior to the effectualization of conversion as also that of reduction in the premium to be paid on a *pro tanto* basis.

AN APPRAISAL

3.104 To be exact, this Issue was oversubscribed by 7.2 times. Considering the fact that it was the Third Series of Company's Debentures in a short span of less than two years this magnitude of oversubscription can be regarded quite satisfactory from the angle of Managers to the Issue and its Underwriters. The Issue, therefore, can be deemed successful from their angles ; oversubscription by more than seven times of an Issue involving Rs. 24 crores has stamped it for the righteousness of planning and the appropriateness of the marketing strategy adopted from the standpoint of Managers to the Issue and made it amply clear to the underwriters that their services would not be needed at all. It must also provide complacence to some extent to the Company and its corporate managemont for it signalizes them that the funds stand augmented and the Company can go ahead in implementing its planned programs, apart reassuring that investors continue to repose confidence in them and they have found the terms of the Issue upto their expectations. The reckoned cost of Debenture through Internal Rate of Return method as 20 per cent per annum can also be taken to have contributed in building up an optimal capital structure for the Company, as it is much below the actual cost of equity capital as measured in terms of dividend rate (35 per cent in 1981) for the sake of simplicity ; the computations relating to the cost of Debenture are as detailed here. Drawing upon the information contained in the Prospectus of the Issue : Tax Liability of the Company calulates at 60 per cent, 'b' at .6*, and Net Subscription Price per Debenture at Rs. 114.58 on spreading the expenses of the Issue worth Rs. 2 crores on 19,20,000 Debentures of Rs. 125/-

*'b' represents the proporation of Mi (Market price per share at the end of ith period) that will be realizable net if the firm were to issue equity shares to public. Accordingly, 'b' $=\frac{153+25}{2}=89$, and $\frac{89}{153}\times 100=58\%$ or approximately .6.

each. Fitting this data in the relevant equation, where 'k' represent cost of capital, we obtain :

$$114.58=\frac{12.02(1-.6)}{(1+k)}+\frac{8.4375(1-.6)}{(1+k)^2}+\frac{6.75(1-.6)}{(1+k)^3}$$

$$+\frac{6.75(1-.6)}{(1+k)^4}+\frac{6.75(1-.6)}{(1+k)^5}+\frac{6.75(1-.6)}{(1+k)^6}+\frac{6.75(1-.6)}{(1+k)^7}$$

$$+\frac{6.75(1-.6)}{(1+k)^8}+\frac{6.75(1-.6)}{(1+k)^9}+\frac{6.75(1-.6)}{(1+k)^{10}}+\frac{6.75(1-.6)}{(1+k)^{11}}$$

$$+\frac{6.75(1-.6)}{(1+k)^{12}}+\frac{6.75(1-.6)}{(1+k)^{13}}+\frac{6.75(1-.6)}{(1+k)^{14}}+\frac{6.75(1-.6)}{(1+k)^{15}}$$

$$+\frac{6.75(1-.6)}{(1+k)^{16}}+\frac{6.75(1-.6)}{(1+k)^{17}}+\frac{6.75(1-.6)}{(1+k)^{18}}+\frac{5.0625(1-.6)}{(1+k)^{19}}$$

$$+\frac{5.0625(1-.6)}{(1+k)^{20}}+\frac{3.375(1-.6)}{(1+k)^{21}}+\frac{3.375(1-.6)}{(1+k)^{22}}$$

$$+\frac{1.6875(1-.6)}{(1+k)^{23}}+\frac{1.6875(1-.6)}{(1+k)^{24}}+\frac{153\times 1\times .6}{(1+k)^2}+\frac{25}{(1+k)^{18}}$$

$$+\frac{0}{(1+k)^{19}}+\frac{25}{(1+k)^{20}}+\frac{0}{(1+k)^{21}}+\frac{25}{(1+k)^{22}}$$

$$+\frac{0}{(1+k)^{23}}+\frac{25}{(1+k)^{24}}$$

=20 per cent approximately;

so the cost of Debenture per annum is 20 per cent.

3.105 The fact that the Company has since then further resorted to this means of raising funds on a continual basis and in a significant manner also goes to prove the success of this Issue not only from the view point of the Company but also from the angle of the economy. On April 10, 1982 Reliance put forwarded its IVth Series of 40,00,000 Convertible Secured Debentures of the face value of Rs. 125 each by way of Rights, aggregating to Rs. 50 crores, for cash at par to every shareholder, Resident Indian Debentureholders of Series I, II, and III, Resident Holders of the Fixed Deposits of the Company and Business Associates of the Company with a proviso to convert 20% of the face value of each Debenture into one Equity Share of Rs. 10 each at a premium of Rs. 15 per share without any further act or application by the Debentureholder on September 30, 1983. The particulars of the remaining Issues are as thus: On October 3, 1984 the Issue of 53,33,333—13.5% Convertible Secured Debentures (Series E)* of the face value of Rs. 150 each for cash at par aggregating to Rs. 80 crores approximately to be offered to the holders of Equity and Preference Shares, Fixed Deposits, and Debentureholders of Series I, II, III, and IV with an obligation to allot One Equity Share of Rs. 10 each at a premium of Rs. 40 per share in exchange of 33.3 per cent of the face value of each Debenture of Rs. 150 without any further act or application by the Debentureholders on 30th April, 1985; On June 3, 1985 the Issue of 100,00,000—15% Secured Redeemable Non-Convertible Debenetures (Series 'F') of the face value of Rs. 100 each for cash at par aggregating Rs. 100 crores on "Rights Basis" to be offered to the holders of equity/preference shares, Debentures of all Series and Fixed Deposits; and, on December 4, 1986 an Issue of 2,75,86,190—13.5% Secured Fully Convertible Debentures (Series 'G') of Rs. 145 each for cash at par aggregating Rs. 400 crores to be offered partly on Rights Basis to the existing Equity Shareholders, Employees/Workers of the Company/Associate Companies and to Non-Resident Indians/Persons of Indian Origin residing abroad on repartriation basis and partly to the Resident Indian Public with a proviso to compulsorily convert the whole of the Debenture into two Equity Shares of Rs. 10 each and a premium of Rs. 62.50 each per share at the expiry of 12 months from the date of allotment of debentures without any further act or application by the debentureholders as also with a right to retain 25 per cent of the subscription amount in case of its oversubscription. This clearly means that Reliance has been successful in floating as many as six Issues of CDs between October 1979 and December 1986 and through them amplify its long term resources to the tune of Rs. 671.80 crores, as also

---

*With effect from this Series of the Issue the Company started designating the debenture issues by the corresponding Alphabet of English to be denoted in capital letters. Thus the fifth series come to be known as Series 'E'. Likewise, the sixth series 'F', and so on.

two issues of NCDs during the aforesaid period and further augment its resources by Rs. 270.03 crores. Gatherin g of Rs. 941.83 crores through Eight Issues of CDs/NCDs in a period of 8 years and 3 months by a single PLC*pr* itself is a record in the history of the corporate finance, and therefore, needs no specific commendation.

3.106 We can now probe in depth into this Issue from the view point of investors so as to understand the logical forces which persuaded them to respond to it in hearty manner. Not relying on 75 per cent expected bencfit as presented in Table 3.6, this Issue even on a quite conservative estimate carried a minimum return of 44 per cent to a short term investor as indicated in Exhibit 3.iii. Still more pertinent in the context are the rate of return and market price obtained on/for the Debenture of this Issue through internal rate of return method.

EXHIBIT 3.iii : Gain to the Short Term Investor

	Rs. P.
Face value of the Debenture	125.00
Convertible portion of the Debenture	25.00
Non-convertible part of the Debenture	100.00
Sate of one Equity Share say at a Market Price of Rs. 100 per Share*	100.00
Sale of Non-convertible part at a Discount of 20 per cent	80.00
Total Money Received	180.00
Net Gain Per Debenture	55.00
Percentage Return on the Debenture	44%

*The Market Price of the Share was as high as Rs. 153 as on 31.7.1982.

MARKET PRICE OF THE CONVERTIBLE DEBENTURE:

3.107 As per the Daily Quotation List of the Bombay Stock Exchange the market price of the Reliance Equity Shares stood at Rs. 153 on 31.7.1982. The required rate of return is assumed as 8 per cent half yearly i.e. 16 per cent per annum. On the basis of these and other informations, the relevant equation stands developed as under :

Market Price of the Debenture=

$$\frac{12.02}{(1.08)}+\frac{8.4375}{(1.08)^2}+\frac{6.75}{(1.08)^3}+\frac{6.75}{(1.08)^4}$$

$$+\frac{6.75}{(1.08)^5}+\frac{6.75}{(1.08)^6}+\frac{6.75}{(1.08)^7}+\frac{6.75}{(1.08)^8}+\frac{6.75}{(1.08)^9}$$

$$+\frac{6.75}{(1.08)^{10}}+\frac{6.75}{(1.08)^{11}}+\frac{6.75}{(1.08)^{12}}+\frac{6.75}{(1.08)^{13}}+\frac{6.75}{(1.08)^{14}}$$

$$+\frac{6.75}{(1.08)^{15}}+\frac{6.75}{(1.08)^{16}}+\frac{6.75}{(1.08)^{17}}+\frac{6.75}{(1.08)^{18}}$$

$$+\frac{5.0625}{(1.08)^{19}}+\frac{5.0625}{(1.08)^{20}}+\frac{3.375}{(1.08)^{21}}+\frac{3.375}{(1\ 08)^{22}}$$

$$+\frac{1.6875}{(1.08)^{23}}+\frac{1.6875}{(1.08)^{24}}+\frac{153}{(1.08)^2}+\frac{25}{(1.08)^{18}}+\frac{0}{(1.08)^{19}}$$

$$+\frac{25}{(1.08)^{20}}+\frac{0}{(1.08)^{21}}+\frac{25}{(1.08)^{22}}+\frac{0}{(1.08)^{23}}+\frac{25}{(1.08)^{24}}$$

=Rs. 225.02 per Debenture

As against the above price, the actual market price of the Debenture stood at Rs. 217 on July 31, 1982. The fact that the actual market price of the Debenture is found on a higher side and quite close to the computed price of Rs. 225.02 strengthens the possibility of the fulfilment of expectation of the investors in respect to the gain visualized by them.

RATE OF RETURN ON THE DEBENTURE

3.108 Placing the required informations at the appropriate places in the equation, where 'r' represent rate of return, we obtain,

$$125=\frac{12.02}{(1+r)}+\frac{8.4375}{(1+r)^2}+\frac{6.75}{(1+r)^3}+\frac{6.75}{(1+r)^4}+\frac{6.75}{(1+r)^5}$$

$$+\frac{6\ 75}{(1+r)^6}+\frac{6.75}{(1+r)^7}+\frac{6.75}{(1+r)^8}+\frac{6.75}{(1+r)^9}+\frac{6.75}{(1+r)^{10}}+\frac{6.75}{(1+r)^{11}}$$

$$+\frac{6.75}{(1+r)^{12}}+\frac{6.75}{(1+r)^{13}}+\frac{6.75}{(1+r)^{14}}+\frac{6.75}{(1+r)^{15}}+\frac{6.75}{(1+r)^{16}}$$

$$+\frac{6.75}{(1+r)^{17}}+\frac{6.75}{(1+r)^{18}}+\frac{5.0625}{(1+r)^{19}}+\frac{5.0625}{(1+r)^{20}}+\frac{3.375}{(1+r)^{21}}$$

$$+\frac{3.375}{(1+r)^{16}}+\frac{1.6875}{(1+r)^{23}}+\frac{1.6875}{(1+r)^{24}}+\frac{153}{(1+r)^{2}}+\frac{25}{(1+r)^{18}}$$

$$+\frac{0}{(1+r)^{19}}+\frac{25}{(1+r)^{20}}+\frac{0}{(1+r)^{21}}+\frac{25}{(1+r)^{22}}+\frac{0}{(1+r)^{23}}$$

$$+\frac{25}{(1+r)^{24}}$$

=28 per cent half yearly or 56 per cent per annum.

The rate of return of 56 per cent per annum is higher than the return estimated vide Exhibit 3.iii. Also, it appears more realistic. Aside, the Issue was accompanied with assurance to receive the benefits of bonus shares, rights allotment of equity shares, preference shares/debentures etc. Moreover, the Reliance shares having been on the volatile list, the liquidity consideration of the debentureholders stood very well cared for. This Issue can therefore logically be considered successful from the view point of investors.

SUMMARIZING THE REASONS FOR SUCCESSFULNESS OF THIS ISSUE :

3.109 The prime reasons which contributed to an all round success of this public issue of CDs may now be encapsu lated. First, the Reliance is a reasonably diversified and managed company. The deliberations with some of the well executives of the Company convinced us beyond doubt that its corporate management is quite dynamic. Consequent to this, second, corporate and financial planning of the Reliance has been quite rigorous and nearer to realities. Third, the terms of conversion, namely, ratio, price and duration were so designed as to well meet the expectations of the investors. The return on the Debentures was kept and maintained at a level satisfying to all categories of investors. Fourth, the volatileness of the Reliance equities not only met the liquidity consideration of investing public but also its desire to earn more and more on each rupee of investment by steadily pushing up the prices of equity shares and debentures at the different Stock Exchanges. Fifth, like that of earlier issues, in this Issue also the Company assured the Debentureholders about several ancillary benefits to be extended to them at some future date in the shape of bonus shares/rights equity/preference shares and/or debentures. And, Reliance created a history of fulfilling its promises either within/earlier than the committed period.

II. AN UNSUCCESSFUL PUBLIC ISSUE OF CDs : THE SUKHJIT STARCH & CHEMICALS LIMITED PUBLIC ISSUE OF 1,00,000—13.5% SECURED CONVERTIBLE DEBENTURES OF Rs. 100 EACH FOR CASH AT PAR AGGREGATING TO Rs. ONE CRORE—JANUARY 18, 1982.

THE HISTORY & BUSINESS

3.110 The Sukhjit Starch and Chemicals Limited (herein after called 'The Sukhjit' or 'The Company') was incorporated on March 16, 1944, under the Indian Companies Act VII, 1913 as adapted by and applicable in the erstwhile State of Kapurthala (now a District in the State of Punjab). On the same day a Certificate of Entitlement to Commence Business was also obtained by the Company. Since incorporation the Company has been engaged in the manufacture of high quality Maize Starch and Liquid Glucose. And Sukhjit at present is one of the leading manufacturers of this product in the Country.

THE MANAGEMENT :

3.111 The Company is managed by Shri Inder Krishan Sardana, Managing Director, subject to the superintendence, control and direction of the Board of Directors and assistance from professional executives and technical staff employed by the Company for the purpose. It may be mentioned here that from out of 8 membees of the Board of Directors 5 belongs to Sardana Family.

FINANCIAL HIGHLIGHTS :

3.112 The financial track record of the Company has been

EXHIBIT 3.iv : The Summary of Financial and Operational Results of the Sukhjit Starch and Chemicals Limited

Particulars	As at the end of December 31				
	1976 (1)	1977 (2)	1978 (3)	1979 (4)	1980 (5)
Sales (Rs. in Lakhs)	256.45	298.37	338 49	327.64	547.78
Profit before Tax (Rs. in Lakhs)	17.96	29.51	28.63	29.96	68.35
Profit after Tax (Rs. in Lakhs)	7.65	12.25	11.60	11.71	26.84
Rate of Dividend (in Per cent)	20.00	25.00	20.00	12.00*	20.00
Equity Capital (Rs. in Lakhs)	17.98**	17.98	17.98	35.97	35.97***
Net Worth (Rs. in Lakhs)	71.79	79.64	87.65	95.04	42.03
Net Block (Rs. in Lakhs)	25.77	25.85	23.76	24.29	42.03
Long Term Debt (Rs. in Lakhs)	—	—	—	—	141.58
Current Assets and Advances (Rs. in Lakhs)	—	—	—	—	368.65
Current Liabilities and Provisions (Rs. in Lakhs)	—	—	—	—	156.28

Notes: *Paid on increased capital after a Bonus Issue of 1 : 1 during the year ended on December 31, 1979.

**The Company came to be incorporated with an Equity Capital of Rs. 6 lakhs.

***The Equity Capital rose to Rs. 47.95 lakhs including Rs. 2.10 lakhs on account of calls in arrears as on June 30, 1981.

Source: Prospectus relating to the Issue of CDs.

displayed in Exhibit 3.iv for the five year period 1976-80. As may be seen in this Exhibit the Equity Capital of the Company rose to Rs. 47.95 lakhs as on June 30, 1981 from Rs. 17.98 lakhs on December 31,1976 and Rs. 6 lakhs on the date of its incorporation. It indicates an increase of 166.7 per cent between December 1976 and June 1981 and 699.2 per cent between the date of incorporation and June 1981. This rise, however, has been facilitated by the three issues of Bonus Shares and one Issue of Rights Equity Shares affected by the Company between December 1947 and November 1980; the Bonus Shares came to be issued on 31.12.1947 in the ratio of 1:2 for a sum of Rs. 2.99 lakhs, on June 12, 1972 in the ratio of 1:1 for Rs. 8.99 lakhs and on February 6, 1979 in ratio of 1:1 for Rs. 17.98 lakhs. The Company also issued Equity Shares at par for Rs. 11.99 lakhs on the Rights basis in the ratio of 1 : 3 on November 20, 1980. The net worth of the Company also rose to Rs. 115.23 lakhs on December 31, 1980 from Rs. 71.79 lakhs on December 31, 1976 i.e. by 60.51 per cent or by an average annual percentage of 15.13. On the side of sources of funds it may also be noted that the Company further raised funds during 1980 by way of secured loans from banks to the tune of Rs. 110.10 lakhs and unsecured loans in the shape of fixed deposits from the public to the extent of Rs. 31.48 lakhs. Certain features concerning with the Company's application of funds and its operational results may now be added. The Net Block of the Company decelerated, though marginally, from Rs. 25.77 lakhs in December 1976 to Rs. 24.29 lakhs in December 1979. They, however, went up to Rs. 43.03 lakhs by the close of December 1980. As on December 31, 1980 the current assets of the Company stood at Rs. 365.65 lakhs against its current liabilities of Rs. 156.28 lakhs. The sales of the Company registered an increase of Rs. 291.33 lakhs or 113.6 per cent during the period 1976-80; profits before tax by Rs. 50.39 lakhs or 280.6 per cent and profits after tax by Rs. 19.19 lakhs or 250.8 per cent during the aforesaid period. The dividend rate has been kept almost constant at 20 per cent during the period being analyzed; it was declared at a higher rate of 25 per cent in 1977 and at a lower rate of 12 per cent in 1979—the lower rate being on account of the issuance of Bonus Shares.

THE ISSUE OF CDs :

3.113 With a view to raise necessary long term funds for financing the diversification program for Rs. 140 lakhs relating to the establishment of a new unit for manufacturing of Dextrose Monohydrate at its existing location at Phagwara, the Company secured consent from the CCI to float 1,00,000—13.5% Secured Convertible Debentures of Rs. 100 each for cash at par aggregating to Rs. 1 crore; the remaining funds to be arranged through Rights Issue of Capital (Rs. 11.98 lakhs), Internal Generation (Rs. 28.02 lakhs), and Term Loan from Bank (Rs. 25 lakhs). Of the 1,00,000 Debentures, 10,000 Debentures of Rs. 100 each were to be kept reserved for allotment to Promotors, Directors of the Company and their friends and relatives. With the Merchant Banking Division of Grindlays Bank Limited, New Delhi as Managers, Bank of Baroda as an agent and trustees of the Debentureholders and Vinod Kumar & Company, New Delhi as Principal Broker and with prior and full arrangement for underwriting, the Issue was open to the public on January 18, 1982 and came to be closed on the last permissible day i.e. January 29, 1982. Other terms and conditions of the Issue were as thus. Applications for Debentures from the Members of the Public were received for a minimum of 5 Debentures or a multiples thereof. And, for each debenture Rs. 50 was to be paid with application and the rest Rs. 50 on allotment. Besides 13.5% there was a proviso to pay an additional interest at the rate of 1 per cent per annum payable if for the immediately preceding financial year the Company declares dividend at a rate exceeding 20 per cent. The interest will be payable every half yearly on June 30 and December 31 of every year. The Company shall convert 20 per cent of the face value of the debenture into 2 Equity Shares of Rs. 10 each at par after the expiry of one year to be counted from the date of allotment. The balance amount of the Debenture of Rs. 80 shall be redeemable at par in 5 equal annual instalments on the last day in the 8th, 9th, 10th, 11th, and 12th years from the date of allotment of the Debentures. The Equity Shares of the Sukhjit was open traded at Delhi Stock Exchange around the market price of Rs. 25 during the short period which preceded the issuance of CDs.

THE FATE :

3.114 The issue did not receive welcome from the investing public. It remained undersubscribed. As reported by the Financial Express in its Daily of March 27, 1982, the underwriters were called upon on March 24, 1982 to accept their liability for the unsubscribed portion of the Issue or settle it otherwise.

3.115 Undersubscription of the Issue clearly means a failure for its managers and underwriters on the one hand and the Company, its corporate management and investors on the other. From the economy's standpoint also it has been a failure on two important scores. One, the amount involved in this Issue is neither significant from the angle of private corporate sector as a whole, nor from the view point of the Indian economy. Second, it has been the first and perhaps the last attempt on the part of the Company to raise long term funds through the means of debentures. In the light of these hard facts, the relatively low cost of the Debenture as computed through Internal Rate of Return Method (7 per cent pėr annum) also becomes irrelevant for the purpose of drawing any inference in respect to the cost of the capital structure of the Company; the details of the assumptions and calculations in respect to the cost of debenture are as adduced hereunder :

Tax liability of the Company is presumed equal to 60 per cent, 'b'=1.0*, and Net Subscription Price equal to Rs. 90 per Debenture after taking into account the expenses of the Issue which aggregated to Rs. 10 lakhs. Utilizing these at the appropriate places in the equation, we get,

$$90=\frac{5.92\times.4}{(1+k)}+\frac{6.75\times.4}{(1+k)^2}+\frac{5.40\times.4}{(1+k)^3}+\frac{5.40\times.4}{(1+k)^4}$$

$$+\frac{5.40\times.4}{(1+k)^5}+\frac{5.40\times.4}{(1+k)^6}+\frac{5.40\times.4}{(1+k)^7}+\frac{5.40\times.4}{(1+k)^8}$$

*'b' represents the proportion of Mi (Market Price per share at the end of ith period) that will be realizable net if the firm were to issue equity shares to public. Accordingly 'b' $=10+10=\frac{20}{2}=10$, $\frac{10\times100}{10}=100\%$ or 1.0.

$$+\frac{5.40\times.4}{(1+k)^{9}}+\frac{5.40\times.4}{(1+k)^{10}}+\frac{5.40\times.4}{(1+k)^{11}}+\frac{5.40\times.4}{(1+k)^{12}}$$

$$+\frac{5.40\times.4}{(1+k)^{13}}+\frac{5.40\times.4}{(1+k)^{14}}+\frac{5.40\times.4}{(1+k)^{15}}+\frac{5.40\times.4}{(1+k)^{16}}$$

$$+\frac{4.32\times.4}{(1+k)^{17}}+\frac{4.32\times.4}{(1+k)^{18}}+\frac{3.24\times.4}{(1+k)^{19}}+\frac{3.24\times.4}{(1+k)^{20}}$$

$$+\frac{2.16\times.4}{(1+k)^{21}}+\frac{2.16\times.4}{(1+k)^{22}}+\frac{1.08\times.4}{(1+k)^{23}}+\frac{1.08\times.4}{(1+k)^{24}}$$

$$+\frac{2\times10\times1}{(1+k)^{2}}+\frac{16}{(1+k)^{16}}+\frac{0}{(1+k)^{17}}+\frac{16}{(1+k)^{18}}$$

$$+\frac{0}{(1+k)^{19}}+\frac{16}{(1+k)^{20}}+\frac{0}{(1+k)^{21}}+\frac{16}{(1+k)^{22}}$$

$$+\frac{0}{(1+k)^{23}}+\frac{16}{(1+k)^{24}}$$

=7 per cent per annum.

FACTORS RESPONSIBLE FOR THE UNSUCCESSFULNESS OF THIS ISSUE :

3.116 The expected gain entailed in the Debenture, on a most optimistic estimate, has been at a low ebb of 24 per cent per annum. (See, Please, Exhibit 3.v). Even this gain is false so long as it is based on the articulated market price of the share of Rs. 30. It is a well known fact that the equity shares of the Sukhjit came to be traded for a few days prior to the opening of the Issue possibily only among the members of Sardana Family. Though not quoted earlier even a single time, its price reached to the peak of Rs. 30/- per share for the regular trading list. But just after the closure of the Issue, trading in it came to an end. The price sharply declined to Rs. 22/- on 31.3.1982, and thereafter neither any trading nor any quotation of Sukhjit equity share has come to our notice. On this basis the actual market price of the equity share can at best be regarded equal to its face value as on the date of conversion. For the sake of argument if the market price is assumed to be Rs. 30 per share on the date of conversion, then it has to be borne in mind that this price was for a regular trading list and the most of the Deben-

EXHIBIT 3.v : Gain per Debenture

	Rs. P.
Face Value of the Debenture	100.00
Convertible portion of the Debenture	20.00
Non-convertible part of the Debenture	80.00
Sale of 2 Equity Shares at the Claimed Market Price of the Share i.e. @ Rs. 30/- per Share	60.00
Sale of Non-convertible part at a discount of 20 per cent	64.00
Total Money Received	124.00
Less Face Value of the Debenture	100.00
Net Gain per Debenture	24.00
Percentage Return on the Debenture	24%

tureholders were to receive equity shares on the date of conversion not in a trading lot. As a consequence, they must accept a price considerably lower than Rs. 30 per share. In view of these circumstances, the return of 24 per cent per annum in this Debenture was falsifying.

MARKET PRICE OF THE DEBENTURE :

3.117 A more realistic picture in respect to the gain on the Debenture may be presented here with the help of computing the market price and rate of return of/on Debenture with the help of the Internal Rate of Return Method. For the purpose of calculating the market price of the Debenture it is presumed that the market price of the equity shares at the time of conversion was equal to its face value i.e. Rs. 10 per share. The required rate of return is assumed as 8 per cent per half year or 16 per cent per annum. Developing the formula with the help of these and other informations pertaining to the rate of interest offered, redemption schedule and conversion ratio etc. as highlighted above, we obtain,

$$+\frac{5.92}{(1.08)}+\frac{6.75}{(1.08)^2}+\frac{5.40}{(1.08)^3}+\frac{5.40}{(1.08)^4}+\frac{5.40}{(1.08)^5}$$

$$+\frac{5.40}{(1.08)^6}+\frac{5.40}{(1.08)^7}+\frac{5.40}{(1.08)^8}+\frac{5.40}{(1.08)^9}+\frac{5.40}{(1.08)^{10}}$$

$$+\frac{5.40}{(1.08)^{11}}+\frac{5.40}{(1.08)^{12}}+\frac{5.40}{(1.08)^{13}}+\frac{5.40}{(1.08)^{14}}+\frac{5.40}{(1.08)^{15}}$$

$$+\frac{5.40}{(1.08)^{16}}+\frac{4.32}{(1.08)^{17}}+\frac{4.32}{(1.08)^{18}}+\frac{3.24}{(1.08)^{19}}+\frac{3.24}{(1.08)^{20}}$$

$$+\frac{2.16}{(1.08)^{21}}+\frac{2.16}{(1.08)^{22}}+\frac{1.08}{(1.08)^{23}}+\frac{1.08}{(1.08)^{14}}+\frac{2\times 10}{(1.08)^{2}}$$

$$+\frac{16}{(1.08)^{16}}+\frac{0}{(1.08)^{17}}+\frac{16}{(1.08)^{18}}+\frac{0}{(1.08)^{19}}+\frac{16}{(1.08)^{20}}$$

$$+\frac{0}{(1.08)^{21}}+\frac{16}{(1.08)^{22}}+\frac{0}{(1.08)^{23}}+\frac{16}{(1.08)^{24}}$$

$$=\text{Rs. } 89.03$$

The market price of Rs. 89.03 per debenture, which is not even sufficient to cover its face value, must clearly mean a discount of more than 20 per cent for its non-convertible portion.

RATE OF RETURN ON THE DEBENTURE

3.118 Presuming again the market price of the equity share as Rs. 10 on the date of conversion, the equation for the rate of return turns out as given below :

$$100=\frac{5.92}{(1+r)}+\frac{6.75}{(1+r)^2}+\frac{5.40}{(1+r)^3}+\frac{5.40}{(1+r)^4}+\frac{5.40}{(1+r)^5}$$

$$+\frac{5.40}{(1+r)^6}+\frac{5.40}{(1+r)^7}+\frac{5.40}{(1+r)^8}+\frac{5.40}{(1+r)^9}+\frac{5.40}{(1+r)^{10}}$$

$$+\frac{5.40}{(1+r)^{11}}+\frac{5.40}{(1+r)^{12}}+\frac{5.40}{(1+r)^{13}}+\frac{5.40}{(1+r)^{14}}+\frac{5.40}{(1+r)^{15}}$$

$$+\frac{5.40}{(1+r)^{16}}+\frac{4.32}{(1+r)^{17}}+\frac{4.32}{(1+r)^{18}}+\frac{3.24}{(1+r)^{19}}+\frac{3.24}{(1+r)^{20}}$$

$$+\frac{2.16}{(1+r)^{21}}+\frac{2.16}{(1+r)^{22}}+\frac{1.08}{(1+r)^{23}}+\frac{1.08}{(1+r)^{24}}+\frac{2\times10}{(1+r)^{2}}$$

$$=\frac{16}{(1+r)^{16}}+\frac{0}{(1+r)^{17}}+\frac{16}{(1+r)^{18}}+\frac{0}{(1+r)^{19}}+\frac{16}{(1+r)^{20}}$$

$$+\frac{0}{(1+r)^{21}}+\frac{16}{(1+r)^{22}}+\frac{0}{(1+r)^{23}}+\frac{16}{(1+r)^{24}}$$

$=13$ per cent per annum.

At an expected return of 13 per cent per annum, possibility of disposing off the non-convertible part of the debenture at a high rate of discount, and insurmountable difficulties likely to be faced in selling out the non-convertible part in view of the non-volatile character of the equity shares, it seems futile to expect a good response from the investing public; the fact that Sukhjit's shares are rarely traded at the Delhi Stock Exchange and are not listed on other important Stock Exchanges of the country make the entire investment in the securities of this Company, be they are of any nature, as most sticky. Despite a good financial track record of the Company the investors' response to the Sukhjit's Issue was miserable on account of several other reasons. The corporate management did not take any step to disclose its credentials to the investing public. On the contrary it has, rightly also, the perception that *de facto* the Company is a closely held Company. The Company came to be promoted by the Sardana family and this family continues to enjoy its dominance in managing the affairs till this day. The liberal policy of dividend/bonus distribution has been adopted in order to encourage this structural feature of the Company. The management also do not keep informed the investing public about its progress/future programs. No measures have been initiated to get the equity shares listed at the different stock exchanges of the country. These reasons in brief led to the debacle of the Sukhjit's Public Issue of CDs.

III. AN ISSUE OF NON-CONVERTIBLE DEBENTURES/ BONDS : J.K. SYNTHETICS LIMITED ISSUE OF 5,00,000 —13.5% SECURED (SECOND SERIES) REDEEMABLE DEBENTURES OF Rs. 100/- EACH FOR CASH AT PAR AGGREGATING Rs. 5 CRORES—AUGUST 10, 1981.

MAY 1943 : J.K. INVESTMENT TRUST LIMITED

3.119 J.K. Synthetics Limited (hereinafter called the Company) came to be promoted by 'Singhania Industrial House' on May 17, 1943, under the name and style, 'J.K. Investment Trust Limited' with its Registered Office at Kanpur (UP). For over one and a half decade it primarily functioned as an investment company.

MAY 9, 1961 : J.K. SYNTHETICS LIMITED

3.120 In 1958 the Company secured, as part of its long run diversification program, a licence to manufacture Nylon and Perlon Yarn. Consequently it ceased to be recognised as an investment trust company and appeared on the corporate scene, with an altered name, 'J.K. Synthetics Limited', as soon as it obtained a fresh Certificate of Incorporation on May 9, 1961. In July 1977, J.K. Steel & Industries Limited further came to be amalgamated with it.

PIONEER IN PRODUCTION OF NYLON YARN

3.121 Quite soon in January 1962 the Company by commencing trial production and a few weeks after the actual production succeeded in emerging as a pioneer of Nylon Yarn in India.

STEADY DIVERSIFICATION

3.122 Since then the Company registered a significant progress in diversifying its activities. And as of now its range of products can very well be considered diverse and market winning. Included in it are : synthetic fibre-nylon, polyster, acrylic, Sulphuric Acid, Cement-Portland and Pozzolona, Aluminium Caps, Polymerisation poly-condensation, Lactum Melter & Waste Recovery and Complete Spgs. Equipments,

Steel Wires and Ropes, and Turnkey Services in the field of Synthetics manufacture.

INDIA WIDE AND GROWING NET WORK

3.123 The Company's net work spreads all through the Nation. There are manufacturing units at Kanpur, Kota and Nimbahera (Rajasthan), Rishra (West Bengal), and Gaziabad. And, J.K.'s marketing net work reaches out all corners of the country—Amritsar to Calcutta to Coimbator to Bombay.

THE MANAGEMENT

3.124. J.K. Synthetics Limited is managed by a Managing Director subject to the superintendence, direction and control of the Board of Directors which is comprised of eminent and professional persons. The day to day management of the various divisions of the company is run by professionally qualified and experienced managerial, technical and administrative personnel at various level. Further, the Company has the advantage of being benefitted by the rich managerial experience possessed by the members of the House of Singhania.

FINANCIAL HIGHLIGHTS

3.125 The progress registered by the Compay over the years and its financial strength can be gauged in terms of commonly used financial and operational measurements as included in Exhibit 3.vi for the period 1977-82. As indicated above, the Company acquired its present name and shape in 1961-62. And, for the purpose it offered to the public 5,23,750 shares of Rs. 10 at par to the public which raised its capital to Rs. 1.25 crores in 1961-62 from Rs. 0.73 crore in 1960. Since then J.K. Synthetics has registered progress on all fronts. To corroborate, the equity capital, preference share capital and reserves and surpluses of the Company rose to Rs. 15.82 crores, Rs. 1.85 crores and Rs. 51.62 crores as on December 31, 1982 from Rs. 15.00 crores, Rs. 0.75 crore and Rs. 26.90 crores as at the close of December 31, 1977, respectively. This indicate an increase of 5.47 per cent in the equity capital, 146.67 per cent in preference share capital, and 91.90 per cent in reserves and surpluses during the aforesaid period. As regards the increase in equity capital

EXHIBIT 3.iv : Financial and Operational Statistics of J.K. Synthetics Limited

(Figures are in Rs. crores)

Particulars	As at the end of December 31,					
	1977	1978	1979	1980	1981	1982
(1)	(2)	(3)	(4)	(5)	(6)	(7)
Sales	114.84	135.72	153.19	170.57	218.81	255.04
Profit before Tax	13.28	16.04	9.74	6.70	12.00	0.34
Profit after Tax	7.78	9.04	9.74	6.70	12.00	0.34
Equity Capital	15.00	15.00	15.00	15.06	15.41	15.82
Preference Share Capital	0.75	0.75	1.75	1.85	1.85	1.85
Reserves and Surpluses	26.90	31.78	38.78	42.76	52.40	51.62
Total Shareholders' Funds	42.65	47.53	55.53	59.67	69.66	69.29
Loan Funds	22.58	30.82	46.11	60.17	82.41	115.54
(Secured Loans)				(10.01)	(9.86)	(12.78)
Fixed Assets*	34.92	49.68	69.30	88.80	109.80	132.92
Current Assets, Loan and Advances				78.54	93.58	113.68
Current Liabilities and Provisions				52.40	58.31	70.19

EXHIBIT 3.iv (Contd.)

1	2	3	4	5	6	7
RATIOS						
%Return on Capital Employed	24.70	23.90	13.90	12.60	15.30	7.60
%Return on Equity	19.50	20.10	17.80	11.30	17.40	0.20
%Profit before Tax to Sales	20.30	22.40	10.70	6.30	8.50	0.10
%Profit after Tax to Sales	12.20	13.10	10.70	6.30	8.50	0.10
Assets Turnover Ratio	1.70	1.60	1.50	1.40	1.40	1.40
Current Ratio	1.90	1.80	1.60	1.50	1.60	1.60
Dividend Rate (In Percentage)	15	18	18	18	18	10
Dividend Per Equity Share (In Rs.)	1.50	1.80	1.80	1.80	1.80	1.00
Earning Per Equity Share (In Rs.)	5.44	6.60	6.40	4.32	7.67	0.10
Book Value Per Equity Share (In Rs.)	27.93	32.82	35.85	38.39	44.02	42.64

Note: *Net Block plus Capital Work in Progress.

Sources: Annual Report of J.K. Synthetics Ltd. for the year 1981 and 1982.
Prospectus Relating to the Issue of CDs.
Bombay Stock Exchange Official Directory.

it may, however, be noted that the Company's equity capital witnessed a sharp growth between 1966 and 1977 on account of as many as five Bonus Issues : first in 1966 in the ratio of 1:5 for Rs. 0.25 crore, second in 1968 in the ratio of 1:3 for Rs. 0.50 crore, third in 1970 in the ratio of 1:2 for Rs. 1 crore, fourth in 1974 in the ratio of 2:1 for Rs. 6 crores and fifth in 1977 in the ratio of 2:3 for Rs 6 crores. Thus from out of the equity capital of Rs. 15 crores in December 1977, Rs. 13.75 crores (91.67 per cent) came to be added on account of capitalization of reserves and surpluses. The loan funds of the Company went up to Rs. 115.54 crores in December 1982 from Rs. 22.58 crores in December 1977 meaning thereby an increase of Rs. 92.96 crores or 411.69 per cent. Share Capital, Reserves and Surpluses and Loan Funds put together constitute the total operational funds with the Company; these stood at Rs. 184.83 crores as on December 31, 1982 as compared to Rs. 65.23 crores as on December 31, 1977 indicating an increase of Rs. 119.60 crores or 183.35 per cent. The fixed assets of the Company went up to Rs. 132.92 crores from Rs. 34.92 crores during the aforesaid period. Although the current assets and liabilities are growing in absolute terms, their relative position is revealed by the current ratio, which reduced to 1.6 in December 1979 from 1.9 in December 1977. It is however unaltered since then. The sales of the Company rose to Rs. 225.04 crores in December 1982 from Rs. 114.84 crores in December 1977. The profit after tax almost steadily increased to Rs. 12 crores during the year ended in December 1981 from Rs. 7.78 crores for the year ended in December 1977; it dwindled to mere Rs. 0.34 crore in 1982. As a result the Earning Per Share and dividend rate which stood at Rs. 7.67 and 18 per cent in 1981, respectively, also steeply came down to Rs. 0.10 and per cent in 1982, respectively. Even so there can not be two opinions about the financial soundness of this Company.

FEATURES OF THE ISSUE

3.126 On August 10, 1981 the Company came out with a public Issue of 5,00,00—13.5% Secured (Second Series) Redeemable Debentures of Rs. 100 each for cash at par with the explicit objective of augmenting the long term resources of the Company for working capital. The main terms of this Issue are as thus. Over and above 13.5% per annum, an additional interest for any financial year will be payable at the rate of 1 per cent per annum, if for the immediately preceding financial year, the Company declares a dividend on its equity capital at a rate exceeding 17 per cent, such rate to be appropriately adjusted in the event of any further issue of bonus shares that the Company may make subsequent to the present issue of debentures. Further, the Company will affect an upward revision in the rate of interest payable on the Debentures in case the same is announced and permitted by the CCI. The Debentures will be redeemed at par in four equal annual instalments immediately on the expiry of seven years from the date of allotment to all the Debentureholders in the 8th, 9th, 10th, and 11th years. The Company further added another attraction to its Issue in the form of 'Buyback Clause'. Under this the Company agreed to repurchase the Debentures at par value from any holder of Debentures on the fulfilment of two conditions by them. One, the face value of the total holdings of the Debentureholder does not exceed Rs. 25,000/- on the date on which the offer for sale is received by the Company. Second, the Debentures which are offered for sale to the Company are held by the Debentureholder at least for a period of three years. The obligation of the Company to repurchase these Debentures shall, however, cease in any accounting year as soon as the aggregate amount of such repurchase reaches Rs. 25 lakhs. While the State Bank of India, Bombay Main Branch, Bombay agreed to act as the Trustees for the Debentureholders, Merchant Banking Division of the State Bank of India acted as Managers to this Issue. Seven Financial Institutions including the Life Insurance Corporation of India, Unit Trust of India, and General Insurance Corporation of India (Rs. 3 crores), 9 Commercial Banks/Cooperative Banks (Rs. 1.62 crores), and 2 Brokers (Rs. 38 lakhs) consented to act as Underwriters of the Issue to the extent of its full amount.

THE OUT COME

3.127 Although abeted by the House of Singhania, which is well known for its managerial proficiency, and by the

Company's overall good track record of its financial deeds, having put forwarded at the most opportune time evidenced by the market price of the equity shares having stood at Rs. 55 per share* and a period characterised by a scramble for debentures, the Issue could come by subscription only of Rs. 2.29 crores as against the total amount of Rs. 5 crores indicating thereby that the investing public proferred only 45.8 per cent of the total amount desired to be raised by the Company.** It may be mentioned that the Issue remained undersubscribed even though the Company's equity shares are of volatile nature and are listed at all the important stock exchanges of the country. The Issue seems to be well planded. But nothing came to the rescue of this Issue. The Underwriters were required to come forward to subscribe the remaining portion of the Issue i.e. Rs. 2.71 crores. The conclusion is obvious. This Issue was unsuccessful from the angle of all, namely, manager and underwriters to the Issue, the Company and its corporate management, the investing public, and evidently, therefore, also of the economy.

THE CRUNCH

3.128 The blase response to this well planned Issue on the part of investing public was primarily on account of the two major factors. One, the NCDs by their very nature do not fall in the category of well-paid securities. They carry a stipulated rate of interest, which of course is higher than CDs, but without any scope for gaining through capital appreciation. Even if the equity shares are of volatile nature, as is the case with the Issue under analysis, neither the NCDs are frequently traded nor they are quoted on most of the stock exchanges. This feature of NCDs in general, and those of J.K. Synthetics in particular, virtually prohibited the chance for any capital appreciation. This aspect further make the investment in NCDs non-liquid. Second, in the wake of carry forward charges (contogo charge or Badla charges) having ranged between 21 to 25 per cent on the one hand, and a maximum interest rate of 15 per cent per annum on NCDs without any other incentives and the market interest rate

*Average market price of the equity share during the year 1981.

**See, please, the Financial Express, Bombay, Feb. 2, 1982.

structure on similar investments promising a minimum return of above 18 per cent per annum, on the other, it would be almost foolish to expect the prudent investors to invest their monies in NCDs.

THE PROSPECTS

3.129 The future seems to be still more dusky for the NCDs in the light of certain developments which have taken place as of late. While the precise details of these are given in last section of this Chapter, we may enumerate them here in brief. The ancillary benefits granted in the form of assurance to issue at some future date the rights equity shares/convertible debentures, and the premium payable at the time of redemption to the NCD holders have been banned. The maximum interest rate payable on them would now be 14 per cent per annum. The bonds which have come to be issued by the Central Government/Public Sector Undertakings are associated with terms which ensure higher liquidity and returns from the angle of investors. These facts coupled with the findings of the case study clearly emphasize that NCDs do not hold good future in the present frame of legal and economic environment. The PLC*pr* themselves can do not do much also unless they are supported by the Government.

SECTION SIX

ANATOMIZATION OF THE RECORDED RESPONSES

CDs/NCDs ISSUING COMPANIES AND THEIR CORPORATE EXECUTIVES

3.130 Of the 284 Questionnaires mailed to the Corporate Executives of the PLC*pr* which floated CDs/NCDs during the period 1978-82, only 105 i.e. 36.97 per cent of the total were finally available to us duly filled. The industry and region-wise break up of the number of Questionnaires mailed, and the distribution of the respondent companies as per the class of debentures and the corresponding respective response rates have been displayed in Table 3.10 and 3.11, respectively. The perusal of the Tables under reference bears out certain striking and worth mentioning hallmarks. While 54 (51.43 per cent of the total) respondent companies resorted to the issuance of

CDs for the purpose of amplifying their long term resources, the remaining 51 (48.57 per cent) preferrred the issuance of NCDs for the purpose. Industry-wise response rate has been highest in the case of 'Silk, Rayon and Woollen' (57 per cent), followed by 'Iron and Steel' (55 per cent), 'Tobacco' and 'Hotel' (50 per cent each) and 'Cotton' (49 per cent), region-wise it has been so for the Northern Region (62 per cent), followed by Central Region (50 per cent), Southern Region (43 per cent), and Western and Eastern Region (33 per cent each).

REASONS WHICH INCITED PLC*pr* FOR THE FLOATATION OF CDs/NCDs

3.131 Multiple responses recorded by the Corporate Executives highlighting the reasons prompting the respondent companies to raise long term funds through issuance of CDs/NCDs have been classified industry-wise in Table 3.12 and region-wise in Table 3.13. As may be seen in these tables the prominent factors which inspired the respondent companies to resort to this means of raising funds include : 'Cheap Cost of Raising Funds' (82 or 27 per cent of the total multiple responses), 'Denial of Credit by Commercial Banks/Other Public Finance Intermediaries (80 or 26.4 per cent), 'Unfitting Terms & Conditions of Institutional Finance' (69 or 22.8 per cent), and 'Most Favoured Method of Raising Corporate Funds in Vogue' (54 or 17.8 per cent). In few other cases, 'Poor Response Depicted by the Public in Depositing their Savings with the Companies' (10 or 3.3 per cent) and 'Difficulties Faced in the Floatation of an Issue of Equity Shares' (8 or 2.6 per cent) also led to the issuance of CDs/NCDs. The industry-, and region-wise corresponding details may be seen in Column 3 through 17 of Table 3.12 and Column 3 through 7 of Table 3.13, respectively. Broadly speaking they indicate the identical pattern of trends both in respect to industry and region-wise classification of the aforesaid factors.

DEPLOYMENT OF FUNDS RAISED THROUGH THE ISSUANCE OF CDs/NCDs

3.132 The respondent companies further revealed that the bulk portion of the funds raised through CDs/NCDs has been utilized either for financing the new/expansion projects (48 or 45.71 per cent of the total number of respondent companies) or for meeting the working capital needs (44 or 41.90 per cent). Some other purposes to which the funds so raised have been put include: financing the modernization schemes (7 or 6.67 per cent), amalgamation programs (4 or 3.81 per cent) and programs of Diluting the Shareholdings of Non-Residents (2 or 1.90 per cent). The industry-group wise break up of the utilization of funds also bears out broadly an indistinguishable pattern. (See, please, for details, Table 3.14). Region-wise distribution of the utilization of the funds raised through such securities indicates that of the 50.48 per cent respondent companies belonging to Western Region, 20.95 per cent employed their funds for the financing of new/expansion projects, 20 per cent for meeting the working capital requirements and 3.81 per cent each for modernization and amalgamation and 1.90 per cent for diluting the foreign shareholdings. In the Eastern Region of the 16.19 per cent, 8.57 per cent used up the funds in financing new/expansion projects, 5.71 per cent in meeting working capital needs, and the remaining 1.90 per cent in implementing their modernization programs. Almost a similar trend is observed for Northern Regions; of the 15.23 per cent, 7.62 per cent concerned with the project financing and expansion, 6.67 per cent with meeting the working capital needs and 0.95 per cent with modernization. In Southern Region, however, of the 11.43 per cent, 6.67 per cent respondent companies utilized the funds for strengthening their working capital sources, and the rest 4.76 per cent for financing new/expansion projects. (For full details, see, please, Table 3.15). (Annexe VI).

METHODS FOR REDEMPTION

3.133 The information given by the respondent companies in regard to the methods employed for redemption of Debentures on their maturity points out that in majority of cases (76 or 72.4 per cent of the total) they have not made any provision either by way of a creation of Reserve Fund or any other provision for the redemption of debentures on their maturity. 16 or 15.2 per cent respondent companies have, however, created Debenture Redemption Funds for the purpose. And the remaining 13 or 12.4 per cent have determined to fall back upon the Sinking Fund Method for the purpose. (Refer please to Table 3.16 for details). (Annexe VI).

OFFICE BEARERS OF THE STOCK EXCHANGES/ MANAGERS AND UNDERWRITERS TO THE ISSUES/BROKERS/EMINENT ACADEMICS

RESPONSE RATE AND THE NATURE OF THE RESPONSES ANALYZED

3.134 As may be perused in Table 3.17, of the 500 Questionnaires mailed to the prominent Office Bearers of the Stock Exchanges/Managers, Underwriters and Brokers to the Issues/ Eminent Academics, responses could actually be gathered only from 126 respondents belonging to this category. This indicate an overall response rate of nearly 25 per cent; region-wise, it being highest (36 per cent) for the Northern Region and lowest (18 per cent) for the Central Region. While we intended to gather views from the respondents of this category in respect to an exhaustive list of issues concerning with the subject, on editing it was found that their responses relating to the ranks assigned by them to the measures that must be taken by a Company floating an Issue of CDs/NCDs and those concerning with the suggestions for making this class of securities more popular are merely worth analyzing.

MEASURES FOR ENSURING SUCCESS OF THE ISSUES OF CDs/NCDs

3.135 Thus from the total respondents as many as 94 (74.6 per cent), 63 (50 per cent), 52 each (41.3 per cent each), and 37 (29.4 per cent) assigned first rank to 'Revising the Rate of Interest Payable on CDs in an Upward Direction from Time to Time', 'Following and Upward Rising Dividend Policy', 'Keeping Informed the Investors about the Company's Progress and Future Plans', and 'Taking Measures for Ensuring an Active Trading in the Associated Equity Shares/CDs at the Different Stock Exchanges', and 'Declaring Interim Dividends and Issuing Bonus Shares' by way of measures that need to be taken by a Company desirous to witness success in entering the market for raising long term funds with an Issue of CDs/NCDs. (For the details of other ranks, see, please, Table 3.18). Furthermore, over nine-tenths of the respondents (122 or 96.8 per cent expressed their opinion that in case these securities are to be made more popular than the interest rate offered on them must be increased apart developing the secondary market for debentures in the country (as per 119 or 94.4 per cent of the respondents) and extending the benefit of Section 80L of the Income Tax Act 1961 on the investment made in CDs/NCDs (as opined by 118 or 93.6 per cent of the total respondents). Also for the purpose, investing public must be educated about the features and the inherent gains in secured debentures—both CDs and NCDs (90 or 71.4 per cent of the respondents), 'Buy Back Facility' must be extended for the non-convertible part of the CDs (84 or 66.7 per cent), conversion period must be kept as short as possible but in no case more than one year (56 or 44.4 per cent) and the benefit available under section 80CC of the Income Tax Act 1961 must be made available to the Debenture-holders (43 or 34.1 per cent). (Pleare see, Table 3.19 for details).

INDIVIDUAL INVESTORS

RESPONSE RATE & OCCUPATIONAL PATTERN OF THE INVESTORS

3.136 The response rate reckoned out 47 per cent in case of individual investors as 704 from out of 1500 actually furnished us with their filled in Questionnaires. This has, however, been higher for Northern (63 per cent), Western (52 per cent), Southern (51 per cent) and Central (50 per cent) Regions excepting the Eastern Region for which it has rather been poor (23 per cent). (See, please, Table 3.20). In the context it should be of interest to mention that 78.6 per cent (553 in number) of the total respondent investors have been found engaged in 'Services' and 21.4 per cent (151) in one or the other kind of Business/Profession. (See, please Table 3.21) (Annexe VI).

VARIETY OF SAVING INSTRUMENTS PREFERED

3.137 However, as may be seen in Table 3.22, the respondents of both categories invest their surplus monies in the variety of saving instruments perhaps, and rightly also, with a view to satisfy their differing motives. The most preferred saving instruments for the service class of investors are : convertible debentures (553 or 78.6 per cent respondents), LIC Policies (492 or 69.9 per cent), Equity Shares (432 or 61.4 per cent), National Savings Certificates (403 or 57.2 per cent), and Fixed Deposits with Banks (312 or 44.3 per cent). Some of them also invest part of their savings in Fixed Deposits with Non-Banking Companies (156 or 22.2 per cent respondents), Fixed Deposits with Post Offices (113 or 16.1 per cent), ULIP Scheme (105 or 14.9 per cent) and in NCDs (52 or 7.4 per cent); the corresponding position of the Business Class of respondent investors is as thus : Convertible Debentures (151 or 21.4 per cent), LIC Policies (116 or 16.5 per cent), National Savings Certificates (112 or 15.9 per cent), Equity Shares (102 or 14.5 per cent), Fixed Deposits with Banks (43 or 6.1 per cent), ULIP Scheme (22 or 3.1 per cent), Fixed Deposits with Post Offices (12 or 1.7 per cent), and Fixed Deposits with Non-Banking Companies (3 or 0.4 per cent).

ABHORRENCE FOR THE NCDs

3.138 On this basis it is evident that while the Business Class of respondent investors do not prefer to invest at all in NCDs, only an insignificant proportion of those who belong to the service class invest in NCDs. Our deliberations with a select group of individual investors revealed that they do not opt for NCDs primarily on account of an overall poor return on them and the difficulties which they have to face in liquidating them in the absence of regular trading and quotations on the important stock exchanges of the country. They further disclosed that even among the service class only those who have no risk bearing capacity and simply wish to receive a return at a fixed rate and at regular intervals prefer NCDs.

INVESTORS' PREDILECTION FOR CDs EXPLICATED

3.139 Ranks assigned by the respondent investors to the variegated reasons favouring the channelization of their savings in CDs have been unveiled in Table 3.23. It's obvious from the contents of this table that over three-fourths of the respondents have either assigned Rank-1 or Rank-2 to the 'Facility of

Conversion' (Rank-1 by 51.42 per cent of the respondents and Rank-2 by 28.55 per cent) and 'Likelihood of the Capital Gains' (Rank-1 by 42.33 per cent and Rank-2 by 35.79 per cent) meaning thereby that the possibility of capital gains have led the majority of the respondents to go in for CDs. Other factors which have been ascribed high in importance from this angle include 'Easy Marketability' (Rank-1 by 14.63 per cent and Rank-2 by 45.6 per cent), 'Rate of Interest Offered' (Rank-1 by 30.68 per cent and Rank-2 by 21.31 per cent), 'Safety of Funds' (Rank-1 by 12.21 per cent, and Rank-2 by 15.62 per cent), 'Assurance of Issuing Equity Shares/CDs on Rights Basis in the Near Future' (Rank-1 by 3.69 per cent and Rank-2 by 14.91 per cent), 'Advise of Investment Consultant/s' (Rank-1 by 7.53 per cent and Rank-2 by 8.52 per cent), and 'Facility of Receiving the Associated Product/s on a Preferential Basis' (Rank-1 by 2.55 per cent and Rank-2 by 3.98 per cent). (For the rest of the details, see, please Column 5 through 9 of the Table under reference).

CRITERIA GOVERNING THE FINAL SELECTION OF THE SPECIFIC ISSUE OF CDs

3.140 The break down of the responses concerning with the factors governing the selection of the various issues of CDs further corroborates the above finding. If the choice is available the final selection rests on such criteria as 'terms of conversion and other auxiliary benefits' (653 or 92.8 per cent of the total respondents), 'market prices of the associated equity shares at the time of the issuance of the CDs' (587 or 83.4 per cent), 'reports about the profitability and other future growth programs of the concerned companies' (501 or 71.2 per cent), 'reputation and goodwill of the associated companies' (448 or 63.64 per cent), 'extent of the prudence found in the policies of the concerned corporate managements' (411 or 58.4 per cent), 'dividend policies of the related companies' (314 or 44.60 per cent), 'volatileness of the concerned equity shares' (147 or 20.9 per cent), and 'non-availability of other worthwhile securities for investment' (65 or 9.23 per cent). (Refer to Table 3.24 for details, please). (Annexe VI).

INVESTORS' PROPOSALS FOR POPULARIZING CDs/NCDs

3.141 And, for popularizing CDs/NCDs respondent investors have recommended several measures such as : extending the benefit of Section 80L of the Income Tax Act, 1961 on the interest earned on debentures (701 or 99.6 per cent of the total respondents), keeping the conversion period as short as possible but not more than one year (587 or 83.38 per cent), developing the secondary market for debentures (523 or 74.29 per cent), increasing the interest rate offered on CDs/NCDs (508 or 72.16 per cent), educating the public about the features and the inherent gains in secured debentures—both CDs/NCDs (385 or 54.7 per cent), extending the purview of Section 80CC of the Income Tax Act, 1961 so as to cover investments in CDs/NCDs (368 or 52.27 per cent) and making applicable the buy back clause to the non-convertible portion of CDs (367 or 52.13 per cent) (Refer to Table 3.25 for details, please). (Annexe VI).

SECTION SEVEN

APPRAISAL OF THE CONTEMPORARY GOVERNMENT POLICY/OFFICIAL GUIDELINES, PERTINENT PROVISIONS OF THE INCOME TAX ACT, 1961 & THE PRESENT STATE OF AFFAIR OF THE SECONDARY MARKET FOR DEBENTURES

THE EXISTING GOVERNMENT POLICY

3.142 The contemporary policy of the Government of India that the private corporate sector should steadily attain self-reliance in point of meeting its requirement of long term funds and reduce dependence on the nation's finance institutions is certainly appropriate and subservient to the present day circumstances as have already been reviewed side by stating the research problem. Ours is a mixed economy in which both public and private sector are expected to go hand in hand as far as the accomplishment of national aspirations are concerned. Right from the beginning of the First Plan, it has been the Union Government's responsibility to provide necessary finance via budgetary allocations to all the public sector enterprizes. As of late there has however been a change in the thinking of the

Government. Even these enterprizes have been required to generate surplus internal funds by escalating their profitability and raise funds from the general public by way of acceptance of Fixed Deposits and issuance of Debentures/Bonds. It is here lies the hub of the prime deficiency in the Government Policy. The Government has laid down differentiating terms for the issuance of Debentures by the public sector undertakings *vis-a-vis* their counterparts belonging to the private sector. The public sector undertakings are permitted to float debentures either at a rate of interest of 10 per cent per annum and exempted from Income Tax without any limit, or at a rate of interest of 14 per cent and carrying the exemption of interest earned on them under Section 80L of the Income Tax Act, 1961 apart exemption from Wealth Tax without any limit; the private sector enterprizes are not allowed to extend such advantages. However, this distinction is simply not tenable on ground of equity.

CCI's GUIDELINES FOR THE ISSUANCE OF DEBENTURES AND THE RELEVANT PROVISIONS OF THE INCOME TAX ACT, 1961

3.143 Beside the above prejudices observed in the Government Policy, the CCI's present Guidelines for the issuance of Debentures are restrictive for our PLC*pr* on several counts. In plain words the PLC*pr* are not allowed to put their debentures on competitive, lucrative and stimulating terms, particularly from the angle of a prudent investor. The PLC*pr* can not extend the benefit of Section 80L and Wealth Tax Exemption to their Debentureholders. The Guidelines issued on October 27, 1980 rightly introduced the provision alongside the interest rate that in order to make the debentures more attractive to the prospective investors, it would be open to the Company to offer suitable incentives like the issue of debentures at a discount or payment of an additional interest of say upto 1 per cent for any year if in that year the Company declares dividend on its equity at a rate exceeding a previously established rate e.g. the highest rate of dividend declared in the three years preceeding the debenture issue. On April 17, 1982 the Government drew a distinction between CDs and NCDs in respect of ceiling on the interest rate. While the then existing 13.5 per cent interest was maintained for the CDs, Government decided to increase the interest rate to 15 per cent per annum for NCDs. But with this the incentive of 1 per cent came to be withdrawn for all debentures; although a premium upto 5 per cent of the face value could be allowed by the Companies on NCDs at the time of their redemption. Even the payment of this premium has been banned now by the Government. On September 17, 1984 a provision was incorporated in the Guidelines that, "in case of non-convertible debentures or non-convertible portion of convertible debentures, a company may have the option of getting the debentures converted into equity fully with the approval of and at such price as may be determined by the Controller of Capital Issues. The debentureholders, will, however, be free not to exercise their right." However, on June 10, 1986, the Government announced a ban on the conversion of non-convertible debentures as also of the non-convertible portion of partially convertible debentures with immediate effect. It is also stipulated that these debentures would in future continue to be extinguished strictly according to the terms of their issue.[17] On March 16, 1987 the Government further announced, as part of the restructuring of the nation's interest rate structure, that with effect from April 1, 1987 the maximum rate of interest payable on CDs and NCDs would be 12.5 per cent and 14 per cent per annum, respectevely. All of these modifications are certainly not appreciable. The specific stipulation that in future debentures are to be blow out exactly in accordance with the terms of the issue is particularly ruinous as the same has introduced inflexibility in the Guidelines. It is to harm all the Companies, Debentureholders and the Economy of the Country.

3.144 The CCI's Guidelines are further deficient in respect to the period of redemption. As per the existing proviso these debentures are redeemable not before the expiry of a period of seven years. And as per the actual terms most of the debentures so far issued are redeemable in five equal annual instalments at the end of 8th, 9th, 10th, 11th, and 12th, years to be counted from the date of allotment. Thus the amount invested in debentures stands redeemed only at the close of

12th year in its entirety. Neither the existing proviso of the Guidelines relating to the period of redemption nor the actul practice in this respect is appealing to the investing public. Repayment of capital in instalments spread over a period of five years is just not acceptable to the debentureholders. Hence, the Guidelines are skimpy in so far as they do not provide for the redemption of debentures issued by PLC*pr* in full just after the expiry of the period of seven years on the lines of Bonds floated by public undertakings. As a matter of fact we can even conceive of alternate plans for the redemption of debentures in the light of variations found in the gestation periods and the profitablity patterns of the variegated projects.

3.145 The Guidelines clearly state that the permission for the issuance of debentures will be given to any PLC*pr* only when (i) the concerned debentures have been listed on the stock exchange, (ii) the shares of the Company proposing to issue the debentures have bcen listed at one or more Stock Exchanges, and (iii) the market quotation of its equity shares heve been at or above par value during the six months prior to the date of application for issue of debentures. These conditions seem to have been injected for taking care of the liquidity aspect of the debentures and of the equity shares to be obtained for the convertible portion of the CDs. Furthuer these appear to accomplish success for the Companies by certifying to the investing public that their wealth in the Company is not only safe but carries chance of growing. Our absorbed investigation into the Isssues of CDs/NCDs floated by PLC*pr* during the period 1978-82 takes us to assume a different position. The above provisions are scanty as they have not been able to guarantee volatileness of the correlated equity shares, an essentiality for achieving the objectives expressed as above; our study has vividly established that a positive and significant relationship is observed between the volatileness of associated equities and the market prices of equities and debentures. Furthermore, it's not enough to evaluate market quotations for the six months period and that the market price has either been at or above par value. For the success of an Issues of CDs the market price of the correlated equity must have been and should be expected to remain above par value:

for an Issue of NCDs to witness a good fate, beside an attractive rate of interest, they must come to be traded and quoted at different Stock Exchanges and their terms should invariably include assurances for the grant of auxiliary benefites. Another flaw of the present Guidelines is the non-existence of the provision covering stipulations concerning with the conversion ratio, price and duration. Our Issue-by-Issue analysis has revealed that, though not primarily, terms of conversion of an Issue does affect its success. To reiterate the main inference, higher the proportion of convertibility and nearer the date of conversion, better would be the response of the invseting public provided the market price of the associated equity is reasonably higher than its face value without resort to any articulation. Further, no mechanism is found in the Guidelines by which the CCI can regulate the misleading advertisements quite often affected via brochures published for private circulation by the Debentures Issuing Companies in regard to the return on investment in them. The exercise finished by us in this regard with the help of IRR Method revealed a significant gap in the publicized and the actual percentages of returns on the various varieties of debentures. Being the custodion of investing public, the CCI must devise some method as part of Guidelines by which such malpractices could be checked.

THE PRESENT STATE OF AFFAIRS OF THE SECONDARY MARKET FOR DEBENTURES

3.146 The Working Group chaired by Shri N. N. Pai, which submitted its report on the subject in January 1982, clearly admitted that the then position of the market for debentures in India has been quite grim. What disturbs us most is the fact that since then the situation has gone down the hill. The availability of market quotations only for the select CDs and nearly absence of market quotations for the NCDs bears out this overriding truth. The issuance of the chunk portion of the total amount involved in different issues of NCDs on rights basis (Rs. 343.16 crores or 80.07 per cent of the total sum raised during the period 1978-82) and quite a good portion in this manner in the case of CDs (Rs. 203.05 crores or 31.53 per cent of the total sum raised during the aforesaid period) further provides an evidence to the effect that the debentures in general and NCDs in particular are not fondling securities to the category of individual investors.

3.147 While there is no need to reiterate the circumstances which explain the urgency for developing an active market for debentures in India, we may count up the factors which have inhibited the development of such a market so far. Until recently debentures have come to be sparingly used for raising long term funds by limited companies of the Indian Corporate Sector; these having become more cherished since 1978 with the PLC*pr* and February 1986 with the public sector undertakings. The Government including the Reserve Bank of India has time and again shown inclination to promote a secondary market for debentures. It was in tune with this keenness that the working group referred to above was set up for suggesting measures far developing a secondary market for debentures. Some of the recommendations were accepted and implemented too at the time of announcing revised guidelines in April 1982. What bewilders us most is that the Report of the Pai Group, which is said to have contained several useful recommendations for making debenture issues popular, has yet not been made public. Quite contrary to the required positive steps, the Government is now allowing public sector undertakings to issue debentures on terms which are more attractive than those designed for the PLC*pr*. The Union Government itself has introduced Indira Vikas Patras and National Savings Certificates VIth and VII Series which carry more enticing terms and tax benefits. Supreimposed over this environment is the unaware ness of our investing populace about the merits and demerits of this security.

3.148 Although listed at one or more Stock Exchanges debentures put forwarded in India by both, PLC*pr* and public enterprizes are not of volatile nature. The total volume of trading in debentures at stock exchanges is rather negligible in magnitude and majority of them are not regularly and frequently quoted. Consequent to this, at times they even fail to satisfy the liquidity motive of the investing public; no doubt, NCDs of PLC*pr* carry Buy Back Clause and Bonds of Public Sector undertakings are freely transferable by endorsement and delivery. Pertinent is this context is another fact. The number of Stock Exchanges in India is inadequate. They are even not sufficient to cater to the needs of urban population. Clearly therefore rural inhabitants are altogether unaware even with the phenomenon of stock exchange.

3.149 The debentures issued by PLC*pr* do not even entitle their holders tax benefits under Section 80L of the Income Tax Act, 1961 and exemption under Wealth Tax Act for which they rightfully deserve. The monetary gain in the from of interest and capital appreciation is incommensurating in the light of their stringent terms of redemption and the opportunity available to the investing public to put surplus monies in more rewarding securities like Indira Vikas Patras/National Savings Certificates/Bonds of Public Sector Enterprizes, etc. Doubling of money without any sort of risk just in five years time,[18] should be preferred by the investors as compared to CDs/NCDs so long as no Income Tax benefit is available either in Indira Vikas Patras or CDs/NCDs and Vikas Patras remain transferable simply by delivery. While in NCDs return is slightly on a higher side, they are redeemable after the expiry of seven years that too in five annual instalments ending with as ahead a twelfth year; the liquidity in NCDs too is far low then that found in Vikas Patras. Likewise, the total return for CDs may certainly calculate at a higher level in contrast to Vikas Patras, but then the maturity period is longer and we find an element of uncertainty in the return in the case of former. The Bonds of public sector undertaking too have an edge over CDs/NCDs on acount of various tax benefits, higher liquidity and redemption in full immediately after the expiry of the period of seven years. And, on account of the coverage of investment in National Savings Certificates under Section 80C of Income Tax Act 1961, these are considered far superior particularly by the section of the people falling under income tax brackets, even though the return is slightly less.

3.150 Irrespective of the stumbling blocks observed in the path of devlopment of an active market for debentures and the experience of our PLC*pr*, investing public and the economy in respect to the issuance of debentures in general and CDs in particular, this mode of security, either in its present or in some modified form, shall have to be made as the one most sought-after by the investing public no matter however comprehensive improvements are required to be affected for the purpose.

NOTES

1. For Example, Spencer & Company Limited entered into a prior arrangement to secure the chunk portion of subscription from military funds for its Issue of NCDs floated on 16.6.1982 for a sum of Rs. One Crore @ 13.5 per cent per annum in order to augment its resources for working capital.
2. The Stock Exchange Official Directory, Bombay, '*Weekly Replacement Service*', Monday, April 20, 1981, p. 34.
3. Ibidem; also, see, please, Kuchhal, S.C., '*Financial Management : An Analytical and Conceptual Approach*', Chaitanya Publishing House, University Road, Allahabad-211 002, pp. 587-607.
4. Kuchhal, S.C., Op. Cit.
5. The age of different companies has been counted from the date of their incorporation. And, the six groups have been constituted as thus. Companies which came into existence upto the close of 1931 have been clubbed at one place so as to indicate an age over 51 years; Companies established during the period 1932-41 reflect an age in the range of 41 to 50 years; companies securing their incorporation certificates between 1942 and 1951 resulted into the creation of an age group of 31 to 40 years; companies which were set up between the years falling in the period 1952-61 represent an age in the range of 21 to 30 years; companies to whom the Certificates of Incorporation were granted between 1962 and 1971 emanated the age class of 11 to 20 years; and, the companies to whom the incorporation certificates were addicted during the period 1972-82 spawned the age group indicating an age up to 10 years. The first age group has been styled, 'Old PLCpr' (OPLCpr); the next three age classes have been clubbed and designated as 'Middle Aged PLCpr' (MAPLCpr); and, the rest of the two age groups have been added and assigned the caption of 'Relatively New PLCpr (RNPLCpr).
6. These Five Regions, 12 States and One Union Territory are : (*i*) Northern Region which covers the States of Haryana, Punjab and the Union Territory of Delhi; (*ii*) Eastern Region which includes the States of Orissa and West Bengal; (*iii*) Central Region which encompasses the States of Madhya Pradesh and Uttar Pradesh; (*iv*) Western Region which comprises the States of Gujarat and Maharashtra; and (*v*) Southern Region which comprehends the States of Andhra Pradesh, Karnataka, Kerala and Tamil Nadu.

7. Bombay Dying and Mfg. Co. Limited, Bombay to which CCI granted its approval on 28.12.1982 has not been regarded as the aftermost company of the period 1978-82 in the issuance of CDs because it's entire issue of Rs. 12 crores was placed on a rights basis. Similarly, the Nagarjuna Steel Limited, Hyderabad to which consent was given by CCI to float an Issue of CDs for Rs. 2.50 crores on 24.12.1982 has been skipped for it could not see its actual placement in the market on account of cancellation of 10.4.1983.
8. Andrew Yule Company Limited, Calcutta, which received CCI's sanction on 13.3.1978, has not been considered as the first company of the period 1978-82 in the sphere of issuing NCDs because the entire subscription of Rs. 25 lakhs was made by West Bengal Industrial Development Corporation Limited. Likewise, Nagarjuna Steel Company, Hyderabad has not been counted as the aftermost company floating NCDs during the aforesaid period on the same ground; the entire consented amount of Rs. 1.25 crores having subscribed by an Army Group.
9. See, please, Annexe I-Part-C 3, of this Study.
10. Ibidem.
11. Grindlays Bank p.i.c., Bombay as Managers to the Issue, 'Prospecuts', Premier Mills Limited, January 27, 1982. pp. 1-4.
12. The Industrial Credit and Investment Corporation of India Limited, the Merchant Banking Division, Bombay, as Managers to the Issue, 'Prospectus', Guest Keen Williams Limited, Calcutta, August 23, 1982, p.1.
13. Champaklal Investment & Financial Consultancy Limited, as Managers to the Issue, 'Prospectus', The Ahmedabad Shri Ramkrishna Mills Company Limited, Ahmedabad, November 30, 1981, p. 3.
14. Grindlays Bank Limited, Merchant Banking Division, New Delhi, as Managers to the Issue, 'Prospectus', The Sukhjit Starch & Chemicals Limited, Phagwara, January 18, 1982, p.3.
15. State Bank of India, Merchant Banking Division, as Managers to the Issue, 'Prospectus' The General Industrial Society Limited, Calcutta, May 10, 1982, p.1.
16. These Issues are the same as those selected by Prasanna Chandra in his title, 'Financial Management : Theory and Practice', Chapter 28, Tata McGraw-Hill Publishing Company Limited, New Delhi, 1984, pp. 635-47. The equations too have been adopted almost with the same symbols, excepting certain minor alterations. However, the assumptions and the inferences drawn are entirely ours.
17. The Journal of the Indian Institute of Bankers, Volume 57, April-June 1986, No. 2, 'Editorial Notes', p. 88.
18. Effective from April 1, 1987 the period of maturity for the Indira Vikas Patras has been extended from five years to five and a half years.

4

THE CONCLUSION

— COALESCENCE
— AFFIRMATION OF HYPOTHESES
— THE REALIZED TASK
— MOST CONDUCIVE THEORETICAL & OPERATIVE FRAMEWORK
— CONGROUS THEORETICAL DISPOSITION
— SUBSERVIENT OPERATIVE FRAME
— FAVOURED AMENDMENTS IN THE INCOME TAX & WEALTH TAX ACTS
— MODIFYING THE CCI'S GUIDELINES
— OPENING OF NEW STOCK EXCHANGES & COUNTERS AT THE STOCK EXCHANGES
— FORTIFICATION OF THE MARKET FOR DEBENTURES
— CONSIDERATIONS TO BE KEPT IN MIND BY THE INVESTING PUBLIC WHILE PURCHASING, SELLING AND RETAINING CDs/NCDs

COALESCENCE

If we put together and intermix the inferences drawn from the marco and microscopic analysis undertaken by us in regard to the CCI's permissions accorded in favour of 284 PLC*pr* for raising long term founds through the issuance of CDs/NCDs between January 1978 and December 1982 on such bases as MRTP and Other than MRTP Companies, Year-, Industry-, Age-, and Region/State/Union Territory-wise distribution, Public and Rights Issues, adjudging successfulness/unsuccessfulness of the Public Issues of CDs from the angle of issuing companies, investors and the economy as a whole, values reckoned out with the help of IRR method of the maket price, rate of return and cost of different variants of CDs and, Case Studies accomplished to represent most successful/unsuccessful Public Issues of CDs and an Issue of NCDs etc. and from the responses recorded by our respondents, then we get to the undermentioned generalized conclusions on the subject chosen for an indepth exploration.

AFFIRMATION OF HYPOTHESES

1. CONVERTIBLE DEBENTURES/BONDS ARE PREFERRED OVER NON-CONVERTIBLE DEBENTURES/BONDS BY BOTH THE INVESTING PUBLIC AND THE CORPORATE MANAGEMENTS

4.2 Enough evidences have been found for avouchment of all the three hypotheses of this research endeavour. Thus the CDs which gained popularity since 1978 are regarded superior *vis-a-vis* NCDs not only by the investing public but also by the corporate managements of PLC*pr*. That the investing public prefers CDs over NCDs is borne out by numerous facts. While all the 704 respondent investors disclosed that they have invested a part of their savings in CDs, only 7.4 per cent of them further have NCDs in their investment portfolio. The interest revealed by then in assigning ranks to the variegated reasons favouring investment in CDs and identifying the factors governing the selection among the various issues the CDs further signify the favour of respondent investors towards this security. The marked predilection of the investing public for CDs is also obvious by a number of trends observed in this work in respect to the Issues of CDs/NCDs affected by PCL*pr* for raising long term funds to meet their variety of needs. During the period 1978-82 PLC*pr* raised nearly Rs. 644 crores through CDs and Rs. 429 crores via NCDs. While over 68 per cent (nearly Rs. 441 crores) of the total funds mobilized by flotation of CDs came from public, the proportion of similar funds in case of NCDs measured about 20 per cent (Rs. 85 crores). Non-appearance of market quotations of NCDs provides a dependable indication of the situation that trading in NCDs at different stock exchanges is negligible; although the position of CDs in this respect is also not very cheering. The case study completed for the Issue of NCDs floated by J.K. Synthetics (August 10, 1981) plausibly brought to our notice that NCDs are not preferred by the investing public on account of certain weaknesses inherent in them. Unless some compensatory benefits are appended to NCDs they may not appeal the prudent investor.

4.3 The corporate managements seem to be quite aware that it's not an easy task to raise funds from the public via NCDs. Hence the aforesaid trend of placing the major portions of the Issues of NCDs on rights bases. Again it has been made possible seemingly in most of cases with prior arrangements with some finance and/or other surplus spending institutions. Of the three categories of PLC*pr*, RNPLC*pr* & OPLC*pr* have raised negligible funds through NCDs. As indicated above, on the whole also the PLC*pr* raised larger funds with the help of CDs during 1978-82 as compared to NCDs; no doubt, in terms of number it is latter's performance (193 Issues) which superceded that of the former (91 Issues) during the aforesaid period. Further the record of Reliance. which augmented maximal funds through secureed debentures, reveals that from out of 8 Issues of Debentures floated by it between October 1979 and December 1986, 6 were of CDs and 2 that of NCDs. The Issues of CDs amplified Reliance resources to the extent of Rs. 671 80 crores and the NCDs by Rs. 270.03 crores. Even so the success of Public Issues of CDs can not be taken as granted. The Companies keen to float CDs must visibly demonstrate their financial superiority to the investing public in terms of payment of dividends regularly and at a steadily rising rate, bonus issues, growing owners' wealth measured by rising trend in market price of equity shares, etc.

2. ISSUES OF CDs ASSOCIATED WITH EQUITY SHARES OF VOLATILE NATURE, CONSTANT/RISING TREND IN MARKET PRICES OF CORRELATED EQUITY SHARES, ALLURING TERMS OF CONVERSION, AUXILIARY BENEFITS AND BACKED BY REGULAR CORPORATE BRIEFS HAVE MET WITH COMMANDING SUCCESS:

4.4 The Hypothesis-2 has been avowed but with certain refinement. The analysis undertaken in respect to the relationship between the prices of equity shares and convertible debentures of 15 PLC*pr* of category 'A' (Volatile) and 12 PLC*pr* of category 'B' (Non-Volatile) with the help of reckoned out values of 'r', 'r^2', '$\bar{V}$', and C.V. and concern of these values with the oversubscription clearly bears out that volatile character of associated equity shares generally have a positive impact on the success of a public issue of CDs. We may recall here that irrespective of the relatively large sums involved in the public issues of CDs floated by 15 PLC*pr* of category 'A' the number of times of oversubscription stood at more than 8 times in 7 cases (46.7 per cent of the total), 6 times in 3 cases (20 per cent) and between 2 and 5 times in the remaining cases (33.3 per cent); the relative position for the 12 PLC*pr* of category 'B' being 3 (25 per cent), 2 (16.7 per cent), and 7 (58.3 per cent), respectively. Volatileness of the correlated equity shares itself, however, is not a sufficient condition for the success of an issue of Public CDs. If the prices of equity shares fluctuate significantly both in upward and downward direction then the chances of witnessing marked success for the concerned Issue/s of CDs are quite dim; relevant details of the public issues of CDs as floated by Delhi Cloth and General Mills Company Limited, Metal Box Company of India Ltd., and TELCO fully confirm what has been said. On the contrary if the volatileness results into a consistent and a steady rise in the market prices of shares followed by those pertaining to CDs then the grand success of the public issues of CDs is certain as evidenced by the concerned details of the Issues of Reliance Textile Industries Limited (Third Series), Straw Products Limited, and Indian Rayon Corporation Limited. The expected gain from an investment in CDs is determined by the market price of the correlated equity shares. Therefore, this price, whatever it is at the time of the issuance of CDs should either remain constant or it should move upward in case the gain is to increase not only on the date of conversion but with the passage of time. The character of volatileness in equity shares, it may be noticed, is simply an instrumental for affecting the expected gains via taking up the degree of liquidity of both the correlated equity shares and CDs at the different stock exchanges of the country. It should therefore be amply clear that the 'Volatileness of the Correlated Equity Shares' influences the success of an Issue through manipulation in the expected rate of return on CDs and the degree of liquidity of CDs and Associated Equity Shares. And volatileness can play a role in the success of a public issue of CDs only in those situations where its impact on expected return is found positive.

4.5 The terms of conversion have also come to influence the fortune of an Issue. Higher the conversion ratio, lower the conversion price, and nearer the date of conversion, better has been the response from the investing public. Since terms of conversion stand represented automatically in the computed percentages of expected gains and the dates of their actual availability to the debentureholders no independent proofs have been possible. Likewise the announced auxiliary benefits in the shape of issuing bonus shares/equity shares/CDs on rights bases and insertion of news items on a regular basis in respect to the progress, future programs of the Company has been found to bear a positive relationship with the success of the issues, although independent negative evidences on this score are missing. This study, therefore, confirms an improved version of Hypothesis-2 which read as thus: Issues of CDs associated with Equity Shares of Volatile nature, constant/rising trend in the market prices of correlated equity shares, alluring terms of conversion, promises to grant auxiliary benefits and backed by regular corporate briefs have met with a commanding success. As a corollory to this it follows that the Issues floated by PLC*pr* of category 'B' and accompanied by relatively less rewarding terms of conversion plus no promise to receive any other kind of benefit/s with no practice of corporate briefs have either come to be undersubscribed or oversubscribed to a little/an insignificant extent; the details of the Issues of Mahindra Mills Limited, Raymond Woollen Mills Limited, Usha Alloys and Steels Limited and Ferro Alloys Corporation Limited may be glanced in the context.

3. ISSUES OF CDs CARRY MISLEADING PUBLICIZED RETURNS AND LESS THAN THE DESIRED DEGREE OF LIQUIDITY:

4.6 The illustrative values of the returns calculated by employing IRR Method confirm that the returns to the holders of CDs as publicized by the PLC*pr* are quite misleading; they have been found significantly low in three cases from out of the five attempted by us. As a matter of fact the publicized returns are reckoned ignoring the time aspect involved in them. In view of the non-appearance of market quotations for as many as 40 Issues of CDs placed on Rights basis and ?4 Issues of Public CDs (64 Issues or 70.3 per cent of the total) it is further affirmed that the degree of liquidity found in CDs is less than what is desired by the investing public. So the Hypothesis-3 of this study also stands testified.

THE REALIZED TASK

4.7 Naskara Jute Company was first to raise capital during the post independence era through debentures. Roughly it was since fifties that Limited Companies of the private corporate sector started, though sporadically, issuing Convertible Debentures. Their efforts, however, did not see any meaningful success until the beginning of Seventies; welcoming response from the investing public having first of all secured by the Standard Mills, Bharat Bijili, Camphore and Allied Products, and National Manufacturing during the period 1971-77.

CONSENTS ACCORDED, AND THE MAGNITUDE OF THE FUNDS RAISED:

4.8 In all CCI granted consents for the floatation of 284 Issues of CDs/NCDs worth nearly Rs. 1,073 crores during the five year period 1978-82. Of these, sanctions for nearly Rs. 644 crores were for 91 Issues of CDs and rest for Rs. 429 crores for 193 Issues of NCDs. The largest beneficiaries of the CCI's permissions have however been the PLC*pr* covered under MRTP Group both in point of the issuance of CDs and NCDs. The year-wise trends indicate that on the whole there has been a steady increase in the number and the amount involved in the permissions granted by the CCI for the floatation of debentures since 1978 and these rose to 90 for over Rs. 516 crores during 1982.

RELATIONSHIP OF INDUSTRY GROUP/NATURE OF PRODUCTS/SERVICES WITH RAISING OF FUNDS THROUGH DEBENTURES:

4.9 Though the industry wise drifts in respect to the different categories of debentures such as public and rights CDs and NCDs are quite inconsistent with each other, on the whole it has been observed that the PLC*pr* occupied in product/service lines providing faster opportunities for growth/diversification like Chemicals, Silk, Rayon, and Woollens, Engineering or which additionally guarantee about attractive and faster returns such as Cotton Textiles, Hotel and Commerce have preferred to augment their resources through debentures as against those found operating in industry groups like 'Tea Plantation', 'Sugar', 'Jute Textiles', 'Rubber and Rubber Mfg', and 'Electricity Generation and Supply'.

AGE OF THE COMPANY AND ITS IMPACT ON THE SELECTION OF THE MODE FOR RAISING LONG TERM FUNDS :

4.10 The Old and Medium-aged PLC*pr*, which *inter alia* represent a group of companies having their age over 21 years, have been found more confident in point of raising long term funds through the public issues of CDs as compared to Relatively New PLC*pr* whose age is upto 20 years. However, it is the Relatively New and Middle Aged PLC*pr* which actually employed CDs in a big way during the period 1978-82. These put together floated 72 Issues of CDs for Rs. 445 crores. The Old PLCpr raised only Rs. 199 crores with the aid of 19 Issues of CDs; probably, they are financially most sound and generate larger internal funds. As against this NCDs find favour with Middle Aged PLCpr perhaps on account of their overall larger needs for funds and the confidence they have in articulating the required support from the investing public/institutions. Relatively New PLC*pr* seem to be hesitant due to the doubt they have about their success, Old PLC*pr* possibly did not feel the need for resorting to this rather shaky means.

LOCATION AND DEBENTURES :

4.11 During the period under review 69 Issues of CDs for over Rs. 517 crores (76 and 80 per cent of the respective totals) were putforwarded by those PLC*pr* which are located in industrially developed States/Metropolitan City like Maharashtra, Gujarat and West Bengal (Calcutta). Almost an identical situation exists in respect to the Issues of NCDs; the aforesaid States/Metropolitan City accounted for 142 Issues (74 per cent of the total) which entailed over Rs. 312 crores (73 per cent).

PURPOSES MET :

4.12 The examination of the CCI's record of approvals unveiled on this score that while CDs have primarlly been employed by the PLC*pr* for gathering long term funds required for meeting working capital requirements and financing expansion/replacement/modernization/diversification projects, NCDs' basic assistance has been for strengthening the companies' base of working capital. In a few cases CDs came to be issued for accumulating medium term funds and the long term funds needed for affecting reduction in the holdings of non-residents, and implementing rehabilitation programs. Likewise, a few Issues of NCDs helped out execution of amalgamation schemes in the private corporate sector.

SCHEMA OF APPROPRIATE YARDSTICKS FOR PRONOUNCING THE SUCCESSFULNESS/UNSUCCESSFULNESS OF THE PUBLIC ISSUES OF CDs :

4.13 From the stand point of Companies, their Corporate Managements, and Managers/Underwriters to the Issues, the success/failure of an Issue of Public CDs needs to be adjudicated in terms of such criteria as oversubscription/undersubscription, number of times an Issue is oversubscribed with reference to the total amount involved, impact of funds raised on the company's capital structure, market prices of correlated equity shares/debentures and volume of trading in them at the parent and other stock exchanges during the period prior to and after the actual allotment of CDs. The prime considerations for the investors are expected rate of return, terms of conversion, auxiliary benefits affixed with the issue, volatile character of the associated equity shares, and the Company's policy to put on corporate briefs on a regular basis. The volume of funds mobilized through all types of debentures by PLC*pr* put together in a given period and the role played by them in restraining inflationary conditions can determine the success of this security from the angle of the nation's economy. On an integrated scale and from the short term perspective a public issue of CDs would be regarded as successful if it involves a sizeable amount; comes to be held widely; secures an overwhelming response from the investing public evidenced by the commendable number of times of oversubscription; leans toward the creation of an optimum capital structure; carries an attractive rate of interest, preferably with a proviso to affect revision alongside the changes made by CCI, and a frame of terms which may ensure debentureholders maximum possible return; backed up by a competent and dynamic corporate management capable of devising worthwhile projects and taking measures necessary for imparting the character of volatileness to the equity shares, and steadily increasing/maintaining their market price, and keeping the shareholders/debentureholders/public well informed about the progress/future programs of the enterprize under its charge. In the long run, debentureholders have further been interested in higher liquidity and redemption yield, fulfilment of the assurance/s extended in the shape of auxiliary benefits, and the survival and prosperity of the Company with its laudable image in the society.

LIST OF SUCCESSFUL/UNSUCCESSFUL PUBLIC ISSUES OF CDs.

4.14. Out of 51 Public Issues of CDs for which consents were accorded by the CCI during 1978-82, 4 did not see theis floatation on account of the non-availment/subsequent cancellation of the permissions. The findings which emerged out on examining the remaining issues on the basis of the integral check list of criteria drawn for the purpose are as follows. 5 Issuer have been unsuccessful; these in descending order include the Issues of Sukhjit Starch and Chemicals, Ahmedabad Shri Ramkrishna Mills Company, Premier Mills, General Industrial Society, and Guest Keen Williams. The rest 42 have been successful placed, as they are, in four categories. The first, which has been named as 'Successful Public Issues of CDs', covers again in a descending order, 7 Issues, put out by Dunlop India, Ahmedabad Advance Mills, Bharat Steel Tubes, Bharat Vijay Mills, Mahindra Mills, Vardhman Spg. and General Mills, and Shri Digvijay Woollen Mills. The second group has been designated as 'Relatively More Successful Public Issues of CDs'. 8 Issues covered under this group in the descending order are those belonging to Keshoram Industries and Cotton Mills, Elecon Engineering, Star Industrial and Textiles Enterprize, Jyoti, Shri Dinesh Mills, Fibre Glass Pilkington, Cellulose Products of India, and Punjab Anand Batteries. 11 Issues are found embraced in another class named as 'Quite Successful Issues'; these are as thus in the aforesaid order: the Issues floated by the ITC, Hindustan Development Corporation, Indian Hotels Company, Kothari (Madras), Ferro Alloys Corporation, Ranbaxy Laboratories, Gujarat Steel Tubes, Raymond Woollen Mills, Camphor & Allied Products, and Rustom Mills and Industries (both occupying ninth rank in the group) and Usha Alloys and Steels. In the last category captioned as, 'Most Successful Issues of CDs', 15* Public Issues of CDs putforwarded by 14 PLC*pr* are included, namely, Reliance Textile

*Excluded the Indian Rayon Corporation's another Issue of CDs floated on 25.1.83.

Industries (Third Series), TELCO, Gwalior Rayon Silk Mfg. (Wvg.) Company, J.K. Synthetics, Indian Rayon Corporation, TISCO, East India Hotels, Delhi Cloth and General Mills, Mukand Iron and Steel Works, Straw Products, Voltas, Zenith, Steel Pipes and Industries, Metal Box Company of India and Lohia Machines.

INVESTMENT OPPORTUNITY ENTAILED IN CDs

4.15 A review of rates of return calculated by employing the IRR Method on the selected issues to represent the different variants of CDs as presented in section four of this Chapter reveals that the return is maximum in the case of fully convertible debenture. It is the minimum in CDs with a Right to Subscribe and position of partly convertible debenture is found in between the two from this angle. As regards this inference we should however note that it is not based on a wider sample and the values under analysis are based on specific market prices of the correlated equity shares. Clearly, therefore, the value would differ depending upon the level of market price of equity share. The rates of returns are further influenced by conversion ratio, price and period. The aggregate return on a specific issue of CDs is further influenced by its expected market price reckoned with the help of IRR Method; and, this in its turn is affected by the maket price of the associated equity shares. Thus the above finding can at best be said to provide a crude estimate about the investment gains offerd by the variegated types of CDs to the investing public.

THE GUIDING LIGHT SPARKED BY THE ACCOMPLISHED CASE STUDIES:

4.16 The Case Study concluded in respect to the most successful public issue of CDs, namly, the Third Series of Debentures of the Reliance, brought to our notice that the main contributing factors to the observed success have been the diversified nature of the activities of the Company, dynamism of the Corporate Management, rigorous and realistic corporate planning including the one undertaken in relation to the Issue. The planning affected in respect to this Issue took care very well of its terms of conversion, volatileness of the correlated equity shares and the resultant market prices of the shares and debentures at different stock exchanges, announced ancillary benefits and the timely fulfilment of the promises made for the purpose, and keeping debentureholders/prospective investors/other interested persons about the company's present progress/future programs of growth. As against this the Case Study sewed up for the most unsuccessful public issue of CDs as floated by Sukhjit Strach & Chemicals Limited disclosed that the basic reasons responsible for its failure have been the low percentage of expected gain, clear possibility of not realizing even this low return on account of the manipulation done by the company's management in artificially pushing up the market price of the equity shares just before the opening of the Issue, sharp decline of the market price of the equity shares during the period following immediately after the closure of the Issue, and virtual absence of trading in equity shares even at the parent stock exchange and the related quotations, non-listing of the equity shares at stock exchanges other than Delhi Stock Exchange, unawareness of the investing public about the credentials of the corporate management the *de facto* status of the the Company being closely held, absence of the practice of putting up corporate briefs on a regular basis, etc.

IMPLICIT WEAKNESSES OF NCDs & THEIR FUTURE PROSPECTS :

4.17 And from the Case Study completed in respect to an Issue of NCDs it's abundantly clear that even the NCDs of well diversified and managed company like J.K. Synthetics are not preferred by the investing public for they are neither well rewarded nor possess desired degree of liqudity despite the associated equity shares being of volatile nature. As a matter of fact they carry a fixed return without having any chance of gaining through capital appreciation or by some other incentive. Aside, the burden of contogo charge is as heavy as 25 per cent. In view of these snags, which have further been accentuated by the changes recently affected in the Guidelines and the developments of money and capital market, the futuer of NCDs does not apear to be bright unless certain strategic measures are taken in order to alter the climate surrounding them.

MOST CONDUCIVE THEORETICAL & OPERATIVE FRAMEWORK

CONGRUOUS THEORETICAL DISPOSITION:

4.18 In India both CDs and NCDs are being employed by PLC*pr* primarily to raise long term debt capital; no doubt, a portion, and in a few selected case, the whole of the amount of CDs has also come to aid in gathering equity capital. Accordingly, the prevalent theoretical notion about CDs/NCDs, both in Government Circle and among corporate financial executives, is to treat them as a means of amplifing 'debt' capital. Nothing wrong in this conception so long as we are concerned with NCDs. This precept, however, needs ratification in regard to CDs. These must be considered basically the fit instrument for augmenting the base of 'equity capital'. The CCI should, therefore, permit either the floatation of NCDs for raising debt capital or Fully Convertible Debentures for strengthening the grounding of equity capital; the permission for the latter being recommendable in the situations where the immediate raising of equity capital is found inconvenient for any reason/undesirable on grounds of principels for sound financial management.

SUBSERVIENT OPERATIVE FRAME:

4.19 Overall policy of the Union Government, legal grounding provided by the CCI's Guidelines, Income Tax and Wealth Tax Acts of this land, and the structure and conditions of the capital market and stock exchanges of the country create the necessary operative frame for the issuance of CDs/NCDs by the PLC*pr*. Given the commended theoretical notion and the deficiencies observed in the present Policy of the Union Government/CCI's Guidelines/relevant provisions of the Income Tax and Wealth Tax Acts on the one hand, and considering on merits the pertinent responses of the corporate executives/academics/investors on the other, we may venture here to suggest as under.

FAVOURED AMENDMENTS IN THE INCOME TAX & WEALTH TAX ACTS:

4.20 The principles of justice and equity warrants that the applicability of Section 80L of the Income Tax Act, 1961 should be extended to cover the interest earned till the date of conversion by the holders of CDs put out by PLC*pr*. Further it should be permissible for the PLC*pr* to extend the option to its debentureholders that the interest earned on CDs could also be exempted completely from income tax in case they are prepared to accept a lower rate of interest on the pattern followed in case of Bonds of Public Sector Undertakings. On the date these CDs are converted into the equity shares, this investment of debentureholders should come to obtain exemption from income tax under a new section to be introduced on the lines of 80CC with a view to encourage investing public to invest CDs intended to raise additional capital by the existing companies. The interest earned by the holders of NCDs till their redemption should be treated alike that of CDs i.e. by covering income on NCDs under Section 80L of the Income Tax Act. PLC*pr* in this case too should be free to grant choice to the debentureholders to go for NCDs totally exempt from income tax, provided, of course, they accept a lower rate of interest. Further, Section 80CC of the Income Tax Act should be amended to include the investment in NCDs provided they are not liquidated prior to the date of redemption. Also the CDs/NCDs of PLC*pr* must be made fully exempted from wealth tax.

MODIFYING THE CCI's GUIDELINES:

4.21 The present guidelines of the CCI pertaining to the issuance of secured debentures by limited companies of the private corporate sector must be modified on the lines recommended hereunder.

(i) Only two varieties of secured debentures should be allowed to be floated by PLC*pr*' namely, Non-Convertible Debentures/Bonds, and Fully Convertible Debentures/Bonds. Obviously, therefore, the CCI must specifically mention it its Guidelines that issuance of Partly Convertible Debentures and the Debentures carrying Rights to Subscribe or Equity Shares in Lieu of Interest Accrued will not be permissible.

(ii) The interest rate which has recently been reduced by 1 per cent per annum on both CDs and NCDs should not only be restored back, but the possibility of raising it further should be seriously examined in view of the persuasive need for adequately compensating the investors at least to the extent the general price level registers rise. The recommended rise is further justified so long as securities like Bonds of public sector undertakings, Indira Vikas Patras and National Savings Certificates continue to enjoy special treatment under Income and Wealth Tax Acts, as also in point of their redemption. The provision for payment of an additional incentive interest upto 1 per cent per annum over and above the usual rate be reintroduced. Furthermore, provision should be made for permitting companies to affect an upward revision in the interest rates on the debentures already found in circulation. Aside, it should be obligatory in terms of law for the debenture issuing PLC*pr* to post in advance the Post-Dated Interest Warrants.

(iii) The premium earlier payable on NCDs at the time of their redemption at a maximum of 5 per cent of their face value should also be restored back and the limit for the payment of premium should be enhanced to 10 per cent of the face value of relevant NCDs.

(iv) The NCDs should be made redeemable after seven years in full and in one instalment like that of the Bonds of public sector undertakings. The convertible debentures on the other hand should be made fully convertible in one or more instalments but within a maximum period of 2 to 3 years.

(v) The permission to float CDs be given only to that PLC*pr* the equity shares of which are of volatile nature and are being quoted at a premium over a minimum period of say one year instead of six months as prescribed now.

(vi) The terms of conversion should also be regulated statutorily in case of CDs. The conversion price may be allowed to be fixed by the concerned company in such a manner which may ensure a gain of at least 10 per cent by way of capital appreciation. Similarly 50 per cent portion of the debentures should come to converted in a maximum period of one year to be counted from the date of actual allotment.

(vii) The ban on announcing auxiliary benefits in the shape of assurance to issue Bonus Shares/Equity Shares/Debentures on a Rights Basis to the debentureholders at some future date with the issues of CDs/NCDs should be lifted. As a matter of fact these benefits may be allowed to diversify.

(viii) It should be made obligatory for all the debenture issuing companies to publish corporate briefs in the important one/two national daily/dailies highlighting their accomplishments and future programs after the lapse of a fixed time interval. And this time interval should not exceed the period of 3 months.

(ix) Only those brochures concerning with the Issues of CDs/NCDs should be allowed to permeate the investing public which have been approved by the CCI. The publication of brochures by the PLCpr under the caption, 'For Private Circulation Only' should not only be banned but treated as cognizable offence.

OPENING OF NEW STOCK EXCHANGES AND COUNTERS AT THE STOCK EXCHANGES :

4.22 The Stock Exchange facility should be made available at all such centres where the population is 5 lakhs or more by opening new stock exchanges at such centres where they do not exist already. Further the Reserve Bank of India should consider the proposal of opening counters at all the stock exchanges where debentures, both CDs and NCDs, could be purchased and sold at pre-determined prices. These counters be established and run by the stock exchange authorities in joint colloboration with commercial banks, other finance institutions, the companies, and brokers. And, it is the consortium of these which would determine buying and selling prices of debentures and also affect changes therein from time to time.

FORTIFICATION OF THE MARKET FOR DEBENTURES

4.23 Aside the aforesaid suggestions which are to contribute to the cause of promoting a market for debentures in India in a big way, further strides in this direction can be made through launching a systematic program, utilizing all available media of communication, for educating the public living in urban as well as rural areas in respect to the debentures/bonds. It can be jointly taken up by the Government, Stock Exchanges, Limited Companies, Commercial Banks, and other finance institutions. The Government should consider two more measures for the purpose. One, permitting the inter-corporate funds and a portion of the provident and superannuation funds to flow into the debentures. Second, allowing the corporate sector to issue "on demand debentures", repayable on demand by a holder and also reissuable to others till the time of redemption. The stock exchange authorities must publish the market quotations of as many as debentures as possible in their Quotation Lists. The PLC*pr* in their turn should open centres at least in metropolitan cities/to give affect to the 'buy back clause' back clause' affixed with the issues of debentures.

CONSIDERATIONS TO BE KEPT IN MIND BY THE INVESTING PUBLIC WHILE PURCHASING, SELLING AND RETAINING CDs/NCDs :

4.24 In a decision for purchasing CDs the investing public must carefully study the concerned company's/companies' location, nature of products/services, extent of diversification, corporate management, financial and operational statistics, status in respect to the volatileness and market price of its equity shares, policy in point of keeping investors informed about its progress/future programs and such features of the Issues as the terms of conversion, and affixed ancillary benefits; but for the terms of conversion same factors have to be given cognizance while selecting NCDs. This study suggests that the investing public must prefer the issues of CDs/NCDs placed in the market by PLC*pr* located in developed states; engaged in such product lines which could provide/guarantee faster growth/diversification/attractive returns like chemicals, silk, rayon, and woollens, engineerings, hotel, cotton textiles, and commerce; managed by competent and dynamic corporate management as evidenced by impressive financial and operational results; the equity shares of which are of volatile character and the market price indicate a steadily rising trend if seen over a period of time; corporate briefs of which are found appearing in one/more national daily/dailies; and the whole gamut of the terms guarantee an overall reasonably high but realistic return. A few words of caution may be added here. The buying decisions should not be allowed to rest on the fascinating advertisements put out by the companies/managers to issues highlighting progress/future prospects in terms of rosy language/alluring returns. These should neither be made on the basis of the returns publicized by the concerned companies through some brochures meant for private circulation. Further, a slightly lower return which has good chances of realization be preferred than a high return with less prospects of it being attained. The question of selling and retaining are inter-related at least in one sense namely, those issues which are not regarded fit for selling can naturally be retained. The CDs whose correlated equity shares show a declining trend in terms of their market prices during the period followed by their allotment and there appears no chance of recovery on the basis of company's current progress/future programs of growth or whose promises for the grant of specific ancillary benefits do not come to materialize in a reasonable period of time, should be dispensed with in due course. The CDs whose associated equity shares are witnessing constant trend in their market prices and there is no hope within the foreseeable future for these prices to rise, then such CDs too can be sold out. Thus the CDs whose equity shares are witnessing an upward trend in their market price, be it small, and whose announced benefits are come to be paid may be retained. The same principles should pay dividends to the investing public in regard to the selling and retaining of NCDs. The investing public should, however, not forget that it must always obey side by side the general principles of investment such as the principle of not putting all eggs into one basket, principle of cycling of investments, etc.

4.25 On implementation of the aforesaid recommendations an internal environment would come to establish which would successfully enable the Indian Private Corporate Sector to take on debentures on a continual basis for mustering long term funds on most conducive terms to it, investors and the economy as a whole.

ANNEXE I

- GUIDELINES FOR THE ISSUANCE OF DEBENTURES
- SEPTEMBER 30, 1978
- OCTOBER 27, 1980
- APRIL 17, 1982
- GUIDELINES FOR THE PROTECTION OF INTEREST OF DEBENTUREHOLDERS—JANUARY, 15, 1987

PART-A

GUIDELINES FOR ISSUE OF "RIGHTS" DEBENTURES BY PUBLIC LIMITFD COMPANIES FOR WORKING CAPITAL REQUIREMENTS : SEPTEMBER 30, 1978.

Government have considered the question of issue of 'rights' debentures by public limited companies for working capital requirements and have formulated the following guidelines in this behalf :

1. These guidelines will apply to only those issues of secured debentures by public limited companies which are "Rights" issues to their shareholders and the objeet of which is to augment the longterm resources of the company for working capital requirements and to reduce its dependence on fixed deposits from the public, loans from shareholders and other short-term borrowings. They will not apply if the issues are not "Rights" issues or if the object of the issue is to raise long-term funds for any other purpose, such as the financing of a new or expansion project, addition to fixed assets, investments, etc.

2. The amount of the debenture issue will not exceed
   (a) 20 per cent of the gross current assets, loans and advances minus the long-term funds presently available for financing working capital, or
   (b) 20 per cent of the paid-up share capital including preference capital, and free reserves, whichever is lower of the two. The amount so arrived at will be rounded off to the nearest multiple of Rs. 25 lakhs.

NOTE : For this purpose,

(i) "Long-term funds" will mean :

(a) Paid-up share capital, including preference capital, and free reserves; and

(b) all term loans, debentures and bonds with an initial maturity period of five years or more including interest accrued thereon. It also includes all deferred payment liabilities, but it does not include short-term bank borrowings and advances, unsecured deposits or loans from the public, shareholders and employees, and unsecured loans or deposits from others.

(ii) "Free reserves" will mean all reserves created out of profits and share premium account. It will not include reserves created out of revaluation of assets, write-back of depreciation provisions, amalgamation, etc.

(iii) "Long-term funds presently available for financing working capital" will mean the long-term funds mentioned under (i) above minus the net block of fixed assets and investments.

3. The debt-equity ratio, including the proposed debenture issue, should not exceed 1:1.

NOTE : For this purpose,

(i) "Debt" will mean the long-term borrowings as defined under para 2 (i) (b) above plus the proposed debenture issue.

(ii) "Equity" will mean paid-up share capital, including preference capital and free reserves, as defined under para 2 (i) (a) above.

(iii) The computations under guidelines 2 and 3 will be based on the latest available audited balance sheet of the company.

4. The bebentures will carry the following rate of interest which will be papablc half-yearly :

(i) 10.5% if the maturity period of the debentures is upto and including 7 years; and

(ii) 11% if the maturity period of the debentures is from 8 to 12 years.

However, in order to make the debentures more attractive to the prospective investors, it is open to a company to offer suitable incentives like, for example, issue of the debentures at a discount or payment of an additional interest of say ½ per cent for any year if, in that year, the company declares dividend on its equity at the rate exceeding a previously established rate, (e.g., the highest rate of dividend declared in the 3 years preceding the debenture issue).

5. The debentures will be redeemed as follows :

   (i) In the case of debentures with a maturity period upto 7 years, 33⅓ per cent of the debentures will be repaid uniformly to all the debenture holders in the 5th, 6th, and 7th years.

   (ii) In the case of debentures with a maturity period upto 12 years, 20 per cent of the debentures will be repaid uniformly to all the debentureholders in the 8th, 9th, 10th, 11th and 12th years.

6. The face value of the debentures will be Rs. 100 with a view to enhancing the scope for subscription, especially by the smaller share holders, and to increase the marketability of the debentures.

7. The debentures shall be listed on the Stock Exchanges.

8. The company should be a listed company and its equity shares must have quoted on the Stock Exchange at or above the par value in the six months prior to the date of the application for the issue of debentures.

9. The debentures shall first be offered to the existing Indian resident shareholders of the company on a pro-rata basis. (The non-resident shareholders will not be entitled to the offer). The offer to the shareholders shall be kept open for a minimum period of two months. The unsubscribed debentures, if any, will be offered on a rational basis to :—

(i) those shareholders of the company interested in taking up additional allotment;

(ii) the depositors of the company; and

(iii) the employees and business associates of the company.

Applications from the above categories can be invited simultaneously with the offer to the shareholders. If any portion of the issue still remains unsubscribed, the Board of Directors of the company can dispose it off in such manner as they deem fit. The depositors of the company could be given an option, if feasible, to convert their unsecured deposits with the company into the secured debentures.

10. The company shall proceed to allot the debentures only after a minimum subscription of 75 per cent of the amount of the debenture issue has been secured.

11. The issue need not be underwritten, but having regard to the above mentioned "minimum subscription" requirement, and the fact that the issue is a "Rights" issue, companies would be well advised to ascertain beforehand the prospects of at least 75 per cent of the issue being taken up by the shareholders of the company, specially the larger shareholders and the other categories mentioned under guideline 9.

12. So long as the debentures are outstanding, the Directors of the company shall certify in their annual Report to the shareholders that the funds raised through the debentures have been utilised for the purpose for which they were raised and that they have not been diverted for any other purpose.

In order to expedite the processing of the applications under the Capital Issues (Control) Act, 1947, companies are advised to make clear the position in respect of each of the guidelines mentioned above either through a covering letter or in their application itself.*

**Source* : Government of India, Ministry of Finanee, Department of Economic Affairs, Investment Division, New Delhi, '*Press Release, September 30th, 1978.*

PART-B

GUIDELINES FOR ISSUE OF DEBENTURES BY PUBLIC LIMITED COMPANIES, OCTOBER 27, 1980.

Government have considered the question of issuing guidelines for issue of debentures by public limited companies and have now formulated the following guidelines in this behalf :—

1. *Objects of Issue :* The guidelines will apply only to those issues of secured debentures by public listed companies to the public. The object of the issue can be either to raise long-term funds for the financing of any expansion or diversification project, or to augment the long-term resources of the company for working capital requirements.

2. *Quantum :* The amount of debentures, in the case of working capital requirements, shall not exceed 20 per cent of the gross current assets, loans and advances. The amount of issue of debentures for project financing will be considered on the basis of the approvals of the scheme of finance by the financial institutions/Government under M.R.T.P. Act, etc.

3. *Debt-Equity Ratio :* The debt-equity ratio, including the proposed debentures issue, shall not exceed 2:1.

NOTE : For this purpose—

(i) 'debt' will mean all term loans, debentures and bonds with an initial maturity period of five years or more, including interest accrued thereon. It also includes all deferred payment liabilities, but it does not include short term bank borrowings and advances, unsecured deposits or loans from the public, shareholders and employees, and unsecured loans or deposits from others. It should also include the proposed debenture issue.

(ii) 'equity' will mean paid up share capital including preference capital and free reserves.

(iii) The computations under guidelines 2 and 3 will be based on the latest available audited balance sheet of the company.

A relaxation in the norm of debt-equity ratio of 2 : 1 will be considered favourably for capital-intensive projects, such as fertilizers, petro-chemicals, cement, paper, shipping, etc.

4. *Interest Rate :* The debentures shall carry a rate of interest not exceeding 12 per cent per annum (increased to 13.5 per cent by Press Release dated the 2nd March, 1981). However, in order to make the debentures more attractive to the prospective investors, it is open to the company to offer suitable incentives like, for exampie, the issue of debentures at a discount, or payment of an additional interest of, say, upto 1 per cent for any year if in that year the company declares dividened on its equity at a rate exceeding a previously established rate (e.g. the highest rate of dividend declared in the three years preceding the debenture issue).

5. *Period :* The debentures shall not be redeemable before the expiry of a period of seven years.

6. The face value of the debentures will ordinarily be Rs. 100 each.

7. The debentures shall be listed on the Stock Exchange.

8. The company proposing to issue the debentures to the public should be a listed one and its equity shares must have been quoted on the Stock Exchange at or above the par value during the six months prior to the date of application for issue of debentures.

9. The issue of debentures shall be underwritten. A relaxation is permitted in this regard if the Controller of Capital Issues is otherwise satisfied that the issue need not be underwritten.

10. Only secured debentures would be permitted for issue to the publlc.*

**Source :* Government of India, Ministry of Finance, Department of Economic Affairs, New Delhi, '*Press Release*', *October 27, 1980.*

PART-C

GUIDELINES FOR ISSUE OF DEBENTURES—REVISED APRIL 17, 1982.

Government have issued revised guidelines for issue of debentures to the public by public limited listed companies. The revised guidelines make a distinction between convertible and non-convertible debentures in respect of ceiling on the interest rate. While the existing 13.5 per cent interest is maintained for the issue of convertible debentures, Government have increased the ceiling on interest rate to 15 per cent per annum in the case of non-convertible debentures. The incentive of 1 per cent has been withdrawn for all debentures. In order to make the non-convertible debentures attractive, a premium upto 5 per cent of the face value of the debentures may also be allowed by companies at the time of redemption of these debentures.

REVISED GUIDELINES FOR ISSUE OF DEBENTURES BY PUBLIC LIMITED COMPANIES

These guidelines are issued in supersession of the guidelines issued by Government on the 27th October 1980.

1. *Apylicability :* The guidelines will apply to issue of secured convertible as well as non-convertible debentures by public listed companies.

2. *Objects of Issues :* The object of the issue can be either to raise long-term funds for the financing of any expansion or diversification project or to augment the long-term resources of the company for worknig capital requirements.

3. *Quantum of Issue :* The amount of issue of debentures in the case of working capital requirements shall not exceed 20

per cent of the gross current assets, loans and advances. The amount of issue of debentures for project financing will be considered on the basis of the approvals of the scheme of finance by the financial institutions/Government under the provisions of the M.R.T.P. Act, etc.

4. *Debt-Equity ratio :* The debt-equity ratio, including the proposed debenture issue will, not normally exceed 2 : 1. For this purpose—

'debt' will mean all term loans, debentures and bonds with an initial maturity period of five years or more, including interest accrued thereon. It also includes all deferred payment liabilities but it does not include short-term bank borrowings and advances, unsecured deposits or loans from the public, shareholders and employees, and unsecured loans or deposits from others. It should also include the proposed debenture issue.

'Equity' will mean paid up share capital including preference capital and free reserves.

NOTE : 1. The computations under guidelines 3 and 4 mentioned above will be based on the latest available audited Balance Sheet of the Company.

2. A relaxation in the norm of debt-equity ratio of 2 : 1 will be considered favourably for capital intensive projects such as fertilizers, petro-chemical, cement, paper, shipping, etc.

5. *Interest rate :* In the case of convertible debentures the rate of interest shall not exceed 13.5 per cent per annum. In the case of non-convertible debentures the rate of interest shall not exceed 15 per cent per annum.

6. *Period at redemption :* The debentures shall not be redeemable before the expiry of a period of seven years.

7. *Price of the time of redemption :* A premium upto 5 per cent of the faee value can be allowed at the time of redemption in the case of non-convertible debentures only.

8. The face valve of the debentures will ordinarily be Rs. 100 each.

9. The debentures shall be listed on the Stock Exchange.

10. Only secured debentures will be permitted for issue to the public.

11. The issue of debentures shall be underwritten. A relaxation is permitted in this regard if the Controller of Capital Issues is otherwise satisfied that the issue need not be underwritten.

12. The shares of the company proposing to issue the debenture must be listed in one or more stock exchanges and the market quotation of its equity shares must have been at or above per value during the six months prior to the date of application for issue of debentures.*

**Source* : Government of India, Ministry of Finance, Department of Economic Affairs, New Delhi, *'Press Release'*, *April 17, 1982.*

PATR-D

GUIDELINES ISSUED BY THE CCI FOR THE PROTECTION OF INTEREST OF DEBENTURE-HOLDERS—JANUARY 15, 1987.

Government have been considering for some time, to issue certain guidelines in the interest of debentureholders, which would facilitate the serviceability and repayment of debentures to the debentureholders on time. The guidelines have now been finalised and are as enumerated below.

1. Servicing of Debentures

A Debenture Redemption Reserve (DRR) shall be created by all companies raising resources through debentures on the following basis :

(a) A moratorium up to the date of commercial production can be provided for creation of the debenture redemption reserve in respect of debentures raised for project finance.

(b) The debenture redemption reserve may be created either in equal instalments for the remaining period or higher amounts if profits permit.

(c) Company should create DRR equivalent to 50 per cent of the amount of debenture issue before debenture redemption commences. Drawal from DRR is permissible for redemption purposes only after 40 per cent of the debenture liability has been actually redeemed by the company.

(d) In case of convertible debentures DRR should be created in respect of non-convertible portion of debenture issue on the same lines as applicable for non-convertible debenture issue.

In respect of convertible issues by new companies, the creation of DRR should commence from the year the company earns profits for the remaining life of debentures.

(e) Companies may distribute dividends out of general reserves in certain years if residual profits after transfer to DRR are inadequate to distributc reasonable dividends.

(f) DRR will be treated as a part of General Reserve for consideration of bonus issue proposals and for price fixation related to post tax return.

(g) In case of new companies distribution of dividend shall require approval of the trustees to the issue and the lead institution, if any.

(h) In the case of existing companies prior permission of the leading institution for declaring dividend exceeding 20 per cent or as per the loan covenents is institutional condition regarding interest and debt service coverage ratio.

(i) Companies may redeem debentures in greater number of instalments. The first instalment may start from 5th instead of seven year.

II. Protection of Debentureholders' Interests :

(i) Trustees to the debenture issue shall be vested with the requisite powers for protecting the interests of debentureholders including a right to appoint a nomince director on the Board of the company in consultation with institutional debentureholders.

(ii) Lead institution/investment institution will monitor the progress in respect of debentures for project finance/modernisation/expansion/diversification/normal capital expenditure. The lead bank for the company will monitor debentures raised for working capital funds.

(iii) Institutional debentureholders and trustees should obtain a certificate from the company's auditors in respect of utilisation of funds during the implementation period of projects. In the case of debentures for working capital purposes the auditor's certificate should be obtained at the end of each accounting year.

(iv) Debenture issues by companies belonging to the groups for financing/replenishing funds or acquiring shareholding in other companies will not be permitted.

(v) The companies shall alongwith their application file to the Controller of Capital Issues prior clearance with certificates from their bankers that the assets on which security is to be created are free from any encumbrances and that necessary permissions to mortgage the assets have been obtained. The security should be created within 12 months from the date of issue of debentures. If for any reason the companies are not in a position to create security within 12 months from the date of issue of debentures the companies shall be liable to pay two per cent penal interest to debentureholders. If security is not created even after 18 months a meeting of the debentureholders should be called within 21 days to explain the reasons thereof and the date by which the security would be created.

(vi) The trustees to the debentureholders will supervise the implementation of the conditions regarding creation of security for the debentures and regarding the debenture redemption reserve.

ANNEXE: II

TABLE 2.1 THROUGH TABLE 2.7

TABLE: 2.1 STATEMENT OF APPROVALS GRANTED BY THE CONTROLLER OF CAPITAL ISSUES UNDER THE CAPITAL ISSUES (CONTROL) ACT, 1947 FOR RAISING CAPITAL BY NON-GOVERNMENT COMPANIES (1978-82)

(AMOUNT IN RUPEES CRORES)

TYPE OF ISSUE	1978		1979		1980		1981		1982		TOTAL	
	NO.OF COMP.	AMOUNT	NO.OF COMP.	AMOUNT	NO.OF COMP.	AMOUNT	NO.OF COMP.	AMOUNT	NO.OF COMP.	AMOUNT	NO.OF COMP.	AMOUNT
(1)	(2)	(3)	(4)	(5)	(6)	(7)	(8)	(9)	(10)	(11)	(12)	(13)
1. Debenture Issue	13 (3.43)	48.75 (17.84)	49 (10.52)	138.75 (27.95)	50 (10.73)	67.75 (8.67)	83 (15.40)	328.88 (45.02)	94 (17.18)	520.20 (45.99)	289* (12.06)	1104.33 (32.36)
2. Others (Initial Issue, Further, Issue, Bonus Issue, Loans, etc.)	366 (96.57	224.44 (82.16)	417 (89.48)	357.69 (72.05)	416 (89.72)	713.66 (91.33)	456 (84.60)	401.71 (54.98)	453 (82.82)	610.94 (54.01	2108 (87.94)	2308.44 (67.64)
Total	379 (100)	273.19 (100)	466 (100)	496.44 (100)	466 (100)	781.41 (100)	539 (100)	730.59 (100)	547 (100)	1131.14 (100)	2397 (100)	3412.77 (100)

* Includes those companies of the private corporate sector which are private limited companies; their number is five.

**Initial issue refers to the issues floated by newly incorporated companies which raised funds from the market by way of either equity shares / perference shares. Further issue likewise refers to those companies which have been in existence and which raised funds either by way of equity shares/perference shares. Bonus issue refers to the bonus issues issued by the existing companies.

SOURCE: Records available in the office of the Controller of Capital Issues.

Annexe II.2

TABLE: 2.2 MEMBERSHIP, PAID-UP CAPITAL AND OWNERSHIP PATTERN OF ALL INDIAN COMPANIES (1977-78 TO 1981-82)

(AMOUNT IS RUPEES CRORES)

YEAR	GOVERNMENT COMPANIES						NON-GOVERNMENT COMPANIES					
	PUBLIC LIMITED		PRIVATE LIMITED		TOTAL		PUBLIC LIMITED		PRIVATE LIMITED		TOTAL	
	NUMBER	PAID-UP CAPITAL (Amount)	NUMBER	PAID-UP CAPITAL (Amount)	NUMBER	PAID-UP CAPITAL (Amount)	NUMBER	PAID-UP CAPITAL (Amount)	NUMBER	PAID-UP CAPITAL (Amount)	NUMBER	PAID UP CAPITAL (Amount)
(1)	(2)	(3)	(4)	(5)	(6)	(7)	(8)	(9)	(10)	(11)	(12)	(13)
1977-78	300	726	445	7,802	745	8,527	8,028	3,113	39,521	957	47,549	4070
1978-79	321	853	461	7,463	782	8,315	8,309	3,240	42,427	1,020	50,736	4260
1979-80	353	1008	472	9,062	825	10,070	8,864	3,445	46,804	1,091	55,668	4536
1980-81	362	1132	499	10,310	851	11,443	9,388	3,550	52,475	1,152	61,863	4701
1981-82	372	1289	522	12,020	894	13,309	10,169	3,716	61,339	1,245	71,508	4961

Annexe II.3

TABLE: 2.2 MEMBERSHIP, PAID-UP CAPITAL AND OWNERSHIP PATTERN OF ALL INDIAN COMPANIES

(1977-78 TO 1981-82)(CONTD..2)

(AMOUNT IN RUPEES CRORES)

YEAR	PUBLIC LIMITED COMPANIES		PRIVATE LIMITED COMPANIES		GRAND TOTAL	
	NUMBER	PAID-UP CAPITAL (Amount)	NUMBER	PAID-UP CAPITAL (Amount)	NUMBER	PAID-UP CAPITAL (Amount)
(1)	(14)	(15)	(16)	(17)	(18)	(19)
1977-78	8,328	3,839	39,966	8,759	48,294	12,598
1978-79	8,630	4,093	42,888	8,482	51,518	12,575
1979-80	9,217	4,453	47,276	10,154	56,493	14,607
1980-81	9,740	4,682	52,974	11,462	62,714	16,144
1981-82	10,541	5,005	61,861	13,265	72,402	18,270

SOURCE:

Government of India, Ministry of Industry and Department of Company Affairs, Research and Statistics Division, Directory of Joint Stock Companies in India, Volume one (A-DEL), New Delhi, 1986,pp. VII to XII.

Annexe II.4

TABLE:2.3 STATEMENT OF APPROVALS GRANTED TO PUBLIC LIMITED COMPANIES OF THE PRIVATE CORPORATE SECTOR BY THE CONTROLLER OF CAPITAL ISSUES FOR RAISING FUNDS THROUGH THE ISSUE OF CONVERTIBLE & NON CONVERTIBLE DEBENTURES DURING THE YEAR 1978.

Sr. No.	Name of Company	Year of Incorporation	Registered office	Nature of Industry	MRTP Company	Con. Dev./Non. Con. Dev.	Date of permission by CCI	Purpose
(1)	(2)	(3)	(4)	(5)	(6)	(7)	(8)	(9)
1.	Andrew Yule Co.Ltd.	1919	Calcutta	Engg.	N.A.	N.C.	13.3.78	W.C.
2.	Kirloskar Oil Engines Ltd.	1946	Pune	Engg.	Yes	N.C.	10.5.78	W.C.
3.	I.C.I.C.I.	1955	Bombay	Finance	N.A.	N.C.	20.5.78	W.C.
4.	Bharat Forge Co.Ltd.	1961	Pune	Steel	Yes	N.C.	31.5.78	W.C.
5.	Metal Box Co.of India Ltd.	1933	Calcutta	Engg.	Yes	Conv.	17.7.78	Expansion
6.	Voltas Ltd.	1954	Bombay	Commerce	Yes	N.C.	7.11.78	Long term Finance.
7.	Tata Oil Mills Co.Ltd.	1917	Bombay	Chemicals	Yes	N.C.	15.11.78	W.C.
8.	Modi Industries Ltd.	1932	Modi Nagar	Steel	Yes	N.C.	17.11.78	W.C.
9.	Mukand Iron & Steel	1937	Bombay	Steel	Yes	N.C.	25.11.78	W.C.
10.	Bombay Dying & Mfg.Co.Ltd.	1879	Bombay	Textile	Yes	N.C.	27.11.78	W.C.
11.	Colour Chemicals Ltd.	1956	Bombay	Chemicals	Yes	N.C.	2.12.78	W.C.
12.	Amar Dys.Chem.Ltd.	1954	Bombay	Chemicals	N.A.	N.C.	7.12.78	W.C.
13.	Polychem Ltd.	1955	Bombay	Chemicals	Yes	N.C.	8.12.78	W.C.

TABLE:2.3 STATEMENT OF APPROVALS GRANTED TO PUBLIC LIMITED COMPANIES OF THE PRIVATE CORPORATE SECTOR BY THE CONTROLLER OF CAPITAL ISSUES FOR RAISING FUNDS THROUGH THE ISSUE OF CONVERTIBLE & NON CONVERTIBLE DEBENTURES DURING THE YEAR 1978. (CONTD..2)

Sr. No.	Name of Company	Face Value of Deb. (Rs.)	Interest Rate (In Per Cent)	Amount			5% Premium on redemption	Aditional information
				Offered to Public (In Rs. Crores)	Offered on Rights basis (In Rs. Crores)	Total (In Rs. Crores)		
(1)	(2)	(10)	(11)	(12)	(13)	(14)	(15)	(16)
1.	Andrew Yule Co.Ltd.	10	10.5	--	0.25	0.25	--	Through West Bengal Ind.Dev.Cor. Ltd.
2.	Kirloskar Oil Engines Ltd.	1000	10.5	--	1.50	1.50	--	11% w.e.f. 16.10.78 & 12% w.e.f. 21.8.81.
3.	I.C.I.C.I.	5000	6.5	--	30.00	30.00	--	--
4.	Bharat Forge Co.Ltd.	500	10.5	-	2.00	2.00	--	11% w.e.f. 6.5.78 & 12% w.e.f. 15.5.81
5.	Metal Box Co.of India Ltd.	10	10.5	1.50	0.50	2.00	--	Converted into 1 Equity share on 31.3.81.
6.	Voltas Ltd.	100	11.0	--	2.00	2.00	--	12% w.e.f. 1.1.82
7.	Tata Oil Mills Co.Ltd.	100	11.0	--	2.25	2.25	--	12% w.e.f. 1.7.81

Annexe II.6

TABLE: 2.3 STATEMENT OF APPROVALS GRANTED TO PUBLIC LIMITED COMPANIES OF THE PRIVATE CORPORATE SECTOR BY THE CONTROLLER OF CAPITAL ISSUES FOR RAISING FUNDS THROUGH THE ISSUE OF CONVERTIBLE & NON CONVERTIBLE DEBENTURES DURING THE YEAR 1978. (CONTD..3)

Sr. No.	Name of Company	Face Value of Deb. (Rs.)	Interest Rate (In Per Cent)	Amount			5% Premium on redemption	Additional information
				Offered to Public (In Rs. Crores)	Offered on Rights basis (In Rs. Crores)	Total (In Rs. Crores)		
(1)	(2)	(10)	(11)	(12)	(13)	(14)	(15)	(16)
8.	Modi Industries Ltd.	100	11.0	--	0.75	0.75	--	Through the LICI, GICI & ICICI.
9.	Mukand Iron & Steel	100	11.0	--	1.50	1.50	--	12% w.e.f.21.5.81.
10.	Bombay Dying & Mfg.Co.Ltd.	100	11.0	--	2.50	2.50	--	
11.	Colour Chemicals Ltd.	100	11.0	--	2.50	2.50	--	
12.	Amar Dys. Chem.Ltd.	100	11.0	--	1.00	1.00	--	
13.	Polychem Ltd.	100	11.0	--	0.50	0.50	--	12% w.e.f.20.3.81.
	TOTAL			1.50	47.25	48.75		

NOTES: 'Con.Deb.' stands for 'Convertible Debentures'

'Non.Con.' & N.C. stand for 'Non Convertible Debentures'.

'N.A.' stands for 'Not applicable'.

'W.C.' stands for 'Working Capital'

SOURCE: Compiled from the information available in the office of the Controller of Capital Issues, Ministry of Finance, Government of India, New Delhi.

Annexe II.7

TABLE : 2.4 STATEMENT OF APPROVALS GRANTED TO PUBLIC LIMITED COMPANIES OF THE PRIVATE CORPORATE SECTOR BY THE CONTROLLER OF CAPITAL ISSUES FOR RAISING FUNDS THROUGH THE ISSUE OF CONVERTIBLE & NON CONVERTIBLE DEBENTURES DURING THE YEAR 1979.

Sr. No.	Name of Company	Year of Incorp-oration	Registered office	Nature of Industry	MRTP Comp-any	Con. Deb./ Non. Con.Deb.	Date of permi - ssion by CCI	Purpose
(1)	(2)	(3)	(4)	(5)	(6)	(7)	(8)	(9)
1.	Sudershan Chem.Ind.Ltd.	1951	Pune	Chemicals	N.A.	N.C.	5.1.79	W.C.
2.	Common Wealth Trust(India) Ltd.	1977	Calicut	Chemicals	N.A.	N.C.	20.1.79	Transfer of Business.
3.	IDL Chemicals Ltd.	1961	Hyderabad	Chemicals	N.A.	N.C.	31.1.79	W.C.
4.	J.K.Chemicals Ltd.	1947	Bombay	Chemicals	Yes	N.C.	6.2.79	W.C.
5.	Machneill Magor Ltd.	1949	Calcutta	Tea	Yes	N.C.	16.12.79	W.C.
6.	G.N.V.F.Co.Ltd.	1976	Baroda	Chemicals	N.A.	N.C.	28.2.79	Long Term Finance.
7.	J.K.Synthetics Ltd.	1943	Kanpur	Chemicals	Yes	N.C.	3.3.79	W.C.
8.	Straw Products Ltd.	1938	JayKaypur (Orissa)	Paper	Yes	N.C.	5.3.79	W.C.
9.	Garware Nylon Ltd.	1957	Bombay	Rayon	Yes	N.C.	12.3.79	W.C.
10.	Mahindra & Mahindra Ltd.	1945	Bombay	Engineering	Yes	N.C.	13.3.79	W.C.
11.	Modi Spg.& Wvg.Mills Co.Ltd	1946	Modi Ngr.	Cotton	Yes	N.C.	28.3.79	W.C.
12.	Calcutta Elect.Supply Corporation (India)Ltd.	1978	Calcutta	Electricity	Yes	N.C.	29.3.79	W.C.
13.	Bombay Dying & Mfg.Co.Ltd.	1879	Bombay	C.Textile	Yes	N.C.	7.[illegible].79	W.C.

TABLE: 2.4 STATEMENT OF APPROVALS GRANTED TO PUBLIC LIMITED COMPANIES OF THE PRIVATE CORPORATE SECTOR BY THE CONTROLLER OF CAPITAL ISSUES FOR RAISING FUNDS THROUGH THE ISSUE OF CONVERTIBLE & NON CONVERTIBLE DEBENTURES DURING THE YEAR 1979. (CONTD..2)

Sr. No.	Name of Company	Face Value of Deb. (Rs.)	Interest Rate (In Per Cent)	Amount: Offered to Public (In Rs. Crores)	Amount: Offered on Rights basis (In Rs. Crores)	Amount: Total (In Rs. Crores)	5% Premium on redemption	Additional information
(1)	(2)	(10)	(11)	(12)	(13)	(14)	(15)	(16)
1.	Sudershan Chem.Ind.Ltd.	100	11.0	--	0.75	0.75	--	--
2.	Common Wealth Trust(India) Ltd.	1000	11.0	--	0.50	0.50	--	Issued to Common Wealth Trust Ltd.U.K.
3.	IDL Chemicals Ltd.	100	11.0	--	1.00	1.00	--	--
4.	J.K.Chemicals Ltd.	100	11.0	--	0.50	0.50	--	--
5.	Machneill Magor Ltd.	100	11.0	--	1.00	1.00	--	--
6.	G.N.V.F.Co.Ltd.	100	11.0	--	2.00	2.00	--	Through Unit Trust of India
7.	J.K.Synthetics Ltd.	100	11.0	--	2.00	2.00	--	12% w.e.f.11.6.81
8.	Straw Products Ltd.	100	11.0	--	2.00	2.00	--	12% w.e.f.21.4.81
9.	Garware Nylon Ltd.	100	11.0	--	1.75	1.75	--	12% w.e.f.14.7.81
10.	Mahindra & Mahindra Ltd.	100	11.0	--	2.00	2.00	--	13.5%w.e.f.7.8.81
11.	Modi Spg.& Wvg.Mills Co.Ltd	100	11.0	--	2.00	2.00	--	13% w.e.f.5.4.81
12.	Calcutta Elect.Supply Corporation(India)Ltd.	100	11.0	--	1.25	1.25	--	--
13.	Bombay Dying & Mfg.Co.Ltd.	100	11.0	--	1.00	1.00	--	--

TABLE:2.4 STATEMENT OF APPROVALS GRANTED TO PUBLIC LIMITED COMPANIES OF THE PRIVATE CORPORATE SECTOR BY THE CONTROLLER OF CAPITAL ISSUES FOR RAISING FUNDS THROUGH THE ISSUE OF CONVERTIBLE & NON CONVERTIBLE DEBENTURES DURING THE YEAR 1979.(CONTD...3)

Sr. No.	Name of Company	Year of Incorporation	Registered office	Nature of Industry	MRTP Company	Con. Deb./ Non. Con. Deb.	Date of permission by CCI	Purpose
(1)	(2)	(3)	(4)	(5)	(6)	(7)	(8)	(9)
14.	Antifriction Bearing Corpn. Ltd.	1961	Bombay	Engineering	N.A.	N.C.	17.4.79	W.C.
15.	Loyal Textile Mills Ltd.	1946	Madras	Textile	Yes	N.C.	19.4.79	W.C.
16.	Excel Industries Ltd.	1960	Bombay	Engineering	N.A.	N.C.	10.5.79	W.C.
17.	Tata Chemicals Ltd.	1939	Bombay	Chemicals	Yes	N.C.	18.5.79	W.C.
18.	Gujarat Steel Tubes Ltd.	1960	Ahemdabad	Steel	N.A.	N.C.	19.5.79	W.C.
19.	Alembic Chemcial Works Co. Ltd.	1907	Baroda	Chemicals	N.A.	N.C.	19.5.79	W.C.
20.	Hindustan Dev.Corpn.Ltd.	1944	Calcutta	Chemicals	N.A.	N.C.	19.5.79	W.C.
21.	Reliance Textile Industries Ltd.	1973	Bombay	Rayon	Yes	Con.	22.5.79	Project Financing.
22.	Indian Explosives Ltd.	1954	Calcutta	Chemicals	Yes	Con.	12.6.79	Financing the Expansion Prog.
23.	Bests Crompton Engg.Ltd.	1911	Madras	Engineering	N.A	N.C.	21.6.79	W.C.
24.	Chloride India Ltd.	1947	Calcutta	Chemicals	Yes	N.C.	21.6.79	W.C.
25.	Jagatjit Industries Ltd.	1944	Kapurthala	Chemicals	N.A.	N.C.	23.6.79	W.C.
26.	Usha Martin Black Ltd.	1960	Calcutta	Steel	Yes	N.C.	26.6.79	W.C.
27.	Tata Finlay Co.Ltd.	1962	Calcutta	Tea	Yes	N.C.	29.6.79	W.C.
28.	Nirlon Synthetic Fibers & Chemicals Ltd.	1958	Bombay	Chemicals	Yes	N.C.	9.7.79	W.C.
29.	Union Carbide India Ltd.	1934	Calcutta	Engineering	Yes	N.C.	11.7.79	W.C.

TABLE: 2.4 STATEMENT OF APPROVALS GRANTED TO PUBLIC LIMITED COMPANIES OF THE PRIVATE CORPORATE SECTOR BY THE CONTROLLER OF CAPITAL ISSUES FOR RAISING FUNDS THROUGH THE ISSUE OF CONVERTIBLE & NON CONVERTIBLE DEBENTURES DURING THE YEAR 1979. (CONTD....4)

Sr. No.	Name of Company	Face Value of Deb. (Rs.)	Interest Rate (In Per Cent)	Amount: Offered to Public (In Rs. Crores)	Amount: Offered on Rights basis (In Rs. Crores)	Amount: Total (In Rs. Crores)	5% Premium on redemption	Additional information
(1)	(2)	(10)	(11)	(12)	(13)	(14)	(15)	(16)
14.	Antifriction Bearing Corpn. Ltd	100	11.0	--	0.50	0.50	--	12% w.e.f.22.6.82.
15.	Loyal Textile Mills Ltd	100	11.0	--	0.25	0.25	--	12% w.e.f.14.11.80.
16.	Excel Industires Ltd.	100	11.0	--	1.00	1.00	--	--
17.	Tata Chemicals Ltd	100	11.0	--	2.50	2.50	--	12% w.e.f.7.7.82.
18.	Gujarat Steel Tubes Ltd.	100	11.0	--	1.00	1.00	--	13.5%w.e.f.4.3.81.
19.	Alembic Chemcial Works Co. Ltd.	100	11.0	--	0.75	0.75	--	13.5%w.e.f.20.1.82.
20.	Hindustan Dev.corpn.Ltd	100	12.0	--	0.75	0.75	--	13.5%w.e.f.28.7.81.
21.	Reliance Textile Industries Ltd.	500	11.0	7.00	--	7.00	--	20% of the face value of the Deb.was converted into 4 equity Shares between 1.10.80 & 30.11.80.
22.	Indian Explosives Ltd.	500	10.5	--	0.25	0.25	--	Through the IDBI; 20% Converted on1.10.82.
23.	Bests Crompton Engg.Ltd	100	10.5	--	0.75	0.75	--	11% w.e.f.28.9.79.
24.	Chloride India Ltd.	100	11.0	--	1.00	1.00	--	--
25.	Jagatjit Industires Ltd.	100	11.0	--	0.75	0.75	--	12%w.e.f.17.1.81& 15%w.e.f.4.5.82.

Annexe:II.11

TABLE:2.4 STATEMENT OF APPROVALS GRANTED TO PUBLIC LIMITED COMPANIES OF THE PRIVATE CORPORATE SECTOR BY THE CONTROLLER OF CAPITAL ISSUES FOR RAISING FUNDS THROUGH THE ISSUE OF CONVERTIBLE & NON CONVERTIBLE DEBENTURES DURING THE YEAR 1979. (CONTD.....5)

Sr. No	Name of Company	Face Value of Deb. (Rs)	Interest Rate (In Per Cent)	Amount			5% Premium on redemption	Additional information
				Offered to Public (In Rs. Crores)	Offered on Rights basis (In Rs. Crores)	Total (In Rs. Crores)		
(1)	(2)	(10)	(11)	(12)	(13)	(14)	(15)	(16)
26.	Usha Martin Black Ltd	100	11.0	--	1.25	1.25	--	--
27.	Tata Finlay Co.Ltd	100	11.0	--	2.50	2.50	--	12% w.e.f.30.1.82.
28.	Nirlon Synthetic Fibers & Chemicals Ltd.	100	11.0	--	2.50	2.50	--	12% w.e.f.26.8 82.
29.	Union Carbide India Ltd	100	11.0	--	2.50	2.50	--	12% w.e.f.10.12.81.

Annexe II.12

TABLE:2.4 STATEMENT OF APPROVALS GRANTED TO PUBLIC LIMITED COMPANIES OF THE PRIVATE CORPORATE SECTOR BY THE CONTROLLER OF CAPITAL ISSUES FOR RAISING FUNDS THROUGH THE ISSUE OF CONVERTIBLE & NON CONVERTIBLE DEBENTURES DURING THE YEAR 1979.(CONTD.....6)

Sr. No.	Name of Company	Year of Incorp-oration	Registered Office	Nature of Industry	MRTP Comp-	Con. Deb./ Non. Con. Deb.	Date of permis-sion by CCI	Purpose
(1)	(2)	(3)	(4)	(5)	(6)	(7)	(8)	(9)
30.	Industrial Cables(India) Ltd.	1956	Rajpura	Engineering	N.A.	N.C.	11.7.79	W.C.
31.	Larsen and Toubro Ltd.	1946	Bombay	Engineering	Yes	N.C.	27.7.79	W.C.
32.	SLM Maneklal Ind.Ltd.	1961	Ahmedabad	Engineering	N.A.	N.C.	10.8.79	W.C.
33.	Ceat Tyres of India Ltd.	1958	Bombay	Rubber	Yes	N.C.	30.8.79	W.C.
34.	General Ind.Socy.Ltd.	1892	Calcutta	Jute	N.A.	N.C.	31.8.79	W.C.
35.	Tata Engg.& Loco. Co.Ltd.	1945	Bombay	Engineering	Yes	Con.	12.9.79	Expansion
36.	Farro Alloys Corp.Ltd.	1955	Tumser	Steel	N.A.	N.C.	12.9.79	W.C.
37.	Goldon Tobacco Co.Ltd.	1955	Bombay	Tobacco	Yes	N.C.	12.9.79	W.C.
38.	Kesoram Ind.&Cotton Mills Ltd.	1919	Calcutta	Cotton	Yes	N.C.	15.9.79	W.C
39.	Zenith Steel Pipes and Ind.Ltd.	1960	Bombay	Steel	Yes	N.C.	15.9.79	W.C.
40.	Ahmedabad Advance Mills Ltd.	1903	Bombay	Cotton	Yes	N.C.	28.9.79	W.C.
41.	Shree Dinesh Mills Ltd.	1935	Baroda	Wollen	N.A.	N.C.	28.9.79	W.C.
42.	Special Steels Ltd.	1958	Bombay	Steel	N.A.	N.C.	28.9.79	W.C.
43.	Tata Robins Frasers Ltd.	1912	Calcutta	Steel	Yes	N.C.	21.10.79	W.C.

Annexe: II.13

TABLE:2.4 STATEMENT OF APPROVALS GRANTED TO PUBLIC LIMITED COMPANIES OF THE PRIVATE CORPORATE SECTOR BY THE CONTROLLER OF CAPITAL ISSUES FOR RAISING FUNDS THROUGH THE ISSUE OF CONVERTIBLE & NON CONVERTIBLE DEBENTURES DURING THE YEAR 1979. (CONTD.......7)

Sr. No.	Name of Company	Face Value of Deb. (Rs.)	Interest Rate (In Per Cent)	AMOUNT: Offered to Public (In Rs. Crores)	AMOUNT: Offered on Rights basis (In Rs. Crores)	AMOUNT: Total (In Rs. Crores)	5% Premium on redemption	Additional information
(1)	(2)	(10)	(11)	(12)	(13)	(14)	(15)	(16)
30.	Industrial Cables(India)Ltd.	100	11.0	--	0.75	0.75	--	--
31.	Larsen and Toubro Ltd.	100	11.0	--	2.50	2.50	--	--
32.	SLM Maneklal Ind.Ltd.	100	11.0	--	0.75	0.75	--	12% w.e.f.13.7.81
33.	Ceat Tyres of India Ltd.	100	11.0	--	1.50	1.50	--	--
34.	General Ind. Socy.Ltd.	100	11.0	--	0.75	0.75	--	--
35.	Tata Engg.& Loco. Co.Ltd.	450	11.0	29.29	17.96	47.25	--	50% converted after 3 years & the rest 50% after 7 years.
36.	Farro Alloys Corp.Ltd.	100	11.0	--	0.75	0.75	--	--
37.	Goldon Tobacco Co.Ltd.	100	11.0	--	0.75	0.75	--	--
38.	Kesoram Ind. & Cotton Mills Ltd.	100	11.0	--	2.50	2.50	--	--
39.	Zenith Steel Pipes and Ind.Ltd.	100	11.0	--	1.25	1.25	--	--
40.	Ahmedabad Advance Mills Ltd.	100	11.0	--	1.00	1.00	--	--
41.	Shree Dinesh Mills Ltd.	100	11.0	--	0.50	0.50	--	--
42.	Special Steels Ltd.	100	11.0	--	1.00	1.00	--	Interest rate raised first to 12%, then to 13.5%, & thereafter to 15%.
43.	Tata Robins Frasers Ltd.	100	11.0	--	0.50	0.50	--	Interest rate raised first to 12% & then to 13.5%.

TABLE :2.4 STATEMENT OF APPROVALS GRANTED TO PUBLIC LIMITED COMPANIES OF THE PRIVATE CORPORATE SECTOR BY THE CONTROLLER OF CAPITAL ISSUES FOR RAISING FUNDS THROUGH THE ISSUE OF CONVERTIBLE & NON CONVERTIBLE DEBENTURES DURING THE YEAR 1979.(CONTD.......8)

Sr. No.	Name of Company	Year of Incorp-oration	Registered Office	Nature of Industry	MRTP Comp-any	Con. Deb. Non. Con. Deb.	Date of permis-sion by CCI	Purpose
(1)	(2)	(3)	(4)	(5)	(6)	(7)	(8)	(9)
44.	Bombay Burmah Trading Corporation Ltd.	1863	Bombay	Trading	N.A.	N.C.	2.11.79	W.C.
45.	Indian D-ystuff Ind-ustries Ltd.	1954	Bombay	Chemicals	Yes	N.C.	16.11.79	W.C.
46.	Bharat Steel Tubes Ltd.	1959	New Delhi	Steel	Yes	N.C.	30.11.79	Long term finance
47.	Ahmedabad Mfg.& Calico Printing Co.Ltd.	1880	Ahmedabad	Cotton	Yes	N.C.	3.12.79	W.C.
48.	Devy Ashmore India Ltd.	1972	Calcutta	Engineering	N.A.	N.C.	4.12.79	W.C.
49.	Rajasthan Spg.& Wvg. Mills Ltd.	1960	New Delhi	Cotton	Yes	N.C.	21.12.79	W.C.

TABLE:2.4 STATEMENT OF APPROVALS GRANTED TO PUBLIC LIMITED COMPANIES OF THE PRIVATE CORPORATE SECTOR BY THE CONTROLLER OF CAPITAL ISSUES FOR RAISING FUNDS THROUGH THE ISSUE OF CONVERTIBLE & NON CONVERTIBLE DEBENTURES DURING THE YEAR 1979. (CONTD.........9)

Sr. No.	Name of Company	Face Value of Deb. (Rs.)	Interest Rate (In Per Cent)	AMOUNT Offered to Public (In Rs. Crores)	Offered on Rights basis (In Rs. Crores)	Total (In Rs. Crores)	5% Premium on redemption	Additional information
(1)	(2)	(10)	(11)	(12)	(13)	(14)	(15)	(16)
44.	Bombay Burmah Trading Corporation Ltd.	100	11	--	1.50	1.50	---	Lateron interest rate raised to 12%
45.	Indian D-ystuff Industries Ltd.	100	11	--	2.50	2.50	---	Lateron interest rate raised to 12%
46.	Bharat Steel Tubes Ltd.	100	11	--	1.25	1.25	---	Lateron interest rate raised to 12%
47.	Ahmedabad Mfg.& Calico Printing Co.Ltd.	100	11	--	2.50	2.50	---	Interest raised first to 12% & then 13.5%
48.	Devy Ashmore India Ltd.	100	11	--	0.50	0.50	---	Interest rate raised first to 12% & then to 13.5%
49.	Rajasthan Spg.& Wvg. Mills Ltd.	100	11	--	1.00	1.00	---	Lateron interest rate raised to 12%
	TOTAL			36.29	77.71	114.00		

NOTES: 'C.C.I.' stands for 'Controller of Capital Issues'.
'Con.Deb.' stands for 'Convertible Debentures'
'Non.Con.' & 'N.C.' stand for 'Non Convertible Debentures'.
'N.A.' stands for 'Not applicable'.
'W.C.' stands for 'Working Capital'

SOURCE: Compiled from the information available in the office of the Controller of Capital Issues, Ministry of Finance, Government of India, New Delhi.

Annexe: II.16

TABLE 2.5 STATEMENT OF APPROVALS GRANTED TO PUBLIC LIMITED COMPANIES OF THE PRIVATE CORPORATE SECTOR BY THE CONTROLLER OF CAPITAL ISSUES FOR RAISING FUNDS THROUGH THE ISSUE OF CONVERTIBLE & NON CONVERTIBLE DEBENTURES DURING THE YEAR 1980.

Sr. No.	Name of Company	Year of Incorp-oration	Registered Office	Nature of Industry	MRTP Comp-any	Con. Deb./ Non. Con. Deb.	Date of permis-sion by CCI	Purpose
(1)	(2)	(3)	(4)	(5)	(6)	(7)	(8)	(9)
1.	Spencer & Co.	1897	Madras	Trading	N.A.	N.C.	2.1.80	W.C.
2.	Hindustan Spg.& Wvg.Mills Ltd.	1882	Bombay	Cotton	Yes	N.C.	4.1.80	W.C.
3.	Kanoria Chem.& Inds.Ltd.	1960	Calcutta	Chemicals	N.A.	N.C.	5.1.80	W.C.
4.	Triveni Engg.Works Ltd.	1961	New Delhi	Sugar	Yes	N.C.	23.1.80	W.C.
5.	Modi Industries Ltd.	1932	Modi Nagar	Sugar	Yes	N.C.	25.1.80	W.C.
6.	Birla Cotton Spg.& Wvg. Mills Ltd.	1920	Delhi	Cotton	N.A.	N.C.	30.1.80	--
7.	Bharat Bijlee Ltd.	1946	Bombay	Engineering	N.A.	N.C.	30.1.80	W.C.
8.	Greaves Cotton & Co.Ltd.	1932	Bombay	Engineering	Yes	N.C.	30.1.80	W.C.
9	Indian Rayon Corporation Ltd.	1956	Veraval	Rayon	Yes	N.C.	30.1.80	W.C.
10.	W.S.Insulators of India Ltd.	1961	Madras	Engineering	N.A.	N.C.	5.2.80	W.C.
11.	Bombay Potteries & Tiles Ltd.	1933	Bombay	Chemcials	N.A.	Con.	6.2.80	W.C.

TABLE:2.5 STATEMENT OF APPROVALS GRANTED TO PUBLIC LIMITED COMPANIES OF THE PRIVATE CORPORATE SECTOR BY THE CONTROLLER OF CAPITAL ISSUES FOR RAISING FUNDS THROUGH THE ISSUE OF CONVERTIBLE & NON CONVERTIBLE DEBENTURES DURING THE YEAR 1980. (CONTD..2).

Sr. No.	Name of Company	Face Value of Deb. (Rs.)	Interest Rate (In Per Cent)	AMOUNT Offered to Public (In Rs. Crores)	Offered on Rights basis (In Rs. Crores)	Total (In Rs. Crores)	5% Premium on redemption	Additional information
(1)	(2)	(10)	(11)	(12)	(13)	(14)	(15)	(16)
1.	Spencer & Co.	100	11,0	--	0.50	0.50	-	--
2.	Hindustan Spg.& Wvg.Mills Ltd.	100	11.0	--	1.25	1.25	-	12% w.e.f.16.1.81 13.5% we.f.27.3.81& 15% w.e.f.17.4.82
3.	Kanoria Chem.&Inds.Ltd.	100	11.0	--	1.00	1.00	-	Interest rate first raised to 12%,& then to 13.5% & thereafter to 15%.
4.	Triveni Engg.Works Ltd.	100	11.0	--	0.50	0.50	-	In the begning applied for Rs.0.75Cr.
5.	Modi Industries Ltd.	100	11.0	--	1.50	1.50	-	--
6.	Birla Cotton Spg.& Wvg. Mills Ltd.	100	11.0	--	2.00	2.00	-	--
7.	Bharat Bijlee Ltd.	100	11.0	--	0.50	0.50	-	12% w.e.f. 12.1.1981
8.	Greaves Cotton & Co.Ltd.	100	11.0	--	1.00	1.00	-	--
9.	Indian Rayon Corporation Ltd.	100	11.0	--	1.00	1.00	#Yes	Interest rate first raised to 13.5% and
10.	*W.S.Insulators of India Ltd	100	10.5	--	0.75	0.75	-	then to 15%
11.	Bombay Potteries & Tiles Ltd.	100	11.0	--	0.10	1.00	-	Interest rate first raised to 12% & then to 13.5%

* Issues was carrying a maturity period of 5 years.

\# Premium allowed on 2.8.82

TABLE :2.5 STATEMENT OF APPROVALS GRANTED TO PUBLIC LIMITED COMPANIES OF THE PRIVATE CORPORATE SECTOR BY THE CONTROLLER OF CAPITAL ISSUES FOR RAISING FUNDS THROUGH THE ISSUE OF CONVERTIBLE & NON CONVERTIBLE DEBENTURES DURING THE YEAR 1980 (CONTD...3)

Sr. No.	Name of Company	Year of Incorp-oration	Registered Office	Nature of Industry	MRTP Comp-any	Con. Deb./Non. Con. Deb.	Date of permi - ssion by CCI	Purpose
(1)	(2)	(3)	(4)	(5)	(6)	(7)	(8)	(9)
12.	Premier Mills Ltd.	1945	Madras	Cotton	N.A.	N.C.	8.2.80	W.C.
13.	Kirloskar Brothers Ltd.	1920	Pune	Engineering	Yes	N.C.	15.2.80	W.C.
14.	Punjab Tractors Ltd.	1970	Roper	Engineering	N.A.	N.C.	28.2.80	W.C.
15.	Duncans Agro Industries Ltd.	1885	Calcutta	Tea	Yes	N.C.	7.3.80	W.C.
16.	Indian Tools Mfgs.Ltd.	1937	Bombay	Engineering	N.A.	N.C.	13.3.80	W.C.
17.	Caprihans India Ltd.	1946	Bombay	Chemcials	Yes	N.C.	14.3.80	W.C.
18.	Blue Star Ltd.	1949	Bombay	Engineering	N.A	N.C.	14.3.80	W.C.
19.	Kirloskar Pneumative Co. Ltd.	1958	Pune	Engineering	Yes	N.C.	14.3.80	W.C.
20.	Hindustan Kokoku Wire Ltd.	1956	New Delhi	Engineering	N.A.	N.C.	20.3.80	W.C.
21.	Asian Cables Corp.Ltd.	1959	Bombay	Engineering	N.A.	N.C.	3.4.80	W.C.
22.	Ajit Mills Ltd.	1945	Ahemdabad	Cotton	N.A.	N.C.	5.4.80	W.C.

TABLE:2.5 STATEMENT OF APPROVALS GRANTED TO PUBLIC LIMITED COMPANIES OF THE PRIVATE CORPCRATE SECTOR BY THE CONTROLLER OF CAPITAL ISSUES FOR RAISING FUNDS THROUGH THE ISSUE OF CONVERTIBLE & NON CONVERTIBLE DEBENTURES DURING THE YEAR 1980. (CONTD....4).

Sr. No.	Name of Company	Face Value of Deb. (Rs.)	Interest Rate (In Per Cent)	AMOUNT Offered to Public (In Rs. Crores)	Offered on Rights basis (In Rs. Crores)	Total (In Rs. Crores)	5% Premium on redemption	Additional information
(1)	(2)	(10)	(11)	(12)	(13)	(14)	(15)	(16)
12.	Premier Mills Ltd.	100	11.0	--	0.50	0.50	--	
13.	Kirloskar Brothers Ltd.	100	11.0	--	1.00	1.00	--	
14.	Punjab Tractors Ltd.	100	11.0	--	0.50	0.50	--	
15.	Duncans Agro Industries Ltd.	100	11.0	--	1.00	1.00	--	Interest rate first raised to 12%, & then to 13.5%
16.	Indian Tools Mfgs. Ltd.	100	11.0	--	0.50	0.50	--	
17.	Caprihans India Ltd.	100	11.0	--	0.75	0.75	--	Interest rate first raised to 12% & then to 13.5%
18.	Blue Star Ltd.	100	11.0	--	0.50	0.50	--	
19.	Kirloskar Pneumative Co. Ltd.	100	11.0	--	0.75	0.75	--	lateron interest rate raised to 12%
20.	Hindustan Kokoku Wire Ltd.	100	11.0	--	0.25	0.25	*Yes	Interest rate first raised to 12%, then to 13.5% & thereafter to 15%
21.	Asian Cables Corp. Ltd.	100	11.0	--	0.50	0.50	--	
22.	Ajit Mills Ltd.	100	11.0	--	0.25	0.25	--	

* w.e.f. 24.6.82

TABLE:2.5 STATEMENT OF APPROVALS GRANTED TO PUBLIC LIMITED COMPANIES OF THE PRIVATE CORPORATE SECTOR BY THE CONTROLLER OF CAPITAL ISSUES FOR RAISING FUNDS THROUGH THE ISSUE OF CONVERTIBLE & NON CONVERTIBLE DEBENTURES DURING THE YEAR 1980 (CONTD.....5)

Sr. No.	Name of Company	Year of Incorp-oration	Registered Office	Nature of Industry	MRTP Comp-any	Con. Deb./ Non. Con. Deb.	Date of permis-sion by CCI	Purpose
(1)	(2)	(3)	(4)	(5)	(6)	(7)	(8)	(9)
23.	Cadbury India Ltd.	1948	Bombay	Chemicals	N.A.	N.C.	18.4.80	W.C.
24.	Devidyal Electronics & Wires Ltd.	1953	Bombay	Engineering	N.A.	N.C.	18.4.80	W.C.
25.	Wimco Ltd.	1923	Bombay	Chemcials	Yes	N.C.	22.4.80	W.C.
26.	Crompton Greaves Ltd.	1937	Bombay	Engineering	Yes	N.C.	2.5.80	W.C.
27.	National Rayon CorporationLtd.	1946	Bombay	Rayon	Yes	N.C.	6.5.80	Long Term Finance
28.	S.I.Viscose Ltd.	1957	Coimbtore	Rayon	Yes	N.C.	8.5.80	W.C.
29.	Anglo India Jute Mills Co.Ltd.	1917	Calcutta	Jute	Yes	N.C.	29.5.80	W.C.
30.	Raja Bahadur Moti Lal Poona Mills Ltd.	1926	Bombay	Cotton	N.A.	N.C.	30.5.80	W.C.
31.	Mahendra Mills Ltd.	1942	Ahemdabad	Cotton	N.A.	N.C.	30.7.80	W.C.
32.	K.G.Khosla Compressors Ltd.	1974	New Delhi	Engineering	N.A.	N.C.	2 8.80	W.C.

Annexe: II.21

TABLE: 2.5 STATEMENT OF APPROVALS GRANTED TO PUBLIC LIMITED COMPANIES OF THE PRIVATE CORPORATE SECTOR BY THE CONTROLLER OF CAPITAL ISSUES FOR RAISING FUNDS THROUGH THE ISSUE OF CONVERTIBLE & NON CONVERTIBLE DEBENTURES DURING THE YEAR 1980. (CONTD......6)

Sr. No.	Name of Company	Face Value of Deb. (Rs.)	Interest Rate (In Per Cent)	AMOUNT Offered to public (In Rs. Crores)	Offered on Rights basis (In Rs. Crores)	Total (In Rs. Crores)	5% Premium on redemption	Additional information
(1)	(2)	(10)	(11)	(12)	(13)	(14)	(15)	(16)
23.	Cadbury India Ltd.	100	11.0	--	1.00	1.00	--	
24.	Devidyal Electronics & Wires Ltd.	100	11.0	--	0.25	0.25	--	Later on interest rate raised to 12%
25.	Wimco Ltd.	100	11.0	--	1.25	1.25	--	
26.	Crompton Greaves Ltd.	100	11.0	--	0.75	0.75	--	
27.	National Rayon Corporation Ltd.	100	11.0	--	2.25	2.25	--	
28.	S.I.Viscose Ltd.	100	11.0	--	2.50	2.50	--	
29.	Anglo India Jute Mills Co. Ltd.	100	11.0	--	0.75	0.75	--	Interest rate first raised to 12% & then to 13.5%
30.	Raja Bahadur Moti Lal Poona Mills Ltd.	100	11.0	--	0.50	0.50	--	
31.	Mahendra Mills Ltd.	100	11.0	--	0.75	0.75	--	Later on interest rate raised to 12%
32.	K.G.Khosla Compressors Ltd.	100	11.0	--	0.50	0.50	--	Interest rate first raised to 13.5% & then to 15%.

Annexe: II.22

TABLE:2.5

STATEMENT OF APPROVALS GRANTED TO PUBLIC LIMITED COMPANIES OF THE PRIVATE CORPORATE SECTOR BY THE CONTROLLER OF CAPITAL ISSUES FOR RAISING FUNDS THROUGH THE ISSUE OF CONVERTIBLE & NON CONVERTIBLE DEBENTURES DURING THE YEAR 1980 (CONTD.......7)

Sr. No.	Name of Company	Year of Incorporation	Registered Office	Nature of Industry	MRTP Company	Con. Deb./ Non. Con. Deb.	Date of permission by CCI	Purpose
(1)	(2)	(3)	(4)	(5)	(6)	(7)	(8)	(9)
33.	Swan Mills Ltd.	1909	Bombay	Cotton	Yes	N.C.	12.8.80	W.C.
34.	Naveen Hotels Ltd.	1975	Hubli (Karnataka)	Hotel	N.A.	N.C.	16.8.80	--
35.	Reliance Textiles Inds.Ltd.	1973	Bombay	Rayon	Yes	Con.	16.8.80	Replacement & Modernization
36.	Glaxo Lab.(India)Ltd.	1924	Bombay	Chemicals	Yes	N.C.	19.8.80	W.C.
37.	Raymond Woollen Mills Ltd.	1925	Bombay	Woollen	Yes	Con.	30.8.80	Expansion
38.	Voltas Ltd.	1954	Bombay	Trading	Yes	N.C.	8.9.80	Amalgamation
39.	Orient Carpet Mfg.(India)Ltd.	1923	Amritsar	Woollen	N.A.	N.C.	11.9.80	W.C.
40.	First Leasing Co.of India Ltd.	1973	Madras	Leasing	Yes	Con.	18.9.80	--
41.	Elel Hotels & Investment Ltd.	1969	Bombay	Hotel	N.A.	N.C.	26.9.80	--
42.	Elel Hotels & Investment Ltd.	1969	Bombay	Hotel	N.A.	Con.	26.9.80	--
43.	Camphor & Allied Prods.Ltd.	1961	Bombay	Chemicals	N.A.	Con.	5.11.80	--

TABLE:2.5 STATEMENT OF APPROVALS GRANTED TO PUBLIC LIMITED COMPANIES OF THE PRIVATE CORPORATE SECTOR BY THE CONTROLLER OF CAPITAL ISSUES FOR RAISING FUNDS THROUGH THE ISSUE OF CONVERTIBLE & NON CONVERTIBLE DEBENTURES DURING THE YEAR 1980. (CONTD........8)

Sr. No.	Name of Company	Face Value of Deb. (Rs.)	Interest Rate (In Per Cent)	AMOUNT Offered to public (In Rs. Crores)	AMOUNT Offered on Rights basis (In Rs. Crores)	AMOUNT Total (In Rs. Crores)	5% Premium on redemption	Additional information
(1)	(2)	(10)	(11)	(12)	(13)	(14)	(15)	(16)
33.	Swan Mills Ltd.	100	11.0	--	0.75	0.75	--	Interest rate first raised to 13.5% & then to 15%.
34.	Naveen Hotels Ltd.	1000	11.0	--	0.20	0.20	--	--
35.	Reliance Textiles Inds.Ltd.	125	11.0	--	10.80	10.80	--	--
36.	Glaxo Lab.(India)Ltd.	100	11 0	--	2.50	2.50	*Yes	Interest rate first raised to 13.5% & then to 15%. Later on interest raised to 12%.
37.	Raymond Woollen Mills Ltd.	400	11.0	4.80	--	4.80	--	
38.	Voltas Ltd.	100	11.0	--	0.30	0.30	--	--
39.	Orient Carpet Mfg.(India)Ltd.	100	11.0	--	0.75	0.75	--	--
40.	First Leasing Co.of IndiaLtd.	100	11.0	--	0.50	0.50	--	Interest rate raised first to 12% & then to13.5%.
41.	Elel Hotels & Investment Ltd.	100	11.0	--	1.00	1.00	--	
42.	Elel Hotels & Investment Ltd.	100	10.5	--	0.50	0.50	--	Later on interest rate raised to 13.5%
43.	Camphor Allied Prods.Ltd.	500	12.0	0.75	0.25	1.00	--	Issue was of unsecured debentures.

*Premium allowed w.e.f. 10.2.81

TABLE:2.5 STATEMENT OF APPROVALS GRANTED TO PUBLIC LIMITED COMPANIES OF THE PRIVATE CORPORATE SECTOR BY THE CONTROLLER OF CAPITAL ISSUES FOR RAISING FUNDS THROUGH THE ISSUE OF CONVERTIBLE & NON CONVERTIBLE DEBENTURES DURING THE YEAR 1980 (CONTD.........9)

Sr. No.	Name of Company	Year of Incorporation	Registered Office	Nature of Industry	MRTP Company	Con. Deb./ Non. Con. Deb.	Date of permission by CCI	Purpose
(1)	(2)	(3)	(4)	(5)	(6)	(7)	(8)	(9)
44.	Kanoria Chem. & Inds.Ltd.	1960	Calcutta	Chemicals	N.A.	N.C.	14.11.80	W.C.
45.	Polychem Ltd.	1955	Bombay	Chemicals	Yes	N.C.	20.11.80	W.C.
46.	Bharat Forge Co.Ltd.	1961	Pune	Steel	Yes	N.C.	24.12.80	W.C.
47.	Punjab Tractors Ltd.	1970	Roper	Engineering	N.A.	N.C.	26.12.80	--
48.	Hindustan Development Corporation Ltd.	1944	Calcutta	Chemicals	N.A.	Con.	26.12.80	Expansion.
49.	Indian Rayon Corporation Ltd.	1956	Veraval	Rayon	Yes	Con.	30.12.80	Expansion.

TABLE:2.5 STATEMENT OF APPROVALS GRANTED TO PUBLIC LIMITED COMPANIES OF THE PRIVATE CORPORATE SECTOR BY THE CONTROLLER OF CAPITAL ISSUES FOR RAISING FUNDS THROUGH THE ISSUE OF CONVERTIBLE & NON CONVERTIBLE DEBENTURES DURING THE YEAR 1980. (CONTD.........10)

Sr. No.	Name of Company	Face Value of Deb. (Rs.)	Interest Rate (In Per Cent)	AMOUNT Offered to public (In Rs. Crores)	AMOUNT Offered on Rights basis (In Rs. Crores)	AMOUNT Total (In Rs. Crores)	5% Premium on redemption	Additional information
(1)	(2)	(10)	(11)	(12)	(13)	(14)	(15)	(16)
44.	Kanoria Chem. & Inds. Ltd.	100	12.0	--	1.25	1.25	--	
45.	Polychem Ltd.	100	12.0	--	0.50	0.50	--	Cancelled on 16.4.81.
46.	Bharat Forge Co.Ltd.	100	12.0	--	2.00	2.00	--	Interest rate first raised to 13.5% & then to 15%
47.	Punjab Tractors Ltd.	100	12.0	--	1.50	1.50	--	Lateron interest rate raised to 13.5%
48.	Hindustan Development Corporation Ltd.	100	12.0	0.75	0.75	1.50	--	Later on interest rate raised to 13.5%
49.	Indian Rayon Corporation Ltd.	100	12.0	5.50	4.50	10.00	--	
	TOTAL			11.80	55.15	66.95		

NOTES: 'C.C.I.' stands for 'Controller of Capital Issues'.
'Con.Deb.' stands for 'Convertible Debentures'.
'Non.Con.' & N.C.' stand for 'Non Convertible Debentures'.
'N.A.' stands for 'Not applicable'.
'W.C.' stands for 'Working Capital'

SOURCE: Compiled from the information available in the office of the Controller of Capital Issues, Ministry of Finance, Government of India, New Delhi.

Annexe: II.26

TABLE:2.6 STATEMENT OF APPROVALS GRANTED TO PUBLIC LIMITED COMPANIES OF THE PRIVATE CORPORATE SECTOR BY THE CONTROLLER OF CAPITAL ISSUES FOR RAISING FUNDS THROUGH THE ISSUE OF CONVERTIBLE & NON CONVERTIBLE DEBENTURES DURING THE YEAR 1981.

Sr. No.	Name of Company	Year of Incorp-oration	Registered Office	Nature of Industry	MRTP Comp-any	Con. Deb./ Non. Con. Deb.	Date of permis-sion by CCI	Purpose
(1)	(2)	(3)	(4)	(5)	(6)	(7)	(8)	(9)
1	Siemens India Ltd.	1957	Bombay	Engineering	Ferra	N.C.	3.1.81	Long Term W.C.
2.	Cheviat Co.Ltd.	1897	Calcutta	Jute	N.A.	N.C.	5.1.81	W.C.
3.	Kirloskar Oil Co.Ltd.	1946	Pune	Engineering	N.A.	N.C.	17.1.81	W.C.
4.	Bhavana Chemcials Ltd.	1962	Bombay	Chemicals	Yes	Con.	16.2.81	--
5.	Madura Coats Ltd.	1974	Madurai	Cotton	Yes	N.C.	18.2.81	W.C.
6.	Daccan Sugar & Abkari Co.Ltd.	1897	Madras	Sugar	N.A.	Con.	24.2.81	Rehabilitation.
7.	Voltas Ltd.	1954	Bombay	Trading	Yes	Con.	27.2.81	W.C.
8.	Indian Aluminium Co.Ltd.	1938	Calcutta	Aluminium	Yes	Con.	13.3.81	Modernization & Expansion.
9.	Macneill & Magor Ltd.	1949	Calcutta	Tea	Yes	N.C.	20.3.81	W.C.
10.	Mukand Iron & Steel Works Ltd.	1937	Bombay	Steel	Yes	N.C.	31.3.81	W.C.

Annexe: II.27

TABLE: 2.6 STATEMENT OF APPROVALS GRANTED TO PUBLIC LIMITED COMPANIES OF THE PRIVATE CORPORATE SECTOR BY THE CONTROLLER OF CAPITAL ISSUES FOR RAISING FUNDS THROUGH THE ISSUE OF CONVERTIBLE & NON CONVERTIBLE DEBENTURES DURING THE YEAR 1981. (CONTD..2)

S. No.	Name of Company	Face Value of Deb. (Rs.)	Interest Rate (In Per Cent)	AMOUNT Offered to public (In Rs. Crores)	AMOUNT Offered on Rights basis (In Rs. Crores)	AMOUNT Total (In Rs. Crores)	5% Premium on redemption	Additional information
(1)	(2)	(10)	(11)	(12)	(13)	(14)	(15)	(16)
1.	Siemens India Ltd.	100	12.0	--	5.00	5.00	--	13.5% w.e.f. 21.8.82&15% w.e.f 17.4.82
2.	Cheviat Co.Ltd.	100	12.0	--	0.75	0.75	--	--
3.	Kirloskar Oil Co.Ltd.	100	12.0	--	0.02	0.02	--	--
4.	Bhavana Chemicals Ltd.	100	--	--	0.20	0.20	--	Issue did not require approval from CCI.
5.	Madura Coats Ltd.	100	12.0	3.50	--	3.50	--	15% w.e.f.17.4.82
6.	Deccan Sugar & Abkari Co.Ltd.	1000	11.0	--	0.50	0.50	--	To Nava Bharat Ferro Alloys Ltd.
7.	Voltas Ltd.	250	12.0	3.00	2.00	5.00	--	13.5% w.e.f. 24.3.81.
8.	Indian Aluminium Co.Ltd.	100	12.0	--	10.45	10.45	--	13.5% w.e.f. 3.7.81. *
9.	Macneill & Magor Ltd.	100	13.5	3.00	--	3.00	--	--
10.	Mukand Iron & Steel Works Ltd	100	13.5	--	1.00	1.00	--	15% w.e.f.26.3.82

* Issued to reduce the holdings of N.R.I.

TABLE:2.6 STATEMENT OF APPROVALS GRANTED TO PUBLIC LIMITED COMPANIES OF THE PRIVATE CORPORATE SECTOR BY THE CONTROLLER OF CAPITAL ISSUES FOR RAISING FUNDS THROUGH THE ISSUE OF CONVERTIBLE & NON CONVERTIBLE DEBENTURES DURING THE YEAR 1981 (CONTD...3)

Sr. No.	Name of Company	Year of Incorp-oration	Registered Office	Nature of Industry	MRTP Comp-any	Con. Deb./Non. Con. Deb.	Date of permis-sion by CCI	Purpose
(1)	(2)	(3)	(4)	(5)	(6)	(7)	(8)	(9)
11.	Aegis Chemcials Inds.Ltd	1956	Vapi	Chemicals	Yes	N.C.	1.4.81	Amalgamation
12.	Straw Products Ltd.	1938	Jaykaypur	Paper	Yes	Con.	1.4.81	New Cement Project.
13.	Titaghur Paper Mills Co.Ltd.	1882	Calcutta	Paper	Yes	N.C.	2.4.81	W.C.
14.	Matulya Mills Ltd.	1961	Ahemdabad	Cotton	Yes	Con.	4.4.81	W.C.
15.	Industrial Cables (India)Ltd.	1956	Rajpura	Engineering	N.A.	N.C.	6.4.81	W.C.
16.	Wimco Ltd.	1923	Bombay	Chemcials	Yes	N.C.	14.4.81	W.C.
17.	Alkali & Chem. Corp.of India Ltd.	1937	Calcutta	Chemicals	Yes	N.C.	20.4.81	W.C.
18.	Associated Bearing Co.Ltd.	1961	Bombay	Engineering	Yes	N.C.	21.4.81	W.C.
19.	Jayshree Tea & Inds.Ltd.	1945	Calcutta	Tea	Yes	N.C.	24.4.81	W.C.
20.	Hindustan Gas & Ind. Ltd.	1944	Calcutta	Chemicals	N.A.	N.C.	2.5.81	W.C.

TABLE:2.6 STATEMENT OF APPROVALS GRANTED TO PUBLIC LIMITED COMPANIES OF THE PRIVATE CORPORATE SECTOR BY THE CONTROLLER OF CAPITAL ISSUES FOR RAISING FUNDS THROUGH THE ISSUE OF CONVERTIBLE & NON CONVERTIBLE DEBENTURES DURING THE YEAR 1981 (CONTD....4)

Sr. No.	Name of Company	Face Value of Deb. (Rs.)	Interest Rate (In Per Cent)	Offered to public (In Rs. Crores)	Offered on Rights basis (In Rs. Crores)	Total (In Rs. Crores)	5% Premium on redemption	Additional information
(1)	(2)	(10)	(11)	(12)	(13)	(14)	(15)	(16)
11.	Aegis Chemicals Inds.Ltd.	100	11.0	--	0.12	0.12	--	Issued to shareholders of Everest Refrigerants Ltd.
12.	Straw Products Ltd.	500	12.0	6.50	3.50	10.00	--	--
13.	Titaghur Paper Mills Co.Ltd.	100	13.5	--	1.00	1.00	--	--
14.	Matulya Mills Ltd.	100	13.5	--	0.50	0.50	--	Issue was of unsecured Deb.
15.	Industrial Cables(India)Ltd.	100	13.5	--	1.00	1.00	--	15% w.e.f.26.7.82
16.	Wimco Ltd.	100	13.5	5.00	--	5.00	--	15% w.e.f.14.7.82
17.	Alkali & Chem.Corp.of India Ltd.	100	13.5	3.00	--	3.00	--	--
18.	Associated Bearing Co.Ltd.	100	13.5	3.00	--	3.00	--	15% w.e.f.11.6.82
19.	Jayshree Tea & Inds.Ltd.	100	13.5	1.50	--	1.50	--	*
20.	Hindustan Gas & Ind.Ltd.	100	13.5	--	0.80	0.80	Yes	15%w.e.f.7.7.82

* Cancelled on account of the refusal to grant extension on 7.10.82.

TABLE:2.6 STATEMENT OF APPROVALS GRANTED TO PUBLIC LIMITED COMPANIES OF THE PRIVATE CORPORATE SECTOR BY THE CONTROLLER OF CAPITAL ISSUES FOR RAISING FUNDS THROUGH THE ISSUE OF CONVERTIBLE & NON CONVERTIBLE DEBENTURES DURING THE YEAR 1981 (CONTD.....5)

Sr. No.	Name of Company	Year of Incorp-oration	Registered Office	Nature of Industry	MRTP Comp-any	Con. Deb. Non. Con. Deb.	Date of /permis-sion by CCI	Purpose
(1)	(2)	(3)	(4)	(5)	(6)	(7)	(8)	(9)
21.	Gramophone Co.of India Ltd.	1946	Calcutta	Engineering	Yes	N.C.	6.5.81	--
22.	Polychem Ltd.	1955	Bombay	Chemicals	Yes	N.C.	8.5.81	--
23.	Kanoria Chem. & Inds.Ltd.	1960	Calcutta	Chemicals	N.A.	N.C.	14.5.81	W.C.
24.	Reliance Textiles Inds.Ltd.	1973	Bombay	Rayon	Yes	Con.	14.5.81	Expansion
25.	Sudarshan Chemicals Ind.Ltd.	1951	Pune	Chemicals	N.A.	N.C.	16.5.81	W.C.
26.	Shri Dinesh Mills Ltd.	1935	Baroda	Woollen	N.A.	Con.	25.5.81	W.C.
27.	Woodcraft Products Ltd.	1943	Calcutta	Engineering	Yes	N.C.	27.5.81	W.C.
28.	Rustom Mills & Inds.Ltd.	1923	Ahemdabad	Cotton	N.A.	Con.	3.6.81	W.C.
29.	Union Carbide India Ltd.	1934	Calcutta	Engineering	Yes	N.C.	15.6.81	W.C.
30.	J.K.Synthetics Ltd.	1943	Kanpur	Chemicals	Yes	N.C.	15.6.81	W.C.

TABLE:2.6 STATEMENT OF APPROVALS GRANTED TO PUBLIC LIMITED COMPANIES OF THE PRIVATE CORPORATE SECTOR BY THE CONTROLLER OF CAPITAL ISSUES FOR RAISING FUNDS THROUGH THE ISSUE OF CONVERTIBLE & NON CONVERTIBLE DEBENTURES DURING THE YEAR 1981 (CONTD......6)

Sr. No.	Name of Company	Face value of Deb. (Rs.)	Interest Rate (In Per Cent)	AMOUNT Offered to public (In Rs. Crores)	Offered on Rights basis (In Rs. Crores)	Total (In Rs. Crores)	5% Premium on redemption	Additional information
(1)	(2)	(10)	(11)	(12)	(13)	(14)	(15)	(16)
21.	Gramophone Co.of India Ltd.	100	13.5	--	1.00	1.00	--	15%w.e.f.7.7.82
22.	Polychem Ltd.	100	13.5	--	1.00	1.00	Yes	15%w.e.f.21.5.82
23.	Kanoria Chem.& Inds.Ltd.	100	13.5	2.00	--	2.00	--	15%w.e.f.3.6.82*
24.	Reliance Textiles Inds.Ltd.	125	13.5	13.00	11.00	24.00	--	
25.	Sudarshan Chemicals Inds.Ltd	100	13.5	--	0.75	0.75	--	15%w.e.f.3.8.82
26.	Shri Dinesh Mills Ltd.	500	13.5	0.60	0.40	1.00	--	**
27.	Woodcraft Products Ltd.	100	13.5	--	0.25	0.25	--	
28.	Rustom Mills & Inds.Ltd.	100	13.5	1.40	0.60	2.00	--	
29.	Union Carbide India Ltd.	100	13.5	5.00	--	5.00	--	15%w.e.f.22.10.82
30.	J.K.Synthetics Ltd.	100	13.5	5.00	--	5.00	--	15%w.e.f.17.4.82

* Consent for Rs.1.25 Cr. cancelled.

** Face value modified to Rs.100 w.e.f.18.4.83.

TABLE:2.6 STATEMENT OF APPROVALS GRANTED TO PUBLIC LIMITED COMPANIES OF THE PRIVATE CORPORATE SECTOR BY THE CONTROLLER OF CAPITAL ISSUES FOR RAISING FUNDS THROUGH THE ISSUE OF CONVERTIBLE & NON CONVERTIBLE DEBENTURES DURING THE YEAR 1981 (CONTD.......7)

Sr. No.	Name of Company	Year of Incorp-oration	Registered Office	Nature of Industry	MRTP Comp-any	Con. Deb./ Non. Con. Deb.	Date of permis-sion by CCI	Purpose
(1)	(2)	(3)	(4)	(5)	(6)	(7)	(8)	(9)
31.	Kirloskar Brothers Ltd.	1920	Pune	Engineering	Yes	N.C.	20.6.81	W.C.
32.	Cloride India Ltd.	1947	Calcutta	Engineering	Yes	N.C.	20.6.81	W.C.
33.	East India Hotel Ltd.	1949	Calcutta	Hotels	Yes	Con.	23.6.81	Expansion &W.C.
34.	Garware Paints Ltd.	1937	Bombay	Chemicals	Yes	N.C.	24.6.81	W.C.
35.	Chemicals & Fibres of India Ltd.	1961	Bombay	Chemicals	Yes	N.C.	25.6.81	W.C.
36.	Ferro Alloy Corporation Ltd.	1955	Tumsar	Steel	N.A.	Con.	29.6.81	Financing New Project.
37.	Ambalal Sarabhai Enterprises Ltd.	1977	Baroda	Chemicals	Yes	N.C.	30.6.81	Amalgamation
38.	Ahemdabad Mfg.& Calico Printing Co. Ltd.	1880	Ahemdabad	Cotton	Yes	N.C.	1.7.81	W.C.
39.	Indian Rayon Corporation Ltd.	1956	Veraval	Rayon	N.A.	N.C.	4.7.81	W.C

TABLE:2.6

STATEMENT OF APPROVALS GRANTED TO PUBLIC LIMITED COMPANIES OF THE PRIVATE CORPORATE SECTOR BY THE CONTROLLER OF CAPITAL ISSUES FOR RAISING FUNDS THROUGH THE ISSUE OF CONVERTIBLE & NON CONVERTIBLE DEBENTURES DURING THE YEAR 1981 (CONTD........8)

Sr. No.	Name of Company	Face value of Deb. (Rs.)	Interest Rate (In Per Cent)	AMOUNT Offered to public (In Rs. Crores)	Offered on Rights basis (In Rs. Crores)	Total (In Rs. Crores)	5% Premium on redemption	Additional information
(1)	(2)	(10)	(11)	(12)	(13)	(14)	(15)	(16)
31.	Kirloskar Brothers Ltd.	100	13.5	1.50	--	1.50	--	*
32.	Cloride India Ltd.	100	13.5	2.00	--	2.00	Yes	
33.	East India Hotel Ltd.	100	13.5	3.00	4.50	7.50	--	
34.	Garware Paints Ltd.	100	13.5	--	0.50	0.50	--	
35.	Chemicals & Fibres of India Ltd.	100	13.5	3.00	--	3.00	--	
36.	Ferro Alloy Cororation Ltd.	250	13.5	5.00	2.50	7.50	--	
37.	Ambalal Sarabhai Enterprises Ltd.	100	9.0	--	3.78	3.78	--	**
38.	Ahemdabad Mfg. & Calico Printing Co.Ltd.	100	13.5	--	2.50	2.50	Yes	15% w.e.f.20.5.82
39.	Indian Rayon Corporation Ltd.	100	13.5	5.00	--	5.00	--	

* Issued without employing any under-writers.
** To shareholders of S.G.Chemicals & Pharmaceutical Co.Ltd.

TABLE: 2.6 STATEMENT OF APPROVALS GRANTED TO PUBLIC LIMITED COMPANIES OF THE PRIVATE CORPORATE SECTOR BY THE CONTROLLER OF CAPITAL ISSUES FOR RAISING FUNDS THROUGH THE ISSUE OF CONVERTIBLE & NON CONVERTIBLE DEBENTURES DURING THE YEAR 1981 (CONTD.........9)

Sr. No.	Name of Company	Year of Incorp-oration	Registered Office	Nature of Industry	MRTP Comp-any	Con. Deb./ Non. Con. Deb.	Date of permis-sion by CCI	Purpose
(1)	(2)	(3)	(4)	(5)	(6)	(7)	(8)	(9)
40.	Morarjee Goculdas Spg.& Mfg.Co.Ltd.	1871	Bombay	Cotton	Yes	N.C.	10.7.81	W.C.
41.	Fiber-glass Pilkington Ltd.	1962	Bombay	Chemicals	Yes	Con.	14.7.81	Modernization & W.C.
42.	Spencer and Co.Ltd.	1897	Madras	Trading	N.A.	N.C.	20.7.81	W.C.
43.	Cheviot Co.Ltd.	1897	Calcutta	Jute	N.A.	Con.	31.7.81	W.C.
44.	Modi Rubber Co.Ltd.	1971	Ghaziabad	Rubber	Yes	N.C.	18.8.81	W.C.
45.	I.T.C.Ltd.	1910	Calcutta	Tobacco	Yes	N.C.	21.8.81	W.C.
46.	K.S.B.Pump Ltd.	1960	Bombay	Engineering	N.A.	Con.	27.8.81	W.C.
47.	Tube Investments of India Ltd.	1949	Madras	Engineering	Yes	N.C.	29.8.81	W.C.
48.	Joyti Ltd.	1943	Baroda	Engineering	N.A.	Con.	19.9.81	Expansion
49.	Cadbury India Ltd.	1948	Bombay	Chemicals	N.A.	N.C.	22.9.81	W.C.
50.	Tata Iron and steel Co.Ltd.	1907	Bombay	Iron & Steel	Yes	Con.	24.9.81	W.C.

TABLE:2.6 STATEMENT OF APPROVALS GRANTED TO PUBLIC LIMITED COMPANIES OF THE PRIVATE CORPORATE SECTOR BY THE CONTROLLER OF CAPITAL ISSUES FOR RAISING FUNDS THROUGH THE ISSUE OF CONVERTIBLE & NON CONVERTIBLE DEBENTURES DURING THE YEAR 1981(CONTD..........10)

Sr. No.	Name of Company	Face value of Deb. (Rs.)	Interest Rate (In Per Cent)	AMOUNT: Offered to public (In Rs. Crores)	AMOUNT: Offered on Rights basis (In Rs. Crores)	AMOUNT: Total (In Rs. Crores)	5% Premium on redemption	Additional information
(1)	(2)	(10)	(11)	(12)	(13)	(14)	(15)	(16)
40.	Morarjee Goculdas Spg. & Mfg. Co.Ltd.	100	13.5	2.50	--	2.50	--	15%w.e.f.1.7.82
41.	Fiber-glass Pilkington Ltd.	156	13.5	1.73	0.90	2.63	--	
42.	Spencer and Co. Ltd.	100	13.5	--	1.00	1.00	--	
43.	Cheviot Co.Ltd.	100	13.5	0.90	0.10	1.00	--	
44.	Modi Rubber Co.Ltd.	100	13.5	6.00	--	6.00	--	15%w.e.f.19.5.82
45.	I.T.C.Ltd	100	13.5	5.00	--	5.00	--	15%w.e.f.31.12.82
46.	K.S.B.Pump Ltd.	75	13.5	--	1.25	1.25	--	
47.	Tube Investments of India Ltd.	100	13.5	--	1.00	1.00	--	Issue was dropped on 2.3.82
48.	Joyti Ltd.	100	13.5	1.00	1.00	2.00	--	
49.	Cadbury India Ltd.	100	13.5	--	2.00	2.00	--	Did not avail consent worth Rs. 1 Crore.
50.	Tata Iron and Steel Co.Ltd.	300	13.5	12.00	18.00	30.00	--	

TABLE:2.6 STATEMENT OF APPROVALS GRANTED TO PUBLIC LIMITED COMPANIES OF THE PRIVATE CORPORATE SECTOR BY THE CONTROLLER OF CAPITAL ISSUES FOR RAISING FUNDS THROUGH THE ISSUE OF CONVERTIBLE & NON CONVERTIBLE DEBENTURES DURING THE YEAR 1981 (CONTD..........11)

Sr. No.	Name of Company	Year of Incorp-oration	Registered Office	Nature of Industry	MRTP Comp-any	Con. Deb./Non. Con. Deb.	Date of permis-sion by CCI	Purpose
(1)	(2)	(3)	(4)	(5)	(6)	(7)	(8)	(9)
51.	Star Industrial & Taxtile Co.Ltd.	1948	Bombay	Cotton	N.A.	Con.	29.9.81	--
52.	Bombay Dying & Mfg.Co.Ltd.	1879	Bombay	Cotton	Yes	N.C.	30.9.81	W.C.
53.	Modipon Ltd.	1965	Modinagar	Chemicals	Yes	N.C.	30.9.81	W.C.
54.	Sukhjit Strach & Chemicals Ltd.	1944	Phagwara	Chemicals	N.A.	Con.	3.10.81	--
55.	El-con Engg. Co. Ltd.	1960	Vidyanagar	Engineering	Yes	Con.	5.10.81	Modernization & Expansion
56.	Indian Organic Chemicals Co. Ltd.	1960	Bombay	Chemicals	Yes	Con.	6.10.81	--
57.	Ahemdabad Shri Rama Krishana Mills Co.Ltd.	1907	Ahemdabad	Cotton	N.A.	Con.	6.10.81	W.C.
58.	Shreyans Paper Mills Ltd.	1979	Jullandhar	Paper	N.A.	Con.	24.10.81	--
59.	I.C.I.C.I.	1955	Bombay	Finance	N.A.	Con.	2.11.81	--

TABLE:2.6 STATEMENT OF APPROVALS GRANTED TO PUBLIC LIMITED COMPANIES OF THE PRIVATE CORPORATE SECTOR BY THE CONTROLLER OF CAPITAL ISSUES FOR RAISING FUNDS THROUGH THE ISSUE OF CONVERTIBLE & NON CONVERTIBLE DEBENTURES DURING THE YEAR 1981 (CONTD............12)

Sr. No.	Name of company	Face value of Deb (Rs.)	Interest Rate (In Per Cent)	AMOUNT Offered to public (In Rs. Crores)	Offered on Rights basis (In Rs. Crores)	Total (In Rs. Crores)	5% Premium on redemption	Additional information
(1)	(2)	(10)	(11)	(12)	(13)	(14)	(15)	(16)
51.	Star Industrial & Textile Co.Ltd.	250	13.5	2.25	2.00	4.25	--	
52.	Bombay Dying & Mfg.Co.Ltd.	100	13.5	4.00	--	4.00	--	15% w.e.f.16.6.82
53.	Modipon Ltd.	100	13.5	5.00	--	5.00	Yes	15% w.e.f.30.6.82
54.	Sukhjit Strach & Chemicals Ltd.	100	13.5	0.90	0.10	1.00	--	
55.	El-con Engg. Co.Ltd.	100	13.5	2.80	2.70	5.50	--	
56.	Indian Organic Chemicals Co.Ltd.	100	13.5	--	3.72	3.72	--	
57.	Ahemdabad Shri Rama Krishana Mills Co.Ltd.	120	13.5	0.48	0.12	0.60	--	
58.	Shreyans Paper Mills Ltd.	100	13.5	--	0.30	0.30	--	To Unit Trust of India.
59.	I.C.I.C.I.	300	13.0	--	13.50	13.50	--	

TABLE:2.6 STATEMENT OF APPROVALS GRANTED TO PUBLIC LIMITED COMPANIES OF THE PRIVATE CORPORATE SECTOR BY THE CONTROLLER OF CAPITAL ISSUES FOR RAISING FUNDS THROUGH THE ISSUE OF CONVERTIBLE & NON CONVERTIBLE DEBENTURES DURING THE YEAR 1981 (CONTD.............13)

Sr. No.	Name of Company	Year of Incorporation	Registered Office	Nature of Industry	MRTP Company	Con. Deb./ Non. Con. Deb.	Date of permission by CCI	Purpose
(1)	(2)	(3)	(4)	(5)	(6)	(7)	(8)	(9)
60.	Delhi Cloth & General Mills Co.Ltd.	1889	Delhi	Cotton	Yes	Con.	3.11.81	W.C.
61.	Punjab Anand Batteries Ltd.	1972	Mohali	Engineering	N.A.	Con.	6.11.81	--
62.	Devy Ashmore India Ltd.	1972	Calcutta	Chemicals	N.A.	N.C.	13.11.81	W.C.
63.	Usha Alloys and Steel Ltd.	1971	Calcutta	Steel	N.A.	Con.	17.11.81	W.C.
64.	Hindustan Brown Boveri Ltd.	1949	Bombay	Engineering	Yes	N.C.	24.11.81	W.C.
65.	Chemicals & Plastics India Ltd.	1962	Madras	Chemicals	N.A.	N.C.	24.11.81	W.C.
66.	Mahindra Spicer Ltd.	1919	Bombay	Engineering	Yes	N.C.	26.11.81	W.C.
67.	J.K.Synthetics Ltd.	1943	Kanpur	Chemicals	Yes	Con.	27.11.81	Expansion & W.C.
68.	Mahavir Spg. Mills Ltd.	1973	Ludhiana	Cotton	N.A.	Con.	27.11.81	--

TABLE: 2.6 STATEMENT OF APPROVALS GRANTED TO PUBLIC LIMITED COMPANIES OF THE PRIVATE CORPORATE SECTOR BY THE CONTROLLER OF CAPITAL ISSUES FOR RAISING FUNDS THROUGH THE ISSUE OF CONVERTIBLE & NON CONVERTIBLE DEBENTURES DURING THE YEAR 1981 (CONTD..............14)

Sr. No.	Name of company	Face value of Deb. (Rs.)	Interest Rate (In Per Cent)	AMOUNT Offered to public (In Rs. Crores)	AMOUNT Offered on Rights basis (In Rs. Crores)	AMOUNT Total (In Rs. Crores)	5% Premium on redemption	Additional information
(1)	(2)	(10)	(11)	(12)	(13)	(14)	(15)	(16)
60.	Delhi Cloth & General Mills Co.Ltd.	125	13.5	6.00	9.00	15.00	--	--
61.	Punjab Anand Batteries Ltd.	100	13.5	0.50	0.50	1.00	--	*
62.	Devy Ashmore India Ltd.	100	13.5	--	1.00	1.00	Yes	15% w.e.f.1.5.82
63.	Usha Alloys and Steel Ltd.	100	13.5	0.90	0.60	1.50	--	
64.	Hindustan Brown Boveri Ltd.	100	13.5	--	1.00	1.00	Yes	15% w.e.f.17.4.82
65.	Chemicals & Plastics India Ltd.	100	13.5	--	1.00	1.00	--	15% w.e.f.24.5.82
66.	Mahindra Spicer Ltd.	100	13.5	--	0.75	0.75	Yes	15% w.e.f20.5.82
67.	J.K.Synthetics Ltd.	160	13.5	12.00	13.00	25.00	--	--
68.	Mahavir Spg. Mills Ltd.	100	13.5	--	0.25	0.25	--	To Unit Trust of India.

* Issue was originally for non-convertible debentures but was made for convertible debentures w.e.f. 25.9.1982.

TABLE:2.6 STATEMENT OF APPROVALS GRANTED TO PUBLIC LIMITED COMPANIES OF THE PRIVATE CORPORATE SECTOR BY THE CONTROLLER OF CAPITAL ISSUES FOR RAISING FUNDS THROUGH THE ISSUE OF CONVERTIBLE & NON CONVERTIBLE DEBENTURES DURING THE YEAR 1981 (CONTD..............15)

Sr. No.	Name of Company	Year of Incorp-oration	Registered Office	Nature of Industry	MRTP Comp-any	Con. Deb./Non. Con. Deb.	Date of permis-sion by CCI	Purpose
(1)	(2)	(3)	(4)	(5)	(6)	(7)	(8)	(9)
69.	Gujarat Steel Tube Ltd.	1960	Ahemdabad	Steel	N.A.	Con.	27.11.81	Finance of Project.
70.	Mahendra Mills Ltd.	1942	Ahemdabad	Cotton	N.A.	Con.	27.11.81	W.C.& Expansion
71.	Premier Mills Ltd.	1945	Udamlpat	Cotton	N.A.	Con.	27.11.81	Expansion
72.	Mukand Iron & Steel Works Ltd.	1937	Bombay	Steel	Yes	Con.	28.11.81	Medium Term Loans.
73.	Swan Mills Ltd.	1909	Bombay	Cotton	Yes	N.C.	28.11.81	W.C.
74.	Bharat Steel Tube Co.Ltd.	1959	N.Delhi	Steel	Yes	Con.	30.11.81	Expansion
75.	Vardhman Spg.& General Mills Ltd.	1962	Ludhiana	Cotton	N.A	Con.	9.12.81	W.C.
76.	Shree Vallabh Glass Works Ltd.	1957	Ahemdabad	Chemicals	N.A.	Con.	17.12.81	Expansion.
77.	Perfect Circle Victor Ltd.	1962	Bombay	Engineering	N.A.	Con.	18.12.81	W.C.

Annexe: II.41

TABLE:2.6 STATEMENT OF APPROVALS GRANTED TO PUBLIC LIMITED COMPANIES OF THE PRIVATE CORPORATE SECTOR BY THE CONTROLLER OF CAPITAL ISSUES FOR RAISING FUNDS THROUGH THE ISSUE OF CONVERTIBLE & NON CONVERTIBLE DEBENTURES DURING THE YEAR 1981 (CONTD.............16)

Sr. No.	Name of company	Face Value of Deb. (Rs.)	Interest Rate (In Per Cent)	AMOUNT Offered to public (In Rs. Crores)	Offered on Rights basis (In Rs. Crores)	Total (In Rs. Crores)	5% Premium on redemption	Additional information
(1)	(2)	(10)	(11)	(12)	(13)	(14)	(15)	(16)
69.	Gujarat Steel Tube Ltd.	500	13.5	3.00	2.00	5.00	--	
70.	Mahendra Mills Ltd.	100	13.5	1.62	1.38	3.00	--	
71.	Premier Mills Ltd.	100	13.5	5.00	--	5.00	--	
72.	Mukand Iron & Steel Works Ltd	200	13.5	4.55	2.45	7.00	---	
73.	Swan Mills Ltd.	100	15.0	2.25	1.50	3.75	--	
74.	Bharat Steel Tube Co. Ltd.	200	13.5	3.00	1.00	4.00	--	
75.	Vardhman Spg. & General Mills Ltd.	100	13.5	1.47	0.53	2.00	--	
76.	Shree Vallabh Glass Works Ltd.	500	13.5	--	2.00	2.00	--	
77.	Perfect Circle Victor Ltd.	100	13.5	--	0.50	0.50	--	

* Company applied for convertible debentures.

TABLE:2.6

STATEMENT OF APPROVALS GRANTED TO PUBLIC LIMITED COMPANIES OF THE PRIVATE CORPORATE SECTOR BY THE CONTROLLER OF CAPITAL ISSUES FOR RAISING FUNDS THROUGH THE ISSUE OF CONVERTIBLE & NON CONVERTIBLE DEBENTURES DURING THE YEAR 1981 (CONTD.................17)

Sr. No.	Name of Company	Year of Incorp-oration	Registered Office	Nature of Industry	MRTP Comp-any	Con. Deb./ Non. Con. Deb.	Date of permis-sion by CCI	Purpose
(1)	(2)	(3)	(4)	(5)	(6)	(7)	(8)	(9)
78.	Kothari (Madras)Ltd.	1970	Madras	Chemicals	Yes	Con.	19.12.81	W.C.
79.	New Gujarati Synthetics Ltd.	1896	Ahemdabad	Cotton	N.A.	N.C.	26.12.81	W.C.
80.	Reliance Textiles Inds.Ltd.	1973	Bombay	Rayon	Yes	N.C.	28.12.81	Amalgamation
81.	Machinery Mfg.Corp.Ltd.	1946	Bombay	Cotton	Yes	Con.	29.12.81	Expansion
82.	Ambalal Sarabhai Enterprises Ltd.	1977	Baroda	Chemicals	N.A.	Con.	31.12.81	W.C.
83.	Perfect Circle Victor Ltd.	1962	Bombay	Engineering	N.A.	N.C.	31.12.81	W.C.

TABLE:2.6 STATEMENT OF APPROVALS GRANTED TO PUBLIC LIMITED COMPANIES OF THE PRIVATE CORPORATE SECTOR BY THE CONTROLLER OF CAPITAL ISSUES FOR RAISING FUNDS THROUGH THE ISSUE OF CONVERTIBLE & NON CONVERTIBLE DEBENTURES DURING THE YEAR 1981.(CONTD..................18)

Sr. No.	Name of Company	Face Value of Deb. (Rs.)	Interest Rate (In Per Cent)	AMOUNT Offered to public (In Rs. Crores)	Offered on Rights basis (In Rs. Crores)	Total (In Rs. Crores)	5% Premium on redemption	Additional information
(1)	(2)	(10)	(11)	(12)	(13)	(14)	(15)	(16)
78.	Kothari (Madras) Ltd.	100	13.5	6.00	4.00	10.00	--	--
79.	New Gujarati Synthetics Ltd.	100	13.5	--	1.50	1.50	Yes	15% w.e.f.20.5.82
80.	Reliance Textiles Inds.Ltd.	8	10.0	--	0.03	0.03	--	To Sidhpur Mills Co Ltd. for amalgamation
81.	Machinery Mfg. Corp. Ltd.	200	13.5	--	3.01	3.01	--	--
82.	Ambalal Sarabhai Enterprises Ltd.	150	13.5	--	9.99	9.99	--	--
83.	Perfect Circle Victor Ltd.	10	13.5	--	0.50	0.50	Yes	15% w.e.f. 9.6.82
	TOTAL			165.85	160.80	326.65		

NOTES: 'C.C.I.' stands for Controller of Capital Issues.
'N.R.I.' stands for Non Resident Indian.
'Con.Deb.' stands for 'Convertible Debentures'.
'Non.Con.' & 'N.C.' stands for 'Non Convertible Debentures'
'N.A.' stands for 'Not applicable'.
'W.C.' stands for 'Working Capital'.

SOURCE: Complied from the information available in the Office of the Controller of Capital Issues, Ministry of Finance, Government of India, New Delhi

TABLE: 2.7 STATEMENT OF APPROVALS GRANTED TO PUBLIC LIMITED COMPANIES OF THE PRIVATE CORPORATE SECTOR BY THE CONTROLLER OF CAPITAL ISSUES FOR RAISING FUNDS THROUGH THE ISSUE OF CONVERTIBLE & NON CONVERTIBLE DEBENTURES DURING THE YEAR 1982.

Sr. No.	Name of Company	Year of Incorporation	Registered Office	Nature of Industry	MRTP Company	Con. Deb./ Non. Con. Deb.	Date of permission by CCI	Purpose
(1)	(2)	(3)	(4)	(5)	(6)	(7)	(8)	(9)
1.	Nagarjuna Steel Ltd.	1974	Hydrabad	Steel	N.A.	Con.	2.1.82	W.C.
2.	Ahmedabad Advance Mills Ltd.	1903	Bombay	Steel	Yes	Con.	7.1.82	-
3.	General Industrial Soc.Ltd.	1892	Calcutta	Chemicals	N.A.	Con.	12.1.82	Expansion
4.	Spencer & Co. Ltd.	1897	Madras	Trading	N.A.	N.C.	14.1.82	W.C.
5.	Kamani Engg.Corporation Ltd.	1945	Bombay	Engineering	Yes	Con.	28.1.82	W.C.
6.	Laxmi Starch Ltd.	1946	Kundara (Kerala)	Steel	N.A.	Con.	30.1.82	W.C.
7.	Rajasthan Spg.&Wvg. Mills Ltd.	1960	N.Delhi	Cotton	N.A.	Con.	30.1.82	Expansion
8.	Real Investment Co.Ltd.	1978	Ahmedabad	Finance	N.A.	Con.	2.2.82	-
9.	Hercules Investment Ltd.	1978	Bombay	Finance	N.A.	Con.	2.2.82	-
10.	Jagadanand Invest. & Trading Co.Ltd.	1979	Bombay	Commerce	N.A.	Con.	2.2.82	-

TABLE: 2.7 STATEMENT OF APPROVALS GRANTED TO PUBLIC LIMITED COMPANIES OF THE PRIVATE CORPORATE SECTOR BY THE CONTROLLER OF CAPITAL ISSUES FOR RAISING FUNDS THROUGH THE ISSUE OF CONVERTIBLE & NON CONVERTIBLE DEBENTURES DURING THE YEAR 1982 (CONTD..2)

Sr. No.	Name of Company	Face Value of Deb. (Rs.)	Interest Rate (In Per Cent)	AMOUNT: Offered to public (In Rs. Crores)	AMOUNT: Offered on Rights basis (In Rs. Crores)	AMOUNT: Total (In Rs. Crores)	5% Premium on redemption	Additional information
(1)	(2)	(10)	(11)	(12)	(13)	(14)	(15)	(16)
1.	Nagarjuna Steel Ltd.	100	13.5	--	1.25	1.25	--	Three shares at par after one year.
2.	Ahmedabad Advance Mills Ltd	400	13.5	2.81	3.19	6.00	--	Rs. 130 converted into one share after 3 years.
3.	General Industrial Soc.Ltd.	100	13.5	2.80	1.20	4.00	--	Rs. 130 converted into 3 shares at par on 1.1.83.
4.	Spencer & Co. Ltd.	100	13.5	--	1.00	1.00	--	--
5.	Kamani Engg.Corp.Ltd.	300	13.5	--	6.00	6.00	--	Rs. 150 converted in 5 shares after 3 years.
6.	Laxmi Starch Ltd.	100	13.5	--	1.00	1.00	--	Rs.20 into 2 shares on 31.12.82
7.	Rajasthan Spg.& Wvg.Mills Ltd.	150	13.5	2.40	2.60	5.00	--	Rs.50 into 5 shares after 1 year.
8.	Real Investment Co. Ltd.	100	13.5	--	0.90	0.90	--	Rs.20 into 2 shares after 7 years.
9.	Hercules Investment Ltd.	100	13.5	--	0.90	0.90	--	-do-
10.	Jagadanand Invest.& Trading Co.Ltd.	100	13.5	--	0.28	0.28	--	-do-

TABLE: 2.7 STATEMENT OF APPROVALS GRANTED TO PUBLIC LIMITED COMPANIES OF THE PRIVATE CORPORATE SECTOR BY THE CONTROLLER OF CAPITAL ISSUES FOR RAISING FUNDS THROUGH THE ISSUE OF CONVERTIBLE & NON CONVERTIBLE DEBENTURES DURING THE YEAR 1982. (CONTD...3)

Sr. No.	Name of Company	Year of Incorporation	Registered Office	Nature of Industry	MRTP Company	Con. Deb./ Non. Con. Deb.	Date of permission by CCI	Purpose
(1)	(2)	(3)	(4)	(5)	(6)	(7)	(8)	(9)
11.	Kedareshwar Invest.& Trading Co.Ltd.	1979	Bombay	Commerce	N.A.	Con.	2.2.82	--
12.	Nikshil Invest.Co.Ltd.	1978	Bombay	Commerce	N.A.	Con.	2.2.82	--
13.	Kamkhal Invest.&Trd.Co.Ltd.	1979	Bombay	Commerce	N.A.	Con.	2.2.82	--
14.	Jagdeshwar Invest.& Trading Co.Ltd.	1979	Bombay	Commerce	N.A.	Con.	2.2.82	--
15.	J.K.Cotton Spg.& Wvg.Mills Co.Ltd.	1924	Kanpur	Cotton	N.A.	N.C.	5.2.82	W.C.
16.	Pams Invest.& Trading Co.Ltd.	1973	Bombay	Commerce	N.A.	Con.	6.2.82	--
17.	Rallis India Ltd.	1948	Bombay	Chemicals	Yes	N.C.	9.2.82	Long Term Funds
18.	Tata Chemicals Ltd.	1939	Bombay	Chemicals	Yes	N.C.	9.2.82	W.C.
19.	Indian Hotels Co.Ltd.	1902	Bombay	Hotel	N.A.	Con.	18.2.82	--
20.	Bharat Vijay Mills Ltd.	1931	Kalol	Cotton	N.A.	Con.	19.2.82	W.C.
21.	Reliance Textile Ind.Ltd.	1973	Bombay	Rayon	Yes	Con.	9.3.82	Expansion

TABLE: 2.7

STATEMENT OF APPROVALS GRANTED TO PUBLIC LIMITED COMPANIES OF THE PRIVATE CORPORATE SECTOR BY THE CONTROLLER OF CAPITAL ISSUES FOR RAISING FUNDS THROUGH THE ISSUE OF CONVERTIBLE & NON CONVERTIBLE DEBENTURES DURING THE YEAR 1982 (CONTD....4)

Sr. No.	Name of Company	Face Value of Deb. (Rs.)	Interest Rate (In Per Cent)	AMOUNT: Offered to public (In Rs. Crores)	Offered on Rights basis (In Rs. Crores)	Total (In Rs. Crores)	5% Premium on redemption	Additional information
(1)	(2)	(10)	(11)	(12)	(13)	(14)	(15)	(16)
11.	Kedareshwar Invest.& Trading Co.Ltd.	100	13.5	--	0.27	0.27	--	Rs.20/-into 2 shares after 7 years
12.	Nikshil Invest.Co.Ltd.	100	13.5	-	0.90	0.90	--	Rs.20/-into 2 shares after 7 years
13.	Kamkhal Invest. & Trading Co. Ltd.	100	13.5	--	0.16	0.16	--	Rs.20/-into 2 shares after 7 years.
14.	Jagdeshwar Invest. & Trading Co. Ltd.	100	13.5	--	0.42	0.42	--	Rs.20/-into 2 shares after 7 years.
15.	J.K.Cotton Spg. & Wvg. Mills Co. Ltd.	100	13.5	--	1.00	1.00	--	--
16.	Pams Invest.& Trading Co.Ltd.	100	13.5	--	0.85	0.85	--	Rs.20/-into 2 shares after 7 years.
17.	Rallis India Ltd.	100	13.5	--	2.50	2.50	Yes	--
18.	Tata Chemicals Ltd.	100	13.5	--	3.50	3.50	Yes	--
19.	Indian Hotels Co.Ltd.	100	13.5	9.33	5.67	15.00	--	Rs.25/-into 1 share after 3 years.
20.	Bharat Vijay Mills Ltd.	500	13.5	1.60	1.80	3.40	--	--
21.	Reliance Textile Ind.Ltd.	125	13.5	--	50.00	50.00	--	20% converted into equity on 30.9.83

TABLE: 2.7 STATEMENT OF APPROVALS GRANTED TO PUBLIC LIMITED COMPANIES OF THE PRIVATE CORPORATE SECTOR BY THE CONTROLLER OF CAPITAL ISSUES FOR RAISING FUNDS THROUGH THE ISSUE OF CONVERTIBLE & NON CONVERTIBLE DEBENTURES DURING THE YEAR 1982. (CONTD.....5)

Sr. No.	Name of Company	Year of Incorp-oration	Registered Office	Nature of Industry	MRTP Comp-any	Con. Deb./Non. Con. Deb.	Date of permi - ssion by CCI	Purpose
(1)	(2)	(3)	(4)	(5)	(6)	(7)	(8)	(9)
22.	Ahmedabad Mfg. & Calico Printing Co.Ltd.	1880	Ahmedabad	Cotton	Yes	Con.	18.3.82	--
23.	Golden Tobacco Co.Ltd.	1955	Bombay	Tobacco	Yes	N.C.	3.4.82	W.C.
24.	Pudunjee Pulp & Paper Mills Ltd.	1964	Pune	Paper	N.A.	Con.	22.4.82	W.C.
25.	Zenith Steel Pipes & Ind.Ltd.	1960	Bombay	Steel	N.A.	Con.	28.4.82	W.C.
26.	Callulose Products of India Ltd.	1959	Ahmedabad	Chemicals	N.A.	Con.	6.5.82	Expansion
27.	Mohta Industries Ltd.	1972	Ludhiana	Steel	N.A.	Con.	10.5.82	W.C.
28.	Graphite India Ltd.	1962	Calcutta	Chemicals	Yes	N.C.	10.5.82	W.C.
29.	Gwalior Rayon Silk Mfg. & Wvg.Co.Ltd.	1947	Nagda(M.P)	Rayon	Yes	Con.	19.5.82	Expansion & W.C.
30.	Standard Mills Co. Ltd	1892	Bombay	Textiles	Yes	Con.	1.6.82	Expansion & W.C.
31.	Ranbaxy Laboratory Co.Ltd.	1961	Ropar (Pb)	Chemicals	N.A.	Con.	2.6.82	Expansion & Modernisation
32.	D.L.F.UniversalLtd.	1963	Faridabad	Engineering	N.A.	N.C.	11.6.82	Expansion

TABLE: 2.7 STATEMENT OF APPROVALS GRANTED TO PUBLIC LIMITED COMPANIES OF THE PRIVATE CORPORATE SECTOR BY THE CONTROLLER OF CAPITAL ISSUES FOR RAISING FUNDS THROUGH THE ISSUE OF CONVERTIBLE & NON CONVERTIBLE DEBENTURES DURING THE YEAR 1982 (CONTD......6)

Sr. No.	Name of Company	Face Value of Deb. (Rs.)	Interest Rate (In Per Cent)	AMOUNT: Offered to public (In Rs. Crores)	Offered on Rights basis (In Rs. Crores)	Total (In Rs. Crores)	5% Premium on redemption	Additional information
(1)	(2)	(10)	(11)	(12)	(13)	(14)	(15)	(16)
22.	Ahmedabad Mfg.& Calico Printing Co. Ltd.	425	13.5	--	15.00	15.00	--	Rs. 125/-to be converted into 1 equity
23.	Golden Tobacco Co.Ltd.	100	13.5 15% w.e.f.29.4.82	3.00	--	3.00	Yes	--
24.	Pudunjee Pulp & Paper Mills Ltd.	100	13.5	--	1.50	1.50	--	Rs.25/-into 2 equities on 31.12.83
25.	Zenith Steel Pipes & Industires Ltd.	120	13.5	2.40	2.40	4.80	--	--
26.	Callulose Products of India Ltd.	200	13.5	0.95	0.55	1.50	--	Rs.100/-into 1 equity on 1.4.83
27.	Mohta Industries Ltd.	100	13.5	0.90	0.40	1.30	--	Rs.50/- into 5 shares on 1.1.83
28.	Graphite India Ltd.	100	13.5 15%w.e.f.26.6.82	--	3.00	3.00	Yes	--
29.	Gwalior Rayon Silk Mfg. & Wvg.Co.Ltd.	160	13.5	10.00	20.00	30.00	--	Rs.40/-into 2 equities on 1.4.83
30.	Standard Mills Co.Ltd.	500	13.5	--	10.00	10.00	--	Rs.200/-into 1 equity on31.7.84
31.	Ranbaxy Laboratory Co.Ltd	200	13.5	1.25	3.25	4.50	--	Rs.50/-into 5 shares on 1.10.83
32.	D.L.F.Universal Ltd.	100	10.00	5.00	--	5.00	--	--

TABLE: 2.7 STATEMENT OF APPROVALS GRANTED TO PUBLIC LIMITED COMPANIES OF THE PRIVATE CORPORATE SECTOR BY THE CONTROLLER OF CAPITAL ISSUES FOR RAISING FUNDS THROUGH THE ISSUE OF CONVERTIBLE & NON CONVERTIBLE DEBENTURES DURING THE YEAR 1982. (CONTD......7)

Sr. No.	Name of Company	Year of Incorp-oration	Registered Office	Nature of Industry	MRTP Comp-any	Con. Deb./ Non. Con. Deb.	Date of permis-sion by CCI	Purpose
(1)	(2)	(3)	(4)	(5)	(6)	(7)	(8)	(9)
33.	Dunlop India Ltd	1926	Calcutta	Rubber	Yes	Con.	17.6.82	Modernisation & W.C.
34.	East India Hotels Ltd.	1949	Calcutta	Hotel	Yes	N.C.	21.6.82	W.C.
35.	Guest Keen Williams Ltd.	1931	Calcutta	Steel	Yes	Con.	21.6.82	--
36.	J.K.Synthetics Ltd.	1943	Kanpur	Chemicals	Yes	N.C.	26.6.82	W.C.
37.	Metal Box of India Co.Ltd.	1933	Calcutta	Engineering	Yes	Con.	28.6.82	W.C.
38.	National Organic Chemic. Indus.Ltd.	1961	Bombay	Chemicals	Yes	N.C.	26.6.82	W.C.
39.	Lohia Machines Ltd.	1972	Kanpur	Engineering	N.A.	Con.	7.7.82	--
40.	Press Metal Corpn.Ltd.	1961	Bombay	Steel	N.A.	N.C.	8.7.82	--
41.	Kelvinator of India Ltd.	1960	N.Delhi	Engineering	N.A.	N.C.	22.7.82	W.C.
42.	Goodlass Narolac Paints Ltd.	1920	Bombay	Chemicals	N.A.	N.C.	24.7.82	W.C.
43.	Geep Industrial Syndicate Ltd.	1948	Allahabad	Engineering	N.A.	N.C.	28.7.82	W.C.
44.	Kesoram Inds.& Cotton Mills Ltd.	1919	Calcutta	Cotton	Yes	N.C.	6.8.82	W.C.

TABLE: 2.7 STATEMENT OF APPROVALS GRANTED TO PUBLIC LIMITED COMPANIES OF THE PRIVATE CORPORATE SECTOR BY THE CONTROLLER OF CAPITAL ISSUES FOR RAISING FUNDS THROUGH THE ISSUE OF CONVERTIBLE & NON CONVERTIBLE DEBENTURES DURING THE YEAR 1982 (CONTD........8)

Sr. No.	Name of Company	Face Value of Deb. (Rs.)	Interest Rate (In Per Cent)	AMOUNT Offered to public (In Rs. Crores)	Offered on Rights basis (In Rs. Crores)	Total (In Rs. Crores)	5% Premium on redemption	Additional information
(1)	(2)	(10)	(11)	(12)	(13)	(14)	(15)	(16)
33.	Dunlop India Ltd.	300	13.5	6.38	5.62	12.00	--	Rs.75/-into 5 equities after 6 months
34.	East India Hotels Ltd.	100	15.0	--	10.00	10.00	--	--
35.	Guest Keen Williams Ltd.	200	13.5	6.50	8.75	15.25	--	--
36.	J.K.Synthetics Ltd.	100	15.0	6.00	--	6.00	Yes	--
37.	Metal Box of India Co.Ltd	100	13.5	--	4.00	4.00	--	Rs.100/-into 10 equities on 30.9.85
38.	National Organic Chemic. IndustriesLtd.	100	15.0	--	12.00	12.00	Yes	--
39.	Lohia Machines Ltd.	200	13.5	4.05	1.60	5.65	--	Rs.70 into 7 equities after 1 year.
40.	Press Metal Corpn.Ltd.	100	15.0	--	0.50	0.50	--	--
41.	Kelvinator of India Ltd	100	15.0	1.00	4.00	5.00	Yes	--
42.	Goodlass Narolac Paints Ltd.	100	15.0	--	1.00	1.00	Yes	--
43.	Geep Industrial Syndicate Ltd.	100	15.0	--	1.50	1.50	Yes	--
44.	Kesoram Inds. & Cotton Mills Ltd.	100	15.0	--	6.00	6.00	Yes	--

TABLE: 2.7 STATEMENT OF APPROVALS GRANTED TO PUBLIC LIMITED COMPANIES OF THE PRIVATE CORPORATE SECTOR BY THE CONTROLLER OF CAPITAL ISSUES FOR RAISING FUNDS THROUGH THE ISSUE OF CONVERTIBLE & NON CONVERTIBLE DEBENTURES DURING THE YEAR 1982. (CONTD.........9)

Sr. No.	Name of Company	Year of Incorp-oration	Registered Office	Nature of Industry	MRTP Comp-any	Con. Deb./ Non. Con. Deb.	Date of permi-ssion by CCI	Purpose
(1)	(2)	(3)	(4)	(5)	(6)	(7)	(8)	(9)
45.	Aluminium Industries Ltd.	1946	Kundara	Aluminium	N.A.	N.C.	17.8.82	W.C.
46.	International Instruments Co.Ltd.	1958	Bangalore	Engineering	N.A.	N.C.	21.8.82	W.C.
47.	Orient Paper & Ind.Co.Ltd.	1936	Brijraj Ngr. (Orissa)	Paper	Yes	N.C.	26.8.82	--
48.	Indian Tools Mfg.Ltd.	1937	Bombay	Engineering	N.A.	N.C.	26.6.82	--
49.	Shree Digvijay Woollen Mills Ltd..	1948	Ah-medabad	Wollen Tex.	N.A.	Con.	30.8.82	--
50.	I.T.C.Ltd.	1910	Calcutta	Tobacco	Yes	N.C.	1.9.82	--
51.	Tata Chemicals Ltd.	1939	Bombay	Chemicals	Yes	N.C.	17.9.82	W.C.
52.	Raja Bhadur Moti Lal Poria Mills Ltd.	1926	Bombay	Cotton	N.A.	N.C.	17.9.82	W.C.
53.	Alkalis Chem.Corpn.of India Ltd.	1945	Calcutta	Chemicals	N.A.	N.C.	23.9.82	W.C.
54.	Larsen & Toubro Ltd.	1946	Bombay	Engineering	Yes	Con.	24.9.82	--
55.	May & Baker Ltd	1928	Bombay	Chemicals	Yes	N.C.	24.9.82	To reduce N.R.Is' contribution & Modernisation

TABLE: 2.7 STATEMENT OF APPROVALS GRANTED TO PUBLIC LIMITED COMPANIES OF THE PRIVATE CORPORATE SECTOR BY THE CONTROLLER OF CAPITAL ISSUES FOR RAISING FUNDS THROUGH THE ISSUE OF CONVERTIBLE & NON CONVERTIBLE DEBENTURES DURING THE YEAR 1982 (CONTD..........10)

Sr. No.	Name of Company	Face Value of Deb. (Rs.)	Interest Rate (In Per Cent)	AMOUNT: Offered to public (In Rs. Crores)	AMOUNT: Offered on Rights basis (In Rs. Crores)	AMOUNT: Total (In Rs. Crores)	5% Premium on redemption	Additional information
(1)	(2)	(10)	(11)	(12)	(13)	(14)	(15)	(16)
45.	Aluminium Ind.Ltd.	100	15.0	--	2.00	2.00	Yes	--
46.	International Instruments Co.Ltd.	100	15.0	--	1.00	1.00	Yes	--
47.	Orient Paper & Ind. Co.Ltd	100	15.0	--	3.60	3.60	--	--
48.	Indian Tools Mfg.Ltd.	100	15.0	--	1.50	1.50	Yes	--
49.	Shree Digvijay Wollen Mills Ltd.	125	13.5	1.19	0.81	2.00	--	Rs.45/-into 3 shares after 8 months.
50.	I.T.C.Ltd.	500	15.0	6.75	23.25	30.00	--	It was the first Co.which issued equity shares in lieu of interest accrued on N.Cs.
51.	Tata Chemicals Ltd.	100	15.0	--	1.00	1.00	Yes	To an army group.
52.	Raja Bhadur Moti Lal Poria Mills Ltd.	100	15.0	--	1.00	1.00	Yes	- -
53.	Alkalis Chem.Corpn.of India Ltd.	100	15.0	--	6.00	6.00	Yes	- -
54.	Larsen & Toubro Ltd.	100	13.5	--	6.00	6.00	--	Rs.40/-into 2 equities after 1 year.
55.	May & Baker Ltd.	100	15.0	0.66	2.34	3.00	--	For reducing the holdings of NRI's

TABLE: 2.7 STATEMENT OF APPROVALS GRANTED TO PUBLIC LIMITED COMPANIES OF THE PRIVATE CORPORATE SECTOR BY THE CONTROLLER OF CAPITAL ISSUES FOR RAISING FUNDS THROUGH THE ISSUE OF CONVERTIBLE & NON CONVERTIBLE DEBENTURES DURING THE YEAR 1982. (CONTD..........11)

Sr. No.	Name of Company	Year of Incorp-oration	Registered Office	Nature of Industry	MRTP Comp-any	Con. Deb./ Non. Con. Deb.	Date of permis-sion by CCI	Purpose
(1)	(2)	(3)	(4)	(5)	(6)	(7)	(8)	(9)
56.	Garware Nylon Co.Ltd.	1957	Bombay	Rayon	Yes	N.C.	30.9.82	W.C.
57.	Modi Industries Ltd.	1932	Modi Ngr.	Steel	N.A.	N.C.	7.10.82	W.C.
58.	Widia (India) Ltd.	1964	Banglore	Steel	N.A.	N.C.	7.10.82	Moderni-zation
59.	Shri Ambica Mills Ltd.	1926	Ahmedabad	Cotton	Yes	N.C.	13.10.82	W.C.
60.	Hindustan Gas & Ind. Ltd.	1944	Calcutta	Chemicals	N.A.	N.C.	14.10.82	W.C.
61.	Bharat Bijlee Ltd.	1946	Bombay	Engineeri-ng	N.A.	N.C.	16.10.82	W.C.
62.	Maheshwari Mills Ltd.	1913	Ahmedabad	Textile	N.A.	Con.	22.10.82	--
63.	Ferro Alloys Corporation Ltd	1955	Tumsar	Steel	N.A.	N.C.	25.10.82	W.C.
64.	Sirpur Paper Mills Ltd.	1938	Hyderabad	Paper	N.A.	Con.	2.11.82	Moderni-zation
65.	Kesoram Inds.& Cotton Mills Ltd.	1919	Calcutta	Textile	Yes	Con.	4.11.82	W.C.& Moderni-zation
66.	SAE India Ltd.	1951	N.Delhi	Engg.	N.A.	N.C.	8.11.82	W.C.
67.	Asian Cables Corp.Ltd.	1959	Bombay	Engg.	Yes	N.C.	8.11.82	W.C.

TABLE: 2.7 STATEMENT OF APPROVALS GRANTED TO PUBLIC LIMITED COMPANIES OF THE PRIVATE CORPORATE SECTOR BY THE CONTROLLER OF CAPITAL ISSUES FOR RAISING FUNDS THROUGH THE ISSUE OF CONVERTIBLE & NON CONVERTIBLE DEBENTURES DURING THE YEAR 1982 (CONTD...........12)

Sr. No.	Name of Company	Face Value of Deb. (Rs.)	Interest Rate (In Per Cent)	AMOUNT Offered to public (In Rs. Crores)	Offered on Rights basis (In Rs. Crores)	Total (In Rs. Crores)	5% Premium on redemption	Additional information
(1)	(2)	(10)	(11)	(12)	(13)	(14)	(15)	(16)
56.	Garware Nylon Co.Ltd.	250	15.0	--	2.50	2.50	Yes	--
57.	Modi Industries Ltd.	100	15.0	--	1.00	1.00	Yes	To an Army Group.
58.	Widia (India)Ltd.	100	15.0	--	1.00	1.00	Yes	To an Army Group.
59.	Shri Ambica Mills Ltd.	100	15.0	--	6.00	6.00	Yes	--
60.	Hindustan Gas & Ind.Ltd.	100	15.0	--	0.50	0.50	Yes	Did not avail the consent.
61.	Bharat Bijlee Ltd.	100	15.0	--	1.50	1.50	--	--
62.	Maheshwari Mills Ltd.	125	13.5		1.20	1.20	--	Rs.12.50 into one equity.
63.	Ferro Alloys Corpn.Ltd.	100	15.0	--	6.00	6.00	--	--
64.	Sirpur Paper Mills Ltd.	1000	14.0	--	1.00	1.00	--	To Unit Trust of India; 20% converted.
65.	Kes-oram Inds.& Cotton Mills Ltd.	100	13.5	4.35	16.65	21.00	--	Rs.10/-into 1 equity after 1 year
66.	SAE India Ltd.	100	15.0	--	2.50	2.50	--	Did not avail the consent.
67.	Asian Cables Corpn.Ltd.	100	15.0	--	1.50	1.50	Yes	--

TABLE: 2.7 STATEMENT OF APPROVALS GRANTED TO PUBLIC LIMITED COMPANIES OF THE PRIVATE CORPORATE SECTOR BY THE CONTROLLER OF CAPITAL ISSUES FOR RAISING FUNDS THROUGH THE ISSUE OF CONVERTIBLE & NON CONVERTIBLE DEBENTURES DURING THE YEAR 1982. (CONTD.............13)

Sr. No.	Name of Company	Year of Incorp-oration	Registered Office	Nature of Industry	MRTP Comp-any	Con. Deb./ Non. Con. Deb.	Date of permiss-ion by CCI	Purpose
(1)	(2)	(3)	(4)	(5)	(6)	(7)	(8)	(9)
68.	Ballarpur Industries Ltd.	1945	N.Delhi	Paper	Yes	N.C.	8.11.82	W.C.
69.	Geep Industrial Syndicate Ltd.	1948	Allahabad	Engg.	N.A.	N.C.	9.11.82	W.C.
70.	Garware Plastic & Poly.Ltd.	1957	Aurangabad	Chemicals	Yes	N.C.	10.11.82	W.C.
71.	Saroja Mills Ltd.	1935	Madurai	Cotton Yarn	N.A.	N.C.	10.11.82	W.C.
72.	Nirlon Synth.&Fibres Co.Ltd.	1958	Bombay	Chemicals	Yes	N.C.	17.11.82	W.C.
73.	Indian Rayon Corpn.Ltd.	1956	Veraval	Rayon	Yes	Con.	23.11.82	W.C. & modernization
74.	Antifriction Bearing Corpn.Ltd.	1961	Bombay	Engg.	N.A.	Con.	24.11.82	W.C.
75.	Mahindra Mills Ltd.	1942	Ahmedabad	Cotton	N.A.	N.C.	26.11.82	W.C.
76.	Ashok Leyland Ltd.	1948	Madras	Engg.	Yes	N.C.	2.12.82	W.C.
77.	Kanoria Chem.& Ind.Ltd.	1960	Calcutta	Chemicals	N.A.	N.C.	10.12.82	W.C.
78.	Tata ChemicalsLtd.	1939	Bombay	Chemicals	Yes	Con.	10.12.82	Modernization

Annexe: II.57

TABLE: 2.7 STATEMENT OF APPROVALS GRANTED TO PUBLIC LIMITED COMPANIES OF THE PRIVATE CORPORATE SECTOR BY THE CONTROLLER OF CAPITAL ISSUES FOR RAISING FUNDS THROUGH THE ISSUE OF CONVERTIBLE & NON CONVERTIBLE DEBENTURES DURING THE YEAR 1982 (CONTD.............14)

Sr. No.	Name of Company	Face Value of Deb. (Rs.)	Interest Rate (In Per Cent)	AMOUNT Offered to public (In Rs. Crores)	Offered on Rights basis (In Rs. Crores)	Total (In Rs. Crores)	5% Premium on redemption	Additional information
(1)	(2)	(10)	(11)	(12)	(13)	(14)	(15)	(16)
68.	Ballarpur Ind.Ltd.	100	15.0	--	10.00	10.00	Yes	--
69.	Geep Ind.Synd.Ltd.	100	15.0	--	0.50	0.50	--	-
70.	Garware Plastic & Poly. Ltd.	100	15.0	--	1.00	1.00	Yes	To an Army Group.
71.	Saroja Mills Ltd.	100	15.0	--	0.50	0.50	--	--
72.	Nirlon Synth.& Fibres Co.Ltd.	100	15.0	--	6.50	6.50	Yes	--
73.	Indian Rayon Corpn.Ltd	140	13.5	4.90	16.10	21.00	--	20% converted into 1 equity on 30.6.83.
74.	Antifriction Bearing Corporation Ltd.	100	13.5	--	1.10	1.10	--	45% converted into 3 shares on 1.4.86.
75.	Mahindra Mills Ltd.	100	15.0	--	0.50	0.50	Yes	--
76.	Ashok Leyland Ltd.	100	15.0	--	10.00	10.00	Yes	--
77.	Kanoria Chem.& Ind. Ltd.	100	15.0	2.50	--	2.50	Yes	--
78.	Tata Chemicals Ltd.	100	13.5	--	30.00	30.00	--	--

TABLE:2.7 STATEMENT OF APPROVALS GRANTED TO PUBLIC LIMITED COMPANIES OF THE PRIVATE CORPORATE SECTOR BY THE CONTROLLER OF CAPITAL ISSUES FOR RAISING FUNDS THROUGH THE ISSUE OF CONVERTIBLE & NON CONVERTIBLE DEBENTURES DURING THE YEAR 1982. (CONTD...............15)

Sr. No.	Name of Company	Year of Incorporation	Registered Office	Nature of Industry	MRTP Company	Con. Deb./ Non. Con. Deb.	Date of permission by CCI	Purpose
(1)	(2)	(3)	(4)	(5)	(6)	(7)	(8)	(9)
79.	Mahindra UgineSteel Co.Ltd.	1962	Bombay	Steel	Yes	N.C.	10.12.82	W.C.
80.	Century Spg.&Mfg.Co.Ltd.	1897	Bombay	Cotton	Yes	N.C.	10.12.82	W.C.
81.	Mukand Iron& Steel Works Ltd.	1937	Bombay	Steel	Yes	N.C.	13.12.82	W.C.
82.	Raymond Woollen Mills Ltd.	1925	Bombay	Woollen	Yes	N.C.	13.12.82	W.C.
83.	Gwalior Rayon & Silk Mills Co.Ltd.	1947	Nagda	Rayon	Yes	N.C.	13.12.82	W.C.& Modernisation.
84.	Aukland International Ltd.	1977	Calcutta	Jute	N.A.	N.C.	15.12.82	--
85.	Jyoti Ltd.	1943	Baroda	Engg.	N.A.	N.C.	17.12.82	W.C.
86.	Bharat Forge Co.Ltd.	1961	Pune	Steel	N.A.	N.C.	24.12.82	Expansion

TABLE: 2.7 STATEMENT OF APPROVALS GRANTED TO PUBLIC LIMITED COMPANIES OF THE PRIVATE CORPORATE SECTOR BY THE CONTROLLER OF CAPITAL ISSUES FOR RAISING FUNDS THROUGH THE ISSUE OF CONVERTIBLE & NON CONVERTIBLE DEBENTURES DURING THE YEAR 1982 (CONTD................16)

Sr. No.	Name of Company	Face Value of Deb. (Rs.)	Interest Rate (In Per Cent)	AMOUNT Offered to public (In Rs. Crores)	Offered on Rights basis (In Rs. Crores	Total (In Rs. Crores	5% Premium on redemption	Additional information
(1)	(2)	(3)	(4)	(5)	(6)	(7)	(8)	(9)
79.	Mahindra Ugine Steel Co. Ltd.	100	15.0	--	6.00	6.00	Yes	--
80.	Century Spg.&Mfg.Co.Ltd.	100	15.0	--	10.00	10.00	Yes	--
81.	Mukand Iron & Steel Works Ltd.	100	15.0	--	8.00	8.00	Yes	Amount of the Issue was reduced by Rs.2 crores on 5.4.83.
82.	Raymond Woolen Mills Ltd.	100	15.0	--	4.50	4.50	Yes	--
83.	Gwalior Rayon & Silk Mills Co.Ltd.	100	15.0	--	15.00	15.00	Yes	--
84.	Aukland International Ltd.	1000	11.0	--	0.12	0.12	--	--
85.	Jyoti Ltd.	100	15.0	--	3.00	3.00	Yes	--
86.	Bharat Forge Co.Ltd.	100	15.0	--	3.60	3.60	Yes	--

Annexe:II.60

TABLE: 2.7 STATEMENT OF APPROVALS GRANTED TO PUBLIC LIMITED COMPANIES OF THE PRIVATE CORPORATE SECTOR BY THE CONTROLLER OF CAPITAL ISSUES FOR RAISING FUNDS THROUGH THE ISSUE OF CONVERTIBLE & NON CONVERTIBLE DEBENTURES DURING THE YEAR 1982. (CONTD................17)

Sr. No.	Name of Company	Year of Incorporation	Registered Office	Nature of Industry	MRTP Company	Con. Deb./ Non. Con. Deb.	Date of permission by CCI	Purpose
(1)	(2)	(3)	(4)	(5)	(6)	(7)	(8)	(9)
87.	Nagarjuna Steel Ltd.	1974	Hyderabad	Steel	N.A.	Con.	24.12.82	--
88.	Nagarjuna Steel Ltd.	1974	Hyderabad	Steel	N.A.	N.C.	24.12.82	--
89.	BASF India Ltd.	1943	Bombay	Chemicals	N.A.	N.C.	28.12.82	--
90.	Bombay Dying & Mfg.Co.Ltd.	1879	Bombay	Cotton	Yes	Con.	28.12.82	Expansion

TABLE: 2.7 STATEMENT OF APPROVALS GRANTED TO PUBLIC LIMITED COMPANIES OF THE PRIVATE CORPORATE SECTOR BY THE CONTROLLER OF CAPITAL ISSUES FOR RAISING FUNDS THROUGH THE ISSUE OF CONVERTIBLE & NON CONVERTIBLE DEBENTURES DURING THE YEAR 1982 (CONTD..................18)

Sr. No.	Name of Company	Face Value of Deb. (Rs.)	Interest Rate (In Per Cent)	AMOUNT: Offered to public (In Rs. Crores)	AMOUNT: Offered on Rights basis (In Rs. Crores)	AMOUNT: Total (In Rs. Crores)	5% Premium on redemption	Additional information
(1)	(2)	(10)	(11)	(12)	(13)	(14)	(15)	(16)
87.	Nagarjuna Steel Ltd.	100	13.50	0.20	2.30	2.50	--	The issue was cancelled on 16.4.83.
88.	Nagarjuna Steel Ltd.	100	15.0	--	1.25	1.25	Yes	To an Army Group.
89.	BASF India Ltd.	100	15.0	--	1.00	1.00	Yes	--
90.	Bombay Dying Mfg.Co.Ltd.	100	13.5	--	12.00	12.00	--	--
	TOTAL			86.92	429.28	516.20		

NOTES: 'C.C.I.' stands for Controller of Capital Issues.
'N.R.I.' stands for Non Resident Indian.
'Con.Deb.' stands for 'Convertible Debentures'
'N.A.' stands for 'Not applicable'
'W.C.' stands for 'Working Capital'.

SOURCE: Compiled from the information available in the Office of the Controller of Capital Issues, Ministry of Finance, Government of India, New Delhi.

ANNEXE III

— PRELUDE TO THE GUIDELINES FOR THE ISSUE OF TAX FREE BONDS BY PUBLIC SECTOR ENTERPRIZES i EXTRACTS FROM THE UNION BUDGET FOR 1985-86 THROUGH 1987-88.

— GUIDELINES FOR THE ISSUE OF "TAX FREE" BONDS BY PUBLIC SECTOR ENTERPRIZES : JULY 16, 1986.

— CATALOGUE OF THE PUBLIC ISSUES OF SECURED REDEEMABLE NON-CONVETIBLE BONDS PUT OUT BY THE PUBLIC SECTOR COMPANIES/CORPORATIONS.

PRELUDE TO THE GUIDELINES FOR THE ISSUE OF TAX FREE BONDS BY PUBLIC SECTOR ENTERPRIZES—EXTRACTS FROM THE UNION BUDGET FOR 1985-86 THROUGH 1987-88

THE UNION BUDGET 1985-86:

PART-A

"The public sector is vital for faster industrialization, balanced regional development, and prevention of concentration of wealth and economic power. Over the years, the public sector has grown rapidly, and an important priority now is to ensure that there is sufficient internal generation of resources for its future growth..." (Para 13).

"An important task for the future is to accelerate industrial growth... Indian industry must also become self-reliant in financing investment..." (Para 22).

"On the financial side, I propose to facilitate the mobilisation of resources from the market by the corporate sector and to reduce its dependence on public financial institutions. With a view to improving the marketability of convertible debentures of non-MRTP and non-FERA companies, the maximum interest payable by them on such issues is being raised from 13.5 per cent to 15 per cent. The Securities Contracts (Regulation) Act, 1956, is being amended to ensure free transfer of securities of listed public limited companies. This measure will particularly benefit small investors spread all over the country. In order to offer wide choice to investors, certain changes are being made in respect of listing requirements of closely held companies. Such companies will be permitted to enlist by offering 40 per cent of their equity capital in two stages over a period of 3 years and capitalise a larger portion of their free reserves before going to the public. In order to diversify the market, a new instrument, namely, Convertible Cumulative Preference Share is being introduced. Several measures to reduce the prevailing high cost of public issues are being announced separately" (Para 25).

(Source : Indian Express, Sunday, March 17, 1985 p. 8).

THE UNION BUDGET : 1986-87:

PART-A

"...An important issue before us is to find sufficient resources for financing the public sector plan. This is not a partisan issue or the problem of a particular Government in power.... In a nutshell, the core of the problem is simply that internal generation in public sector enterprizes is not measuring upto the task of financing a plan of the size that is essential for our development.

The severity of the problem can be illustrated by the experience of the current year. The Seventh plan visualizes that 53 per cent of the central plan be financed through resources of public enterprizes, and 47 per cent will be financed through the budget. In the first year of the plan, in view of the paucity of internal resources, the budget had to finance 66 per cent of the central plan, and not 47 per cent. We have been successful in increasing tax revenues sharply, but higher revenues have been more than offset by increase in food and fertilizer subsidies and assistance to States. The higher budgetary support to the plan, therefore, had to come from additional domestic borrowings...."

"An important innovation to tap people's savings particularly rural savings for public sector projects was announced by me last year. Public Sector Companies in telecommunications and power sectors have been permitted to raise funds from the public through a new series of bonds. These bonds provide an attractive rate of interest and are quoted in the Stock Exchange. As a further innovation in the next year, the government will introduce another series of public sector bonds with a tax-free return. In addition, other benefits such as wealth tax exemption will also be available."

"The proposed outlay for the department of telecommunications for 1986-87 is Rs. 915 crores. With a view to improving the operational efficiency of the telecommunication net work, the government have decided to set up a public sector corporation to manage and operate the telephone services of the metropolitan cities of Bombay and Delhi. This Corporation will also raise funds through the issue of bonds."

(Source : Commerce, Volume 152, No. 3903, March 8, 1986 pp. 440-65).

THE UNION BUDGET : 1987-88

PART-A

"The public sector is the core of our industrial economy. I am also convinced that our public sector enterprizes can be made as efficient as any in the world. I am glad to say that the infrastructure industries in the public sector are showing distinctly better performance. There has been a significant improvement in productivity in coal, power and railways. The improvement in thermal power generation is particularly striking. The plant load factor in the current year is the highest since 1976-77. The improvement in the functioning of infrastructure has been brought about by a change in the management culture, and better performance on the shop floor."

"The capital markets in India have shown tremendous growth in the last few years. Approvals for capital issues have exceeded Rs. 5,000 crores in 1986-87. They were only about Rs. 500 crores in 1980-81. For a healthy growth of capital markets, investors' rights must be fully protected. Trading malpractices must be prevented. Government have decided to set up a separate Board for the regulation and orderly functioning of Stock Exchanges and the securities industry."

"The deficit is high and I do not like it. I have decided that the deficit in the Budget estimates for 1987-88 shall not be exceeded. Some supplementary demands are unavoidable; I am instructing the Ministries and other Central Government Organisations to ensure that additional demands are offset by equivalent savings or through measures to raise more resources. We will review the financial performance of public sector units to ensure that targets for internal resource generation are met...."

PART-B

"The capital markets have shown remarkable buoyancy. I propose to make some changes in the tax laws which will support healthy development of the capital markets. The existing provision of allowing deduction in respect of investment in equity shares of certain categories of new companies was to be withdrawn with effect from 1st April, 1987. In view of the need to continue support for issues of new companies, I propose to extend this concession for 3 more years. I also propose to reduce the holding period of these shares from 5 years to 3 years.... At present shares have to be held for a period of 36 months before capital gains on their transfer qualify for the concessional treatment allowed for long term capital gains. It is proposed to reduce the holding period to 12 months.

(Source : The Hindustan Times, Sunday, March 1, 1987. pp. 8-9).

GUIDELINES FOR THE ISSUE OF "TAX FREE" BONDS BY PUBLIC SECTOR ENTERPRISES: JULY 16, 1986

Government had issued guidelines regarding floatation of bonds by public sector undertakings in the Telecommunications and Power sectors in the last financial year. In the Budget Speech this year, the Finance Minister had announced that Government will introduce another series of public sector bonds with a tax free return.

2. In pursuance of this, it has been decided to allow Government, Corporate bodies, as may be permitted by the

Government, to issue bonds for setting up of new projects, expansion or diversification of existing projects, capital expenditure for modernisation or for augmenting the resources of the company for working capital requirements, subject to Government's clearance. This series will be in addition to the earlier series for Power and Telecom. Bonds.

3. In the new series, the interest rate shall be upto a maximum of 10%. The period of redemption will normally be upto 10 years, which could be increased in suitable cases. However, the interest rate and period of redemption shall be approved by the Government on a case-by-case basis. The income from these bonds shall be completely free from income-tax. The bonds will be exempt from wealth tax without any limit. They will be transferable by endorsement and delivery. Decision on qnantum etc. will be taken by the Ministry of Finance on a case-by-case basis.

Source : Ministry of Finance, Office of the Controller of Capital Issues vide their F. No. SII (16)-CCI (II)/86, dated 16.7.86.

Catalogue of The Public Issues of Secured Redeemable Non-Convertible Bonds Put Out By The Public Sector Companies/Corporations

Sr. No.	*Name and Address of the Company/ Corporation*	*Month/ Date of the opening of the Issue*	*Face value of the Bond (Amount in Rs.)*	*No. of Bonds*	*Total Amount (Amount in Rs. crores)*	*Interest rate offered per annum (In per-cent)*	*KEY HIGHLIGHTS*
(1)	(2)	(3)	(4)	(5)	(6)	(7)	(8)
1.	The Hindustan Machine Tools Limited	August, 1977	100.00	5,50,000	5.50	14.0 & 10.5	—Redeemable after the lapse of 10 years at par.
2.	The National Thermal Power Corporation Limited, NTPC Square, 62-63, Nehru Place, New Delhi-110019	February 12, 1986	1000.00	10,00,000	100.00	14.0	—Managers to Issue : The Merchant Banking Divisions of the SBI & ICICI, Bombay. —First Power Sector Bonds Issued by the premier Government undertaking.

—Two Schemes of Interest : Cumulative & Non-Cumulative.

—Annual Yield of 22.5 percent under Cumulative Interest Payment Scheme.

—Total exemption from Wealth Tax without any limit.

—No tax deduction at source irrespective of the amount of interest.

—Income tax exemption under Section 80 L.

—Special tax benefits for Charitable and Religious Trusts under Section 11 of the Income Tax Act.

—Interest from Day One payable from the date of realisation of application money.

(1)	(2)	(3)	(4)	(5)	(6)	(7)	(8)
							—Interest Warrants in Advance : Post-dated interest warrants alongwith the Bonds. —Redemption at the end of 7th year. —Buy back arrangement for small investors upto a limit of Rs. 40,000 after One Year. —Fully secured by a charge on the fixed assets of the company. —Easy liquidity : Freely transferable by endorsement—listed at Delhi, Bombay, Ahmedabad, Calcutta, Bangalore, Madras and Kanpur Stock Exchanges.

3.	The Rural Electrification Corporation Limited, DDA Building, Nehru Place, New Delhi-110 019	March 3, 1986	In Two Denominations—Rs. 1,000/- & Rs. 10.000/-	—	65.00	14.0	—Managers to the Issue : Central Bank of India, Canara Bank and Punjab National Bank. —Redeemable at par after the expiry of 7 years from the date of allotment. —Choice between cumulative & non-cumulative interest schemes. —Interest income eligible for Section 80 L deduction. —Wealth tax exemption without limit. —No tax deduction at source irrespective of amount of interest. —Easy marketability :

(1)	(2)	(3)	(4)	(5)	(6)	(7)	(8)
							—Transferable by endorsement & delivery. —Bonds listed on Delhi, Bombay & Ahmedabad Stock Exchanges. —Buy back facility at par upto Rs. 40,000/- after one year ; however, the company will buy back such Bonds on First-cum-first served basis upto a maximum of Rs. 2 crores per financial year. —In the case of opting for the non-cumulative scheme, the Post-dated interest coupons for half yearly payment of interest will be attached with the Bonds.

4.	The National Hydro-Electric Power Corporation Ltd., Hemkunt Tower, 98, Nehru Place, New Delhi-110019.	August 18, 1986	1,000.00	6,00,000	60.00	14.0	—Managers to the Issue : The Merchant Banking Divisions of the SBI and the ICICI Limited, Bombay. —*Tax Benefits :* —Income tax exemption under Section 80 L. —No tax deduction at source irrespective of amount of interest. —Total exemption from Wealth Tax without any limit. —Special tax benefits for Charitable and Religious Trusts under Section 11 of the Income Tax Act. —*Interest :* —Two schemes of interest : Non-cumulative : inte-

(1)	(2)	(3)	(4)	(5)	(6)	(7)	(8)
							rest payable Half Yearly; Post-dated Interest Warrants sent in advance alongwith the Bonds; Cumulative : Annual yield of 22.5 per cent. —Interest payable from the date of realisation of application money. —*Security* : —Fully secured by a charge on the Fixed Assets of the Company. —Accepted by NPHC as security in Lieu of Bid Guarantees/Earnest Money/Bank Guarantees. *Liquidity* : —Freely Transferable by

endorsement and delivery.

—Listing at Delhi, Bombay, Ahmedabad, Calcutta, Madras, Kanpur, Ludhiana and Bangalore Stock Exchanges.

—Buy back facility for small investors upto a limit of Rs. 40,000/- after the first year, subject to a limit of Rs. 2 crores per year.

—Full redemption at par at the end of 7th year.

(1)	(2)	(3)	(4)	(5)	(6)	(7)	(8)
5.	The Indian Petrochemicals Corporation Limited, P.O. Petrochemicals Pincode-391346 District Vadodara (Gujarat)	October 9, 1986	1,000.00	4,00,000	40.00	14.0	—Managers to the Issue : SBI Capital Markets Limited, Bombay, and the Merchant Banking Division of the ICICI Limited, Bombay. —Interest Income eligible for Section 80 L deduction. —No deduction of Tax at source. —Full Wealth Tax exemption. —Bonds are secured against assets of the company. —Transferable by endorsement and delivery. —Assured buy-back facility at 8 centres.

							—Listing on six major stock exchanges. —Cumulative scheme-interest compounded half yearly. —Non-cumulative scheme offers half yearly, post-dated interest warrants in advance. —Special tax benefits for charitable and religious trusts. —Redeemable at par on expiry of 7 years. —Interest from Day One.
6.	The Mahanagar Telephone Nigam Limited, Khurshid Lal Bhawan, Janpath, New Delhi-110 050	November 25 ,1985	1,000	15,00,000	150.00	14.0 & 10.0 (Tax Free)	—Managers to the Issue : SBI & Capital Markets Limited, Bombay, and The Merchant Banking Divisions of Canara Bank, New Delhi, and

(1)	(2)	(3)	(4)	(5)	(6)	(7)	(8)
							The Industrial Credit and Investment Corporation of India Limited, Bombay. —14% Bonds exempted under Section 80 L of Income Tax Act, 1961. —10% (Tax Free) Bonds exempt from Income Tax without any limit. —Wealth Tax exemption without any limit. —Special Tax benefits for Charitable and Religious Trusts. —No deduction of Tax at source. —Fully secured against assets of the company. —Interest from Day One.

—Choice between cumulative & non-cumulative under both the schemes.

—14% bonds under cumulative scheme yield 22.5% simple interest & 10% bonds yield an annual return of 16.5% Tax Free.

—Non-cumulative scheme offers half-yearly, post-dated interest warrants in advance.

—Bonds accepted by MTNL as security, in Lieu of Bid Guarantee/Earnest Money/Bank Guarantee.

—Transferable by endorsement and delivery.

(1)	(2)	(3)	(4)	(5)	(6)	(7)	(8)
							—Assured by back facility at 7 centres from individual investors after a lockin period of three years upto Rs. 40,000 subject to a maximum of Rs. 4 crores in a financial year. —Listing on seven major stock exchanges.
7.	The National Thermal Power Corporation Ltd., NTPC Square, 62-63, Nehru Place, New Delhi-110019.	January 22, 1987	1,000	12,00,000	120.00	14.0 & 10.0 (Tax Free)	Managers to the Issue : SBI Capital Markets Limited, Bombay, and Merchant Banking Divisions of the ICICI, Bombay, and the Canara Bank, New Delhi. *Scheme 'A' : 10% Bonds :* —For all assessees, inte-

rest exempt from Income Tax without any limit.

—Interest @10% per annum payable at six monthly intervals for Non-Cumulative Bonds.

—Redeemable after 10 years at par.

—Under Cumulative Plan, total interest of Rs. 1653/-, yielding an annual return of 16.5%.

—Unique annual return of 33% for Companies, Banks and other High Income Groups with 50% tax rate. Guaranteed buy-back at par, available after 3 years, with full interest to investors with holdings of upto Rs. 40,000/-

(1)	(2)	(3)	(4)	(5)	(6)	(7)	(8)
							Scheme 'B' : 14% Bonds: —Interest exempt from Income Tax under Section 80L of the Income Tax Act, 1961. —Interest @ 14% per annum payable at six monthly intervals for Non-Cumulative Bonds. —Redeemable after 7 years at par. —Under Cumulative Plan, total interest of Rs.1578/- yielding an annual return of 22.5%. —Guaranteed buy-back at par available after 1 year, with full interest to investors with holdings of up to Rs. 40,000/-.

Common Features for 10% and 14% Bonds :

—Investment totally exempt from Wealth Tax.

—No deduction of Income Tax at source.

—Special Income Tax benefits for Charitable and Religious Trusts.

—Under non-cumulative plans Bonds will be issued with post-dated warrants which can be encashed automatically on due dates.

—Interest payable right from the date of realisation of application money.

—Easily transferable by simple endorsement and delivery.

(1)	(2)	(3)	(4)	(5)	(6)	(7)	(8)
							—Listed on 7 major Stock Exchanges of India. —Fully secured against assets of the company. —Accepted by NTPC as security in lieu of Bid/Performance Guarantees/Earnest Money and Security Deposits.
8.	The Indian Telephone Industries, Ltd., 16, Museum Road, Bangalore-560001	February 11, 1987	1,000	10,00,000	100.00	14.0 & 10.0 (Tax-Free)	—Managers to the Issue : SBI Capital Markets Limited, Bombay, & Merchant Banking Bureau of Canara Bank, Bangalore and the Merchant Banking Division of the ICICI Limited, Bombay. *Category-I : 10% Bonds* : —For all assessees, interest

exempt from Income Tax without any limit.

—Redeemable after 10 years at par.

—Interest @ 10% per annum payable at six-monthly intervals for non-cumulative bonds.

—Under cumulative scheme, total interest of Rs. 1653/- yielding an annual return of 16.5%.

—Buy-back facility at par after 3 years subject to a ceiling of Rs. 40,000/-.

Category-II : *14% Bonds* :

—Interest exempt from Income Tax under Section 80L of the Income Tax Act, 1961.

—Redeemable after 7 years at par.

(1)	(2)	(3)	(4)	(5)	(6)	(7)	(8)
							—Interest @14% per annum payable at six-monthly intervals for non-cumulative bonds. —Under Cumulative Scheme, total interest of Rs. 1578/-, yielding an annual return of 22.5%. —Buy back facility after one year upto a ceiling of Rs. 40,000. *Common Features for 10% & 14% Bonds* : —No deduction of Income Tax at source. —Special Income Tax benefits for Charitable & Religious Trusts. —Under non-cumulative

Scheme, Bonds will be issued with post-dated interest warrants which can be encashed automatically on due dates.

—Interest payable right from the date of realization of application money.

—Easily transferable by simple endorsement and delivery.

—Stamp duty exemption for transfer of Bonds.

—Listed on 9 major Stock Exchanges of India.

—Fully secured against assets of the Company.

—Accepted by ITI as security in lieu of Bid/Performance Guarantee, Earnest Money & Security Deposits.

(1)	(2)	(3)	(4)	(5)	(6)	(7)	(8)
9.	Indian Railway Finance Corporation Limited, Palika Bhavan, Sector-XIII, R.K. Puram, Delhi-110066	March 2, 1987	1,000	25,00,000	250 00	10.0 (Tax Free)	—Lead Managers to the Issue : SBI Capital Markets Limited Bombay, and the Merchant Banking Division of the Indian Bank, New Delhi. —Interest from Income Tax exempt without any limit. —Choice of 2 interest schemes —Cumulative & Non-Cumulative. —10% per annum interest, payable at six-monthly intervals under non-cumulative scheme. —Under cumulative scheme, total interest yield of Rs. 1653/-, an annual return of 16.5%.

—Under non-cumulative scheme, Bonds will be issued alongwith post-dated interest warrants which can be encashed automatically on due dates.
—No deduction of Income Tax at source.
—Interest payable right from the date of realization of application money.
—Investment totally exempt from Wealth Tax.
—Easily transferable by simple endorsement and delivery.
—Listing at all major Stock Exchanges.
—Redeemable after 10 years.
—Buy back at par after 3 years for individuals.

(1)	(2)	(3)	(4)	(5)	(6)	(7)	(8)
							—Fully secured. —Accepted by Indian Railways as security in lieu of Bid/Performance Guarantees, Earnest Money and Security Deposits.

Source : Compiled from the respective Prospectuses.

ANNEXE IV

— **QUESTIONNAIRE : 1**

ADDRESSED TO THE CHAIRMAN/FINANCE EXECUTIVES OF THE COMPANIES WHICH HAVE ISSUED CONVERTIBLE/NON-CONVERTIBLE DEBENTURES/BONDS.

— **QUESTIONNAIRE : 2**

ADDRESSED TO THE OFFICE BEARERS OF THE RECOGNISED STOCK EXCHANGES/ MANAGERS TO ISSUES/EMINENT ACADEMICS/UNDERWRITERS TO ISSUES.

— **QUESTIONNAIRE : 3**

ADDRESSED TO SELECT GROUP OF INVESTORS.

QUESTIONNAIRE : 1 CONFIDENTIAL

TO BE ADDRESSED TO THE CHAIRMAN/FINANCE EXECUTIVES OF THE COMPANIES WHICH HAVE ISSUED CONVERTIBLE/NON-CONVERTIBLE DEBENTURES/BONDS

(*If the space provided for answers in the questionaire is insufficient, please give data in a separate sheet mentioning the serial number of the questlon.*)

1. Name and address of the company :
2. Year of establishment :
3. Please check (√) the class of industry to which your company belongs :

   Basic Industry
   Consumer Goods Industry
   Intermediate Goods Industry
   Capital Goods Industry

4. Please indicate (√) the Industry/Group to which your company belongs :

   (i) Aluminium
   (ii) Cement
   (iii) Chemicals, Dyes and Pharmaceuticals
   (iv) Coal and Mining
   (v) Electricity Generation & Supply
   (vi) Engineering, Metal and Alloys
   (vii) Hotel
   (viii) Iron and Steel

(ix) Jute
(x) Mineral oils
(xi) Oil
(xii) Paper and Paper products
(xiii) Rubber
(xiv) Shipping
(xv) Sugar
(xvi) Textiles
(xvii) Tobacco
(xviii) Transport
(xix) Tea
(xx) Trading
(xxi) Others (Please specify)

5. Please check (√) the nature of ownership applicable to your company :

(i) Indian Owned
(ii) Foreign owned
(iii) Foreign equity participation
(iv) Foreign subsidiary
(v) Others (Please specify)

6. Please rank the following financial objectives in order of their importance to your company :

(Most important=1, Next Most Important=2, etc.)

FINANCIAL OBJECTIVES	RANK
(i) To maximise per cent return on investment in assets	=
(ii) To maximise aggregate earnings	=
(iii) To achieve a desired growth rate in earnings per share (EPS)	=
(iv) To maximise ordinary share prices	=
(v) Others (Please specify)	=

7. Indicate precisely the objectives laid down by your company in the following areas :

   (i) Profit requiretments
   (ii) Marketing
   (iii) Innovation (Research and Development)
   (iv) Human Organisation
   —Personnel recruitment
   —Training and Development
   (v) Physical resources
   (vi) Financial resources
   (vii) Productivity
   (viii) Social responsibility

8. Kindly indicate broadly the nature of strategies and policies that the management of your company proposes to follow for accomplishing the objectives laid down in the above areas.

9. Please give an outline of the organisational structure of your company.

10. Kindly append the copies of your company's published Annual Report alongwith the Chairman's speeches for the year 1978 through 1982.

11. In what directions you are planning your further growth? Kindly indicate in brief the nature of such plans prepared by your management.

12. What preliminary problems did your company face in finalising the issues of convertible/non-convertible debentures/bonds? Please highlight them in detail.

13. How did you plan the "terms of Issue/s" of debentures/bonds ? Kindly indicate in detail about the terms of conversion (including conversion price), amount and timing of issue in the case of convertible debentures/bonds.

14 Please enclose the copy/copies of the prospectuses issued by the company for floating convertible/non-convertible debentures/bonds since 1978.

15. Also append, please, the copy/copies of the Trust Deed/s for the relevant issues of convertible/non-convertible debentures/bonds.

16. Please furnish us with the details of the capital structure of your company as per the following table :

Capital structure	At the time of issuance of convertible/non-convertible debentures/bonds.				
	First Series	Second Series	Third Series	Fourth Series	Fifth Series
(1)	(2)	(3)	(4)	(5)	(6)
Equity Shares					
Preference Shares					
Reserves					
Debt :					
Loans from commercial banks					
Loans from other finance institutions					
Debentures :					
Non-convertible					
Convertible					
Deposits from Public					
Other Sources (please specify)					

17. Kindly also furnish us with the data as per the following table :

Issues of convertible/non-convertible debentures/bonds	Debit-Equity Ratio	
	Prior to the Issue	After the Issue has been affected
(1)	(2)	(3)
First Series		
Second Series		
Third Series		
Fourth Series		
Fifth Series		

18. In case the Prospectuses for the Issues of convertible/non-convertible debentures/bonds are not available, kindly furnish us with the data as per Tables 1 and 2 (fill in the column 7 through 10 only if the Prospectuses have been appended).

TABLE : 1

Convertible debentures	Date on which consent given by the Controller of Capital issues	Actual date of floatation	Amount of Issue	
			Offered to public	Offered to existing shareholders
(1)	(2)	(3)	(4)	(5)
First Series				
Second Series				
Third Series				
Fourth Series				
Fifth Series				

TABLE : 1 (Contd.)

Convertible debentures	Name and addresses of the Managers to Issue	Actual amount subscribed by	
		Public	Existing shareholders
(1)	(6)	(7)	(8)
First Series			
Second Series			
Third Series			
Fourth Series			
Fifth Series			

TABLE : 1 (Contd.)

Convertible debentures	Number of times the issue was over-subscribed	Amount required to be subscribed by the under-writers in case of under-subscription	Terms and conditions of the Issue
(1)	(9)	(10)	(11)
First Series			
Second Series			
Third Series			
Fourth Series			
Fifth Series			

TABLE : 2

Non-convertible debentures	Date on which consent given by the Controller of Capital Issues	Actual date of floatation	Amount of Issue Offered to Public	Amount of Issue Offered to existing shareholders
(1)	(2)	(3)	(4)	(5)
First Series				
Second Series				
Third Series				
Fourth Series				
Fifth Series				

TABLE : 2 (Contd.)

Non-convertible debentures	Name and addresses of the Managers to Issue	Actual amount subscribed by Public	Actual amount subscribed by Existing shareholders
(1)	(6)	(7)	(8)
First Series			
Second Series			
Third Series			
Fourth Series			
Fifth Series			

TABLE : 2 (Contd.)

Non-convertible debentures	Number of times the issue was over-subscribed	Amount required to be subscribed by the under-writers in case of under subscription	Terms and Conditions of issue
(1)	(9)	(10)	(11)
First Series			
Second Series			
Third Series			
Fourth Series			
Fifth Series			

19. Please check (√) the purpose/s for which funds so raised were utilised/are intended to be used :

Convertible debentures/ bonds	First Series	Second Series	Third Series	Fourth Series	Fifth Series
(1)	(2)	(3)	(4)	(5)	(6)
Meeting working capital needs					
Modernization					
Expansion					
Diversification					
Raising the base of equity capital					
Diluting the foreign shareholdings					
Others (Please specify)					

Non-convertible debentures/bonds	First Series	Second Series	Third Series	Fourth Series	Fifth Series
(1)	(2)	(3)	(4)	(5)	(6)
Meeting working capital needs					
Modernization					
Expansion					
Diversification					
Others (Please specify)					

20. Kindly check (√) the reasons mentioned below which prompted your company to resort to this means of financing. Please rank the various reasons in order of their importance.

(Most Important=1, Next Most Important=2, etc.)

REASONS	RANK
Cheep cost of raising funds	=
Difficulty in issuing Equity Shares	=
Poor response of public in depositing money with the company	=
Denial of credit by other finance institutions	=
Inappropriate terms and conditions of the institutional finance	=
Others (Please specify)	=

21. Please check (√) the following steps which might have been taken by the management of your company for securing good response to the Issue/Issues of convertible debentures/bonds.

Steps Taken	First Series	Second Series	Third Series	Fourth Series	Fifth Series
(1)	(2)	(3)	(4)	(5)	(6)
Keeping the conversion price at a low level					
Allowing the conversion on the expiry of an early period					
Giving wide and regular publicity to the progress registered by the company in general and in respect to the project for which funds have been raised through this instrument					
Taking appropriate measures (such as declaring of interim dividend and/or bonus shares) from time to time to boost up the market price of the company's equity/debentures					
Inclusion of the company's shares in the cleared list of stock exchange/s					
Others (Please specify)					

22. What alternate strategies were adopted by your management for making the issues of non-convertible debentures/bonds successful ? Please mention them clearly.

23. Which method your company adopted/intends to adopt for the redemption of the debentures on the maturity date. Please check (√) the following.

Method	First Series	Second Series	Third Series	Fourth Series	Fifth Series
(1)	(2)	(3)	(4)	(5)	(6)
Sinking Fund Method					
Profit & Loss					
Appropriation method					
Any other (please specify)					

24. What steps do you propose to take for safeguarding the interests of the debenture/bondholders ? Kindly check (√) the following list.

= Restricting the creation of new long-term debts

= Maintaining a specific debt-equity ratio

= Restricting the pay-out ratio

= Maintaining a specified level of working capital

= Any other (Please specify)

25. Are you satisfied with the official guidelines related to the issuing of secured convertible/non-convertible debentures/bonds ? Please check (√) your answer.

YES/NO

26. If the answer to above is 'No', please indicate the lines on which you would like to modify the currently applicable official guidelines. Kindly substantiate your answer with appropriate reasons.

27. Name and designation of the person from whom further clarification, if any, may be sought :

Please mail the above completed questionnaire to :

Dr. OM PRAKASH GOYAL
Head,
Department of Commerce,
M. D. University,
Rohtak-124 001
Haryana, India
Tel : 5641

QUESTIONNAIRE : 2 CONFIDENTIAL

TO BE ADDRESSED TO THE OFFICE BEARERS OF THE RECOGNISED STOCK EXCHANGES/ MANAGERS TO ISSUES/EMINENT ACADE-MICS/UNDER-WRITERS TO ISSUES

(*If the space provided for answers in the questionnaire is insufficient, please give information/data in a separate sheet mentioning the Serial Number of the question*).

1. Name and address :
2. Professional status :
3. Name of the institution with which associated :
4. Span of professional experience :
5. How do you look at the debentures/bonds, particularly the convertible debentures/bonds as means of corporate financing and as a saving instrument in the context of Indian environment ? Kindly state your views keeping in view the other available means of raising long-term funds such as accepting deposits from public, floating preference and/or equity shares, borrowing from finance institutions, etc.
6. For what purposes and under what diverse situations this instrument of raising funds should be employed by the private corporate sector ?
7. What reasons do you consider are responsible for the issuance of convertible debentures/bonds in a big way by the public limited companies of the Indian private corporate sector in last few years ? Please mention them in order of importance.

8. What factors, in your opinion, should be taken into account by the corporate managements/managers to issues while issuing such securities ?

9. What do you feel about the terms and conditions on which such securities are being offered at present? Please state your views in the light of short and long run interests of the issuing companies and those of the investing public.

10. At what level the conversion price should be kept while offering the issues of convertible debentures/bonds to public? Should it be lower, equal or higher than the market price of the relevant equity as found at the time of floating such debentures ?

11. On what yardsticks the successfulness or unsuccessfulness of issues of such securities should be measured? Please mention the different criteria in order of their importance.

12. Either in the interest of the issuing company or that of investors would you like to modify the presently attached terms and conditions? If yes, what modifications are needed any why ?

13. What is your considered opinion about the official guidelines issued from time to time by the Controller of Capital Issues in respect to the issue of secured convertible/non-convertible debentures/bonds? Are these in accordance with the sound financial management principles on the one hand, and in tune with the psychology and motivations of the Indian investors, on the other ?

    Kindly mention your views in detail.

14. If the existing official guidelines are deficient in any manner what improvements you would like to affect in these and what would be the consequent repercussions of the suggested improvements ?

15. Kindly indicate your views on the following :

    (i) The appropriate maturity period for the convertible/non-convertible debentures/bonds in the Indian context.

(ii) The appropriate alternate strategies that should be adopted by corporate managements/managers to issues for making a successful issue of debentures (Convertible/ Non-convertible).

(iii) Do you feel the necessity of taking certain follow up measures by the convertibles' issuing company? If yes, please rank the following measures in order of importance.

MEASURES	RANK
Keeping informed the investors about the progress and future plans of the company through inserting news in the different news papers from time to time	=
Making effort to see that there is an active trading in the shares of the company at as many as possible recognised stock exchanges of the country.	=
Maintaining a constant dividend policy	=
Following an upward rising dividend policy	=
Declaring interim dividends and bonus shares	=
Revising the rate of interest payable on convertibles as and when there is an upward revision in the permissible interest rates	=
Any other measures (Please specify)	=

16. What do you feel about the following provisions of the Income-Tax Act ?

(i) Section 80 cc : Can we think of making it applicable to the debentures of new units ?

(ii) Section 80 L : Would it be advisable to bring interest earned on debentures also within the purview of this section so as to treat it at par with the earnings in the shape of dividends on shares and interest on saving accounts for tax exemption purposes ?

(iii) Section 194 (A) : Would it be logical to apply this section to debentures for harmonizing the treatment of interest on debentures and company deposits for purposes of tax deduction at source ?

(iv) Would you further like to suggest any other modification in the existing provisions of the Income Tax Act of this land with a view to increase the effective return on debentures ? If 'yes', please mention them.

17. In what other ways the marketability of such securities and the effective return on them can be improved ? Please state your views at length.

18. What could be the role of finance intermediaries in popularising this instrument of corporate financing in India ?

19. What measures do you consider would lead to the creation and development of an effective secondary market for debentures in India ?

20. Can we think of drawing some lessons on the subject from the experience of American and/or British Corporations? If 'yes', kindly indicate the areas in detail.

Please mail the above completed questionnaire to :

OM PRAKASH GOYAL
Head,
Department of Commerce
M. D. University
Rohtak-124001
Haryana, INDIA.
Tel : 5641

QUESTIONNAIRE : 3 CONFIDENTIAL

TO BE ADDRESSED TO A SELECT GROUP OF INVESTORS

(If the space provided for answers in the questionnaire is insufficient, please give information/data in a separate sheet mentioning the serial number of the question.)

1. Kindly check (√) your category :

   Individual investor

   Institutional investor

2. Please answer this question, if you are an individual investor :

   (a) Name and address

   (b) Occupation

   (c) Age

   (d) Please check (√) the following items in which you might have invested your savings during the period 1978-82 :

      Fixed Deposits with Commercial Banks

      Fixed Deposits with Post Offices

      Fixed Deposits with Companies

      National Savings Certificates

      ULIP Purchased

      LIC Premium Paid

      Equity Shares

      Preference Shares

Debentures/bonds
Convertible
Non-convertible
Others (Please specify)

3. Kindly answer this question, if you are an institutional investor :

   (a) Name and address :

   (b) Nature of business :

   (c) Year of incorporation :

   (d) Please furnish us with the data as per the following table :

Investments made in	During the year				
	1978	1979	1980	1981	1982
Term deposits with banks					
Term deposits with companies					
Government securities :					
Central Government					
State Governments					
Equity Shares of the companies					
Preference shares of the companies					
Debentures/Bonds :					
Convertible					
Non-convertible					
Others (Please specify)					
TOTAL					

4. Please rank the following reasons in order of importance

which led you/your institution to invest in convertible/ non-convertible debentures/bonds :

(Most Important=1, Next Most Important=2, etc.)

REASONS	RANK
Rate of interest offered	=
Possibility of capital gains	=
Facility of conversion	=
Easy Marketability	=
Safety of funds	=
Advice of your investment consultant	=
Assurance of getting convertible debentures/bonds at some future date (applicable only in the case of non-convertible debentures/ bonds) .	=
Facility of preferential allotment of a scooter/moped	=
Non-availability of other investible securities	=
Other reason/s (Please specify)	=

5. Kindly check (√) the following factors on the basis of which you select the specific issue/s of convertible debentures/ bonds :

Favourable terms and conditions

Reputation and Goodwill of the Company

Prudent policy of the management

Market price of the shares of the concerned company

Volatile nature of the shares of the company

Encouraging reports about the profitability and other growth plans of the company

Non-availability of good equity shares

Past dividend policy of the company

Any others (please specify)

6. Would you prefer convertible debentures/bonds over non-convertible debentures/bonds ? Kindly check (√) the appropriate answer.

YES/NO

7. Do you prefer convertible debentures/bonds over equity shares ? Please check (√) the appropriate answer.

YES/NO

8. Would you prefer to invest in convertible debentures/ bonds if the conversion price is kept either equal or above the prevailing market price of the relevant equity? Please check (√) the appropriate answer.

YES/NO

9. Do you invcst in convertible debentures/bonds to retain them in your portfolio till the date of their redemption or to sell these out as soon as a good opportunity arises or to retain them till the date of conversion ?

10. How do you calculate 'profit' ?

   (i) in the case of convertible debentures/bonds :

   (ii) in the case of non-convertible debentures/bonds :

11. Kindly state your reactions on the following :

   (i) 'buy back clause' usually appended by the companie issuing convertible debentures/bonds.

   (ii) recent withdrawal of the facility of allowing 1 pe cent incentive interest rate on the issues of convertible debentures/bonds.

12. Are you satisfied with the terms and conditions on which the various companies are currently floating convertible debentures/bonds ? Kindly check (√) your answer.

YES/NO

13. If your answer to above is NO, please indicate the lines on which you would like to modify the present framework of terms and conditions of the convertible debentures/bonds. Please state your views in detail.

14. Do you observe any deficiency in the instrument of convertible/non-convertible debenture/bond ? If yes, please state it at length.

15. How do you find the attractively designed announcements made by the corporate managements/managers-to-issues while issuing such securities to the public ? Do you find them in any way misleading the investing public ? Kindly state your views frankly and in detail.

16. In your opinion what could be the possible ways through which debentures could be made attractive to common investor, in particular to the small investor? Kindly categorise your suggestions into the following :

    (i) Steps to be taken by the corporate managements/ managers to-issues :

    (ii) Steps to be taken by the Controller of Capital Issues and the Ministry of Finance :

    (iii) Other measures (Please specify) :

Please mail the above completed questionnaire to:

Dr. OM PRAKASH GOYAL
Head
Department of Commerce
M. D. University
Rohtak-124 001
Haryana, India
Tel. 5641

ANNEXE V

— LIST OF EMINENT CORPORATE EXECUTIVES, OFFICE BEARERS OF STOCK EXCHANGES AND ACADEMICS.

LIST OF EMINENT CORPORATE EXECUTIVES, OFFICE BEARERS OF STOCK EXCHANGES AND ACADEMICS

CORPORATE EXECUTIVES

1. Shri Aditya Birla Chairman	Indian Rayon Corporation Ltd., Veraval.
2. Shri A. Hoser Managing Director	Siemens India Ltd., Bombay.
3. Shri Anand Pradeep Managing Director	Punjab Anand Batteries Ltd., Mohali. (Pb).
4. Shri B R Trivedi Accounts Manager	The Ahmedabad Mfg. & Calico Printing Co. Ltd., Ahmedabad.
5. Shri Charat Ram Vice Chairman	The Delhi Cloth & General Mills Ltd., Delhi.
6. Shri D.B. Jhaveri Joint Managing Director	The Camphor & Allied Products Ltd., Bombay.
7. Shri D.C. Kothari Chairman-cum- Managing Director	The Kothari Industries Ltd., Madras.
8. Shri D.G. Khatri Chief Accountant	The Great Eastern Shipping General Co. Ltd., Bombay.
9. Shri D.K. Oswal Managing Director	The Vardhman Spinning & General Mills Ltd., Ludhiana (Pb).

10.	Shri D.L. Pradhan Vice President	The Larsen and Toubro Ltd., Bombay.
11.	Shri D.P. Mandelia Adviser	The Birla Group of Companies
12.	Shri D.S. Kaji Financial, Controller	The Raymond Woollen Mills Ltd., Bombay.
13.	Shri F.C. Rustugi Financial Controller	J.K. Synthetics Ltd., Kanpur.
14.	Shri G.D. Arora Controller of Accounts	The Ballarpur Industries Ltd., Calcutta.
15.	Shri G.R. Handa Manager Finance— Administration	The Siemens India Ltd., Bombay.
16.	Shri J.R. Desai Managing Director	The Kelvinator of India Ltd., New Delhi.
17.	Shri J.R. Joshi Managing Director	The Kirloskar Oil Engines Ltd., Bombay.
18.	Shri K.B. Dadi Seth Finance Controller	The Hindustan Lever Ltd., Bombay.
19.	Shri M.C. Patel Whole Time Director	Elecon Engineering Co. Ltd. Vallabh Vidhya Nagar 388120.
20.	Shri M.D. Ambani Executive Director	The Reliance Industries Ltd. Bombay.
21.	Shri M.K. Modi Managing Director	The Modipon Ltd., Modi Nagar.
22.	Shri M.P. Birla Chairman	The Birla Jute & Mfg. Co. Ltd., Calcutta.
23.	Shri M.S. Oberoi Chirman-cum- Managing Director	The East India Hotels Ltd., Calcutta.
24.	Shri N.A. Soonewala Director—Advisor	The Tata Group of Companies.

25.	Shri O.S. Kanwar Managing Director	The BST Ltd., New Delhi.
26.	Shri P.K. Sunderasan Financial Controller	The Kothari Industries Ltd., Madras.
27.	Shri P.R, Gandhi Finance Accountant	The Mafatlal Industries Ltd., Bombay.
28.	Shri R C Bhandari Chief Accountant	The Dempo Steam Ships Ltd., Goa.
29.	Shri R.M. Mehta Company Director	The Gujarat Steel Tubes Ltd., Ahmedabad.
30.	Shri R.N. Kapoor Secretary	The Shri Digvijaya Woollen Mills Ltd., Jamnagar-361006 (Gujarat)
31.	Shri R. Seshasayee Director Finance	The Ashok Leyland Ltd., Madras.
32.	Shri S.P. Dalal Chief Finance Officer	The Mahindra & Mahindra Ltd., Bombay.
33.	Shri U.C. Khanna Manager Finance—Taxation.	The Hindustan Lever Ltd., Bombay.
34.	Shri V.K. Modi Managing Director	The Modi Rubber Ltd., Modi Nagar.

OFFICE BEARERS OF STOCK EXCHANGES

1.	Shri E.R. Krishnamurthy Executive Director	The Madras Stock Exchange, Madras.
2.	Shri R.K. Panday Executive Director	The Delhi Stock Exchange New Delhi.
3.	Shri V.D. Sarde Former Chairman	The Bombay Stock Exchange Bombay.

EMINENT ACADEMICS

1.	Professor A.V.K. Iyenger	Institute for Financial Management and Research, Madras.

2.	Professor Behabatosh Benerji	Calcutta University, Calcutta.
3.	Doctor Besant Raj	Madras
4.	Professor B.N. Mehrotra	Department of Business Management, University of Jammu, Jammu Tawi
5.	Professor B.S. Bhatia	Department of Business Management Punjab University, Patiala.
6.	Professor B.S. Goyal	Institute of Management and Social Change Patna.
7.	Professor B.S. Sharma	Indira Gandhi Open University New Delhi.
8.	Professor C.B. Gupta Ex-Director	Institute of Management Technology, Gaziabad.
9.	Professor D.D. Narula Ex-Secretary	Indian Council of Social Sciences Research, New Delhi.
10.	Professor Dool Singh Ex-Dean, Faculty of Commerce & Business Management	Kurukshetra University, Kurukshetra.
11.	Professor D.R. Singh	Department of Business Management, Punjab Agricultural University, Ludhiana.
12.	Professor Harish C. Sharma Ex-Head	Department of Economic Administration and Financial Management, University of Rajasthan, Jaipur.

13.	Professor H.P. Chokshy	Faculty of Commerce M.S. University, Baroda
14.	Shri H.P. Raina Tax Consultant	Bombay.
15.	Shri Hanumanta Rao Associate Professor	Institute for Financial Management & Research, Madras
16.	Professor K.S. Mathur Ex-Professor of Accountancy & Business Statistics	University of Rajasthan, Jaipur.
17.	Professor L.C. Gupta	Management Development Institute Gurgaon.
18.	Professor Lal C. Jagetia Professor of Accounting	Cleveland State University Ohio (USA).
19.	Shri L.K. Jha Economic Adviser to Prime Minister of India	New Delhi
20.	Professor L.V.L.N. Sharma	I.I.T. Madras.
21.	Professor M.C. Khandelwal	Department of Accountancy and Business Statistics, University of Rajasthan, Jaipur.
22.	Professor M.D. Sharma	Department of Banking & Finance, M.S. University, Baroda.
23.	Professor M.L. Kothari	Faculty of Commerce and Business Management, Vikram University, Ujjain.

24.	Professor M. Saeed	Department of Commerce, Jamia Millia University, New Delhi.
25.	Professor N.R. Seth Director	Indian Institute of Management, Ahmedabad.
26.	Professor N.S. Gupta	University of Jammu, Jammu Tawi.
27.	Professor Prasanna Chandra	Indian Institute of Management, Banglore.
28.	Professor P.K. Ghosh	Department of Commerce, University of Delhi, Delhi.
29.	Professor P.P. Singh	Centre of Management Studies, I.I.T., New Delhi.
30.	Professor R.B.L. Aggarwal	Faculty of Commerce & Management Studies. L.M. Sukhadia University, Udaipur.
31.	Porfessor R.B. Upadhyaya, Vice-Chancellor	Ajmer University, Ajmer.
32.	Professor R.K. Jena	Department of Commerce, Utkal University, Bhuvneshwar (Orissa).
33.	Professor R.K. Lele	Department of Commerce, University of Delhi, Delhi.
34.	Professor S.C. Kuchhal	Indian Institute of Management, Ahmedabad.
35.	Professor S.M. Sukla	Kanpur University, Kanpur.
36.	Professor V.E. Ramamoorthy	Administrative Staff College, Hyderabad.

37.	Professor V.N. Hukku	University of Jodhpur, Jodhpur.
38.	Professor Y.K. Bhushan, Director	Narsee Monjee Institute of Management Studies, Juhu Development Scheme, Bombay.

ANNEXE: VI

Table 3.1 Through Table 3.25

Annexe VI.1

TABLE 3.1 : APPROVALS GRANTED BY THE CONTROLLER OF CAPITAL ISSUES TO PUBLIC LIMITED COMPANIES OF THE PRIVATE CORPORATE SECTOR FOR RAISING FUNDS THROUGH THE ISSUANCE OF DEBENTURES. (1978-82)

(Amount in Rupees Crores)

Sr. No.	YEAR	NON CONVERTIBLE DEBENTURES		
		Offered to Public. (Amount)	Offered on Rights Basis. (Amount)	Total (Amount)
(1)	(2)	(3)	(4)	(5)
1.	1978	- (-)	46.75 (12)	46.75 (12)
2.	1979	- (-)	59.50 (46)	59.50 (46)
3.	1980	- (-)	37.75 (41)	37.75 (41)
4.	1981	67.25 (24)	30.75 (20)	98.00 (44)
5.	1982	18.16 (5)	168.41 (45)	186.57 (50)
	TOTAL	85.41 (29)	343.16 (164)	428.57 (193)

TABLE 3.1 : APPROVALS GRANTED BY THE CONTROLLER OF CAPITAL ISSUES TO PUBLIC LIMITED COMPANIES OF THE PRIVATE CORPORATE SECTOR FOR RAISING FUNDS THROUGH THE ISSUANCE OF DEBENTURES.(Contd..2).

(1978-82)

(Amount in Rupees Crores)

Sr. No.	YEAR	CONVERTIBLE DEBENTURES			Total
		Offered to Public (Amount)	Offered on Rights Basis (Amount)	Total (Amount)	(Col. 5 + Col. 8) (Amount)
(1)	(2)	(6)	(7)	(8)	(9)
1.	1978	2.00 (1)	- (-)	2.00 (1)	48.75 (13)
2.	1979	54.25 (2)	0.25 (1)	54.50 (3)	114.00 (49)
3.	1980	17.30 (4)	11.90 (4)	29.20 (8)	66.95 (49)
4.	1981	182.48 (26)	46.17 (13)	228.65 (39)	326.65 (83)
5.	1982	184.90 (18)	144.73 (22)	329.63 (40)	516.20 (90)
	TOTAL	440.93 (51)	203.05 (40)	643.98 (91)	1,072.55 (284)

NOTE: Figures in parentheses under Column 3 through 9 indicate the number of companies.

SOURCE: Compiled from the information available in the Office of the Controller of Capital Issues, Ministry of Finance, Government of India, New Delhi.

Annexe VI.7

TABLE 3.3 : INDUSTRY-WISE DISTRIBUTION OF THE APPROVALS GRANTED BY THE CCI FOR THE ISSUANCE OF CONVERTIBLE/NON-CONVERTIBLE DEBENTURES/BONDS.(Contd...3).

(Amount in Rupees Crores) (1978-82)

1980

Sr. No.	INDUSTRY GROUP	NCDs.	CONVERTIBLE DEBENTURES			Total Issues of NCDs/ CDs.
			Public Issues	Rights Issues	Total	
		(Amount)	(Amount)	(Amount)	(Amount)	(Amount)
(1)	(2)	(13)	(14)	(15)	(16)	(17)
1.	Tea Plantation	1.00 (1)	- (-)	- (-)	- (-)	1.00 (1)
2.	Sugar	2.00 (2)	- (-)	- (-)	- (-)	2.00 (2)
3.	Tobacco	- (-)	- (-)	- (-)	- (-)	- (-)
4.	Cotton Textiles	6.00 (7)	- (-)	- (-)	- (-)	6.00 (7)
5.	Jute Textiles	0.75 (1)	- (-)	- (-)	- (-)	0.75 (1)
6.	Silk,Rayon&Woollen Textiles.	6.50 (4)	14.80 (2)	10.80 (1)	25.60 (3)	32.10 (7)
7.	Iron,Steel& Non-Ferrous Metal(Basic)	2.00 (1)	- (-)	- (-)	- (-)	2.00 (1)
8.	Aluminium	- (-)	- (-)	- (-)	- (-)	- (-)
9.	Engineering	9.25 (14)	- (-)	- (-)	- (-)	9.25 (14)
10.	Chemicals	8.25 (7)	2.50 (2)	0.10 (1)	2.60 (3)	10.85 (10)
11.	Rubber&Rubber Mfg.	- (-)	- (-)	- (-)	- (-)	- (-)
12.	Paper&Paper Products	(-)	(-)	(-)	(-)	(-)
13.	Electricity Generation & Supply	- (-)	- (-)	- (-)	- (-)	- (-)
14.	Commerce	0.80 (2)	- (-)	0.50 (1)	0.50 (1)	1.30 (3)
15.	Hotel	1.20 (2)	- (-)	0.50 (1)	0.50 (1)	1.70 (3)
	TOTAL	37.75 (41)	17.30 (4)	11.90 (4)	29.20 (8)	66.95 (49)

Annexe VI.8

TABLE 3.3. : INDUSTRY-WISE DISTRIBUTION OF THE APPROVALS GRANTED BY THE CCI FOR THE ISSUANCE OF CONVERTIBLE/NON-CONVERTIBLE DEBENTURES/BONDS.(Contd....4).

(Amount in Rupees Crores) (1978-82)

Sr. No.	INDUSTRY GROUP	1981				
		NCDs.	CONVERTIBLE DEBENTURES			Total Issues of NCDs/ CDs.
			Public Issues	Rights Issues	Total	
		(Amount)	(Amount)	(Amount)	(Amount)	(Amount)
(1)	(2)	(18)	(19)	(20)	(21)	(22)
1.	Tea Plantation	4.50 (2)	- (-)	- (-)	- (-)	4.50 (2)
2.	Sugar	- (-)	- (-)	0.50 (1)	0.50 (1)	0.50 (1)
3.	Tobacco	5.00 (1)	- (-)	- (-)	- (-)	5.00 (1)
4.	Cotton Textiles	17.75 (6)	31.85 (7)	3.76 (3)	35.61 (10)	53.36 (16)
5.	Jute Textiles	0.75 (1)	1.00 (1)	- (-)	1.00 (1)	1.75 (2)
6.	Silk,Rayon & Woollen Textiles	5.03 (2)	25.00 (2)	- (-)	25.00 (2)	30.03 (4)
7.	Iron,Steel & Non-Ferrous Metal(Basic)	1.00 (1)	55.00 (6)	- (-)	55.00 (6)	56.00 (7)
8.	Aluminium	- (-)	- (-)	10.45 (1)	10.45 (1)	10.45 (1)
9.	Engineering	22.02 (13)	8.50 (3)	1.75 (2)	10.25 (5)	32.27 (18)
10.	Chemicals	33.95 (15)	38.63 (4)	15.91 (4)	54.54 (8)	88.49 (23)
11.	Rubber&Rubber Mfg.	6.00 (1)	- (-)	- (-)	- (-)	6.00 (1)
12.	Paper&Paper Products	1.00 (1)	10.00 (1)	0.30 (1)	10.30 (2)	11.30 (3)
13.	Electricity Generation & Supply.	- (-)	- (-)	- (-)	- (-)	- (-)
14.	Commerce	1.00 (1)	5.00 (1)	13.50 (1)	18.50 (2)	19.50 (3)
15.	Hotel	- (-)	7.50 (1)	- (-)	7.50 (1)	7.50 (1)
	TOTAL	98.00 (44)	182.48 (26)	46.17 (13)	228.65 (39)	326.65 (83)

Annexe VI.9

TABLE 3.3 : INDUSTRY-WISE DISTRIBUTION OF THE APPROVALS GRANTED BY THE CCI FOR THE ISSUANCE OF CONVERTIBLE/NON-CONVERTIBLE DEBENTURES/BONDS.(Contd.....5).

(Amount in Rupees Crores) (1978-82)

Sr. No.	INDUSTRY GROUP	1982 NCDs.	CONVERTIBLE DEBENTURES			Total Issues of NCDs/ CDs.
			Public Issues	Rights Issues	Total	
		(Amount)	(Amount)	(Amount)	(Amount)	(Amount)
(1)	(2)	(23)	(24)	(25)	(26)	(27
1.	Tea Plantation	- (-)	- (-)	- (-)	- (-)	- (-)
2.	Sugar	- (-)	- (-)	- (-)	- (-)	- (-)
3.	Tobacco	3.00 (1)	30.00 (1)	- (-)	30.00 (1)	33.00 (2)
4.	Cotton Textiles	25.00 (7)	29.40 (3)	38.20 (4)	67.60 (7)	92.60 (14)
5.	Jute Textiles	- (-)	- (-)	- (-)	- (-)	- (-)
6.	Silk,Rayon& Woollen Textiles	22.00 (3)	53.00 (3)	50.00 (1)	103.00 (4)	125.00 (7)
7.	Iron,Steel & Non-Ferrous Metal(Basic)	27.35 (8)	29.85 (5)	2.25 (2)	32.10 (7)	59.45 (15)
8.	Aluminium	2.00 (1)	- (-)	- (-)	- (-)	2.00 (1)
9.	Engineering	33.00 (11)	5.65 (1)	17.10 (4)	22.75 (5)	55.75 (16)
10.	Chemicals	49.50 (14)	10.00 (3)	30.00 (1)	40.00 (4)	89.50 (18)
11.	Rubber&Rubber Mfg.	- (-)	12.00 (1)	- (-)	12.00 (1)	12.00 (1)
12.	Paper&Paper Products	13.60 (2)	- (-)	2.50 (2)	2.50 (2)	16.10 (4)
13.	Electricity Generation & Supply	0.12 (1)	- (-)	- (-)	- (-)	0.12 (1)
14.	Commerce	1.00 (1)	- (-)	4.68 (8)	4.68 (8)	5.68 (9)
15.	Hotel	10.00 (1)	15.00 (1)	- (-)	15.00 (1)	25.00 (2)
	TOTAL	186.57 (50)	184.90 (18)	144.73 (22)	329.63 (40)	516.20 (90)

Annexe VI.10

TABLE 3.3. : INDUSTRY-WISE DISTRIBUTION OF THE APPROVALS GRANTED BY THE CCI FOR THE ISSUANCE OF CONVERTIBLE/NON-CONVERTIBLE DEBENTURES/BONDS.(Contd......6).

(Amount in Rupees Crores) (1978-82)

Sr. No.	INDUSTRY GROUP	1978-82 NCDs. (Amount)	CONVERTIBLE DEBENTURES Public Issues (Amount)	Rights Issues Amount)	Total Amount)	Total Issues of NCDs/ CDs. (Amount)
(1)	(2)	(28)	(29)	(30)	(31)	(32)
1.	Tea Plantation	9.00 (5)	- (-)	- (-)	- (-)	9.00 (5)
2.	Sugar	2.00 (2)	- (-)	0.50 (1)	0.50 (1)	2.50 (3)
3.	Tobacco	8.75 (3)	30.00 (1)	- (-)	30.00 (1)	38.75 (4)
4.	Cotton Textiles	61.50 (27)	61.25 (10)	41.96 (7)	103.21 (17)	164.71 (44)
5.	Jute Textiles	2.25 (4)	1.00 (1)	- (-)	1.00 (1)	3.25 (5)
6.	Sils,Rayon&Woollen Textiles.	35.78 (11)	99.80 (8)	60.80 (2)	160.60 (10)	196.38 (21)
7.	Iron,Steel&Non-Ferrous Metal(Basic)	41.60 (20)	84.85 (11)	2.25 (2)	87.10 (13)	128.70 (33)
8.	Aluminium	2.00 (1)	- (-)	10.45 (1)	10.45 (1)	12.45 (2)
9.	Engineering	77.27 (49)	63.40 (6)	18.85 (6)	82.25 (12)	159.52 (61)
10.	Chemicals	115.45 (53)	51.13 (9)	46.26 (7)	97.39 (16)	212.84 (69)
11.	Rubber&Rubber Mfg.	7.50 (2)	12.00 (1)	- (-)	12.00 (1)	19.50 (3)
12.	Paper&Paper Products	16.60 (4)	10.00 (1)	2.80 (3)	12.80 (4)	39.40 (8)
13.	Electricity Generation & Supply	1.37 (2)	- (-)	- (-)	- (-)	1.37 (2)
14.	Commerce	36.30 (7)	5.00 (1)	18.68 (10)	23.68 (11)	59.98 (18)
15.	Hotel	11.20 (3)	22.50 (2)	0.50 (1)	23.00 (3)	34.20 (6)
	TOTAL	428.57 (193)	440.93 (51)	203.05 (40)	643.98 (91)	1072.55 (284)

BLE 3.3. : INDUSTRY-WISE DISTRIBUTION OF THE APPROVALS GRANTED BY THE CCI FOR THE ISSUANCE OF CONVERTIBLE/NON-CONVERTIBLE DEBENTURES/BONDS.(Contd.......7).

NOTES : 1. 'CCI' stands for Controller of Capital Issues.

'NCDs' stands for Non-Convertible Debenture /Bonds.

'CDs' stands for Convertible Debentures/ Bonds.

Figures in parentheses under Column 3 through Column 32 indicate the Number of Companies.

SOURCE: Compiled from the information contained in Table 2.3 through Table 2.7 of Annexe II.

TABLE 3.4 : AGE-WISE CATEGORIZATION OF THE PLCpr WHICH WERE GRANTED APPROVALS FOR THE ISSUANCE OF CONVERTIBLE/ NON-CONVERTIBLE DEBENTURES/BONDS.

(1978-82)

Amount in Rupees Crores.

1978

Sr. No.	AGE-GROUPS	NCDs. (Amount)	CONVERTIBLE DEBENTURES Public Issues (Amount)	Rights Issues (Amount)	Total Issues of CDs. (Amount)	Total Issues of NCDs/CDs. (Amount)
(1)	(2)	(3)	(4)	(5)	(6)	(7)
A.	**RNPLCpr**	- (-)	- (-)	- (-)	- (-)	- (-)
1.	Upto 10 years	- (-)	- (-)	- (-)	- (-)	- (-)
2.	11-20 years.	- (-)	- (-)	- (-)	- (-)	- (-)
B.	**MAPLCpr**	41.75 (9)	2.00 (1)	- (-)	2.00 (1)	43.75 (10)
3.	21-30 years	39.50 (7)	- (-)	- (-)	- (-)	39.50 (7)
4.	31-40 years	- (-)	- (-)	- (-)	- (-)	- (-)
5.	41-50 years	2.25 (2)	2.00 (1)	- (-)	2.00 (1)	4.25 (3)
C.	**OPLCpr**	5.00 (3)	- (-)	- (-)	- (-)	5.00 (3)
6.	51 and above	5.00 (3)	- (-)	- (-)	- (-)	5.00 (3)
	TOTAL	46.75 (12)	2.00 (1)	- (-)	2.00 (1)	48.75 (13)

TABLE 3.4 : AGE-WISE CATEGORIZATION OF THE PLCpr WHICH WERE GRANTED APPROVALS FOR THE ISSUANCE OF CONVERTIBLE/ NON-CONVERTIBLE DEBENTURES/BONDS. (Contd..2).

Amount in Rupees Crores. (1978-82)

Sr. No.	AGE-GROUPS	1979				Total Issues of NCDs/CDs.
		NCDs.	CONVERTIBLE DEBENTURES			
			Public Issues	Rights Issues	Total Issues of CDs.	
		(Amount)	(Amount)	(Amount)	(Amount)	(Amount)
(1)	(2)	(8)	(9)	(10)	(11)	(12)
A.	RNPLCpr	4.25 (4)	7.00 (1)	- (-)	7.00 (1)	11.25 (5)
1.	Upto 10 years.	4.25 (4)	7.00 (1)	- (-)	7.00 (1)	11.25 (5)
2.	11-20 years.	- (-)	- (-)	- (-)	- (-)	- (-)
B.	MAPLCpr	44.00 (33)	47.25 (1)	0.25 (1)	47.50 (2)	91.50 (35)
3.	21-30 years	27.00 (20)	- (-)	0.25 (1)	0.25 (1)	27.25 (21)
4.	31-40 years.	9.50 (9)	47.25 (1)	- (-)	47.25 (1)	56.75 (10)
5.	41-50 Years.	7.50 (4)	- (-)	- (-)	- (-)	7.50 (4)
C.	OPLCpr	11.25 (9)	- (-)	- (-)	- (-)	11.25 (9)
6.	51 and above.	11.25 (9)	- (-)	- (-)	- (-)	11.25 (9)
	TOTAL	59.50 (46)	54.25 (2)	0.25 (1)	54.50 (3)	114.00 (49)

TABLE 3.4 : AGE-WISE CATEGORIZATION OF THE PLCpr WHICH WERE GRANTED APPROVALS FOR THE ISSUANCE OF CONVERTIBLE/ NON-CONVERTIBLE DEBENTURES/BONDS.(Contd...3).

Amount in Rupees Crores. (1978-82)

Sr. No.	AGE-GROUPS	1980				Total Issues of NCDs/ CDs.
		NCDs.	CONVERTIBLE DEBENTURES			
			Public Issues	Rights Issues	Total Issues of CDs.	
		(Amount)	(Amount)	(Amount)	(Amount)	(Amount)
(1)	(2)	(13)	(14)	(15)	(16)	(17)
A.	RNPLCpr	3.70 (5)	- (-)	11.80 (3)	11.80 (3)	15.50 (8)
1.	Upto 10 years	0.70 (2)	- (-)	11.30 (2)	11.30 (2)	12.00 (4)
2.	11-20 years	3.00 (3)	- (-)	0.50 (1)	0.50 (1)	3.50 (4)
B.	MAPLCpr	21.80 (25)	12.50 (3)	0.10 (1)	12.60 (4)	34.40 (29)
3.	21-30 years	11.55 (13)	11.00 (2)	- (-)	11.00 (2)	22.55 (15)
4.	31-40 years	6.50 (8)	1.50 (1)	- (-)	1.50 (1)	8.00 (9)
5.	41-50 years	3.75 (4)	- (-)	0.10 (1)	0.10 (1)	3.85 (5)
C.	OPLCpr	12.25 (11)	4.80 (1)	- (-)	4.80 (1)	17.05 (12)
6.	51 and above	12.25 (11)	4.80 (1)	- (-)	4.80 (1)	17.05 (12)
	TOTAL	37.75 (41)	17.30 (4)	11.90 (4)	29.20 (8)	66.95 (49)

TABLE 3.4 : AGE-WISE CATEGORIZATION OF THE PLCpr WHICH WERE GRANTED APPROVALS FOR THE ISSUANCE OF CONVERTIBLE/ NON-CONVERTIBLE DEBENTURES/BONDS.(Contd....4).

Amount in Rupees Crores. (1978-82)

Sr. No.	AGE-GROUPS	1981				Total Issues of NCDs/ CDs.
		NCDs.	CONVERTIBLE DEBENTURES			
			Public Issues	Rights Issues	Total Issues of CDs.	
		(Amount)	(Amount)	(Amount)	(Amount)	(Amount)
(1)	(2)	(18)	(19)	(20)	(21)	(22)
A.	RNPLCpr	20.81 (8)	41.13 (6)	11.24 (5)	52.37 (11)	73.18 (19)
1.	Upto 10 years	8.31 (4)	25.00 (2)	10.54 (3)	35.54 (5)	43.85 (9)
2.	11-20 years	12.50 (4)	16.13 (4)	0.70 (2)	16.83 (6)	29.33 (10)
B.	MAPLCpr	47.94 (24)	92.75 (15)	34.43 (7)	127.18 (22)	175.12 (46)
3.	21-30 years	20.12 (8)	27.00 (5)	20.97 (5)	47.97 (10)	68.09 (18)
4.	31-40 years	18.32 (12)	47.75 (7)	3.01 (1)	50.76 (8)	69.08 (20)
5.	41-50 years	9.50 (4)	18.00 (3)	10.45 (1)	28.45 (4)	37.95 (8)
C.	OPLCpr	29.25 (12)	48.60 (5)	0.50 (1)	49.10 (6)	78.35 (18)
6.	51 and above	29.25 (12)	48.60 (5)	0.50 (1)	49.10 (6)	78.35 (18)
	TOTAL	98.00 (44)	182.48 (26)	46.17 (13)	228.65 (39)	326.65 (83)

Annexe VI.16

TABLE 3.4 : AGE-WISE CATEGORIZATION OF THE PLCpr WHICH WERE GRANTED APPROVALS FOR THE ISSUANCE OF CONVERTIBLE/ NON-CONVERTIBLE DEBENTURES/BONDS.(Contd.....5).

Amount in Rupees Crores. (1978-82)

Sr. No.	AGE-GROUPS	1982				Total Issues of NCDs/ CDs.
		NCDs.	CONVERTIBLE DEBENTURES			
			Public Issues	Rights Issues	Total Issues of CDs.	
		(Amount)	(Amount)	(Amount)	(Amount)	(Amount)
(1)	(2)	(23)	(24)	(25)	(26)	(27)
A.	RNPLCpr	16.37 (16)	9.45 (3)	57.43 (11)	66.88 (14)	83.25 (30)
1.	Upto 10 years	1.37 (12)	9.45 (3)	55.93 (10)	65.38 (13)	66.75 (25)
2.	11-20 years	15.00 (4)	- (-)	1.50 (1)	1.50 (1)	16.50 (5)
B.	MAPLCpr	136.70 (35)	68.80 (7)	49.10 (7)	117.90 (14)	254.60 (49)
3.	21-30 years	45.10 (12)	36.80 (5)	1.10 (1)	37.90 (6)	83.00 (18)
4.	31-40 years	72.50 (16)	32.00 (2)	13.00 (3)	45.00 (5)	117.50 (21)
5.	41-50 years	19.10 (7)	- (-)	35.00 (3)	35.00 (3)	54.10 (10)
C.	OPLCpr	33.50 (9)	106.65 (8)	38.20 (4)	144.85 (12)	178.35 (21)
6.	51 and above	33.50 (9)	106.65 (8)	38.20 (4)	144.85 (12)	178.35 (21)
	TOTAL	186.57 (50)	184.90 (18)	144.73 (22)	329.63 (40)	516.20 (90)

Annexe VI.17

TABLE 3.4 : AGE-WISE CATEGORIZATION OF THE PLCpr WHICH WERE GRANTED APPROVALS FOR THE ISSUANCE OF CONVERTIBLE/ NON-CONVERTIBLE DEBENTURES/BONDS.(Contd......6)

Amount in Rupees Crores. (1978-82)

Sr. No.	AGE-GROUPS	1978-82				Total Issues of NCDs/ CDs.
		NCDs.	CONVERTIBLE DEBENTURES			
			Public Issues	Rights Issues	Total Issues of CDs.	
		(Amount)	(Amount)	(Amount)	(Amount)	(Amount)
(1)	(2)	(28)	(29)	(30)	(31)	(32)
A.	RNPLCpr	45.13 (23)	57.58 (10)	80.57 (19)	138.15 (29)	183.28 (52)
1.	Upto 10 years.	14.63 (12)	41.45 (6)	77.77 (15)	119.22 (21)	133.85 (33)
2.	11-20 years	30.50 (11)	16.13 (4)	2.70 (4)	18.83 (8)	49.33 (19)
B.	MAPLCpr	292.19 (126)	223.30 (27)	83.88 (16)	307.18 (43)	599.37 (169)
3.	21-30 years	143.27 (60)	74.80 (12)	22.32 (7)	97.12 (19)	240.39 (79)
4.	31-40 years	106.82 (45)	128.50 (11)	16.01 (4)	144.51 (15)	251.33 (60)
5.	41-50 years	42.10 (21)	20.00 (4)	45.55 (5)	65.55 (9)	107.65 (30)
C.	OPLCpr	91.25 (44)	160.05 (14)	38.70 (5)	198.75 (19)	290.00 (63)
6.	51 and above.	91.25 (44)	160.05 (14)	38.70 (5)	198.75 (19)	290.00 (63)
	TOTAL	428.51 (193)	440.93 (51)	203.05 (40)	643.98 (91)	1,072.49 (284)

TABLE 3.4 : AGE-WISE CATEGORIZATION OF THE PLCpr WHICH WERE GRANTED APPROVALS FOR THE ISSUANCE OF CONVERTIBLE/ NON-CONVERTIBLE DEBENTURES/BONDS.(Contd.......7).

NOTES : (1) 'PLCpr' stands for Public Limited Companies of the Private Corporate Sector.

'NCDs' stands for Non-Convertible Debentures.

'CDs' stands for Convertible Debentures.

'RNPLCpr' stands for Relatively New Public Limited Companies of the Private Corporate Sector.

'MAPLCpr' stands for Middle Aged Public Limited Companies of the Private Corporate Sector.

'OPLCpr' stands for Old Public Limited Companies of the Private Corporate Sector.

(2) Figures in parentheses under Column 3 through Column 32 indicate the Number of Companies.

SOURCE : Compiled from the information included in Table 2.3 through Table 2.7.

TABLE 3.5 : REGION-WISE DISTRIBUTION OF THE PLCpr WHICH WERE GRANTED APPROVALS FOR THE ISSUANCE OF CDs/NCDs.
(1978-82)

(Amount in Rupees Crores)

Sr. No. REGION	1978				
	NCDs.	CONVERTIBLE DEBENTURES			Total Issues of NCDs/CDs.
		Public Issues	Rights Issues	Total	
	(Amount)	(Amount)	(Amount)	(Amount)	(Amount)
(1) (2)	(3)	(4)	(5)	(6)	(7)
I. NORTHERN REGION	- (-)	- (-)	- (-)	- (-)	- (-)
1. Haryana	- (-)	- (-)	- (-)	- (-)	- (-)
2. Punjab	- (-)	- (-)	- (-)	- (-)	- (-)
3. Delhi	- (-)	- (-)	- (-)	- (-)	- (-)
II. EASTERN REGION	0.25 (1)	2.00 (1)	- (-)	2.00 (1)	2.25 (2)
4. Orissa	- (-)	- (-)	- (-)	- (-)	- (-)
5. West Bengal	0.25 (1)	2.00 (1)	- (-)	2.00 (1)	2.25 (2)
III. CENTRAL REGION	0.75 (1)	- (-)	- (-)	- (-)	0.75 (1)
6. Madhya Pradesh	- (-)	- (-)	- (-)	- (-)	- (-)
7 Uttar Pradesh	0.75 (1)	- (-)	- (-)	- (-)	0.75 (1)
IV. WESTERN REGION	45.75 (10)	- (-)	- (-)	- (-)	45.75 (10)
8. Gujarat	- (-)	- (-)	- (-)	- (-)	- (-)
9. Maharashtra	45.75 (10)	- (-)	- (-)	- (-)	45.75 (10)
V. SOUTHERN REGION	- (-)	- (-)	- (-)	- (-)	- (-)
10. Andhra Pradesh	- (-)	- (-)	- (-)	- (-)	- (-)
11. Karnataka	- (-)	- (-)	- (-)	- (-)	- (-)
12. Kerala	- (-)	- (-)	- (-)	- (-)	- (-)
13. Tamil Nadu	- (-)	- (-)	- (-)	- (-)	- (-)
TOTAL	46.75 (12)	2.00 (1)	- (-)	2.00 (1)	48.75 (13)

Annexe VI.20

TABLE 3.5 : REGION-WISE DISTRIBUTION OF THE PLCpr WHICH WERE GRANTED APPROVALS FOR THE ISSUANCE OF CDs/NCDs.(Contd..2).

(Amount in Rupees Crores) (1978-82)

Sr. No.	REGION	1979 NCDs. (Amount)	CONVERTIBLE DEBENTURES Public Issues (Amount)	Rights Issues (Amount)	Total (Amount)	Total Issues of NCDs/CDs. (Amount)
(1)	(2)	(8)	(9)	(10)	(11)	(12)
I.	NORTHERN REGION	3.75 (4)	- (-)	- (-)	- (-)	3.75 (4)
1.	Haryana	- (-)	- (-)	- (-)	- (-)	- (-)
2.	Punjab	1.50 (2)	- (-)	- (-)	- (-)	1.50 (2)
3.	Delhi	2.25 (2)	- (-)	- (-)	- (-)	2.25 (2)
II.	EASTERN REGION	16.50 (12)	- (-)	0.25 (1)	0.25 (1)	16.75 (13)
4.	Orissa	2.00 (1)	- (-)	- (-)	- (-)	2.00 (1)
5.	West Bengal	14.50 (11)	- (-)	0.25 (1)	0.25 (1)	14.50 (12)
III.	CENTRAL REGION	4.00 (2)	- (-)	- (-)	- (-)	4.00 (2)
6.	Madhya Pradesh	- (-)	- (-)	- (-)	- (-)	- (-)
7.	Uttar Pradesh	4.00 (2)	- (-)	- (-)	- (-)	4.00 (2)
IV.	WESTERN REGION	32.75 (24)	54.25 (2)	- (-)	54.25 (2)	87.00 (26)
8.	Gujarat	8.25 (7)	- (-)	- (-)	- (-)	8.25 (7)
9.	Maharashtra	24.50 (17)	54.25 (2)	- (-)	54.25 (2)	78.75 (19)
V.	SOUTHERN REGION	2.50 (4)	- (-)	- (-)	- (-)	2.50 (4)
10.	Andhra Pradesh	1.00 (1)	- (-)	- (-)	- (-)	1.00 (1)
11.	Karnataka	- (-)	- (-)	- (-)	- (-)	- (-)
12.	Kerala	0.50 (1)	- (-)	- (-)	- (-)	0.50 (1)
13.	Tamil Nadu	1.00 (2)	- (-)	- (-)	- (-)	1.00 (2)
	TOTAL	59.50 (46)	54.25 (2)	0.25 (1)	54.50 (3)	114.00 (49)

TABLE 3.5 : REGION-WISE DISTRIBUTION OF THE PLCpr WHICH WERE GRANTED APPROVALS FOR THE ISSUANCE OF CDs/NCDs.(Contd...3).

(Amount in Rupees CRores) (1978-82)

Sr. No.	REGION	1980 NCDs.	CONVERTIBLE DEBENTURES Public Issues	Rights Issues	Total	Total Issues of NCDs/CDs.
		(Amount)	(Amount)	(Amount)	(Amount)	(Amount)
(1)	(2)	(13)	(14)	(15)	(16)	(17)
I.	NORTHERN REGION	6.00 (7)	- (-)	- (-)	- (-)	6.00 (7)
1.	Haryana	- (-)	- (-)	- (-)	- (-)	- (-)
2.	Punjab	2.75 (3)	- (-)	- (-)	- (-)	2.75 (3)
3.	Delhi	3.25 (4)	- (-)	- (-)	- (-)	3.25 (4)
II.	EASTERN REGION	4.00 (4)	1.50 (1)	- (-)	1.50 (1).	5.50 (5)
4.	Orissa	- (-)	- (-)	- (-)	- (-)	- (-)
5.	West Bengal	4.00 (4)	1.50 (1)	- (-)	1.50 (1)	5.50 (5)
III.	CENTRAL REGION	1.50 (1)	- (-)	- (-)	- (-)	1.50 (1)
6.	Madhya Pradesh	- (-)	- (-)	- (-)	- (-)	- (-)
7.	Uttar Pradesh	1.50 (1)	- (-)	- (-)	- (-)	1.50 (1)
IV.	WESTERN REGION	21.80 (24)	15.80 (3)	11.40 (3)	27.20 (6)	49.00 (30)
8.	Gujarat	2.00 (3)	10.00 (1)	- (-)	10.00 (1)	12.00 (4)
9.	Maharashtra	19.80 (21)	5.80 (2)	11.40 (3)	17.20 (5)	37.00 (26)
V.	SOUTHERN REGION	4.45 (5)	- (-)	0.50 (1)	0.50 (1)	4.95 (6)
10.	Andhra Pradesh	- (-)	- (-)	- (-)	- (-)	- (-)
11.	Karnataka	0.20 (1)	- (-)	- (-)	- (-)	0.20 (1)
12.	Kerala	2.50 (1)	- (-)	- (-)	- (-)	2.50 (1)
13.	Tamil Nadu	1.75 (3)	- (-)	0.50 (1)	0.50 (1)	2.25 (4)
	TOTAL	37.75 (41)	17.30 (4)	11.90 (4)	29.20 (8)	66.95 (49)

TABLE 3.5 : REGION-WISE DISTRIBUTION OF THE PLCpr WHICH WERE GRANTED APPROVALS FOR THE ISSUANCE OF CDs/NCDs. (Contd....4).

(Amount in Rupees Crores) (1978-82)

Sr. No.	REGION	1981				
		NCDs.	CONVERTIBLE DEBENTURES			Total Issues of NCDs/ CDs.
		(Amount)	Public Issues (Amount)	Rights Issues (Amount)	Total (Amount)	(Amount)
(1)	(2)	(18)	(19)	(20)	(21)	(22)
I.	NORTHERN REGION	1.00 (1)	23.00 (5)	0.55 (2)	23.55 (7)	24.55 (8)
1.	Haryana	- (-)	- (-)	- (-)	- (-)	- (-)
2.	Punjab	1.00 (1)	4.00 (3)	0.55 (2)	4.55 (5)	5.55 (6)
3.	Delhi	- (-)	19.00 (2)	- (-)	19.00 (2)	19.00 (2)
II.	EASTERN REGION	26.30 (13)	20.00 (4)	10.45 (1)	30.45 (5)	56.75 (18)
4.	Orissa	- (-)	10.00 (1)	- (-)	10.00 (1)	10.00 (1)
5.	West Bengal	26.30 (13)	10.00 (3)	10.45 (1)	20.45 (4)	46.75 (17)
III.	CENTRAL REGION	16.00 (3)	25.00 (1)	- (-)	25.00 (1)	41.00 (4)
6.	Madhya Pradesh	- (-)	- (-)	- (-)	- (-)	- (-)
7.	Uttar Pradesh	16.00 (3)	25.00 (1)	- (-)	25.00 (1)	41.00 (4)
IV.	WESTERN REGION	48.20 (23)	99.48 (14)	34.67 (9)	134.15 (23)	182.35 (46)
8.	Gujarat	12.90 (5)	26.60 (8)	12.49 (3)	39.09 (11)	51.99 (16)
9.	Maharashtra	35.30 (18)	72.88 (6)	22.18 (6)	95.06 (12)	130.36 (30)
V.	SOUTHERN REGION	6.50 (4)	15.00 (2)	0.50 (1)	15.50 (3)	22.00 (7)
10.	Andhra Pradesh	- (-)	- (-)	- (-)	- (-)	- (-)
11.	Karnataka	- (-)	- (-)	- (-)	- (-)	- (-)
12.	Kerala	- (-)	- (-)	- (-)	- (-)	- (-)
13.	Tamil Nadu	6.50 (4)	15.00 (2)	0.50 (1)	15.50 (3)	22.00 (7)
	TOTAL	98.00 (44)	182.48 (26)	46.17 (13)	228.65 (39)	326.65 (83)

TABLE 3.5 : REGION-WISE DISTRIBUTION OF THE PLCpr WHICH WERE GRANTED APPROVALS FOR THE ISSUANCE OF CDs/NCDs.(Contd.....5).

(Amount in Rupees Crores) (1978-82)

		1982				
Sr. No.	REGION	NCDs. (Amount)	CONVERTIBLE DEBENTURES Public Issues (Amount)	Rights Issues (Amount)	Total (Amount)	Total Issues of NCDs/CDs. (Amount)
(1)	(2)	(23)	(24)	(25)	(26)	(27)
1.	NORTHERN REGION	22.50 (4)	10.80 (3)	- (-)	10.80 (3)	33.30 (7)
1.	Haryana	5.00 (1)	- (-)	- (-)	- (-)	5.00 (1)
2.	Punjab	- (-)	5.80 (2)	- (-)	5.80 (2)	5.80 (2)
3.	Delhi	17.50 (3)	5.00 (1)	- (-)	5.00 (1)	22.50 (4)
II.	EASTERN REGION	31.72 (8)	82.25 (5)	4.00 (1)	86.25 (6)	117.97 (14)
4.	Orissa	3.60 (1)	- (-)	- (-)	- (-)	3.60 (1)
5.	West Bengal	28.12 (7)	82.25 (5)	4.00 (1)	86.25 (6)	114.37 (13)
III.	CENTRAL REGION	25.00 (6)	35.65 (2)	- (-)	35.65 (2)	60.65 (8)
6.	Madhya Pradesh	15.00 (1)	30.00 (1)	- (-)	30.00 (1)	45.00 (2)
7.	Uttar Pradesh	10.00 (5)	5.65 (1)	- (-)	5.65 (1)	15.65 (6)
IV.	WESTERN REGION	90.60 (25)	53.70 (7)	137.48 (18)	191.18 (25)	281.78 (50)
8.	Gujarat	15.50 (4)	27.90 (4)	17.10 (3)	45.00 (7)	60.50 (11)
9.	Maharashtra	75.10 (21)	25.80 (3)	120.38 (15)	146.18 (18)	221.28 (39)
V.	SOUTHERN REGION	16.75 (7)	2.50 (1)	3.25 (3)	5.75 (4)	22.50 (11)
10.	Andhra Pradesh	3.25 (2)	2.50 (1)	2.25 (2)	4.75 (3)	8.00 (5)
11.	Karnataka	2.00 (2)	- (-)	- (-)	- (-)	2.00 (2)
12.	Kerala	- (-)	- (-)	1.00 (1)	1.00 (1)	1.00 (1)
13.	Tamil Nadu	11.50 (3)	- (-)	- (-)	- (-)	11.50 (3)
	TOTAL	186.57 (50)	184.90 (18)	144.73 (22)	329.63 (40)	516.20 (90)

TABLE 3.5 : REGION-WISE DISTRIBUTION OF THE PLCpr WHICH WERE GRANTED APPROVALS FOR THE ISSUANCE OF CDs/NCDs.(Contd......6).

(Amount in Rupees Crores) (1978-82)

Sr. No.	REGION	1978-82 NCDs. (Amount)	CONVERTIBLE DEBENTURES Public Issues (Amount)	Rights Issues (Amount)	Total (Amount)	Total Issues of NCDs/ CDs. (Amount)
(1)	(2)	(28)	(29)	(30)	(31)	(32)
1.	NORTHERN REGION	33.25 (16)	33.80 (8)	0.55 (2)	34.35 (10)	67.60 (26)
1.	Haryana	5.00 (1)	- (-)	- (-)	- (-)	5.00 (1)
2.	Punjab	5.25 (6)	9.80 (5)	0.55 (2)	10.35 (7)	15.60 (13)
3.	Delhi	23.00 (9)	24.00 (3)	- (-)	24.00 (3)	47.00 (12)
II.	EASTERN REGION	78.77 (38)	105.75 (11)	14.70 (3)	120.45 (14)	199.22 (52)
4.	Orissa	5.60 (2)	10.00 (1)	- (-)	10.00 (1)	15.60 (3)
5.	West Bengal	73.17 (36)	95.75 (10)	14.70 (3)	110.45 (13)	183.62 (49)
III.	CENTRAL REGION	47.25 (13)	60.65 (3)	- (-)	60.65 (3)	107.90 (16)
6.	Madhya Pradesh	15.00 (1)	30.00 (1)	- (-)	30.00 (1)	45.00 (2)
7.	Uttar Pradesh	32.25 (12)	30.65 (2)	- (-)	30.65 (2)	62.90 (14)
IV.	WESTERN REGION	239.10 (106)	223.23 (26)	183.55 (30)	406.78 (56)	645.88 (162)
8.	Gujarat	38.65 (19)	64.50 (13)	29.59 (6)	94.09 (19)	132.74 (38)
9.	Maharashtra	200.45 (87)	158.73 (13)	153.96 (24)	312.69 (37)	513.14 (124)
V.	SOUTHERN REGION	30.20 (20)	17.50 (3)	4.25 (5)	21.75 (8)	51.95 (28)
10.	Andhra Pradesh	4.25 (3)	2.50 (1)	2.25 (2)	4.75 (3)	9.00 (6)
11.	Karnataka	2.20 (3)	- (-)	- (-)	- (-)	2.20 (3)
12.	Kerala	3.00 (2)	- (-)	1.00 (1)	1.00 (1)	4.00 (3)
13.	Tamil Nadu	20.75 (12)	15.00 (2)	1.00 (2)	16.00 (4)	36.75 (16)
	TOTAL	428.57 (193)	440.93 (51)	203.05 (40)	643.98 (91)	1072.55 (284)

ABLE 3.5 : REGION-WISE DISTRIBUTION OF THE PLCpr WHICH WERE GRANTED APPROVALS FOR THE ISSUANCE OF CDs/NCDs.(Contd.......7).

NOTES : 1. 'PLCpr' stands for Public Limited Companies of the Private Corporate Sector.
'NCDs' stands for Non-Convertible Debentures/Bonds.
'CDs' stands for Convertible Debentures/Bonds.
2. Figures in parentheses under Column 3 through Column 32 indicate the Number of Companies.

SOURCE: Compiled from the information included in Table 2.3 through Table 2.7 of Annexe II.

TABLE 3.6 STATEMENT SHOWING THE DETAILS OF THE APPROVALS GRANTED BY CCI FOR THE ISSUANCE OF CDs & OTHER INFORMATIONS PERTINENT FOR EVALUATING THEIR SUCCESSFULNESS/UN-SUCCESSFULNESS.

(1978-82)

(Amount in Rupees Crores)

Sr. No.	Name of Company	Year of Incorporation	Registered Office	Industry Group.	MRTP/ Other than MRTP Company.	Purpose of the Issue.	Date of CCI's consent	Actual date of Issuance
(1)	(2)	(3)	(4)	(5)	(6)	(7)	(8)	(9)
1.	Metal Box Co. of India Ltd.	1933	Calcutta	Engineering	MRTP	Expansion	17.07.1978	02.11.1978
2.	Reliance Textile Industries Ltd.	1973	Bombay	Rayon	MRTP	Project Finance	22.05.1979	03.10.1979
3.	TELCO	1945	Bombay	Engineering	MRTP	Project Finance	12.09.1979	06.10.1980
4.	Raymond Woollen Mills Ltd.	1925	Bombay	Woollen	MRTP	Expansion	23.08.1980	11.12.1980
5.	Camphor & Allied Products Ltd.	1961	Bombay	Chemicals	N.A.	Expansion	05.11.1980	29.01.1981
6.	Hindustan Development Corpn. Ltd.	1944	Calcutta	Chemicals	N.A.	Expansion	26.12.1980	06.05.1981
7.	Indian Rayon Corpn. Ltd.	1956	Veraval	Rayon	MRTP	Expansion	30.12.1980	16.03.1981
8.	Voltas Ltd.	1954	Bombay	Trading	MRTP	W.C.	27.02.1981	06.05.1981
9.	Straw Products Ltd.	1938	Jaykaypur	Paper	MRTP	New Project	01.04.1981	18.08.1981
10.	Reliance Textile Industries Ltd.	1973	Bombay	Rayon	MRTP	Project Finance	14.05.1981	10.06.1981

TABLE 3.6 : STATEMENT SHOWING THE DETAILS OF THE APPROVALS GRANTED BY CCI FOR THE ISSUANCE OF CDs & OTHER INFORMATIONS PERTINENT FOR EVALUATING THEIR SUCCESSFULNESS/ UN-SUCCESSFULNESS. (Contd..2)

(1978-82)

(Amount in Rupees Crores)

Sr. No.	Name of Company	Face Value of CDs. +	Nature of conversion.	Conversion Ratio	Date /period of conversion	Interest Rate ++	AMOUNT Offered to Public	Offered on Rights Basis.	Total
(1)	(2)	(10)	(11)	(12)	(13)	(14)	(15)	(16)	(17)
1.	Metal Box Co. of India Ltd.	10	Fully Convertible.	1 E.S.For 1 C.D. At Par	31.03.81	10.5	1.50	0.50	2.00
2.	Reliance Textile Industries Ltd.	500	Partly Convertible	4 E.S.For 20% F.V.of CD at Premium of Rs.15.	1.01.81	11.0	7.00	--	7.00
3.	TELCO	450	Fully Convertible	2 E.S.for 1 CD at a Premium of Rs.125.	3 & 7 years	11.0	29.29	17.96	47.25
4.	Raymond Woollen Mills Ltd.	400	Right to Subscribe	5 E.S. for 1 CD at a Premium of Rs.10.	31.07.81	11.0	4.80	--	4.80
5.	Camphor & Allied Products Ltd.	500	Partly Convertible	2 E.S. for 60% F.V. of CD at a premium of Rs. 50.	4 years	12.0	0.75	0.25	1.00
6.	Hindustan Development Corpn.Ltd.	100	Right to Subscribe	6 E.S.for 1 CD at a premium of Rs.7.50	3 years	12.0	0.75	0.75	1.50
7.	Indian Rayon Corporation Ltd.	100	Partly Convertible	1 E.S. for 20% F.V. of CD at a premium of Rs.10.	30.06.82	12.0	5.50	4.50	10.00
8.	Voltas Ltd.	250	Partly Convertible	1 E.S.for 40% F.V.of CD at par	3 years	13.5	3.00	2.00	5.00
9.	Straw Products Ltd.	500	Fully Convertible	25E.S.for 1 CD at a premium of Rs.10.	3 years	12.0	6.50	3.50	10.00
10.	Reliance Textile Industries Ltd.	125	Partly Convertible	1 E.S.for 20% F.V. of CD at a premium of Rs.15.	31.8.82	13.5	13.00	11.00	24.00

TABLE 3.6 : STATEMENT SHOWING THE DETAILS OF THE APPROVALS GRANTED BY CCI FOR THE ISSUANCE OF CDs & OTHER INFORMATIONS PERTINENT FOR EVALUATING THEIR SUCCESSFULNESS/UN-SUCCESSFULNESS.(Contd...3).

(1978-82)

(Amount in Rupees Crores)

Sr. No.	Name of Company	Over Sub-scr-ipt-ion. ¢	Aux-ili-ary Ben-efits. ¢¢	Market price of E.S. $	Announced Conversion price. $$	News Items (Yes/No) *	Benefit indices #	Expected Benefit ##	Remarks
(1)	(2)	(18)	(19)	(20)	(21)	(22)	(23)	(24)	(25)
1.	Metal Box Co.of India Ltd.	2	N.M.	1.70	AT PAR	NO	70.00	7.00	--
2.	Reliance Textile Industries Ltd.	6	YES	10.00	2.50	YES	300.00	60.00	--
3.	TELCO	6	@@	3.00	2.25	YES	33.50	33.50	--
4.	Raymond Woollen Mills Ltd.	4	YES	4.50	2.00	NO	150.00	37.50	--
5.	Camphor & Allied Products Ltd.	12	YES	2.20	1.50	NO	46.70	28.00	--
6.	Hindustan Development Corporation Ltd.	72	YES	7.50	1.75	NO	328.57	345.00	--
7.	Indian Rayon Corporation Ltd.	8	YES	7.80	2.00	YES	290.00	58.00	--
8.	Voltas Ltd.	8.7	NO	2.70	AT PAR	NO	170.00	68.00	--
9.	Straw Products Ltd.	25	YES	4.80	2.00	NO	140.00	140.00	--
10.	Reliance Textile Industries Ltd.	8	YES	10.00	2.50	YES	300.00	75.00	--

Annexe VI.37

TABLE 3.6 : STATEMENT SHOWING THE DETAILS OF THE APPROVALS GRANTED BY CCI FOR THE ISSUANCE OF CDs & OTHER INFORMATIONS PERTINENT FOR EVALUATING THEIR SUCCESSFULNESS/UN-SUCCESSFULNESS.(Contd............12).

(1978-82)

(Amount in Rupees Crores)

Sr. No.	Name of Company	Over Sub-script-ion. ¢	Aux-ili-ary Ben-efits. ¢¢	Market price of E.S. $	Announced Conversion Price. $$	News Items (YES/NO) *	Benefit Indices #	Expected Benefit ##	Remarks
(1)	(2)	(18)	(19)	(20)	(21)	(22)	(23)	(24)	(25)
31.	Bharat Steel Tubes Ltd.	E.D.A. O.N.A.	YES	2.00	AT PAR	NO	100.00	25.00	R.Q.E.S.
32.	Vardhman Spg.& General Mills Ltd.	E.D.A. O.N.A.	YES	3.60	1.80	NO	100.00	18.00	R.Q.E.S.
33.	Kothari (Madras) Ltd.	7	YES	3.50	1.80	NO	94.44	34.00	--
34.	Ahmedabad Advance Mills Ltd.	E.D.A. O.N.A.	YES	2.45	1.30	NO	88.46	28.75	E.S. is rarely Traded & No Quotations for CD.
35.	General Industrial Society Ltd.	U.S.	NO	2.20	AT PAR	NO	120.00	36.00	R.Q.E.S. NO QUOTATION OF CD.
36.	Rajasthan Spg.& Wvg. Mills Ltd.	APPROVAL			NOT	AVAILED			--
37.	Indian Hotels Co. Ltd.	6.63	YES	6.00	2.50	NO	140.00	35.00	--
38.	Bharat Vijay Mills Ltd.	E.D.A. O.N.A.	YES	5.00	2.50	NO	100.00	50.00	--
39.	Zenith Steel Pipes & Industries Ltd.	3.8	YES	4.80	1.50	NO	220.00	55.00	--
40.	Cellulose Products of India Ltd.	2.3	YES	1.75	AT PAR	NO	75.00	37.50	--

TABLE 3.6 : STATEMENT SHOWING THE DETAILS OF THE APPROVALS GRANTED BY CCI FOR THE ISSUANCE OF CDs & OTHER INFORMATIONS PERTINENT FOR EVALUATING THEIR SUCCESSFULNESS/UN-SUCCESSFULNESS.(Contd.............13)

(1978-82)

(Amount in Rupees Crores)

Sr. No.	Name of Company	Year of Inco-rpor-ation	Registered Office	Industry Group	MRTP/ Other than MRTP Comp-any.	Purpose of the Issue	Date of CCI's consent	Actual date of Issuance
(1)	(2)	(3)	(4)	(5)	(6)	(7)	(8)	(9)
41.	Mohta Industries Ltd.	1972	Ludhiana	Steel	N.A.	W.C.	10.05.1982	NOT ISSUED
42.	Gwalior Rayon Silk Mfg. (Wvg.)Co.Ltd.	1947	Nagda	Rayon	MRTP	Exp.& W.C.	19.05.1982	14.07.1982
43.	Ranbaxy Lab. Ltd.	1961	Roper	Chemicels	N.A.	Exp. & Mod.	02.06.1982	15.09.1982
44.	Dunlop India Ltd.	1926	Calcutta	Rubber	MRTP	Mod. & W.C.	17.06.1982	24.09.1982
45.	Guest Keen Williams Ltd.	1931	Calcutta	Steel	MRTP	Long Term Funds	21.06.1982	23.08.1982
46.	Lohia Machines Ltd.	1972	Kanpur	Engg.	N.A.	Expansion	07.07.1982	07.09.1982
47.	Shree Digvijay Woollen Mills Ltd.	1948	Ahmedabad	Woollen	N.A.	Expansion	30.08.1982	02.11.1982
48.	I.T.C.Ltd.	1910	Calcutta	Tobacco	MRTP	Expansion	01.09.1982	29.11.1982
49.	Keshoram Industries & Cotton Mills Ltd.	1919	Calcutta	Cotton	MRTP	W.C.& Mod.	04.11.1982	09.02.1983
50.	Indian Rayon Corporation Ltd.	1956	Veraval	Rayon	N.A.	W.C.& Mod.	23.11.1982	25.01.1983
51.	Nagarjuna Steel Ltd.	1974	Hyderabad	Steel	N.A.	--------	24.12.1982	Approval cancelled

TABLE 3.6 : STATEMENT SHOWING THE DETAILS OF THE APPROVALS GRANTED BY CCI FOR THE ISSUANCE OF CDs & OTHER INFORMATIONS PERTINENT FOR EVALUATING THEIR SUCCESSFULNESS/UN-SUCCESSFULNESS.(Contd..............14).

(1978-82)

(Amount in Rupees Crores)

Sr. No.	Name of Company	Face Value of CDs. +	Nature of Conversion.	Conversion Ratio	Date/ period of conversion.	Interest Rate. ++	AMOUNT Offered to Public.	Offered on Rights Basis	Total
(1)	(2)	(10)	(11)	(12)	(13)	(14)	(15)	(16)	(17)
41.	Mohta Industries Ltd.	100	Partly Convertible	5 E.S.for 50%F.V.of CD	1.1.83	13.5	0.90	0.40	1.30
42.	Gwalior Rayon Silk Mfg.(Wvg.)Co.Ltd.	160	Partly Convertible	2 E.S.for 25%F.V.of CD at a premium of Rs.10.	1.4.83	13.5	10.00	20.00	30.00
43.	Ranbaxy Lab. Ltd.	200	Partly Convertible	5 E.S.for 25%F.V.of CD at par.	1.10.83	13.5	1.25	3.25	4.50
44.	Dunlop India Ltd.	300	Partly Convertible	10E.S.for 50%F.V.of CD at a premium of Rs.5.	After 6 & 12 months	13.5	6.38	5.62	12.00
45.	Guest Keen Williams Ltd.	200	Partly Convertible	5 E.S.for 25%F.V.of CD at par.	After 6 months & 1 year	13.5	6.50	8.75	15.25
46.	Lohia Machines Ltd.	200	Partly Convertible	7 E.S.for 35%F.V.of CD at par.	2 years and 6 months	13.5	4.05	1.60	5.65
47.	Shree Digvijay Woollen Mills Ltd.	125	Partly Convertible	3 E.S.for 36%F.V.of CD at a premium of Rs.5.	1.7.83	13.5	1.19	0.81	2.00
48.	I.T.C.Ltd.	500	E.S.in Lieu of Accrued Interest	10 E.S.in lieu of interest accrued at par	1.7.84 & 1.7.85	15.00	6.75	23.25	30.00
49.	Keshoram Ind.& Cotton Mills Ltd.	100	Partly Convertible	1 E.S.for 10%F.V. of CD at par.	30.9.83	13.5	4.35	16.65	21.00
50.	Indian Rayon Corpn. Ltd.	140	Partly Convertible	1 E.S.for 20%F.V. of CD at a premium of Rs.18.	30.6.83	13.5	4.90	16.10	21.00
51.	Nagarjuna Steel Ltd.	100	APPROVAL CANCELLED			13.5	0.20	2.30	2.50

Annexe VI. 40

TABLE 3.6 : STATEMENT SHOWING THE DETAILS OF THE APPROVALS GRANTED BY CCI FOR THE ISSUANCE OF CDs & OTHER INFORMATIONS PERTINENT FOR EVALUATING THEIR SUCCESSFULNESS/UN-SUCCESSFULNESS.(Contd...............15).

(1978-82)

(Amount in Rupees Crores)

Sr. No.	Name of Company	Over Sub-scr-ipt-ion. £	Aux-ili-ary Ben-efits. ££	Market price of E.S. $	Announced Conversion Price. $$	News Items (YES/NO) *	Benefit Indices #	Expected Benefit ##	Remarks
(1)	(2)	(18)	(19)	(20)	(21)	(22)	(23)	(24)	(25)
41.	Mohta Industries Ltd.	APPROVAL			NOT		AVAILED		
42.	Gwalior Rayon Silk Mfg.(Wvg.)Co.Ltd.	6	N.D.O.	5.00	2.00	NO	150.00	37.50	--
43.	Ranbaxy Lab.Ltd.	6.8	YES	2.50	AT PAR	NO	150.00	37.50	--
44.	Dunlop India Ltd.	E.D.A. O.N.A.	N.D.O.	2.60	1.50	NO	73.33	36.60	NO QUOTATIONS FOR CDs ARE AVAILABLE.
45.	Guest Keen Williams Ltd.	U.S.	YES	2.40	AT PAR	NO	140.00	35.00	NO QUOTATIONS FOR CDs ARE AVAILABLE.
46.	Lohia Machines Ltd.	13	YES	2.35	AT PAR	YES	135.00	47.25	--
47.	Shree Digvijay Woollen Mills Ltd.	E.D.A. O.N.A.	N.D.O.	3.20	1.50	NO	113.33	40.80	--
48.	ITC Ltd.	8.9	N.D.O.	3.68	AT PAR	NO	268.00	53.60	--
49.	Keshoram Industries & Cotton Mills Ltd.	6.7	N.D.O.	6.50	AT PAR	NO	550.00	55.00	--
50.	Indian Rayon Corpn. Ltd.	8	N.D.O.	9.00	2.80	YES	221.43	44.20	--
51.	Nagarjuna Steel Ltd.	APPROVAL			CANCELLED OUT ON 16.04.1983.				

Annexe VI.41

TABLE 3.6 STATEMENT SHOWING THE DETAILS OF THE APPROVALS GRANTED BY CCI FOR THE ISSUANCE OF CDs & OTHER INFORMATIONS PERTINENT FOR EVALUATING THEIR SUCCESSFULNESS/ UNSUCCESSFULNESS (Contd................16).

NOTES: 1. 'CCI' stands for Controller of Capital Issues.
'CDs' stands for Convertible Debentures.
'N.A.'stands for Not Applicable.
'W.C.'stands for Working Capital.
'Engg.'stands for Engineering.
'Exp.' stands for Expansion.
'Mod.' Stands for Modernization.
'E.S.' Stands for Equity Share.
'F.V.' Stands for Face Value.
'N.M.' Stands for Not Mentioned.
'N.Q.A.' Stands for No Quotations Available.
'U.S.' Stands for Undersubscribed.
'E.D.A.O.N.A.' Stands for Exact Details About Oversubscription Not Available.
'N.D.A.' Stands for Not Detailed Out.
'R.Q.E.S.' Stands for Rare Quotations for Equity Shares are Available.

2. + Face Value of CDs is in Rupees.

3. ++ Interest Rate is in percentage.

TABLE 3.6 STATEMENT SHOWING THE DETAILS OF THE APPROVALS GRANTED BY CCI FOR THE ISSUANCE OF CDs & OTHER INFORMATIONS PERTINENT FOR EVALUATING THEIR SUCCESSFULNESS/UNSUCCESSFULNESS (Contd................17).

NOTES: 4. @@ Premium to be Charged for Conversion will be Reduced.

5. ¢ Oversubscription has been shown in number of times an Issue came to be oversubscribed.

6. ¢¢ Auxiliary Benefits to the Debentureholders are promises affixed with the concerned Issue to be fulfilled during the conversion period and are generally in the shape of issuance of Bonus Shares/Equity Shares/Convertible Debentures on Rights Basis.

7. $ Market Price of Equity Shares here represents the price of the associated equity shares to their face value in number of times at the time of the floatation of the relevant Issue of CDs.

8. $$ Announced Conversion Price is in Number of Times to the Face Value of the Associated Equity Shares.

9. * 'News Items' here refer to the Company's Practice of Inserting Corporate Briefs on a regular basis in the important National Daily/Dailies Highlighting its Progress and Future Plans.

10. # Benefit Index= $\frac{\text{Amount of Benefit Per Equity Share}}{\text{Conversion Price}} \times 100$

TABLE 3.6 STATEMENT SHOWING THE DETAILS OF THE APPROVALS GRANTED BY CCI FOR THE ISSUANCE OF CDs & OTHER INFORMATIONS PERTINENT FOR EVALUATING THEIR SUCCESSFULNESS/UNSUCCESSFULNESS (Contd..................18).

NOTES: 11. ## Expected Benefit here denotes the benefit to the debentureholders at the time of actual conversion on account of difference found in the market price of associated equity share and the announced conversion price expressed as percentage to the face value of CD.

SOURCES:

1. Records available in the Office of the Controller of Capital Issues, New Delhi.
2. Prospectuses & Press Releases put out by the concerned companies in the different news papers.
3. Quotation Lists of Various Stock Exchanges of India.

TABLE 3.7 : SUMMARY OF STATISTICAL RESULTS/INFORMATION PERTAINING TO THE INCREASE/DECREASE REGISTERED IN THE PRICES OF ASSOCIATED EQUITY SHARES/CONVERTIBLE DEBENTURES.

(1978-82)

Sr. No.	Name of Company	Coefficient of Correlation ('r')	Coefficient of Determination ('r^2')	STANDARD DEVIATION ('σ')		COEFFICIENT OF VARIATION (C.V.)		Percentage increase/decrease in the prices of associated E.S. since the enlistment of CDs.	Percentage increase/decrease in the prices of CDs.
				Equity Shares.	CDs.	Equity Shares.	CDs.		
(1)	(2)	(3)	(4)	(5)	(6)	(7)	(8)	(9)	(10)
	CATEGORY 'A'								
1.	Metal Box Company of India Limited.	+0.92	0.85	2.59	3.42	16.80	21.00	+150.00	+140.00
2.	Reliance Textile Industries Ltd. (Series-I)	+0.78	0.61	8.62	16.34	7.50	10.70	+023.00	+065.00
3.	TELCO	+0.82	0.70	9.87	8.62	30.80	22.56	+120.00	+077.00
4.	Voltas Ltd.	+0.89	0.80	47.63	76.40	15.44	19.95	+034.18	+064.52
5.	Indian Rayon Corporation Ltd.	+0.67	0.45	4.24	17.78	6.80	6.26	+026.00	+042.00
6.	Straw Products Ltd.	+0.91	0.83	4.42	167.68	9.23	17.88	+006.98	+018.79
7.	Reliance Textile Industries Ltd. (Series-III)	+0.82	0.67	14.63	25.84	10.16	14.56	+033.33	+052.00

TABLE 3.7 : SUMMARY OF STATISTICAL RESULTS/INFORMATION PERTAINING TO THE INCREASE/DECREASE REGISTERED IN THE PRICES OF ASSOCIATED EQUITY SHARES/CONVERTIBLE DEBENTURES. (Contd..2).

(1978-82)

Sr. No.	Name of Company	Coefficient of Correlation ('r')	Coefficient of Determination ('r2')	STANDARD DEVIATION ('σ')		COEFFICIENT OF VARIATION(C.V.)		Percentage increase/decrease in the prices of associated E.S.since the enlistment of CDs.	Percentage increase/decrease in the prices of CDs.
				Equity Shares.	CDs.	Equity Shares.	CDs.		
(1)	(2)	(3)	(4)	(5)	(6)	(7)	(8)	(9)	(10)
8.	East India Hotels Ltd.	+0.94	0.89	4.24	17.78	12.12	11.96	+030.00	+034.62
9.	TISCO	+0.56	0.31	42.50	44.05	14.50	10.35	-004.22	+025.61
10.	D.C.M.Co.Ltd.	+0.97	0.96	19.75	13.54	40.64	10.98	+179.41	+036.52
11.	J.K.Synthetics Ltd.	-0.37	0.14	1.17	2.42	2.01	1.22	-001.72	+002.02
12.	Mukand Iron & Steel Works Ltd.	+0.60	0.36	1.43	4.38	6.06	2.23	-012.50	-002.56
13.	Zenith Steel Pipes & Industries Ltd.	+0.82	0.67	3.61	7.64	12.43	6.45	+006.67	-040.00
14.	Gwalior Rayon Silk Mfg. (Wvg.)Co.Ltd.	+0.64	0.41	3.00	4.15	5.88	2.35	-012.73	-001.11
15.	Lohia Machines Ltd.	+0.98	0.97	7.89	132.41	12.09	28.79	+031.03	+080.00
	CATEGORY 'B'								
1.	Raymond Woollen Mills Ltd.	+0.21	0.04	1.56	12.80	2.70	3.50	+006.80	+010.00
2.	Camphor & Allied Products Ltd.	-0.57	0.32	22.85	9.83	14.24	2.35	-014.71	+005.50

TABLE 3.7 : SUMMARY OF STATISTICAL RESULTS/INFORMATION PERTAINING TO THE INCREASE/DECREASE REGISTERED IN THE PRICES OF ASSOCIATED EQUITY SHARES/CONVERTIBLE DEBENTURES. (Contd...3).

(1978-82)

Sr. No.	Name of Company	Coefficient of Correlation ('r')	Coefficient of Determination ('r2')	STANDARD DEVIATION ('σ')		COEFFICIENT OF VARIATION(C.V.)		Percentage increase/decrease in the prices of associated E.S. since the enlistment of CDs.	Percentage increase/decrease in the prices of CDs.
				Equity Shares.	CDs.	Equity Shares.	CDs.		
(1)	(2)	(3)	(4)	(5)	(6)	(7)	(8)	(9)	(10)
3.	Hindustan Development Corpn. Ltd.	-0.19	0.04	2.08	4.68	3.60	4.20	-014.70	+240.00
4.	Rustom Mills & Industries Ltd.	-0.03	0.001	0.90	2.27	4.83	2.78	-015.79	+002.50
5.	Ferro Alloys Corpn.Ltd.	+0.79	0.62	23.41	8.68	13.06	3.66	-036.67	-008.33
6.	Usha Alloys & Steels Ltd.	+0.87	0.75	2.47	5.62	10.85	5.48	-029.63	-013.33
7.	Gujarat Steel Tubes Ltd	+0.60	0.36	19.18	12.16	7.12	2.42	-022.03	-005.04
8.	Mahindra Mills Ltd.	+0.83	0.68	12.97	5.46	6.75	5.27	+019.41	+013.13
9.	Kothari (Madras)Ltd.	+0.45	0.20	2.14	4.39	8.79	4.79	-080.00	-009.09
10.	Indian Hotels Co.Ltd.	+0.86	0.74	9.82	11.85	16.00	10.08	+072.73	+035.24
11.	Ranbaxy Laboratories Ltd.	+0.71	0.51	2.99	23.00	7.61	7.76	+013.51	+021.91
12.	I.T.C.Ltd.	+0.44	0.17	1.22	17.16	3.64	5.44	+006.06	+020.81

SOURCE : Computed on the basis of weekly/monthly price quotations of associated equity shares/CDs of the concerned companies as available on their parent stock exchanges.

TABLE 3.8 : VOLUME OF LONG TERM FUNDS RAISED THROUGH PUBLIC ISSUES OF CDs BY THE SUCCESSFUL PLCpr+.

(1978-82)

(Amount in Rupees Crores)

Sr. No.	Name of Company	Date of CCI's approval	AMOUNT OF FUNDS RAISED: Through offering to Public (Amount)	AMOUNT OF FUNDS RAISED: Through offering on Rights Basis (Amount)	AMOUNT OF FUNDS RAISED: Total (Amount)
(1)	(2)	(3)	(4)	(5)	(6)
1.	Metal Box Company of India Ltd.	17.7.1978	1.50	0.50	2.00
		28.6.1982	-	4.00	4.00
2.	Reliance Textile Industries Ltd.	22.5.1979	7.00	-	7.00
		16.8.1980	-	10.80	10.80
		14.5.1981	13.00	11.00	24.00
		(28.12.1981)	(-)	(0.03)	(0.03)
		9.3.1982	-	50.00	50.00
3.	Tata Engineering & Locomotive Company ltd.	12.9.1979	29.29	17.96	47.25
4.	Raymond Woollen Mills Ltd.	23.3.1980	4.80	-	4.80
		(13.12.1982)	(-)	(4.50)	(4.50)
5.	Camphor & Allied Products Ltd.	5.11.1980	0.75	0.25	1.00
6.	Hindustan Development Corporation Ltd.	(19.5.1979)	(-)	(0.75)	(0.75)
		26.12.1980	0.75	0.75	1.50
7.	Indian Rayon Corporantion Ltd.	(30.10.1980)	(-)	(1.00)	(1.00)
		30.12.1980	5.50	4.50	10.00
		23.11.1982	4.90	16.10	21.00
8.	Voltas Ltd.	(8.9.1980)	(-)	(0.30)	(0.30)
		27.2.1981	3.00	2.00	5.00
		(4.7.1981)	(5.00)	(-)	(5.00)
9.	Straw Products Ltd.	(5.3.1978)	(-)	(2.00)	(2.00)
		1.4.1981	6.50	3.50	10.00

TABLE 3.8 : VOLUME OF LONG TERM FUNDS RAISED THROUGH PUBLIC ISSUES OF CDs BY THE SUCCESSFUL PLCpr+. (Contd..2). (1978-82)

(Amount in Rupees Crores)

Sr. No.	Name of Company	Date of CCI's approval	AMOUNT OF FUNDS RAISED		
			Through Offering to Public (Amount)	Through Offering on Rights Basis (Amount)	Total (Amount)
(1)	(2)	(3)	(4)	(5)	(6)
10.	Shree Dinesh Mills Ltd.	(28.09.1979) 25.05.1981	(-) 0.60	(0.50) 0.40	(0.50) 1.00
11.	Rustom Mills & Industries Ltd.	03.06.1981	1.40	0.60	2.00
12.	East India Hotels Ltd.	23.06.1981 (21.06.1982)	3.00 (-)	4.50 (10.00)	7.50 (10.00)
13.	Ferro Alloys Corporation Ltd.	(12.09.1979) 29.06.1981 (25.10.1982)	(-) 5.00 (-)	(00.75) 2.50 (06.00)	(00.75) 7.50 (06.00)
14.	Fibre Glass Pilkington Ltd.	14.07.1981	1.73	0.90	2.63
15.	Jyoti Ltd.	19.09.1981 (17.12.1982)	1.00 (-)	1.00 (03.00)	2.00 (03.00)
16.	Tata Iron & Steel Company Ltd.	24.09.1981	12.00	18.00	30.00
17.	Star Industrial & Textile Enterprizes Ltd.	29.09.1981	2.25	2.00	4.25
18.	Elecon Engineering Company Ltd.	05.10.1981	2.80	2.70	5.50
19.	Delhi Cloth & General Mills Company Ltd.	03.11.1981	6.00	9.00	15.00

TABLE 3.8 : VOLUME OF LONG TERM FUNDS RAISED THROUGH PUBLIC ISSUES OF CDs BY THE SUCCESSFUL PLCpr+. (Contd...3). (1978-82)

(Amount in Rupees Crores)

Sr. No.	Name of Company	Date of CCI's approval	AMOUNT OF FUNDS RAISED: Through Offering to Public (Amount)	Through Offering on Rights Basis (Amount)	Total (Amount)
(1)	(2)	(3)	(4)	(5)	(6)
20.	Punjab Anand Batteries Ltd.	06.11.1981	0.50	0.50	1.00
21.	Usha Alloys & Steels Ltd.	17.11.1981	0.90	0.60	1.50
22.	J.K. Synthetics Ltd.	(03.03.1979)	(-)	(2.00)	(2.00)
		(15.06.1981)	(5.00)	(-)	(5.00)
		27.11.1981	12.00	13.00	25.00
		(26.06.1982)	(6.00)	(-)	(6.00)
23.	Gujarat Steel Tubes Ltd.	(19.05.1979)	(-)	(1.00)	(1.00)
		27.11.1981	3.00	2.00	5.00
24.	Mahindra Mills Ltd.	(30.07.1980)	(-)	(0.75)	(0.75)
		27.11.1981	1.62	1.38	3.00
		(26.11.1982)	(-)	(0.50)	(0.50)
25.	Mukand Iron & Steel Works Ltd.	(25.11.1978)	(-)	(1.50)	(1.50)
		(31.03.1981)	(-)	(1.00)	(1.00)
		28.11.1981	4.55	2.45	7.00
		(13.12.1982)	(-)	(4.50)	(4.50)
26.	Bharat Steel Tubes Ltd.	(30.09.1979)	(-)	(1.25)	(1.25)
		30.11.1981	3.00	1.00	4.00

TABLE 3.8 : VOLUME OF LONG TERM FUNDS RAISED THROUGH PUBLIC ISSUES OF CDs BY THE SUCCESSFUL PLCpr+. (Contd....4).

(1978-82)

(Amount in Rupees Crores)

Sr. No.	Name of Company	Date of CCI's approval.	AMOUNT OF FUNDS RAISED		
			Through offering to Public (Amount)	Through offering on Rights Basis. (Amount)	Total (Amount)
(1)	(2)	(3)	(4)	(5)	(6)
27.	Vardhman Spg. & General Mills Ltd.	09.12.1981	1.47	0.53	2.00
28.	Kothari(Madras) Ltd.	19.12.1981	6.00	4.00	10.00
29.	Ahmedabad Advance Mills Ltd.	(28.09.1979) 7.01.1982	(-) 2.81	(1.00) 3.19	(1.00) 6.00
30.	Indian Hotels Company Ltd.	18.02.1982	9.33	5.67	15.00
31.	Bharat Vijay Mills Ltd.	19.02.1982	1.60	1.80	3.40
32.	Zenith Steel Pipes & Industries Ltd.	(15.09.1979) 28.04.1982	(-) 2.40	(1.25) 2.40	(1.25) 4.80
33.	Cellulose Products of India Ltd.	6.05.1982	0.95	0.55	1.50
34.	Gwalior Rayon Silk Mfg. (Wvg.)Company Ltd.	19.05.1982 (13.12.1982)	10.00 (-)	20.00 (15.00)	30.00 (15.00)
35.	Ranbaxy Laboratories Ltd.	02.06.1982	1.25	3.25	4.50
36.	Dunlop India Ltd.	17.06.1982	6.38	5.62	12.00
37.	Lohia Machines Ltd.	7.07.1982	4.05	1.60	5.65

TABLE 3.8 : VOLUME OF LONG TERM FUNDS RAISED THROUGH PUBLIC ISSUES OF CDs BY THE SUCCESSFUL PLCpr+. (Contd.....5). (1978-82)

(Amount in Rupees Crores)

Sr. No.	Name of Company	Date of CCI's approval	AMOUNT OF FUNDS RAISED		
			Through offering to Public. (Amount)	Through offering on Rights Basis. (Amount)	Total (Amount)
(1)	(2)	(3)	(4)	(5)	(6)
38.	Shree Digvijay Woollen Mills Ltd.	30.08.1982	1.19	0.81	2.00
39.	ITC Ltd.	(21.08.1981) 01.09.1982	(5.00) 6.75	(-) 23.25	(5.00) 30.00
40.	Keshoram Industries & Cotton Mills Ltd.	(15.09.1979) (06.08.1982) 4.11.1982	(-) (-) 4.35	(2.50) (6.00) 16.65	(2.50) (6.00) 21.00

Notes: (1) + These include those PLCpr which emerged successful on the criterion of 'oversubscription' in the floatation of Public Issues of CDs.

(2) Figures in brackets relate to the Issues of NCDs which came to be floated by the respective companies.

Source: Compiled from the information contained in Table 2.3 through 2.7 of Annexe II.

TABLE 3.9 : LONG TERM FUNDS MOBILIZED BY SUCCESSFUL PLCpr+: A COMPOSITE PICTURE. (1978-82)

(Amount in Rupees Crores)

Sr. No.	Name of Company	VIA FLOATATION OF		Total Mobilized Funds.
		Convertible Debentures. (Amount)	Non-Convertible Debentures. (Amount)	(Amount)
(1)	(2)	(3)	(4)	(5)
1.	Metal Box Company Ltd.	6.00	-	6.00
2.	Reliance Textile Industries Ltd.	91.80	0.03	91.83
3.	Tata Engineering & Locomotive Company Ltd.	47.25	-	47.25
4.	Raymond Woollens Mills Ltd.	4.80	4.50	9.30
5.	Camphor & Allied Products Ltd.	1.00	-	1.00
6.	Hindustan Development Corporation Ltd.	1.50	0.75	2.25
7.	Indian Rayon Corporation Ltd.	31.00	1.00	32.00
8.	Voltas Ltd.	5.00	5.30	10.30
9.	Straw Products Ltd.	10.00	2.00	12.00
10.	Shree Dinesh Mills Ltd.	1.00	0.50	1.50
11.	Rustom Mills & Industries Ltd.	2.00	-	2.00
12.	East India Hotels Ltd.	7.50	10.00	17.50
13.	Ferro Alloys Corporation Ltd.	7.50	6.75	14.25
14.	Fibre Glass Pilkington Ltd.	2.63	-	2.63
15.	Jyoti Ltd	2.00	3.00	5.00
16.	Tata Iron & Steel Company Ltd.	30.00	-	30.00

TABLE 3.9 : LONG TERM FUNDS MOBILIZED BY SUCCESSFUL PLCpr+: A COMPOSITE PICTURE.(CONTD..2). (1978-82)

(Amount in Rupees Crores)

Sr. No.	Name of Company	VIA FLOATATION OF		Total Mobli-zed Funds. (Amount)
		Converti-ble Debe-ntures. (Amount)	Non-Conver-tible Debe-ntures. (Amount)	
(1)	(2)	(3)	(4)	(5)
17.	Star Industrial & Textiles Enterprize Limited.	4.25	-	4.25
18.	Elcon Engineering Company Ltd.	5.50	-	5.50
19.	Delhi Cloth & General Mills Company Ltd.	15.00	-	15.00
20.	Punjab Anand Batteries Ltd.	1.00	-	1.00
21.	Usha Alloys & Steels Limited	1.50	-	1.50
22.	J.K.Synthetics Ltd.	25.00	13.00	38.00
23.	Gujarat Steel Tubes Ltd.	5.00	1.00	6.00
24.	Mahindra Mills Ltd.	3.00	1.25	4.25
25.	Mukand Iron & Steel Works Ltd.	7.00	7.00	14.00
26.	Bharat Steel Tubes Ltd.	4.00	1.25	5.25
27.	Vardhman Spg. & General Mills Ltd.	2.00	-	2.00
28.	Kothari(Madras)Ltd.	10.00	-	10.00
29.	Ahmedabad Advance Mills Ltd.	6.00	1.00	7.00
30.	Indian Hotels Company Ltd.	15.00	-	15.00
31.	Bharat Vijay Mills Ltd.	3.40	-	3.40
32.	Zenith Steel Pipes India Ltd.	4.80	1.25	6.05

TABLE 3.9 : LONG TERM FUNDS MOBILIZED BY SUCCESSFUL PLCpr+: A COMPOSITE PICTURE.(CONTD...3). (1978-82)

(Amount in Rupees Crores)

Sr. No.	Name of Company	VIA FLOATATION OF		Total Mobilized Funds.
		Convertible Debentures. (Amount)	Non-Convertible Debentures. (Amount)	(Amount)
(1)	(2)	(3)	(4)	(5)
33.	Cellulose Products of India Ltd.	1.50	-	1.50
34.	Gwalior Rayon Silk Mfg. (Wvg.)Company Ltd.	30.00	15.00	45.00
35.	Ranbaxy Laboratories Ltd.	4.50	-	4.50
36.	Dunlop India Limited	12.00	-	12.00
37.	Lohia Machines Ltd.	5.65	-	5.65
38.	Shree Digvijay Woollen Mills Limited.	2.00	-	2.00
39.	I.T.C.Ltd.	30.00	5.00	35.00
40	Keshoram Industries & Cotton Mills Ltd.	21.00	8.50	29.50

Note: + These include those PLCpr which emerged successful on the criterion of oversubscription in the floatation of Public Issues of CDs.

Source: Compiled from the information included in Table 3.8 of this Annexe.

TABLE 3.10 : INDUSTRY-WISE DISTRIBUTION OF RESPONDENT COMPANIES WHICH RESORTED TO THE ISSUANCE OF CONVERTIBLE/NON-CONVERTIBLE DEBENTURES/BONDS: (1978-82)

Sr. No.	Industry	Number of Question-naires Mailed.	Number of Respondent Companies. NCDs Issuing Compa-nies.	CDs. Issuing Compa-nies.	Total (Col. 4+5).	Response Rate* (In %)
(1)	(2)	(3)	(4)	(5)	(6)	(7)
1.	Tea	5	1	-	1	20
2.	Sugar	3	1	-	1	33
3.	Tobacco	4	1	1	2	50
4.	Cotton Textiles	45	10	12	22	49
5.	Jute Textiles	5	-	-	-	-
6.	Silk, Rayon & Woollen Textiles	21	3	9	12	57
7.	Iron & Steel & Non-Ferrous	33	8	10	18	55
8.	Aluminium	2	-	-	-	-
9.	Engineering	61	9	7	16	26
10.	Chemicals	68	14	10	24	35
11.	Rubber & Rubber Products	3	-	1	1	33
12.	Paper & Paper Products	8	1	1	2	25
13	Electricity Generation & Supply	2	-	-	-	-
14	Commerce	18	2	1	3	17
15	Hotel	6	1	2	3	50
	TOTAL	284	51	54	105	36.97

Note: * Response Rate has been computed as percentage of Column (6) to Column (3).

Source: Organized from the pertinent information secured from Respondent Companies in Questionnaire:1.

TABLE 3.11 : REGION-WISE CATEGORIZATION OF RESPONDENT CONVERTIBLE/NON-CONVERTIBLE DEBENTURES'/ BONDS' ISSUING COMPANIES. (1978-82)

Sr. No.	Region	Number of Questionnaires Mailed.	Number of Respondent Companies.			Response Rate* (In %)
			Non-Convertible Debentures/Bonds Issuing Companies.	Convertible Debentures/ Bonds Issuing Companies.	Total (4+5)	
(1)	(2)	(3)	(4)	(5)	(6)	(7)
1.	Northern Region	26	9	7	16	62
2.	Eastern Region	52	6	11	17	33
3.	Central Region	16	4	3	7	44
4.	Western Region	162	24	29	53	33
5.	Southern Region	28	8	4	12	43
	TOTAL	284	51	54	105	36.97

Note: * Response Rate represents the percentage of the actual total number of respondent companies (Column 6) to the total number of Questionnaires mailed (Column 3).

Source: Compiled from the relevant information filled in Questionnnaire:1 by the respondent companies.

TABLE 3.12 : CDs/NCDs ISSUING RESPONDENT COMPANIES: INDUSTRY-WISE & AGGREGATE CATALOGUING OF THE REASONS/CIRCUMSTANCES WHICH PROMPTED THEM TO RAISE LONG TERM FUNDS THROUGH DEBENTURES.

(1978-82)

(Figures are in Number)

Sr. No.	Reasons/ Circumstances	INDUSTRY GROUPS								
		Tea	Sugar	Tobacco	Cotton Tex.	Jute Tex.	Silk, Rayon & Woollen Tex.	Iron & Steel & non ferrous	Aluminium	Engineering
(1)	(2)	(3)	(4)	(5)	(6)	(7)	(8)	(9)	(10)	(11)
1.	CDs/NCDs are able to augment long term funds at a cheap cost.	1	1	2	18	-	10	11	-	13
2.	Poor Response Depicted by the Public in Depositing their savings with them.	-	1	-	3	-	1	2	-	1
3.	Denial of Credit by Commercial Banks/ Other Public Finance Intermediaries.	1	1	2	19	-	8	13	-	11
4.	Difficulties faced in the Floatation of an Issue of Equity Shares.	-	-	-	2	-	2	1	-	1
5.	Unfitting Terms & conditions of the Institutional Finance.	1	1	1	12	-	11	10	-	12
6.	Most Favoured Method of Raising Corporate Funds in Vogue.	1	-	1	15	-	6	9	-	7

TABLE 3.12 : CDs/NCDs ISSUING RESPONDENT COMPANIES: INDUSTRY-WISE & AGGREGATE CATALOGUING OF THE REASONS/CIRCUMSTANCES WHICH PROMPTED THEM TO RAISE LONG TERM FUNDS THROUGH DEBENTURES.(CONTD.....2)
(1978-82)

(Figures are in Number)

Sr. No.	Reasons/ Circumstances	INDUSTRY GROUPS						Total number of respondent companies.
		Chemicals	Rubber & Rubber Products.	Paper & paper Products.	Electricity Generation & Supply.	Commerce	Hotel	
(1)	(2)	(12)	(13)	(14)	(15)	(16)	(17)	(18).
1.	CDs/NCDs are able to augment long term funds at a cheap cost.	20	1	1	-	2	2	32
2.	Poor Response Depicted by the Public in Depositing their savings with them.	2	-	-	-	-	-	10
3.	Denial of Credit by Commercial Banks/ Other Public Finance Intermediaries.	17	1	2	-	3	2	80
4.	Difficulties faced in the Floatation of an Issue of Equity Shares.	2	-	-	-	-	-	8
5.	Unfitting Terms & conditions of the Institutional Finance.	16	1	1	-	2	1	69
6.	Most Favoured Method of Raising Corporate Funds in Vogue.	13	-	-	-	1	1	54

Note: The aggregate number of these responses comes to 303 which does not tally with the total number of respondent companies on account of their multiple responses.

Source: Compiled from the primary information gathered through Questionnaire:1.

TABLE 3.13 : REGION-WISE CATEGORIZATION OF THE REASONS/ CIRCUMSTANCES PROMPTING THE CDs/NCDs ISSUING RESPONDENT COMPANIES TO AUGMENT THEIR LONG TERM FUNDS THROUGH SUCH SECURITIES. (1978-82)

Sr. No.	Reasons/ Circumstances.	REGIONS					Total number of Respondent Companies.
		Northern.	Eastern.	Central	Western.	Southern.	
(1)	(2)	(3)	(4)	(5)	(6)	(7)	(8)
1.	CDs/NCDs are able to augment long term funds relatively at a Cheap Cost.	11	11	6	45	9	82
2.	Poor Response depicted by the Public in Depositing their Savings with them.	1	3	2	3	1	10
3.	Denial of credit by Commercial Banks/Other Public Finance Intermediaries.	22	12	2	38	6	80
4.	Difficulties faced in the floatation of an Issue of Equity Shares.	1	2	1	2	2	8
5.	Unfitting Terms & Conditions of the Institutional Finance.	8	13	3	36	9	69
6.	Most favoured Method of Raising corporate funds in Vogue.	8	7	4	30	5	54

Note: The aggregate number of these responses comes to 303 which does not tally with the total number of respondent companies on account of the multiple responses recorded by several of them.

Source: Compiled from the primary information gathered via Questionnaire:1.

TABLE 3.14 : INDUSTRY-WISE DISTRIBUTION OF THE UTILIZATION OF FUNDS RAISED THROUGH THE ISSUANCE OF CONVERTIBLE/NON-CONVERTIBLE DEBENTURES/BONDS BY THE RESPONDENT COMPANIES.

(1978-82)

(Figures are in Number)

Sr. No.	Purpose	INDUSTRY GROUPS							
		Tea	Sugar	Tobacco	Cotton Textiles	Jute Textiles	Silk, Rayon & Woollen Textiles	Iron & Steel & basic Non-Ferrous Metal	Aluminium.
(1)	(2)	(3)	(4)	(5)	(6)	(7)	(8)	(9)	(10)
1.	Meeting the working capital requirements.	1	1	1	8	-	5	8	-
2.	Modernization	-	-	-	2	-	-	2	-
3.	Project Finance and Expansion.	-	-	1	5	-	7	10	-
4.	Amalgamation	-	-	-	-	-	1	-	-
5.	Diluting the Shareholdings of non-residents	-	-	-	-	-	-	-	-
	TOTAL	1	1	2	15	-	13	20	-

TABLE 3.14 : INDUSTRY-WISE DISTRIBUTION OF THE UTILIZATION OF FUNDS RAISED THROUGH THE ISSUANCE OF CONVERTIBLE/ NON-CONVERTIBLE DEBENTURES/BONDS BY THE RESPONDENT COMPANIES.(Contd.....2)

(1978-82)

(Figures are in Number)

Sr. No.	Purpose	INDUSTRY GROUPS							Total Number of Respondent Companies.
		Engineering	Chemicals	Rubber & Rubber Products.	Paper & Paper Products	Electricity Generation & Supply	Commerce	Hotel	
(1)	(2)	(11)	(12)	(13)	(14)	(15)	(16)	(17)	(18)
1.	Meeting the working capital requirements.	8	8	-	1	-	2	1	44
2.	Modernization.	2	1	-	-	-	-	-	7
3.	Project Finance & Expansion.	9	13	-	1	-	-	2	48
4.	Amalgation	-	2	-	-	-	1	-	4
5.	Diluting the Shareholdings of non-residents.	-	1	1	-	-	-	-	2
	TOTAL	19	25	1	2	-	3	3	105

Source: Compiled from the relevant information filled in by the respondent companies.

TABLE 3.15 : REGION-WISE UTILIZATION OF THE FUNDS RAISED THROUGH THE ISSUANCE OF CDs/NCDs BY THE RESPONDENT COMPANIES. (1978-82)

Sr. No.	Purpose/s	REGIONS Northern	Eastern	Central	Western	Southern	Total
(1)	(2)	(3)	(4)	(5)	(6)	(7)	(8)
1.	Meeting the Working Capital Requirements.	7 (6.67)	6 (5.71)	3 (2.86)	21 (20.00)	7 (6.67)	44 (41.90)
2.	Modernization	1 (0.95)	2 (1.90)	- (-)	4 (3.81)	- (-)	7 (6.67)
3.	Project Finance and Expansion.	8 (7.62)	9 (8.57)	4 (3.81)	22 (20.95)	5 (4.76)	48 (45.72)
4.	Amalgamation	- (-)	- (-)	- (-)	4 (3.81)	- (-)	4 (3.81)
5.	Diluting the Shareholdings of Non-Residents.	- (-)	- (-)	- (-)	2 (1.90)	- (-)	2 (1.90)
	TOTAL	16 (15.23)	17 (16.19)	7 (6.67)	53 (50.48)	12 (11.43)	105 (100.00)

Note : Figures in brackets indicate the percentages to the total number of respondent companies which stands at 105.

Source: Compiled from the relevant information filled in the Questionnaire:2 by the companies which have floated secured debentures during the period 1978-82.

TABLE 3.16 : METHODS ADOPTED FOR THE REDEMPTION OF DEBENTURES ON MATURITY: BREAK UP OF THE NUMBER OF RESPONDENT COMPANIES. (1978-82)

Sr. No.	Method of Redemption of Debentures on Maturity.	Number of Respondent Companies.	Percentage to total number of Respondent Companies.
(1)	(2)	(3)	(4)
1.	Through the Creation of Debenture Redemption Fund.	16	15.2
2.	By Adoption of Sinking Fund Method.	13	12.4
3.	Not Creating Any Sort of Reserves for the Purpose, but Redeeming them through any other means considered most appropriate on the maturity date.	76	72.4
	TOTAL	105	100.0

Source: Compiled through classifying the relevant information of the filled in Questionnaire:2.

TABLE 3.17 : REGION WISE DISTRIBUTION OF RESPONDENT OFFICE BEARERS OF THE STOCK EXCHANGES/ MANAGERS TO ISSUES/EMINENT ACADEMICS / UNDERWRITERS TO ISSUES/BROKERS.

Sr. No.	REGION	Number of Question-naires Mailed.	Number of Concerned Respondents who actually filled in the addressed Questionnaire.	Percentage of Column (3) to (2)
(1)	(2)	(3)	(4)	(5)
1.	Northern Region	100	36	36.0
2.	Eastern Region	100	22	22.0
3.	Central Region	50	9	18.0
4.	Western Region	190	41	22.0
5.	Southern Region	60	18	30.0
	TOTAL	500	126	25.0

Source : Enumerated on the basis of the information filled in Questionnaire:2 actually secured from the Office Bearers of the Stock Exchanges/Managers to Issues/Eminent Academics/ Underwriters to Issues/Brokers.

TABLE 3.18 : RANKS ASSIGNED TO THE DIFFERENT MEASURES NEED TO BE TAKEN BY THE COMPANIES ISSUING CONVERTIBLE DEBENTURES/ BONDS:CLASSIFICATION OF THE RESPONSES RECORDED BY THE RESPONDENT OFFICE BEARERS OF STOCK EXCHANGES/ MANAGERS TO ISSUES/EMINENT ACADEMICS/UNDERWRITERS TO TO ISSUES/BROKERS.

Sr. No.	Reasons	RANKS						Total
		I	II	III	IV	V	VI	
(1)	(2)	(3)	(4)	(5)	(6)	(7)	(8)	(9)
1.	Revising the rate of interest payable on CDsin an upward direction.	94 (74.6)	30 (23.8)	2 (1.6)	- (-)	- (-)	- (-)	126 (100.0)
2.	Keeping informed the investors about the Company's progress and future plans.	52 (41.3)	48 (38.1)	13 (10.3)	8 (6.3)	5 (4.0)	- (-)	126 (100.0)
3.	Maintaining a constant Dividend Policy.	36 (28.6)	40 (31.7)	38 (30.2)	3 (2.4)	8 (6.3)	1 (0.8)	126 (100.0)
4.	Following an upward rising Dividend Policy.	63 (50.0)	20 (15.9)	41 (32.5)	- (-)	2 (1.6)	- (-)	126 (100.0)
5.	Declaring Interim Dividends/Bonus Shares.	37 (29.4)	48 (38.1)	22 (17.5)	7 (5.6)	12 (9.5)	- (-)	126 (100.0)
6.	Taking measures for ensuring an active trading in the Associated Equity Shares/ CDs at S.E+	52 (41.3)	13 (10.3)	48 (38.1)	11 (8.7)	2 (1.6)	- (-)	126 (100.0)

Notes: (1) + S.E. stands for the different stock exchanges in India.
(2) Figures in brackets indicate the percentages to total.

Source: Compiled from the information filled in Questionnaire: 2 by the concerned respondents.

TABLE 3.19 : POPULARIZING CONVERTIBLE DEBENTURES/NON-CONVERTIBLE DEBENTURES: CLASSIFICATION OF THE SUGGESTIONS OFFERED BY THE RESPONDENT OFFICE BEARERS OF THE STOCK EXCHANGES/MANAGERS TO ISSUE/EMINENT ACADEMICS/UNDER-WRITERS TO ISSUES/BROKERS.

Sr. No.	Suggestion	Number of Respondents	Percentage to total number of respondents.*
(1)	(2)	(3)	(4)
1.	Extending the benefit of Section 80L of the Income Tax Act, 1961 to the investments made in CDs/NCDs.	118	93.6
2.	Extending the purview of Section 80CC of the Income Tax Act, 1961 so as to cover investments in CDs/NCDs.	43	34.1
3.	Making applicable the Buy Back Clause to the Non-Convertible Portion of CDs.	84	66.7
4.	Increasing the interest rate offered on CDs/NCDs.	122	96.9
5.	Educating the public about the features and the inherent gains in secured debentures-both CDs and NCDs.	90	71.4
6.	Keeping the conversion period as short as possible but not more than one year.	56	44.4
7.	Developing the secondary market for debentures for enhancing their liquidity/return.	119	94.4

Notes: * Total number of respondents stand at 126.
SOURCE: Compiled from the information filled in Questionnaire:2.

TABLE 3.20 : REGION WISE DISTRIBUTION OF RESPONDENT INVESTORS.

Sr. No.	Region	Number of Questionnaires Mailed.	Number of Investors who actually responded.	Percentage of Column (3) to (2)
(1)	(2)	(3)	(4)	(5)
1.	Northern Region	400	254	63
2.	Eastern Region	400	90	23
3.	Central Region	100	50	50
4.	Western Region	400	208	52
5.	Southern Region	200	102	51
	TOTAL	1500	704	47

Source : Enumerated on the basis of the information filled in Questionnaire:3 actually secured from the Investors.

TABLE 3.21 : BREAK - UP OF RESPONDENT INVESTORS ON THE BASIS OF THEIR OCCUPATION.

Sr. No.	Occupation	Number of Respondent Investors	Percentage to total number of respondent investors
(1)	(2)	(3)	(4)
1.	Service+	553	78.55
2.	Business*	151	21.45
	TOTAL	704	100.00

Notes: + All those investors who are engaged in one or the other kind of job for which a fixed salary and other allowances are paid by any institution found functioning both in the public and private sector on the one hand and organized and unorganized on the other have been included in the category of'service'.

* The investors who are engaged in manufacturing /provision of product/s and/or service/s irrespective of size/form of investment/organization and number of persons employed have been deemed to have been doing 'Business'; they cover all self employed respondent investors too.

Source: Categorized on the basis of information filled in Questionnaire:3 addressed to Investors.

TABLE 3.22 : INVESTMENT IN DIFFERENT SAVINGS INSTRUMENTS: DISTRIBUTION OF THE RESPONDENT INVESTORS.

(1978-82)

Sr. No.	Saving Instrument	Number of Respondent Investors.		
		Those engaged in services.	Those engaged in Business.	Total (3+4)
(1)	(2)	(3)	(4)	(5)
1.	Fixed Deposits with Banks.	312 (44.3)	43 (6.1)	355 (50.4)
2.	Fixed Deposits with Post Offices.	113 (16.1)	12 (1.7)	125 (17.8)
3.	Fixed Deposits with Non-Banking Companies.	156 (22.2)	3 (0.4)	159 (22.6)
4.	National Savings Certificates.	403 (57.2)	112 (15.9)	515 (73.1)
5.	ULIP Scheme.	105 (14.9)	22 (3.1)	127 (18.0)
6.	LIC Policies.	492 (69.9)	116 (16.5)	608 (86.4)
7.	Equity Shares.	432 (61.4)	102 (14.5)	534 (75.9)
8.	Convertible Debentures	553 (78.6)	151 (21.4)	704 (100.0)
9.	Non-Convertible Debentures.	52 (7.4)	- (-)	52 (7.4)
10.	Preference Snares	- (-)	- (-)	- (-)

Note: Figures in brackets indicate the percentages to total number of respondent investors which stands at 704.

Source: Compiled from the responses filled in Questionnaire:3 addressed to the Investors.

TABLE 3.23 : RANKS ASSIGNED BY THE RESPONDENT INVESTORS TO THE VARIEGATED REASONS FAVOURING INVESTMENT OF THEIR SAVINGS IN CONVERTIBLE DEBENTURES/BONDS: BREAK UP OF THE INVESTORS' RESPONSES.

Sr. No.	Reasons	RANKS						Total
		I	II	III	IV	V	None	
(1)	(2)	(3)	(4)	(5)	(6)	(7)	(8)	(9)
1.	Rate of Interest Offered.	216 (30.68)	150 (21.31)	276 (39.20)	46 (6.53)	- (-)	16 (2.27)	704 (100.00)
2.	Likelihood of the Capital Gains.	362 (51.42)	201 (28.55)	84 (11.93)	42 (5.96)	- (-)	15 (2.13)	704 (100.00)
3.	Fa-cility of conversion.	298 (42.33)	252 (35.79)	102 (14.49)	43 (6.10)	- (-)	9 (1.28)	704 (100.00)
4.	Easy Market-ability	103 (14.67)	321 (45.60)	212 (30.11)	58 (8.24)	8 (1.12)	2 (0.28)	704 (100.00)
5.	Safety of the Funds.	86 (12.21)	110 (15.62)	231 (32.81)	156 (22.16)	89 (12.64)	32 (4.55)	704 (100.00)
6.	Advise Given by the investment consultant/s	53 (7.53)	60 (8.53)	- (-)	21 (2.98)	6 (0.85)	564 (80.11)	704 (100.00)
7.	Facility of receiving the associated product/s on a preferential basis.	18 (2.55)	28 (3.98)	32 (4.54)	205 (29.12)	20 (2.84)	401 (56.96)	704 (100.00)
8,	Assurance of issuing equity shares /convertible debentures on rights basis.	26 (3.69)	105 (14.91)	212 (30.11)	315 (44.74)	24 (3.41)	22 (3.12)	704 (100.00)

Note: Figures in brackets indicate percentages to total.

Source: Compiled from the responses filled in Questionnaire: 3 addressed to the investors.

TABLE 3.24: FACTORS GOVERNING THE SELECTION AMONG THE VARIOUS ISSUES OF CONVERTIBLE DEBENTURES: BREAK UP OF THE RESPONSES OF THE RESPONDENT INVESTORS.

Sr. No.	FACTORS GIVEN WEIGHTAGE	NUMBER OF RESPONDENT INVESTORS			PERCENTAGE TO TOTAL NUMBER OF RESPONDENT INVESTORS*
		THOSE ENGAGED IN SERVICE.	THOSE ENGAGED IN BUSINESS.	TOTAL (3+4)	
(1)	(2)	(3)	(4)	(5)	(6)
1.	Favourable Terms of conversion & other auxiliary benefits.	531	122	653	92.76
2.	Reputation & Goodwill of the Company.	346	102	448	63.64
3.	Prudent Policies of the Management.	313	98	411	58.38
4.	Market Price of the equity share of the Company.	486	101	587	83.38
5.	Encouraging Reports about the Profitability and other future growth programs of the Company.	412	89	501	71.16
6.	Dividend Policy of the Company.	245	69	314	44.60
7.	Volatile Nature of the associated Equity Share.	121	26	147	20.88
8.	Non-availability of other worthwhile securities for investment.	53	12	65	9.23

* Total Number of Respondent Investors stands at 704.

Source: Compiled from the Responses filled in Questionnaire:3 addressed to the Investors.

TABLE 3.25: POPULARIZING CONVERTIBLE DEBENTURES/NON-CONVERTIBLE DEBENTURES: BREAK UP OF THE INVESTORS' SUGGESTIONS.

Sr.No.	Suggestion	Number of Respondent Investors.	Percentage to total+
(1)	(2)	(3)	(4)
1.	Extending the benefit of Section 80L of the Income Tax Act, 1961 to the investments made in CDs/NCDs.	701	99.57
2.	Extending the purview of Section 80CC of Income Tax Act, 1961 so as cover investments in CDs/NCDs.	368	52.27
3.	Making applicable the buy back clause to the non-convertible portion of CDs.	367	52.13
4.	Increasing the interest rate offered on CDs/NCDs.	508	72.16
5.	Educating the public about the features and the inherent gains in secured debentures both CDs/NCDs.	385	54.69
6.	Keeping the conversion period as short as possible but not more than one year.	587	83.38
7.	Developing the Secondary Market for Debentures in order to enhance their liquidity/return.	523	74.29

+ Total Number of Respondent Investors Stands at 704.

Source: Compiled from the Responses filled in Questionnaire:3 addressed to the Investors.

BIBLIOGRAPHY

— BOOKS

— ARTICLES

— REPORTS

— MAGAZINES/JOURNALS/DAILIES

BOOKS

Archer, Stephen H., Choate, G. Marc, and Racette, George, 'Financial Management', New York, John Wiley & Sons, Second Edition, 1983.

Babbie, Earl R., 'Survey Research Methods', California, Belmont, Wadsworth Publishing Company, Inc., 1973.

Brigham, Eugene F., (in Collaboration with Gapenski, Louis C.), 'Financial Management : Theory and Practice', Tokyo, Holt-Saunders Japan Limited, Fourth Edition, 1985.

Chandra Prasanna, 'Financial Management : Theory and Practice' New Delhi, Tata McGraw-Hill Publishing Company Limited, 1984.

Christy, George A., and Clendenin, John C., 'Introduction to Investments', New York, Mc-Graw-Hill Book Company, Seventh Edition, 1978.

Fisher, Donald E., and Jordon, Ronald J., 'Security Analysis and Portfolio Management', Englewood Cliffs, New Jersey, Prentice-Hall, Inc., Third Edition, 1983.

Francis, Jack Clark, 'Investments : Analysis and Management', New York, Mc-Graw-Hill Book Company, Second Edition, 1976.

Franks J.R., and Scholefield, H.H., 'Corporate Financial Management', Gower Press, Teak Field Limited, England, Second Edition.

Gitman, Lawrence J., 'Principles of Managerial Finance', New York, Harper and Row Publishers, Third Edition, 1982.

Graham, Benjamin, Dodd, David L., and Cottle, Sidney, (with the collaboration of Charles Tatham), 'Security Analysis :

Principles and Techniques', New York, McGraw-Hill Book Company, Inc., Fourth Edition, 1962.

Hampton, John J., 'Financial Decision Making: Concepts, Problems and Cases', New Delhi, Prentice-Hall of India Private Limited, Second Edition, 1980.

Huang Stanley, 'Investment Analysis and Management', Winthrog Publishing Inc., Cambridge, Massachusetts, 1981.

Jayapandian, S., 'Convertibility Clause and Investment Climate —An IFMR Survey', Madras, Institute for Financial Management and Research, November 1980.

Johnson Timothy E., 'Investment Principles', Prentice-Hall Inc., Englewood Cliffs, N.J., Second Edition, 1683.

Kapur, D.K., 'Management of Capital Issues', New Delhi, PHD Chamber of Commerce and Industry, Third Edition, May 1983.

Keown, Arthur J., Scott, David F. Jr. Martin. John D. and William Petty J., 'Basic Financial Management', Englewood Cliffs, N.J , Prentice-Hall, Inc., Third Edition, 1985.

Kuchhal, S C., 'Financial Management: An Analytical and Conceptual Approach', Allahabad, Chaitanya Publishing House, Eighth Edition, 1982.

Levy, Hain and Sarnat, Marshall, 'Capital Investment and Financial Decisions', Englewood Cliffs, N.J., Prentice-Hall, Inc., Third Edition, 1986.

Mayo, Herbert B., 'Basic Investments: An Introduction', Illinois, Hinsdale, Dryden Press, 1980.

Mehta, S.S., and Honavar, R.M., 'Some Aspects of the Indian Capital Market', a Confidential Report Submitted to the World Bank, Madras, Institute for Financial Management and Research, 1984.

Pike, Richard and Dobbins, Richard, 'Investment Decisions and Financial Strategy', Oxford Philip Allan Publishers Limited, First Edition, 1986.

Sharpe, William F., 'Investments', Englewood Cliffs, New Jersey, Prentice-Hall, Inc., Second Edition, 1981.

Simha S.L.N., Hemalatha D. and Balakrishnan S., 'Investment Management : Introduction to Securities Analysis', Institute for Financial Management and Research, Madras, December, 1979.

Solomon, Ezra and Pringle, Jonn J., 'An Introduction to Financial Management', Prentice-Hall of India Pvt. Ltd., 1978.

Sur, A.K., 'The Stock Exchange', Calcutta, The World Press Private Limited, 1979.

The Institute of Company Secretaries of India, New Delhi, 'Dividend and Interest', Secretarial Practice Series-3, First Edition, April 1981.

Vanhorne, James C., 'Fundamentals of Financial Management' New Delhi, Prentice-Hall of India Private Limited, Fourth Edition, 1980.

Weston, J. Fred and Brigham, Eugene F., 'Managerial Finance', Tokyo, Holt-Saunders Japan Limited, Seventh Edition, 1981.

ARTICLES

Alexander, Gordon J., Stover, Rager D. and Kuhnoee, D. B., 'Market Timing Strategies in Covertible Debt Financing', Journal of Finance 9, March 1979, pp. 143-55.

Alexander Gorden J., and Sotver, Roger D., 'The Effect of Forced Conversion on Common Stock Prices', Financial Management, Spring 1980, pp. 39-45.

Balakrishnan, P.K., 'Rate of Return On Convertible Debentures', Financial Express, Bombay, January 3, 1981.

Banerjee, Nantoo, 'Big Debentures in Trouble', Business Standard, July 13, 1981.

Bierman, Harold Jr., 'Convertible Bonds as Investments', Financial Analysts Journal 36, March-April 1980, pp. 59-61.

Bond, F.M., 'Yields on Convertible Securities : 1969-74', Journal of Business Finance and Accounting 3, Summer 1976, pp. 93-114.

Brennan M.J., and Schwartz, E.S., 'Convertible Bonds : Valuation and Optimal Strategies for Call and Conversion', Journal of Finance 32, December 1977, pp. 1699-1975.

Brigham, Eugene F., 'An Analysis of Convertible Debentures: Theory and Some Empirical Evidence', Journal of Finance, 21, March 1966, pp.35-54.

Chandratre, K.R., 'Non-Convertible Debentures *vis a vis* Company Deposits', The Economic Times, Bombay, June 27, 1983.

Chaudhuri, Swapan Kanti, 'Convertible Debentures: Components of Yield', The Economic Times, October 16, 1982.

Cretien, P.D. Jr., 'Premiums on Convertible Bonds: Comment', Journal of Finance, Volume 25, September 1970, pp. 917-22.

Datar, V.D., 'Convertible Debentures : A Utility Analysis', Mid-Week Review on Investment, The Economic Times, Bombay, April 7, 1982.

Desai, Darshan S., 'Convertible Debentures : Financial and Tax Implications', The Chartered Accountant, Vol. XXXI, No. 2, August 1982, pp. 123-26.

Dewani, M. D., 'One More Debenture Issue Fails', The Financial Express, Bombay, January 8, 1983.

Duvel, David Tell, 'Premiums on Convertible Bonds: Comment', Journal of Finance 25, September 1970, pp. 923-27.

Goyal, O.P. and Agarwal V.K., 'Convertible Debentures/Bonds : Experience of Private Corporate Sector', Saturday Supplement on Finance, The Economic Times, Bombay, May 8, 1982.

Hedge D.R., 'Guidelines on Debentures: Historical Perspective', Finance Supplement, The Economic Times, October 16, 1982.

Ingersoll, Jonathan E., 'A Contingent Claims Valuation of Convertible Securities', Journal of Financial Economics, May 1977, pp. 289-322.

Kashekar S.R., 'Bonds—The British Way', Special Survey on Investment, The Economic Times, April 23, 1981.

Kutty M. Krishnan, 'Bonds of Public Bodies', Special Survey on Investment, The Economic Times, April 23, 1981.

Mehta, Dileep R., 'The Impact of Outstanding Convertible Bonds on Corporate Dividend Policy', Journal of Finance 31, May 1976, pp. 489-506.

Miller, A.B., 'How to Call Your Convertible', Harvard Business Review, Vol. 49, May-June 1971, pp. 66-70.

Moses, A. S., 'Convertible Debenture Profit', The Financial Express, Bombay, May 15, 1982.

Mukhi, M.D., 'Debentures : Prolific Source of Funds for Companies', Financial Express, Bombay, April 28, 1983.

Mukhi, M.D., 'Debentures : Steps Needed to Develop It', Part I, The Economic Times, Bombay, January 23, 1981; and, 'Debentures : Need for a Secondary Market', Part II, The Economic Times, Bombay, January 24, 1981.

Norgaard, Richard L., 'An Examination of The Yields of Corporate Bonds and Stocks', Journal of Finance, September 1974, pp. 1275-1286.

Prasad, G., and Rao, K. Viyyanna, 'Management of Convertible Debentures-I', and 'Convertible Debentures-II', Financial Express, Bombay, October 27 & 28, 1981.

Ramachandran, K.S., 'Why this Scramble for Convertible Debentures?' Financial Express, Bombay, February 2, 1982.

Research Bureau, Business Standard, 'Debenture Issues and Equity Prices : A Case Study of Seven Companies', Business Standard, January 29, 1982.

Sengupta, Sudhi R., 'Working Capital: Debentures and Deposits as Sources', The Economic Times, Bombay June 4, 1981; and 'Working Capital: Interests of Investors', The Economic Times, Bombay, June 5, 1981.

Seth, Narendra J., 'Convertible Debentures, Bonds : Relevance to Financing of New Projects', The Economic Times, Bombay, October 7, 1980.

Seth, Narendra J., 'Convertible Bonds : A Perspective on Conversion Price', Saturday Supplement, The Economic Times, Bombay, April 10, 1982.

Sinha, N.P., 'Convertible Debentures—An Analytical Study', The Chartered Accountant, Volume XXXI, No 3, September 1982.

Sharma, L.V.L.N., Murali, Nagalakshmi, 'Corporate Debt Capacity—A Simulation Approch', The Chartered Accountant, Vol. XXIX, No. 12, June 1981, pp. 881-87.

Venkataraman, N.V., 'Debentures : Rising Importance', The Special Survey on Investmant, The Economic Times, Bombay, April 23, 1981.

Walter, James E. and Que, Agustin V., 'The Valuation of Convertible Bonds', Journal of Finance 28, June 1963, pp. 713-32.

REPORTS

Annual Reports of Different Public Limited Companies of the Private Corporate Sector.

Government of India, Ministry of Finance, Economic Division, 'Economic Survey', 1975-76 through 1985-86, New Delhi.

Government of India, Ministry of Industry and Department of Company Affairs, Research and Statistics Division, 'Directory of Joint Stock Companies in India', Volume One (A-DEL), New Delhi, 1986.

Government of India, Ministry of Law, Justice and Company Affairs, Department of Company Affairs, Research and Statistics Division, 'Directory of Joint Stock Companies in India', Volume I, New Delhi, 1980.

Government of India, Ministry of Law, Justice and Company Affairs, Department of Company Affairs, Research and Statistics Division, 'Registrations and Liquidations of Joint Stock Companies in India 1980-82', New Delhi, 1982.

Government of India, Ministry of Law, Justice and Company Affairs, Department of Company Affairs 'Report of the High-Powered Expert Committee on Companies and MRTP Acts', New Delhi, August 1978.

Government of India, Ministry of Law, Justice and Company Affairs, 'The Companies Act, 1956'.

Government of India, Planning Commission, New Delhi, Drafts of First Five Year Plan through Sixth Five Year Plan, New Delhi,

Government of India, Planning Commission, 'The Seventh Five Year Plan: 1985-90', Volume I & *II*, 1985.

Government of India, 'Report of the Industrial Licensing Policy Inquiry Committee', New Delhi, 1969.

Reserve Bank of India, 'Report of Study Group to Frame Guidelines for Follow up of Bank Credit', Bombay, 1975.

Reserve Bank of India, 'Report of the Working Group to Review the System of Cash Credit', Bombay, 1979.

Reserve Bank of India, 'Report of the Commitee to Review the Working of the Monetary System', Bombay, April 1985.

Rescrve Bank of India, 'Report on Currency & Finance 1969-70 through 1983-84', Bombay.

Stock Exchange Official Directory, Bomay.

Stock Exchange Official Year Book, Delhi.

Stock Exchange Official Year Book, Madras.

Quotation Lists of Market Prices of Equity shares and Debentures of Different Stock Exchanges of India.

MAGAZINES/JOURNALSD/AILIES

Business Standard

Chartered Accountant

Commerce

Capital

Financial Management

Financial Analysts

Journal of Business Finance & Accounting.

Journal of Finance

The Economic Times

The Financial Express

The Hindustan Times

The Indian Express

The Times of India

INDEX